Masters
of
Animation

Masters
of
Animation

John Grant

BT BATSFORD • LONDON

Acknowledgements

The following went above and beyond the call of duty in helping me lay hands on rare videotapes: Janet Benn, Byron Clooney, Dean Kalman Lennert, and Nancy and Russell Lewis. Vincent Di Fate gave me exciting new information about the origins of storyboard just as this book was going to press. Three of the animators discussed in this book spared valuable time to give me help: Ralph Bakshi, Bruno Bozzetto and John Canemaker. David R. Smith of the Disney Archives was as always helpful; CJ Glazer of the Will Vinton Studios emulated Dave in helpfulness. Andrew Osmond was as always an enthusiastic supporter. Some of the movie synopses are based on those in *The Encyclopedia of Fantasy* (1997), edited by myself and John Clute: my thanks for John Clute for this. Richard Reynolds commissioned this book; he departed before having to face the actual manuscript, but I forgive him anyway. Roger Huggins and especially Tina Persaud of Batsford have been amazingly forgiving as deadline after deadline has slipped by. My wife, Pamela D. Scoville, not only helped in literally countless incidentals but also, even more impressively, continued to live with an often grumpy, stressed-out husband throughout this book's tortured creation.

If I were fully to express my gratitude to all these folk the book would be several pages longer.

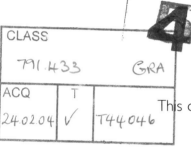
Dedication

This one's for Nancy and Russ, with thanks for many, many things,
but most particularly for being themselves.
And also, like life itself, it's for Pam.

A catalogue record for this book is available from the British Library.

ISBN 0 7134 8554 X
Printed in Spain

Volume © B T Batsford 2001

First published in 2001 by
B T Batsford
9 Blenheim Court
Brewery Road
London N7 9NY

A member of the Chrysalis Group plc

Page 2: Self-portrait of Chuck Jones with Wile E. Coyote and the Road Runner.
Photograph: Chuck Jones Enterprises. © Warner Bros.

Contents

INTRODUCTION

What is it about animation that so fascinates us?

The standard reply to that question is that animated figures can do things no live-action figure could, but the technology of special effects has now reached such a level that this answer can no longer be valid. Seemingly live-action characters now do on screen virtually anything an animated character could, and yet far from seeing a diminution of the animation industry over recent years we have in fact seen a great resurgence. If it were merely a question of seeing impossible things done in seeming live-action, then animation would be a dead art. Similarly, while some of the modern CGI animations do manage to create the illusion of life using overtly non-living characters, they are only a part of the scene: five of the most lauded animated features of recent years – *Princess Mononoke* (1997), *Tarzan* (1999), *The Iron Giant* (1999), *Chicken Run* (2000) and *Titan A.E.* (2000) – display characters and environments on-screen that make no pretense at being anything other than animated. The great new movies coming out of the anime tradition are likewise overtly *animated*, for example *Perfect Blue* (2000) and *My Neighbors the Yamadas* (1999).

So there has to be another answer. Something to do with the surrealistic possibilities of animation, perhaps?

My own proposed answer may seem rather too obvious if we express it at its simplest: we like animation because we *know* it is animation. All through studies of speculative literature there is tacit or stated acceptance that part of its appeal to the reader is the necessity for the willing suspension of disbelief. If we read a mimetic novel we may praise the author for the skill with which reality is portrayed. Reading a fantasy novel appeals to a quite different sense within us: we *know* we are reading about the impossible occurring in a world that doesn't exist, yet at the same time we willingly *permit* ourselves to believe entirely, while the pages are open, that this is the real world. This dichotomy of perception is what gives us the tingle we get when reading (good) fantasy. We go to see animation because we want that same extra tingle, born out of a willing double perception, that we get from reading fantasy.

Of course, this is a generalization; it takes no account of abstract animation, for one thing. But then abstract animation has always been in a class of its own: it is liquid art. Yet it explains why even the gravest and stateliest of us can find genuine, deep fascination in Bugs Bunny or *Bambi*.

Most of us first encounter animation in childhood, which can be a good or a bad thing, because too many of us assume that this means animation is purely a childish interest. With such people, one can only sympathize; as I later state in my discussion within this book of Hayao Miyazaki's marvelous movie-for-all-ages *My Neighbor Totoro*, its young heroine "learns not only how to begin becoming an adult but also how to *hold onto her childhood* – something all adults must do if they are to be complete human beings." Yet this identification of animation as "merely" for juveniles has dogged the medium since about the 1930s. Before that it was regarded as for all ages, and some of the early entertainment animations are in fact astonishingly risqué. Today, the bizarre situation seems to be that while the general public willingly accepts animation as a medium for adults as much as for children, the cinema establishment lags some way behind this sea-change of opinion. *South Park* and its ilk are encouraged to be as scatological as possible because they represent "adult animation," but almost everything else is expected to be kiddie fodder, with no allowance between these extremes for animated movies that are just ... well, intelligent movies.

Intelligence shines through the creations of nearly all of the animators whose work is discussed in these pages. This observation does not exclude those animators widely regarded as at the "entertainment" end of a disparate spectrum. There is as much intelligence in the marvelous inventiveness of, say, the animators of the Warners stable or the storytelling power of, say, the Disney crew as there is in the abstractions of Norman McLaren, the aesthetics of Frédéric Back or Lotte Reiniger, or the surrealism of Jan Švankmajer, or ... Yes, there *have* been animators who have produced only the dull and the dreary, but their names have been largely forgotten. The animators from whose work shines the gleam of intelligence are the ones who become regarded as "masters."

It was clear from the very outset that this book would have to be selective in its choice of master animators, as otherwise it could fill several volumes. It has turned out to be a much bigger – and, I hope, better – enterprise than either I or my blessedly tolerant publisher ever dreamed it would be. In our initial innocence we assumed there might be about 25 figures within the animation industry who could rightly be given the description "master". We discovered we were hopelessly wrong in that reckoning. The essays in this book cover a total of over 35 master animators in some detail and countless others in passing, and *still* I am more than aware of all the others who could have been added: modern masters like Michael Sporn, Mike Judge, Brad Bird, Isao Takahata, Katsuhiro Otomo, John Lasseter, Mamoru Oshii, and the Brothers Quay and Bolex; masters from animation's Golden Age like Frank Tashlin, Shamus Culhane, Dick Huemer, Art Babbitt, Grim Natwick and all of Walt Disney's Nine Old Men (although the team principle in operation at Disney has always made it hard to distinguish their individual contributions); special-effects and stop-motion animators like Willis O'Brien, George Pal, Art Clokey and Ray Harryhausen; and masters of animation's dawn, such as Earl Hurd and J. Stuart Blackton (who can be claimed to have started it all in 1906 with his *Humorous Phases of Funny Faces*) ... although even he was predated by Arthur Melbourne Cooper with *Matches: An Appeal* (1899).

All of these are important figures in the story of animation, but a book can sensibly be only so long. To have included everyone would have been to do an injustice to all through the superficial treatment necessarily given to each; after all, many of the animators included here – and many more besides – have been the subjects of complete books to themselves. Ultimately, the selection had to be subjective.

As it is, welcome to the world of animation's masters. If you enjoy this book, it is because of them.

John Grant

TEX AVERY (1908–1980)

Setup for *Droopy's Double Trouble* (1951) showing Droopy.
Photograph: Howard Lowery. © MGM, Warner Bros.

Born on February 26, 1908, in Taylor, Texas, Frederick Bean Avery became an animator revered within the profession for his elevation of the irreverent, gag-packed, surrealistic short cartoon to a height which will probably never again be equaled, let alone surpassed. But during his lifetime he was comparatively little known to the public at large.

The earliest of his artworks we know about are the cartoons he did for his high-school yearbook, *The Viking*. On leaving school his dream was to become a cartoonist. He tried his luck at the local Dallas newspapers and with local cartoonists before being advised that he might do better if he had some formal art training. Accordingly, he went to the Art Institute of Chicago, but lasted there only a month as he found the work irrelevant to his dream. The Chicago cartoonists were just as unresponsive to his offers as the Dallas ones had been. He moved to Los Angeles, where he got a job on the night shift at the docks and slept on the beach, all the time trying fruitlessly to sell himself as a strip cartoonist. Someone tipped him off that the nearby animation studio belonging to Charles Mintz was hiring, and so he got a temporary job there as an ink-and-painter. When that was over he managed to get another, similar job at the Walter Lantz Studio, this time working his way up to become an in-betweener (an animator who does drawings 'in-

between' the key ones, which are normally done by a senior animator) and backgrounder on the Oswald the Rabbit shorts. It was around this time that he became convinced that his future lay in animation rather than cartooning.

A sequence of lucky events then led to his rapid promotion at Lantz. But lucky events have nothing to do with the development of Avery's brilliantly surreal sense of humor, both verbal and visual, which was what truly distinguished him as an animator and which, through those he later influenced, had such a profound effect on the whole art of shorts animation. Lesser creators in any artistic field always have very firm ideas as to what you can and can't do. Possibly it was because Avery was pushed so rapidly up the ladder of animation that he was unfettered by such ideas, but more likely this quality – essentially a channel for rebelliousness – was something innate to him. Whatever the case, Avery very early understood that the essence of visual or other humor is surprise, and so he aimed always to startle the audience into laughter, by whatever means and whatever the rulebook said. Although in his

later years he had the tiresome habit of repeating the same surprises, so that they surprised no longer; most of his short movies offer the audience not only laughter and fun but also an exhilarating, *imaginatively liberating* experience. His characters are often perfectly aware that they are performers in an entertainment, and frequently pause to address the audience, complain about the working conditions, admit that they've strayed into the wrong cartoon, and protest about the corniness of the plot. They might run off the edge of the frame, revealing the synch holes at the edge of the film, or go past the boundary where Technicolor is available to find themselves in a black-and-white world, or … It has been said time and time again that what distinguishes Avery's work from the rest is that he was prepared to do anything for a laugh, but this is a false oversimplification. The real element that marks his work is this sense of joyous *liberation* from restrictions – in point of fact, from the restrictions of animation's unwritten rulebook, but in point of *affect* (which is the more significant consideration, since the important thing about an artwork is what it does to the audience) from the restrictive pathways of everyday, conventional thinking, and hence from the narrow limits of everyday life. The subliminal message from others was that, in effect, you could do only *so much*, whereas Avery was saying you could do *anything you wanted to*.

It was lucky for him that the Lantz Studio didn't much care what the results were so long as the shorts continued to sell – had Avery been at Disney, for example, his "excesses" would almost certainly have been curtailed. As it was, he was permitted to take his animation in any direction his muse led him.

He gained his amazing sense of surrealism at the Lantz Studio, but it was there that he also lost something: his left eye, during one of the frequent rounds of studio horseplay. (The animators often flicked spitballs at each other, and one of them, tragically, one day substituted a paper clip.) This had a psychological effect on him that lasted his whole life – where he had been vain of his physique, he became a bit of a slob – and probably affected the nature of his humor as well. Many of the sharpest humorists, from Swift onward, are driven by one unhappiness or another. Later on he would be deeply insecure: at Warners, even though he was the studio's most valuable property, he was so afraid of being fired that he would carry papers with him whenever he strayed from his desk so that he could look as if he were working should the boss spot him. He also became increasingly obsessive; again at Warners he was once so absorbed in a piece of work (according to Chuck Jones) that he put off urinating so long that he had to be taken to hospital to have his bladder emptied.

In 1935, when Lantz failed to give him a pay raise he wanted, Avery persuaded Leon Schlesinger at Warners to employ him as an animation director (initially for just one movie, but the contract was extended without quibble) alongside Friz Freleng and Hal King. More to the point, two of the animators assigned to his team were Chuck Jones and Bob Clampett. Both men in later years talked effusively of what they learned from Avery; what is less often noted is that he was equally publicly grateful for what he got from them,

which was a youthfully exuberant and wholehearted support in his determination to make funny movies. They offered him fertile ground for the further growth of his exciting surrealism in the telling of stories and the communication of gags, not to mention in the gags themselves.

Avery's team was given a termite-infested bungalow in which to work – it and they collectively became known as Termite Terrace, an appellation they bore with pride. Significantly, Leon Schlesinger was not an interfering producer, being generally content to let his animation directors do what they thought best and judging only by results. If Avery wanted to make his cartoons zanier and faster than anybody else's, that was fine by Schlesinger – especially since audiences loved the results. In consequence, the output of Warners in general became quite markedly sharper and faster than that of any of the other studios, as his colleagues at Warners followed Avery's successful lead. It was important that the Warner cartoons should have such a distinction. Walt Disney had managed to make the Disney cartoons markedly different by his concentration on story and character. The Warners animators would probably have lost any direct market contest if they had attempted to follow along those same lines. They therefore had to find some other avenue through which they could outclass Disney, some other reason why audiences should prefer a Warners cartoon to anyone else's; and Avery's flamboyant surrealism and rapidity of pacing proved to be that avenue.

His first movie for Warners was *Gold Diggers of '49* (1936), a vehicle for the existing, rather lackluster Warners characters Porky and Beans. (It was done, as were many of his movies, under the name Fred Avery rather than Tex Avery; here I make no differentiation between the two.) Both characters had been introduced in the likewise rather lackluster short *I Haven't Got a Hat* (1935; see page 82), done by Friz Freleng. Beans, a cheeky little black cat, had been plucked from that short to be groomed for stardom, and had appeared in a further couple of 1935 black-and-white shorts, *A Cartoonist's Nightmare* and *Hollywood Capers*; for his part, Porky Pig, likewise selected as a potential series hero, had appeared further in 1935's *Into Your Dance*. However, the future was not looking especially bright for them – they were not characters with any great appeal – and in any event Beans soon went off to join Flip the Frog and Oswald the Rabbit in that curious heaven there must be for forgotten cartoon heroes.

Porky Pig would probably have gone the same way had it not been for Avery. His first move was to turn Porky and Beans from cute little infants into a fully grown pig and cat. This immediately sent the message that *Gold Diggers of '49* was not just for children but for adults as well. In the longer term it meant that eventually Avery and the rest were able to use a much more adult form of humor with Porky than might otherwise have been the case; Disney, he reckoned, had the smaller kids, so Warners should go for the older kids and adults. Again, this notion was something that spread through Warners as a whole and then eventually through much of the U.S. commercial animation industry.

Miss Glory (1936)

🎨 color /animated ⏱ 7½ minutes
Merrie Melodies
Famous star Miss Glory is coming to visit Hicksville, and dimwitted bellhop Abner in the local fleapit hotel fantasizes about his chances with this presumably glamorous entertainer. Waiting, he falls asleep and dreams the hotel is a magnificent Art Deco structure in the big city; the entire style of the cartoon moves into splendid Art Deco at this point. There are various gags and hijinks before the svelte thespian arrives and is mobbed by eager men in scenes reminiscent of a Busby Berkeley musical. When Abner awakes back in Hicksville it is to discover that Miss Glory is a child star — a tiny tot. Avery was uncredited on this movie. The striking "moderne" art (i.e., Art Deco) was conceived and created by Leodora Congdon.

Daffy Duck and Egghead (1938)

🎨 color /animated ⏱ 7½ minutes
Merrie Melodies/Daffy Duck & Egghead
Daffy Duck's second appearance and his first in the starring role. He is being hunted by Egghead. A disclaimer at the short's start reads: "The events and ducks depicted in this photoplay are fictitious. Any similarity to actual ducks, either living or roasted, is purely coincidental." After exasperatedly shooting a silhouetted audience member who refuses to sit down, Egghead uses various stratagems (e.g., a clockwork lure) in attempts to catch Daffy. Amidst these, the two fight a comic duel in which Egghead proves incapable of hitting Daffy even when the duck stands right in front of him.

Cinderella Meets Fella (1938)

🎨 color /animated ⏱ 8¼ minutes
Merrie Melodies/Egghead
One of Avery's several scrambled, gag-packed revamps of traditional tales. A feisty Cinderella, fully conscious of her role in the story, calls the cops to get them to deliver her fairy godmother, who arrives severely the worse for alcoholic wear. The latter creates the prescribed coach and horses, only Wild West style (her first try produces Santa Claus complete with sleigh and reindeer), and off Cinders goes to "The Royal Ball (Free Parking Till Midnight)." Egghead is the goofy Prince Charming; he arrives drunk in a rolled-up carpet. Midnight striking, Cinders deliberately leaves a glass slipper and flees. Egghead/Charming pursues, finding Cinderella's house lit up by a battery of neon signs. But she has tired of waiting, and gone to watch a screening of this very cartoon; as he weeps in despair, she rushes up from the auditorium and back into the short. The lovers decide to go and snog (kiss) in the tenth row.

Cel for *Little Walking Hood* (1937), showing Grandma.
© Warner Bros.

Porky became the first Warners star with any staying power after the now-forgotten Bosko. (To replace Bosko, Warners had tried Buddy, of whom Chuck Jones, who cut his animating teeth on the series, remarked: "Nothing in the way of bad animation could make Buddy worse than he was anyway.") His trademark stammer was originally done by a genuinely stammering actor, Joe Dougherty, but from the start there was something distressing rather than funny about Dougherty's voicetracks, and after a couple of years he was replaced by the young Mel Blanc in his first major voicing role; it was he who gave Porky his famous "Th-th-th-that's all, folks" closing line.

The first new character to be created by Avery for Warners was Daffy Duck, who made a rather rebarbative debut in *Porky's Duck Hunt* (1937) but was soon toned down just enough to become one of animation's finest creations. This was not the would-be-suave-but-accident-prone Daffy whom we later came to know, but an utterly uncontrollable zany who was capable of doing anything on screen that an animator could draw and who had an almost elemental lack of responsibility. Although Avery was to develop the idea of the trickster much further in Bugs Bunny, Daffy represents the first full-blooded introduction of this archetype into animation — a statement that needs rapid qualification. Earlier animation is full of examples of characters whose whole *raison d'être* was that they were tricky little imps, but Daffy harks back to a much older and much more fundamental meaning of the word "trickster." In his capriciousness and his seeming omnipotence — he can manipulate reality on a whim — he is an incarnation of the

tricksters of our deepest folklore and even some of our Creation myths, from the Garden of Eden's Serpent (and later Satan) to the Norse trickster god Loki to the spider Anansi in African traditions to the figure of Coyote in the lore of the Native Americans of the Southwest. Daffy is thus both infinitely attractive, on the one hand, and a figure of considerable dread, on the other. He is quite distinct from tricky characters like Mickey or Flip the Frog or countless other animated characters, whose attraction is that they are the little clever guy who outwits the powerful bully: Daffy *is* the powerful bully, and the humor comes about because Porky or Egghead or Elmer Fudd doesn't *realize* it.

The name Egghead in that list may cause some readers to stop short. Egghead was another Avery creation, first appearing in *Egghead Rides Again* (1937). For the Avery short *Dangerous Dan McFoo* (1939) an actor called Arthur Q. Bryan was employed for the voicing of the title role. The voice was such a success that the animators determined to build a character around it, and for this purpose they began to remodel Egghead into Elmer Fudd. Because of confusion about this, one often comes across the mistaken claim that *Dangerous Dan McFoo* represents Elmer Fudd's debut as a renamed Egghead; in fact neither appears in the short. Elmer first appeared by name in the Chuck Jones short *Elmer's Candid Camera* (1940), although he was still more Egghead than Elmer, as it were; of considerable interest in this movie was a rabbit adversary. Elmer's real debut can probably best be regarded as in the Avery short *A Wild Hare* (1940), which can also be seen as the true debut of the most significant Warners star of them all, Bugs Bunny.

A precursor of Bugs can be seen in three earlier shorts, *Porky's Hare Hunt* (1938) – which is basically just a remake of the Avery short *Porky's Duck Hunt*, using a rabbit/hare in place of a duck – *Hare-um Scar-um* (1939), plus the aforementioned *Elmer's Candid Camera*, in which the character is beginning to approach the Bugs we know. However, it was *A Wild Hare* that fixed him as a definite personality, very recognizably the same character as the modern incarnation, even though the details of the features may have altered a bit. Leaving aside for the moment such peripherals as the catchphrase "What's Up, Doc?" – appropriated by Avery from smartasses in the school playground – here was another of those elemental trickster figures. Far, far more than Daffy Duck, Bugs touched those deep parts of the human psyche that demand one of the components of the understood universe – i.e., one of the gods – be trickster. It is not at all a coincidence that the Bugs Bunny shorts can together be regarded as forming a quasi-mythology.

It was a Bugs Bunny short that led to Avery's downfall at Warners. During his time at the studio he had never got on particularly well with Leon Schlesinger; at one point Schlesinger laid him off for a couple of months over the arguments about an idea of Avery's that Schlesinger vetoed (live-action animals saying funny things with animated mouths; the series was eventually produced by Paramount). But Schlesinger was not normally guilty of the sin which most often causes animators to resent their

Original poster for *The Shooting of Dan McGoo* (1945). Private collection. © MGM, Warner Bros.

Dangerous Dan McFoo (1939)

🎨 color / animated ⏱ 7¼ minutes
Merrie Melodies

A parody of the Robert Service ballad "The Shooting of Dan McGrew." At the back of a snowbound bar in, er, Malibu, Dangerous Dan McFoo (a little dog) plays a taut game of bagatelle . . . "and watching his fate was his heavy date, the girl who was known as Sue." Out of the snow comes a bigger dog, whose eye is caught by the Katharine Hepburn-voiced Sue; she, in his mind's eye, briefly morphs into an alluring Bette Davis. The two males have a boxing match for her favors in which both fight dirty – as is revealed by the camera freeze-framing. Finally they shoot it out in the dark, Dan surviving. In 1945 Avery made, for MGM, the Droopy cartoon *The Shooting of Dan McGoo*. Having been fired in the interim by Warners, no doubt he felt no guilt about revisiting the territory.

Thugs with Dirty Mugs (1939)

color / animated / 8 minutes
Merrie Melodies

A witty, surreally plotted parody of the gangster movies that Warners had made famous. Killer Diller (played by Ed G. Robemsome) and his gang rob more banks than can be counted. Killer at one point even successfully holds up a pay phone. Chief of Police Flat Foot Flanigan (played by F.H.A. [Sherlock] Homes) is ineffectual in attempting to catch the bad guy. In the end, Killer is caught when a member of the audience who has sat through the movie twice snitches on him to Flanigan.

Cross Country Detours (1940)

color / animated / 9½ minutes
Merrie Melodies

One of Avery's spoof travelogs, parodying Disney's live-action wildlife shorts, this takes us to Yosemite National Park. The bears yell angrily at tourists who ignore the DO NOT FEED THE BEARS signs; a cute little Bambi-like deer morphs into a vamp; a fire-fighting ranger rushes to where a careless tourist has thrown down a lighted cigar . . . only in order to finish smoking it himself. Then the scene shifts to other National Parks, showing us, for example, the wondrous natural bridge in Bryce Canyon, complete with teeth (bridge — geddit?). Elsewhere, among many further gags, a vaunted close-up of a frog croaking shows the frog pull out a gun and shoot himself. A lizard shedding her skin does so as a tantalizing striptease — concluded by a heavy CENSORED label. Eventually the screen is split, the gila monster in the left side being assumed too frightening for the children in the audience, who are exhorted instead to watch a little girl reciting "Mary Had a Little Lamb" on the right; the little girl terrifies the gila monster.

bosses: interfering with the movies. Indeed, Schlesinger gave the crew on Termite Terrace almost total freedom. For some reason, however, he did decide to interfere with Avery's *The Heckling Hare* (1941). The version of the short that was released ends, quite noticeably, abruptly and untidily, with Bugs and the dog he has been trickstering surviving a long fall; there is the feeling when watching it that the cartoon is unfinished. This is more or less true, because Avery's original ending had the two falling again, this time apparently to their doom. Schlesinger was reluctant to leave audiences believing their beloved star might have died, and so, to Avery's fury, cut the last 40 feet of the short. Relations between the two men swiftly got so bad that Avery was fired from Warners.

He was immediately signed up by MGM. This might not seem remarkable — he was a hot property whom surely any animation studio would gladly hire — but in fact it was: MGM was one of the stodgiest studios in the business, having built its recent reputation on such solid family fare as *The Wizard of Oz* (1939). Moreover,

MGM animation producer Fred Quimby was a man of unrelenting humorlessness, who had difficulty understanding why the Tom & Jerry movies, then being made for the studio by William Hanna and Joseph Barbera, were funny and who found Avery's surrealistic humor completely incomprehensible and therefore, by definition, *wrong*. So with hindsight it is bizarre that MGM and Quimby ever employed Avery, and even more bizarre that while there he managed to produce, despite all the restrictions — including those imposed on the industry as a whole by the Hays Office — what are certainly the most subversive cartoons ever made for the commercial U.S. cinema.

As animation directors are supposed to do, Avery did create some new series characters for MGM: Screwy Squirrel, George and Junior, Spike the gentle bulldog and, the only two with much permanence, Droopy, the little depressive bloodhound, and the Wolf. Viewing most of Avery's MGM series shorts today, one has the strong sense that in some ways he was merely going through the motions, that the main focus of his attentions was elsewhere. Many of the Droopy shorts provide the major exception to this pseudo-rule (the shorts featuring the Wolf are in a rather different category). One of the greatest of the Droopy cartoons, *Northwest Hounded Police* (1946), gives the seemingly characterless little dog all the power of a haunt: whatever the fugitive Wolf does and wherever he goes, Droopy is somehow there with him. Again Avery was, whether consciously or not, drawing upon deep-rooted mythological tropes: all over mythology we find embodiments of guilt, usually in the form of supernatural entities of some type or another, that are unshakable. Thus *Northwest Hounded Police* is not only funny — it most definitely is — but also in a way as disquieting as Poe's story "The Tell-Tale Heart," which draws on very similar primal fears. And the movie is also extremely imaginative, especially bearing in mind that essentially it's founded on no more than the running gag of Droopy's ubiquity.

But, as indicated, series characters were not what Avery's time at MGM was all about. What gave the best of Avery's cartoons their strength was that they kicked away the crutch of the series star and drew instead upon a cast of characters who seemed created afresh for each new movie but many of whom were in fact (again) archetypal. Avery was deeply emotionally involved in the animation of character, to the point where he realized that outer form was not the defining element of a character. So, when the Wolf appears in a Tex Avery short, he is important not because of his ears or teeth or tail but because he is a sort of visual shorthand for an archetypal character (who, of course, in folklore is often also a wolf). The physical features of the babe who can be Red Hot Riding Hood or Swing Shift Cinderella are not in themselves important: she is simply a code that conveys to us that this is an erotic archetype.

The most famous of his MGM shorts are the ones that pervert folktales, and of these the most famous is *Red Hot Riding Hood* (1943). This fell foul of the Hollywood censors, the Wolf's violently lustful reaction to the nightclub-singing Red being viewed as in part

too phallic; oddly, they seem not to have noticed the overtly phallic reaction of the stranger to "the girl who was known as Sue" back in 1939's *Dangerous Dan McFoo*. In *Red Hot Riding Hood* some of the Wolf's sexual pantomime had to be cut; much later, even this cut version was banned for a while from American television. What is not generally realized is that Avery was producing some of these overtly sexy cartoons as part of MGM's war effort: they were designed to entertain not children but the troops. They were the most popular animated shorts that MGM ever produced, and Preston Blair – who animated the character and thus deserves much of the credit – would recall that the curvaceous, provocative Red herself was so much admired that on one occasion someone even stole some cels featuring her that were waiting on the camera stand to be photographed.

Avery was obviously much enamored of the Little Red Riding Hood tale in general. Aside from *Red Hot Riding Hood* there were *Little Red Walking Hood* (1937) and *Little Rural Riding Hood* (1937), plus appearances of the Wolf and Red in such other movies as *Swing Shift Cinderella* (1945), *The Bear's Tale* (1940), and *The Screwy Truant* (1945).

As at Warners, Avery's innovations rubbed off on the other animators. In particular, his pacing – whereby as many gags as possible were crammed into as short an interval as possible – started to be imitated by MGM's other unit, the one run by Hanna and Barbera devoted to the production of the Tom & Jerry shorts. These were already fine examples of the animated short and very popular, but the introduction of faster pacing as well as sharper, Avery-style humor made them even better. It is ironic that seven of the Hanna–Barbera shorts won Oscars for MGM while Avery won only one, for *Blitz Wolf* (1942), a war-effort reworking of the Three Little Pigs story and his first movie for the studio.

The strain of life in general and of working at MGM – and for Fred Quimby in particular – took a major toll on an increasingly unhappy and self-isolating man. In 1950 he took a year off in order to try to recover from the stress of his workplace, but things were little better when he returned. It was a time of stress throughout the industry, as animated shorts – and indeed shorts in general – became less economical due to the erosion of movie audiences by television. Some animators, in particular Avery's MGM colleagues Hanna and Barbera, saw television as opening up a new and vastly larger field of opportunities, but Avery was not one of them. As much of a perfectionist as Walt Disney but without the clout to be able to mold television to his own liking, Avery was dedicated to theatrical animation. When MGM closed down his unit in 1954, he moved to the Walter Lantz Studio, effectively rejoining the company where he had started. However, he rapidly came to feel that he was being ripped off financially, and stayed at Lantz only long enough to direct the two Chilly Willy shorts – *I'm Cold* (1954; vt *Some Like It Not*), which was an Oscar nominee, and *The Legend of Rock-A-Bye Point* (1955; vt *Rockabye Legend*) – plus a couple of others.

By 1955 he was out on the street. He joined the small Hollywood studio Cascade, which specialized in producing

a Wild Hare (1940)

♫ color / animated ⏱ 8 minutes
Merrie Melodies/Bugs Bunny
Although a madcap rabbit had appeared in a few earlier Warners shorts, this is widely regarded as the first "real" appearance of Bugs Bunny. In fact, Bugs still has a way to go before reaching the form in which we have come to love him, but his perpetual antagonist, the numbskull hunter Elmer Fudd, is more or less completely formed and the trickster character of Bugs, complete with catchphrase "What's up, Doc?", is here. The action is fairly standard for the series: after opening verbal jousts, Elmer catches a skunk rather than Bugs in his carrot-baited rabbit trap; Bugs then promises Elmer a clear shot and stages a histrionic death scene; as Elmer weeps in repentance, Bugs kicks his behind.

all This and Rabbit Stew (1941)

♫ color / animated ⏱ 6³/₄ minutes
Merrie Melodies/Bugs Bunny
Bugs's sixth outing would be a regularly seen part of the canon were it not for the appalling racial stereotyping: in place of Elmer Fudd we have a caricatured black hunter characterized as lazy, stupid, shiftless, and mindlessly addicted to gambling. He is manipulated all over the landscape by Bugs in the way that all hunters inevitably are, having unpleasant encounters with a skunk and a bear, before the mere sight of a pair of dice in the rabbit's hand sends him into a gambling frenzy. Needless to say, he loses all his clothes, even, at the very last moment when the iris has contracted far enough that modesty may prevail, his remaining fig leaf.

Blitz Wolf (1942)

♫ color / animated ⏱ 9³/₄ minutes
Avery's first movie for MGM is a revamping of the tale of the Three Little Pigs: where the first two pigs build their houses of straw and wood respectively, Practical Pig surrounds his with artillery and trenches. The two feckless pigs mock him, but he warns them they should buy bombs and weapons in preparation for the invasion planned by the Big Bad Wolf – who is Hitler. They reply that they have a nonaggression treaty with Adolf Wolf, but of course that proves worthless and the Blitz begins. The two flimsy houses demolished, the three pigs hide in Practical Pig's entrenchment, with its "No Japs Allowed" sign. Only Practical Pig's military might, a copy of *Esquire* and a bottle of vitamin B-1 tablets can prevail against the villain. The *coup de grace* is administered by the pigs' secret weapon, Defense Bonds, and Adolf Wolf is blown to Hell.

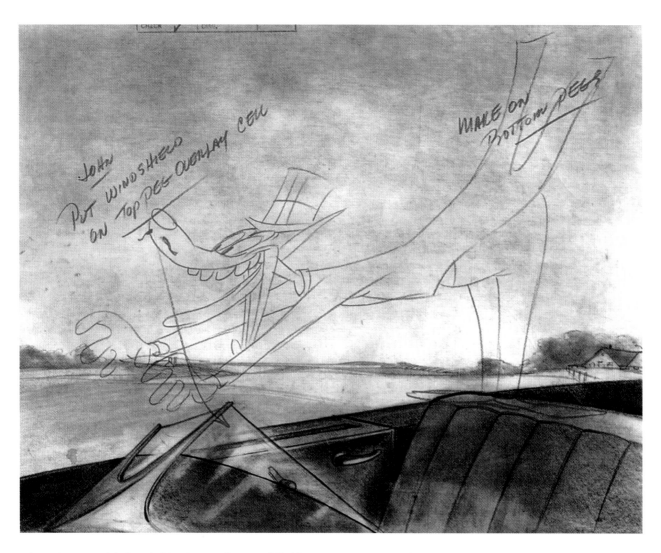

Layout drawing for *Little Rural Riding Hood* (1949) showing the Wolf. Photograph: Howard Lowery. © MGM, Warner Bros.

animated commercials for television; he actually won a Television Commercials Council Award in 1960. In many ways he seemed perfectly happy with this undistinguished twilight of a glorious career, but he began drinking heavily. Soon after his son Tim died of a drug overdose in 1972, at the age of 24, Avery and his wife of four decades, Patricia, separated. For the last three years of his life he worked at Hanna–Barbera as a gagman and character developer, and it was at the Hanna–Barbera office one day in 1980 that he collapsed. William Hanna himself drove Avery to the hospital. On August 26, 1980, Avery died in the hospital of lung cancer.

In a way Tex-Avery-the-man had died before this. By the end of his life he had, for a long time, had no faith in either himself or his accomplishments, looking back on his career with doubt that it had all mattered very much or that anything he had done had been of any worth whatsoever. But Tex Avery the *animator* did not die on that day in August 1980. His work is more popular now than it has probably ever been, and in France in particular he has attained the status of a cult hero – you might almost think he'd been French! The best of his cartoons are still as fresh today as when they were made, and it is arguable that his particular style of animation – with the surrealism, the exuberance, and the lightning pacing and gaggery – has never been surpassed, even in the homage to him by another of animation's great masters, Richard Williams, at the start of *Who Framed Roger Rabbit* (1988). And whenever, be it centuries hence – which it very well might be – one person says to another "What's up, Doc?" and thinks of a trickster who was also a grey rabbit, Frederick Bean Avery will still be alive.

Red Hot Riding Hood (1943)

🔈color / animated ⏱ 7¼ minutes

A short that caused a furore. It starts with an exaggeratedly cutesy version of the standard tale, but then the Wolf explodes: "I'm fed up with all that cissy stuff." Red and Granny join in the protests. The director gives in, and the story is revamped: the Wolf is a wolf in the sense of "lecher," Granny is a sexpot and Red, rechristened "Red Hot Riding Hood," works in a Hollywood nightclub. Half a century later, in *The Mask* (1994), Jim Carrey, watching Cameron Diaz's act, pays homage to the Wolf's reaction to Red's performance. Red refusing the Wolf's post-show blandishments, he pursues her to Granny's house, where Granny uses various slapstick methods in attempts to seduce him. Beaten and battered, the next night he is back at the nightclub. When Red starts to perform, rather than have anything more to do with women he shoots himself. But his ghost emerges and hoots and howls exactly as before.

Happy-Go-Nutty (1944)

🔈color / animated ⏱ 7¼ minutes
Screwy Squirrel

The second Screwy Squirrel short. Screwy, who thinks he's Napoleon, escapes from an institution for insane squirrels — Moron Manor, whose four tower blocks are shaped to spell out NUTZ — and goads the dimwitted blue dog designated the Nut Catcher into chasing him. The gags come fast and furious — too fast and furious, in fact, for the cartoon actually to be funny. The ending comes after the pair race past the screen saying "The End" and come back to it, bidding each other farewell from the movie; then the dog tells Screwy he's been pursuing him because Screwy must be nuts to think he's Napoleon — the dog himself is Napoleon.

Swing Shift Cinderella (1945)

🔈color / animated ⏱ 7¾ minutes

The short starts with a wild chase of Little Red Riding Hood by the Wolf. They zoom past the title screen, and she drags him back to explain that they're in the wrong cartoon. Ushering Red off, the Wolf transforms himself into a lecher-wolf and goes to visit the sexy Cinders. She repels his advances violently, then phones for help from the Fairy Godmother — who is boozily similar to her counterpart in Warner's *Cinderella Meets Fella* (1938) and is only too happy, to his huge dismay, at the prospect of sampling the Wolf's masculine charms. She transforms Cinders into a replica of Red from *Red Hot Riding Hood* (1943) and packs her off to the ball, which is at the luxurious Castle Mañana. Wolf and Godmother pursue. After much stuff that could be from *Red Hot Riding Hood*, midnight strikes: Cinders rushes off to catch her job on the midnight shift at Lockweed, only to find that all her fellow workers are . . . wolves.

Northwest Hounded Police (1946)

🔈color / animated ⏱ 7½ minutes

The Wolf is incarcerated in "Alka-Fizz Prison — No Noose is Good Noose," a sign in which says, "Come In — Have a Seat," pointing to an electric chair. He breaks out, courteously leaving a "Vacancy" sign at the gate, and heads north to the icy landscape of Canada — to Mounty County. Droopy, as Sergeant McPoodle, is the mountie given the job of catching him. There is much chasing; at one point the Wolf seeks sanctuary in an eyrie at the peak of the highest mountain, only for Droopy to emerge from the egg there. The chase leads all the way to New York (and indeed momentarily off the edge of the film) and into a movie theater, where the Wolf assumes he will be safe; but no, because what's being shown is, inevitably, a Droopy cartoon. Plastic surgery unavailing (he's given Droopy's face, and demands his own face back), he throws himself suicidally into a zoo lion's mouth, only to discover Droopy there. Finally back in prison, he wonders aloud if there could have been more than just one Droopy on his heels; outside his cell we see hundreds of them.

Little Tinker (1948)

🔈color / animated ⏱ 7¼ minutes

In a scenario reminiscent of one of Chuck Jones's Pepe Le Pew cartoons, a little skunk falls in love with a glamourous lady-squirrel, but she rejects him because of his stench. Same for a cute little girl-bunny. Even Cupid, who drops by to advise, must put on a gas mask. Cupid gives him a book, *Advice to the Love-Worn*, and he follows its advice to try out a Pepe Le Pew French accent on a chipmunk with no luck. Various other book-advised stratagems include disguising himself as Frank Sinatra, but even this fails once the dames get a whiff. He is about to commit suicide when Cupid insists he read the book's last chapter: "Camouflage." Disguised as a fox, he picks up a svelte lady-fox — only to find she is actually a disguised lady-skunk, so the two can live happily ever after.

TV of Tomorrow (1953)

🔈color / animated with live-action tv scenes ⏱ 7 minutes

One of Avery's occasional series, begun with *House of Tomorrow* (1949), parodying the popular futurology of the day. Among the futuristic features: the model that eliminates picture distortion caused by passing aircraft by shooting down the offending aircraft; and the set built into the front of the washing machine to take the tedium out of laundry day. One modern problem is pinpointed as a man switches from channel to channel to channel, each time finding the same monotonous Wild West chase. The finale is "a direct telecast from the planet Mars" . . . but Martian tv proves to be showing that same boring cowboy chase!

FRÉDÉRIC BACK (1924–)

Still from *Crac* (1981).

Frédéric Back was born on April 8, 1924, in Saarbrücken, Germany, the son of an orchestral timpanist. He grew up in Strasbourg before studying art in Paris from 1937 and, from the outbreak of World War II, in Rennes – all of which might lead one to think that he was a European animator. In fact, he moved to Montreal in 1948, intending to paint landscapes, but in the event joining the School of Furniture Design there. His first association with the screen came in 1952, when the Canadian Broadcasting Corporation (Société Radio-Canada) hired him as a graphic artist. He remained in Canada, and now is perhaps the most Canadian – *French*-Canadian – of all animators.

His early years at the CBC were devoted largely to art direction and set design; such material as he did produce for the screen was mainly in the form of still paintings and drawings, special effects, and miniatures, although he did do some animation for educational programs. Through his job he learned about painting on glass, which he practiced in his spare time. In 1968 the CBC opened up an animation department, and Back joined it; its director, Hubert Tison, has collaborated with Back in his animation work ever since. In 1970 the CBC started a film-exchange program with various tv stations in Europe. Because of this spreading of costs, the CBC animators, including Back, could spend time producing animation intended for programing rather than just station IDs and the like. Between 1970 and 1993, when he left the CBC, Back created nine animated movies and won two Oscars, for *Crac* (1981) and *The Man who Planted Trees* (*L'homme qui plantait des arbres*; 1987). He

was Oscar-nominated for two more. Since then he has continued to create animated movies. He has come to be regarded as *the* animators' animator (because of obsessive working he has lost the sight of his right eye). Through the love of nature expressed in his movies, he is known as a spearhead of environmentalist movements. In a 1997 interview Didier Ghez, Disney's Glen Keane, was asked which animated movie he admired the most:

> *The Man who Planted Trees* by Frédéric Back. He is doing what I want to do. He is saying something personal, because he believes it and his drawing is a passion for him. You look at his work and it's a moving impressionist painting with the light dappling across characters. This is what I want to do. I would like to be him.

Back's first animated movie, done with Graeme Ross, was *Abracadabra* (1970), the tale of a little girl who retrieves the sun from the sorcerer who has stolen it. This was followed by *Inon, or The Conquest of Fire* (*Inon ou la conquête du feu*; 1971), based on the Algonquin legend of how man obtained fire from the thunder god Inon. *The Creation of the Birds* (*La création des oiseaux*; 1973) is based on a Micmac legend that explains the changing seasons. *Illusion* (1974) shows how consumerism, greed, and urban sprawl

Crac (1981)

color / animated ⏱ 15 minutes

A century or more ago in Québec, a peasant chops down a tree, and from its wood crafts a rocking chair as a gift to his beloved. After their grand wedding celebration, he tends the fields while she sits in the rocker knitting garments for their firstborn. More and more children come, each delivered — including the twins — by a magical Native American messenger. For the children the old rocker is a place where they can enact their fantasies of being a train driver or a fisherman or a warrior. When the peasant is an old man, the chair breaks and he throws it out. Decades pass, and still the chair lies abandoned as an industrial city grows up where once there was farmland. One of the buildings is an art gallery, and the attendant appropriates the old chair that someone has found on the land for his own use, rocking on it as visitors ponder the impenetrable exhibits on the walls. But the children see through all the pretension and have eyes only for the rocking chair. At night, when no one is looking, the chair rocks to itself, remembering all the peasant revelry and joy it has seen, and dances with the pictures from the walls.

are destroying nature, but offers the hope that our children will reverse this trend. In *Taratata* (*Taratata la parade*; 1977) a child mimics a grand parade, making up in love what his recreation lacks in splendor. *All–Nothing* (*Tout–rien*; vt *Nothing–All–Nothing*; 1980), the first of Back's movies to be nominated for an Oscar, concerns the relationship between man and nature since the dawn of time. The English variant title, *Nothing–All–Nothing*, perhaps best expresses the overall "if this goes on" theme. He had also, in 1979, done the animated sequences for an Emmy-winning tv rendition of Stravinsky's *The Firebird*.

The animation historian Giannalberto Bendazzi and others identify *All–Nothing* as marking the end of the first phase of Back's animated creativity, in that all six of these movies, no matter how exquisitely made, are didactic in tone. His next three works somehow seem more mature. Hereafter he was prepared to let more of Frédéric Back the man shine through, so that watching any of these three movies is not just an aesthetic but an emotional experience; the fact that it's hard to isolate the source of the emotional reaction just makes the movies more captivating. Back is content with this ambiguity: in an interview with Dean Kalman Lennert in *The Paper Snarl* in 2000 he remarked that:

> when you say something after a film, sometimes you limit the vision of what you have [shown]. When a hundred people see a film you have a hundred different films going out because each [person] has a different reaction depending on his experience . . . so it is difficult to . . . add something by speaking.

The initial movie of this new phase was 1981's *Crac*, which won Back his first Oscar plus about twenty other international awards.

Through the history of a rocking chair — the title represents the *crack!* as the tree is felled that will make the chair — the *sense of* Québec peasant culture is conveyed to us, as well as the message that we discard such culture in favor of the modern at our own loss. In the concluding segment of the movie the old rocker, which has now become almost a sentient personality in its own right, persuades the abstract, soulless paintings on the walls of the modern art gallery that may be its final home to join in a wild rustic dance. As they dance, their cold, geometric abstraction dissolves into swirls of wild, energetic earth colors. There are moments of humor, too, and references to the Native American legends that predated by centuries the peasant community.

Back's next movie, *The Man who Planted Trees*, which garnered him his second Oscar and about thirty other international awards, was not finished until 1987. The reason the half-hour movie took him five years to make was not just the fact that he animated it almost entirely himself, doing about 80 percent of all the drawings with a solitary inbetweener (see page 83) to do the rest, but the painstaking method of animation he generally employs, using colored pencils with turpentine on frosted cels. The method makes his lines blur together, so that the animation seems almost painted; one difficulty is that modern frosted acetate is less coarsely grained than the older varieties, and thus doesn't hold the colors so well.

A story by Jean Giono is read aloud, uncut, as the soundtrack of *The Man who Planted Trees*. It begins with a young man walking through Alpine countryside. He encounters an old shepherd, Elzeard Bouffier, who tells him how, through two world wars, he has, singlehandedly and simply for love rather than reward, patiently planted and cultivated a whole forest of trees, creating an oasis of life from wasteland. It is tempting to see Elzeard Bouffier as an analogy for Back himself, who patiently crafted many thousands of drawings, and in so doing brought something out of nothing. The art in the movie seems derived from the styles of a number of great European painters, and the luminosity of the color makes watching *The Man who Planted Trees* an experience touched by enchantment.

Back's final movie for the CBC was the 24-minute *The Mighty River* (*Le fleuve aux grandes eaux*; 1993). It's the story of the St. Lawrence River and the wildlife surrounding it, and how these have been endangered or enhanced by the activities of humanity, from the earliest Native Americans onward. The narration of this animated quasi-documentary is by Donald Sutherland. It is regarded as a lesser work than the previous two movies, but nevertheless has passages of great beauty. It was nominated for an Oscar and received about twenty other awards.

Back has not confined himself to animation, having also done interior decoration, murals, and church restoration and ornamentation. He illustrated the book version of *Crac* (1982), with text by his wife, Ghylaine Paquin-Back, an edition of *L'homme qui plantait des arbres* (1989), and *Glimpses of an Arctic Past* (1995). Back is an Officer of the Order of Canada, a Knight of the Order of Québec, and an Officier de l'Ordre des Arts et Lettres de la France.

RALPH BAKSHI (1938–)

Setup for *The Lord of the Rings* (1978), showing Gandalf and Shadowfax. © 1978 Saul Zaentz Company. All rights reserved.

Of Palestinian descent, Ralph Bakshi was born in the Brownsville area of Brooklyn on October 29, 1938. It was soon obvious that he was artistically talented – one likes to imagine that the fledgling cartoonist Michael Corleone in *Heavy Traffic* (1973) is in part a self-portrait – and in due course he received formal art training at Manhattan's High School of Industrial Arts. He emerged with a diploma in cartooning and swiftly got a job as a cel painter with the Terrytoons Animation Studio, which had recently been bought by CBS. By the age of 21 he was an animator, working on some of the most popular of the Terrytoons tv characters – Mighty Mouse, Deputy Dawg, Heckle & Jeckle – as well as the theatrical James Hound series. Soon he was directing such series, and by his mid-20s he was the studio's Creative Director. In 1966 he was made its Supervising Director. It had been a meteoric rise, made possible in part by his own quirky genius and in part by the fact that CBS was constantly shuffling and reshuffling the Terrytoons activities around this time, so the right young man in the right place at the right time had every opportunity.

The true extent of that quirkiness first made itself publicly obvious in 1966, when the tv series *The Mighty Heroes* premiered. CBS had noticed that superhero series were popular and demanded that Terrytoons produce one. Bakshi responded in satirical vein to the proposal, coming up with a scheme for a program starring superheroes like Diaper Man, Cuckoo Man, and Rope Man. To general astonishment, the execs loved the idea, and 20 half-hour episodes were produced (of which ten were released as theatrical shorts in 1969–71). Although lacking conventional – or indeed useful – superpowers, somehow the Mighty Heroes bumbled through to triumph over equally bizarre villains such as The Enlarger, The Stretcher, The Toy Man, The Frog, and The Shocker.

Shortly afterward, in 1967, Terrytoons folded, and Bakshi was asked to join Paramount Cartoon Studios – the old Fleischer Studio – as a producer and director. This job lasted only a matter

of months before Paramount closed down its animation operation, but that was long enough for Bakshi to produce a few theatrical shorts. He was immediately taken on by Steve Krantz Productions to do some work on their animated tv series *Rocket Robin Hood* (1966–69), which relocated the adventures of Robin and his Merry Men into the year 3000, from Sherwood Forest to Sherwood Asteroid, and so forth. More importantly, Krantz made him co-producer, director, and story consultant for the *Spider-Man* animated tv series. This ran in weekly half-hour episodes – 52 in all – for two seasons from September 1967 to August 1969, with a third season running from March to September 1970. Grantray–Lawrence Animation of Toronto did the first season; Krantz Productions, with Bakshi at the helm, took over for the second and third seasons. Viewers noticed the difference: where the first season tended to pit Spider-Man against villains drawn straight from the pages of the Marvel comics and to follow the formula pretty closely, the second and third seasons saw a greater unpredictability in terms of both storyline and antagonists. As with *The Mighty Heroes*, a restless imagination like Bakshi's was incapable of any enduring patience with the standard plots, situations, formulaic characterizations, clichés, and conventions of the superhero genre.

He was impatient, too, with another convention: that animation was a children's medium. And he was keen to get away from the Disney approach of "clean-line animation," which necessarily affected much of the other work he had been doing. As is noted elsewhere in this book, one of the great burdens on animation has been the relentless pressure by tv executives, distributors, critics/reviewers, and even consumers that animation should be "like Disney" (or, at a lower level, "like Hanna–Barbera"). "Not like Disney" is taken to mean "not as good as Disney." (Bakshi is actually a great admirer of Disney animation, and raves in particular about the studio's *Tarzan* [1999].) In this context the reference "not like Disney" is to the autographic approach taken by most independent and most European animators but by few commercial US animators aside from Bakshi. In essence, he'd been trained in the autographic approach by default: required for budgetary reasons to produce 50 feet of animation and all their own layouts each week, the Terrytoons animators had no choice but to abandon such niceties as pencil tests and opt for an autographic style. In an *Animation World News* article in July 1999 Bakshi describes this, and also stresses the influence on him of the animator Jim Tyer, who, far from bemoaning the enforced looseness of the Terrytoons animation, realized what great strengths it gave to the end result. This lesson stuck with Bakshi when, in 1970–71, he worked on his first feature, *Fritz the Cat* (1972), which he wrote as well as directed:

> On *Fritz the Cat, Heavy Traffic, Hey Good Lookin', Wizards,* we had no pencil tests. What I did have was the brilliant golden age animators on my side. Who loved what they

Fritz the Cat (1972)

color / animated ○ 77 minutes

Fritz (a cat) starts this episodic movie as a student at New York University. In the course of various adventures associated with sex and dope, he falls foul of the attentions of the police, and decides to cut and run for the West Coast with his girlfriend. The girlfriend having abandoned him in the middle of nowhere, he falls in with a bunch of urban terrorists, whose stated leftist, anarchist ideals barely mask their true, Nazi agenda. Nearly kiled in one of their bombing raids, he is visited in the hospital by a trio of willing bimbo cats, and realizes he should stick to his original hedonist philosophy and let the rest of the world take care of itself.

Heavy Traffic (1973)

color / animated/live-action ○ 76 minutes

Michael is an aspiring New York cartoonist who somehow manages to work despite the interminable fighting between his low-level-mafioso father and his shrill Jewish mother. He manages to madden both parents by taking up with a beautiful black girlfriend, and leaves home to live with her. However, life is hard for the young pair; they take on a succession of direr and direr jobs, eventually descending to the sex industry, she luring men as a prostitute and then he robbing them before she actually sleeps with them. From here the descent to more violent crime is rapid, and at the close of the animated story a retaliatory death awaits both of them. But all this has been framed by live-action sequences in which the animated story is a quasi-precognitive dream of footloose Michael; at the end of the movie he encounters the beautiful black woman of his dream and decides that loving her is worth the risk of the dream "warning" coming true.

were doing – finally. Virgil Ross, Irv Spence, Manny Perez, Bob Carlson, John Sperry, Ed Barge, Tex Avery (he was Irv Spence's best friend and used to come in and hang out a couple of times a week until he left the planet), John Vita . . . These guys loved what we were doing. They were free to create, to say anything, and man, could they animate. Not the slick, boring, perfect stuff, but the "I really feel this scene" kinda stuff. I believe in what I am drawing. I believe in what I am drawing.

Fritz the Cat was "adult" animation with a vengeance – at least in the sense that it contained cursing, nudity, drugs, sex, rock'n'roll, and everything else that might inflame our moral guardians – and even before production started it had created a furor in the industry. Bakshi's confederate in the venture was Steve Krantz, who produced not only this and the subsequent Bakshi feature but also the vastly inferior, non-Bakshi *Fritz* sequel, *The Nine Lives of Fritz the Cat* (1974).

Based on the characters created by wayward comics genius Robert Crumb – although the movie was in fact disowned by

him – *Fritz the Cat* (1972) is generally and too easily dismissed as a self-indulgently scatological romp through the hippy clichés of the 1960s. It is, however, something more than that. As a portrayal of a particular stratum of Western society during a particular era, it is often almost disturbingly accurate, and as such it has dated very well. Moreover, Bakshi's love–hate relationship with the people and mores of that microcosm is fully evident in the satirical bite of much of the movie. Hippies may have watched it in the 1970s for nostalgic reasons and laughed aloud at the (very funny) clowning of a pair of dimwitted cops who, in the first half of the movie, represent Fritz's potential nemesis and are appropriately (for this ethos) depicted as pigs. But other audiences, and particularly viewers today, will be more struck by the frequent savagery with which Ralph Bakshi depicts his male principals.

Fritz himself, a student at New York University (the opening scenes are played out in nearby Washington Square Park), is, behind a veneer of *faux* sophistication, an innocent abroad in the tradition of Henry Fielding's characters Joseph Andrews and, more especially, Tom Jones. There is something of the feel of the 18th-century novel, too, in the movie's structure, which is disjointedly episodic rather than linear – there is no overarching plot and, consequently, neither is there any resolution of themes, stories, or developments. Fritz starts as a randy, pot-smoking but fundamentally innocent hedonist, and is dragged along haphazardly as the movie explores some of the seamier and darker aspects of the hippie revolution of love. He sniggers at the pretty girls (rabbits and cats), who over-adulate black men (crows) because Black Is Beautifully Fashionable, and whose empty anti-racism can be encapsulated by their question "Why does a great actor like James Earl Jones always have to play black men?" Yet his own attempts to bridge the racial divide are every bit as naive and ham-fisted – and in the end demeaning to blacks. Later in the movie he is taken in – in both senses of that expression – by card-carrying hippies who are nevertheless out-of-the-closet neo-Nazis, urban terrorists, and misogynistic sadists. He realizes the true nature of their evil only fractions of a second before being blown up by the terrorist bomb he has helped plant, because to have done otherwise would have involved making a mental leap out of the hippie ambience, an ambience as rule-laden as the "more conventional" society he has histrionically chosen to reject. At the end of his adventures, as he makes a Lazarus-like recovery in the hospital and immediately initiates an orgy with three airhead girls, his philosophical conclusion is, in essence, that all that's important in life is getting laid a lot – which was exactly the extent of his personal ethical formulation at the movie's outset. Like the true innocent abroad, he has been impervious to the world around him and, ultimately, is completely unaffected by his experiences.

Fritz the Cat was, as it was doubtless intended to be, a *cause célèbre* from the moment it was released. To the pillars of that long-ago society it was a red rag, seemingly designed to annoy almost everybody except the "degenerates" who were their whipping boys anyway. The real reason for the furor was that society had got it into its head that animation was a cutesy medium whose sole purpose was to cater to children. The ribaldry inherent in the work of such established masters of the form as Tex Avery and even the early Disney was either glossed over or ignored – or, it's tempting to believe, simply not *perceived*, invisible to a mindset which had *already* concluded that animation was innocuous. Bakshi overturned all these preconceptions in a single stroke: his characters were grotesque rather than twee, scummy rather than cute; and when they showed their bottoms it was not, as with the cupids at the end of the *Pastoral* section of Disney's *Fantasia* (1940), for the purpose of adding yet further saccharine but to present an erotic (at least to the other grotesques) or offensive image. Hence the fury: it was the rage that the unexpected always sparks in the rigid-minded.

It is not necessary to *like* this movie in order to recognize the colossal service Bakshi performed with it for animation in general, and certainly commercial animation: whole areas of modern animation could never have come about had he not taken the plunge. It wasn't just a revolution in terms of subject matter; perhaps even more important was that the movie showed there was an alternative to the Disney ethos, that animation need not be designed purely to warm the heart or moisten the cheeks or keep the kids quiet; that animated characters need not be cute and cuddlesome and merchandisable by the millions – indeed, Bakshi's characters are most often distinctly *unlovable*. What he did, through animation style, dialogue and character design, was to show that far too many of his contemporaries were careering down a blind alley in their attempts to become more Disney-like than Disney. Although the term "adult animation" is usually used of *Fritz the Cat* in euphemistic or derogatory reference to its sex and cursing, the movie can also be seen as a pioneer of adult animation in the more literal sense – the breakthrough movie that opened brand new vistas to the commercial animator in the United States.

Having established a territory for himself, Bakshi was left with the problem of whether to extend its borders or simply to explore it more thoroughly. With *Heavy Traffic* (1973), his follow-up movie, he chose a blend of the two options. One of the most violent animations ever screened, this is another New York lament, filmed with some sequences in live action and some in limited animation. It tells of young Michael, wannabe cartoonist son of a mob-connected, racist, promiscuously adulterous Italian father and a (justifiably) shrewish Jewish mother. Escape from their prejudices and their bloody battles is clearly essential, yet Michael does very little about it – he is as much an unempowered participant as Fritz – until he is almost driven out by his father's racism: the lovely Carole, who could have her pick of any man but who has willy-nilly chosen

Michael, is in his father's eyes just a black woman, and hence an inferior form of life. Carole and Michael try virtually everything in their efforts to subsist together, finally sinking to quasi-prostitution and violent crime; moreover, the father takes out a contract on his son to end the exogamy. The story seems to conclude as Michael has his brains blown out; but then we discover all has been a dream. He meets the real Carole but meekly accepts a rebuff from her; goes home to discover that his nightmare version of life was no exaggeration; and pursues and assertively woos her. Even if degradation and sudden death will lie at the end of the story, he feels that's a small price to pay for the treasure of escape from the present.

Again, however, Bakshi is reaching beyond the individual in his tale, for *Heavy Traffic* is not just about Michael: it is about a generation discarding the trash of its predecessor generation – the development is inevitable, decreed and instigated by no one. The metaphor that runs throughout the movie is of pinball, pinball being a game over whose outcome the player has only limited control and which has the option, any time the player seems to be about to win, of declaring TILT.

There are some glorious flights of fancy in the midst of what is otherwise a much more tightly controlled and self-disciplined movie than *Fritz the Cat*. A brief hallucinatory sequence as the animated Michael meets his death is animated beautifully, semi-surrealistically and highly imaginatively . Told in limited animation in the middle of the movie, as an example brought partly to life in Michael's cartooning, is the futuristic and deliciously blasphemous post-Apocalypse saga (a foretaste here of Bakshi's *Wizards*) of Wanda the Last, the most beautiful woman in this desolated world, and the eventually parricidal son she conceives through orthodox coitus with a horny God. But despite these sequences, and the upbeat live-action conclusion, it is difficult to conclude that this is other than a pessimistic movie: the streets of a mindlessly violent New York form the backdrop, and there is a sense that, whatever the aspirations of the fledgling generation, things will never change.

Apparently, Bakshi initially intended to base this movie project on Hubert Selby's controversial novel *Last Exit to Brooklyn* (1964); however, negotiations for the screen rights fell through at a late stage in the proceedings, and so Bakshi hastily put together a story with the same setting and ethos.

After *Heavy Traffic* Bakshi and Krantz parted ways, and Bakshi formed his own company, Bakshi Productions Inc.

With 1974's *Coonskin* (retitled *Streetfight* for video release) Bakshi finally became too controversial for his own good: although Paramount had contracted to distribute the movie, they shied away from its frank portrayal of racism. Eventually it was released by industry minnows Bryanston, and then only for a brief run. Once again mixing animation and live-action, the movie adopts some tropes and indeed some subplots from Joel Chandler Harris (the creator of Brer Rabbit) but could hardly be more distanced from the folksy homespun wisdom of the Brer

Coonskin (1974)

(vt *Streetfight*)
⚲color / animated/live-action ◷ 82 minutes
In live action, two black men plan to spring a third from a dour, concentration-camp-style Southern prison and flee to Harlem, where they will do their best to make good. The parallel animated tale — of what could happen after the escape — has a prison-bound Scatman Crothers narrating in lieu of Uncle Remus and the three central characters rendered as Brother Bear, Brother Fox and Brother Rabbit, the latter being as one might expect the trickster of the trio.

Wizards (1977)

⚲color with some b/w / animated with live-action archive footage ◷ 80 minutes
Two million years after a holocaust, Delia, Queen of the Fairies, gives birth to twins, Avatar and Blackwolf, who shall become wizards; even at birth the two are "polarized" — Avatar attractive and good, Blackwolf repellent and evil. Delia's death, years later, generates a magical battle between the two which Avatar wins, Blackwolf being driven to hide and scheme in the city of Scortch, in the mutant (human) lands, swearing vengeance. Three thousand years later the real story begins . . . Blackwolf has parties of assassins roaming the land, exterminating those who believe in the power of nature and magic. He launches against the Free States a mighty war machine, overtly modeled on Nazi Germany. Blackwolf has also invented a strange device, the Dream Machine, which can mentally possess the troops of the forces of Good. Those forces are led by — and at times seem to comprise solely — the bumbling, hippie-ish, elderly wizard Avatar, the scantily clad ingenue fairy queenlet Elinore, the plucky elf Weehawk, and the robotic Peace, once Blackwolf's premier assassin, Necron 99, but renamed by Avatar when turned from Evil to Good.

The Lord of the Rings (1978)

(vt *J.R.R. Tolkien's The Lord of the Rings*)
⚲color / animated ◷ 131 minutes
This follows the plot of the first half of Tolkien's trilogy. Created in an earlier time by an evil sorcerer, the Ring corrupts everyone who possesses it, and all who have once owned it and lost it yearn uncontrollably to repossess it. It was believed finally lost to all, but then, before this movie begins, it was found by the hobbit Bilbo. He passes it to his nephew, Frodo, who is charged — under the instruction and occasional leadership of the wizard Gandalf — with taking it to a place of safety. The movie chronicles the adventures of Frodo and the band of friends who choose to accompany him as they attempt to effect this, meanwhile being hounded by various embodiments of Evil, most notably the awesomely undead armies of the Dark Lord Sauron. Unfortunately the tale ends mid-swashbuckle, albeit with the promise of a (never to be made) conclusion.

American Pop (1981)

color with some b/w / animated with live-action archive footage ⬤ 80 minutes

The story of 20th-century pop music as told through the lives of four participants in that history, an immigrant Russian Jew child, Zalmie, and his son Benny, grandson Tony and great-grandson Little Pete. Zalmie is more of a music-hall/burlesque act than a singer, especially after his voice box is injured during World War I; he also becomes inextricably entwined with the mob. Benny is the true musical genius of the family, but dies young, shot in the back by a German soldier in France during World War II. Itinerant rebel-without-a-cause Tony drifts into Sixties hippie rock almost by accident, and becomes a casualty of its drugs-and-booze philosophy — though not before he has passed on the torch to his illegitimate son Pete, perhaps the only one of the quartet to match hard-headed determination and business nous to musical talent, and consequently the only one to achieve genuine success — which he does as a mainstream punk rocker.

Hey Good Lookin' (1982)

color /animated ⬤ 87 minutes

Brooklyn in 1953, and the Italian gangs hate the black gangs. Vinny, leader of the Italian gang the Stompers, is endowed with more dress sense than valour; his best friend Crazy Shapiro, son of the local racist cop, proves to be crazy not as in zany but as in psychopathic, and murders a pair from the rival Black Chaplains. There are various rumbles, until in the end Vinny must flee town. The main tale is framed by an encounter, thirty years later, between Vinny and his 1950s girlfriend Roz.

Fire & Ice (1983)

color /animated ⬤ 81 minutes

Young muscleman Larn — the last of all his slaughtered tribe — strives with the aid of the enigmatic Darkwolf (who looks disconcertingly like a loinclothed Batman with mannerisms borrowed from the Lone Ranger) to save the lovely Princess Teegra (whose entire attire, sewn up together, might just make a lady's handkerchief), daughter of the vacillatory king of the civilized but beleaguered city Fire Keep, from the nonexistent mercies of the Elric-style albino necromancer, Ice Lord and would-be world conqueror Nekron, who uses swiftly mobile glaciers and subhuman warriors to subjugate the lands he covets and tyrannizes. In the end Larn succeeds against all the odds, but only thanks to the unexplained interventions of Darkwolf.

Rabbit stories – or from the Disney live-action/animated riff on them, *Song of the South* (1946).

The three animated friends move through a Harlem populated by pimps, whores, pushers, murderous thugs, muggers, gangsters, false prophets, garbage-pickers, all using the f-word (not to mention the n-word) as often as they breathe . . . this is no idealized vision of black society, yet it is, warts and all, an astonishingly loving one. While white society – personified as the seductively promiscuous Miss America, available to black men only through threatened rape and then proving clap-ridden – is, because of the repression it imposes, the ultimate villain of the piece, there are black villains too, whose actions serve only to exacerbate that repression, a point made by Brother Rabbit: "It's tough enough fighting Miss America without bullshit from my own brothers."

Controversy was one thing, but *Coonskin* made the bad mistake of losing money; the U.S. movie industry can tolerate a lot, but not that. There was an overwhelming sense that Bakshi had overstayed his welcome as Hollywood's bad boy – he'd been a flash in the pan, a one-hit wonder, the hit being one of those idiosyncratic freaks that just come along every now and then. He had established no track record. What was a much more genuine concern was that Bakshi had spent three movies exploring much the same turf – the lowlife of Manhattan – and seemed pusillanimous about the prospect of leaving it. One can imagine, then, how cries of joy failed to fill the corridors of the distributors at the news that a fourth Bakshi movie, seemingly repeating the formulae of the first three, was on its way.

That movie was *Hey Good Lookin'*, largely completed by 1975 but due to lack of industry interest not released until 1982. What is not evident is that Bakshi had indeed planned to make a breakthrough with this movie: it was to be his first all-live-action feature. However, mid-production it was evident that the project as a whole was in deep trouble. He was told that, to give it any chance at all, he should play to his strength – animation. As a result, *Hey Good Lookin'* continues so precisely, in terms of visual style, from where *Coonskin* left off that it's hard to remember one is watching a different movie.

There is very little plot to this slight but rather appealing movie. If controversy played a part in its failure to find a distributor, then it can only have been the controversy raised by Bakshi's previous movies, in particular *Coonskin*, for there's little here to which one can take much exception (although some have sounded off about its fairly tame violence). In fact, there's little here at all, which may be the real problem.

In parts of *Hey Good Lookin'* one becomes more conscious than before that Bakshi is using rotoscoping as a shortcut

rather than an effect. Bakshi did not invent this process (see page 81) – essentially, shooting sequences in live action and then tracing the resulting frames for animation – but his name was to become much associated with it, especially after his next couple of movies.

With the failure of *Coonskin* and the disaster of *Hey Good Lookin'* fresh in his mind, it would have been obvious to an animator far less intelligent than Bakshi that he was overdue to leave his self-delineated ghetto, and this is exactly what he did. His next movie, *Wizards* (1977), is a charmingly whimsical yet bitterly *felt* post-apocalyptic fantasy. The animation is recognizably Bakshi's while being quite different in style from that of his previous movies – rather, different in *styles*, because he uses a diversity of them here. Rotoscoping is deployed extensively and to fine effect, especially in the portrayal of the armies of Evil as they approach the Final Conflict. But aside from this the overall affect of the animation is akin to that of the great anime creators – one has to keep reminding oneself that *Wizards* predates Miyazaki's *The Castle of Cagliostro* (1979), not the other way round. The backgrounds – supervised by the British fantasy artist Ian Miller, and on occasion showing his own distinctive, meticulous style and draftsmanship – are especially lovely, even the simplest of them; and in general the movie has a strong visual *brio* despite occasional technical hurriedness. Bakshi even takes time out for a brief parody or two of the Disney treatment of fantasy.

Wizards loses nothing of its power for being a small movie: it is *The Red Badge of Courage* alongside *All Quiet on the Western Front*. But at the same time there is a sense, sharpened by hindsight, that this is a movie done in preparation for something else. Sure enough *The Lord of the Rings* (1978) and *Fire & Ice* (1983) were on their way. It is not the first time that a dry-run movie has outshone the later and supposedly greater creation. Moreover, *Wizards* surprised everyone by being a minor box-office hit; it made much more of a profit than anyone had anticipated, and its video sales are still relatively buoyant.

In my conversations with him, Bakshi admitted, openly and unprompted, that *The Lord of the Rings* was a disaster. In small part the blame must be attributed to the producers, who lost faith; but he acknowledged that the real fault lies at his own door – and that the studio bosses' loss of faith was, certainly from their perspective, entirely understandable. The problem was that Bakshi was too much in awe of the material he was adapting for the screen. At the start of the project the movie was to be the acme of his career, the ultimate cinematic treatment of a novel that he personally adored and worshiped as a masterpiece of literature, J.R.R. Tolkien's massive, three-volume *The Lord of the Rings* (1954–55). This reverential approach served him ill. He found himself reluctant to cut or change so much as a single word of the original. Since Tolkien's novel is perhaps three-quarters of a million words in length and the average movie script is perhaps 10,000 words long, it was obvious that this

reluctance to adapt was a recipe for catastrophe. Production slowed, stuttered, and constipated; Bakshi, who could be as difficult as any creator, became impossible to deal with. There were constant changes of personnel – not only for this reason, of course, but also often because key staff had other professional commitments and simply couldn't stay with the project any longer. Naturally, costs soared; and to the studio personnel it must have seemed more and more money was flooding into a bottomless pit, with very little to show for it. In the end Bakshi was forced to finish fast, fudging and shortcutting in all directions and having to be satisfied with an adaptation that barely covers the contents of Tolkien's first volume, *The Fellowship of the Ring* (1954).

All of these measures are only too evident in the final result, which is a botched, disorganized, unsatisfying, muddily animated and generally confused and confusing movie. The use of rotoscoping, which had done Bakshi so proud in *Wizards*, here looks exactly like what it was: a means of speeding up production. The overuse of the technique, which increases pronouncedly toward the end of the movie, becomes progressively more rebarbative and has the additional irritation that characters whose portrayals have by now been well established slip well off-model during the rotoscoped sequences. The rotoscoping of the supposedly hyper-terrifying Balrog renders the monster banal and deeply unfrightening.

And the rotoscoping is far from the only irritation. The various hobbits are personified in the early stages of the movie as ebullient small children rather than adults – for example, to express joy they jump up and down or dance around in circles – and their voicing, especially that of Sam Ganji, is profoundly annoying. Offsetting that are the excellent characterizations of players like Aragorn, Gandalf, and especially Gollum, who are finely voiced by John Hurt, William Squire, and Peter Woodthorpe respectively.

The problems go deeper. There are various ways in which Tolkien's novel can be read, and one of them is as heroic fantasy (often called, outside scholarly circles, Sword & Sorcery); it is perfectly legitimate that Bakshi should have chosen this option. However, a great difficulty with filming heroic fantasy is that the lofty pronouncements, portentous deeds, archetypal characters, mighty feats, and general melodrama, all of which can glow with layers of meaning on the printed page, tend to look a bit ... well, *silly* on the screen. It is a fictional subgenre that gains part of its strength from constantly teetering on the edge of the ridiculous; if the suspension of disbelief falters for one moment, the whole structure falls apart. Bakshi would have had a hard enough task maintaining that credibility throughout what is, at a whopping 131 minutes, perhaps the longest animated movie ever produced outside Japan, but it was made impossible for him both by the rotoscoping (yet again) and, not to mince words, by the use of Peter S. Beagle as the primary screenwriter. Beagle is deservedly regarded as one of the pivotal figures in 20th-century written

Still from *The Lord of the Rings* (1978) showing Gandalf and Frodo.

fantasy; but, as shown particularly in the animated movie *The Last Unicorn* (1982), based on his own superb 1968 novel, he has considerable difficulty translating his concepts to the cinema. The dialogue that works so well on the page all too often comes over on screen as trite, pompous, or both – almost to the point of seeming self-parody. Thus the very Beagle-ish sequence in the enchanted land of Lothlorien, which is not especially well animated, somehow comes across as a school play in which the teachers' little darling has been cast as the good fairy.

The degree of plotting chaos cannot be overemphasized. We are all familiar with bad storytellers – bar or party bores – who know their tale so well that they're incapable of telling it: they blithely omit much of the important information on the unconscious assumption that, it being known to them, it must also be known to their glazed listeners. This is exactly the fault with the plotting here. The movie's final great battle is, when all has seemed lost, won by the good guys – but for no apparent reason other than that the air is suddenly filled with pure notes from a trumpet and the sun comes out. Indeed, whole swathes of plot events

happen for no apparent reason. Even if one is familiar with Tolkien's massive novel (which can itself be pretty confusing) it is exceptionally difficult to follow what is going on in the movie. The motivations of our heroes are unclear: although one understands why Frodo wants to take the Ring out of the Shire, there is no perceptible reason why he and his companions should then embark on their gruelling quest except that the quest is one of the staples of heroic fantasy (and other generic forms of fantasy). And the motivations of the bad guys, except for the Dark Lord Sauron's overarching desire to lay his hands on the Ring and with it conquer the world for Evil, are even less on view. Just to add to the general shambles, the movie has no conclusion or resolution: it just stops mid-gasp with the abrupt announcement that "Here ends the first part of the history of the War of the Rings," which must have mightily rattled those who shelled out good money for their first-run movie theater ticket expecting the whole thing . . . especially since no further part has appeared, or will. Overall, then, the work is reminiscent – often visually too – of one of those crummy old B-movie Westerns in which everyone gallops around interminably to no detectable purpose.

Yet Bakshi's *The Lord of the Rings* does have some virtues. There are some lovely sequences of animation, and, where

dialogue and animation marry well together, one can get a deeply rewarding glimpse of Bakshi's underlying vision of the tale. It's as if what we're being presented with is a set of notes and jottings toward the completed work; and there's always a fascination in studying a creator's notes and jottings, some of which are exquisitely brilliant, some relatively humdrum, and many destined to be wisely ditched during the final act of creation. For this reason alone the movie is worth watching. One can only dream longingly of the 10- or 12-hour epic which Bakshi might have made, and certainly had the ability to make, had he been given unlimited supplies of time and money. Full credit is due to him for having had the enormous ambition to conceive the enterprise, even if the end-result is so disheartening.

One senses that the experience of *The Lord of the Rings* scalded and shattered its director. Although in fact the movie turned a respectable profit – presumably because of the Tolkien connection – the critical flak must have been almost unbearable for him, especially coupled with the colossal hype the studio had generated for the movie in advance of its release. Worse still must have been the daily confirmation, as the chorus of vituperation rose, that his great dream lay in ruins. He was not to say goodbye to fantasy, or even to heroic fantasy, but for the moment he retreated to the safe territory he had marked out in such movies as *Heavy Traffic* and *Coonskin*. (Despite popular misconception, he was not involved in the 1981 Gerald Potterton-directed animated science-fiction compilation *Heavy Metal*, although his thematic and visual influence is overt throughout that movie.)

Yet his return to home ground was with a highly – and refreshingly – ambitious movie, *American Pop* (1981). Here he uses the history of U.S. 20th-century popular music, as told through the stories of four generations begun by a Jewish child refugee from Russian pogroms at the start of the century, to portray in microcosm a much broader theme: a social history of the American Century, of the sourer aspects of the American Dream. Almost a by-product is the grand historical *justification* that gradually builds up of modern (1980s) rock music, which Bakshi clearly sees not as the facile nonsense it was so often taken to be but more as the topmost floor to date of a great and integrally architected edifice that is forever under further construction. This is underlined in the final sequence, as an almost hallucinogenic kaleidoscope of images drawn from all periods of the 20th century underpins a driving rock rhythm.

American Pop has been Bakshi's most commercially successful movie, almost certainly not because of its many cinematic virtues but because of its soundtrack, which comprises an expertly chosen and interwoven sequence of popular song. A cynic might suggest that this was exactly as intended, that the whole enterprise was directed toward producing a soundtrack that would draw vast audiences, with the movie as merely a necessary ancillary. Whatever the case, over twenty years after *American Pop*'s release it is still a

standard item on the shelves of any self-respecting video store, a situation to which most of the recognized classic movies of that era can only aspire. But what this success obscures is the fact that *American Pop* is actually itself deserving of classic status: Bakshi failed to achieve his sweeping ambition with *The Lord of the Rings* but here, taking on a vision very nearly as ambitious, he fully succeeded. If there is one criticism that can be made, it is a very mild one: that he is less at ease with the smallish parts of his multigenerational story that are set outside his beloved East Coast, specifically outside New York. Even so, his thumbnail portrayal of 1960s San Francisco, when there was a hippie band being formed and rehearsing and splitting up on every corner, is quite masterful in its capturing of mood. (This central section, as Tony, grandson of the original immigrant Zalmie, makes it as a songwriter but then throws everything away for the great god Drugs, is something of a movie *à clef*, with a main character who owes much to Janis Joplin.) The narrative as a whole is driven forward by quite exceptional characterization, with each new son, like it or not, becoming his father . . . until Tony almost violently rejects this role in the nick of time, abandoning his bastard son Little Pete rather than risk forcing him into his own broken mold – only for Little Pete to follow the pattern anyway, this time not just accepting his father's role but magnificently transcending it, beating considerable odds to become the music star his male ancestors had dreamed of being.

The animation is never poor and often terrific, and the additional visual elements Bakshi uses in tandem with it are also of great interest: archival live-action footage drawn from the various eras; collage work primarily using photographs; and painted stills, some of which offer a tantalizing forecast of the fine-art oil paintings which Bakshi, having declared his moviemaking days to be behind him, currently produces.

At some point over the years Bakshi had fallen in love with the art of Frank Frazetta, the Michelangelo of Sword & Sorcery painting. After over a decade's distinguished work in the comics, Frazetta emerged in the early 1960s as a book-cover artist for works by authors such as Edgar Rice Burroughs and Robert E. Howard. He now concentrates largely on fine art. In the late 1970s Bakshi contacted Frazetta suggesting that they collaborate on a movie. To his astonishment Frazetta replied positively, and, as soon as the two men could manage to synchronize their schedules, they began work together planning *Fire & Ice* (1983), an animated movie based in what could loosely be thought of as Frazetta's world; appropriately, the movie had the working title *The Sword and the Sorcery*. This is a world of Conan-like warriors, lusciously underclad heroines, pterodactyl-like dragons that can be ridden into battle, lesbian (but of course) sorceresses, dinosaur-like water-monsters, sinister, tormentedly self-loathing villains . . . a savage and primitive world where mighty barbarians battle each other in an enactment of the time-old struggle between the principles of Good and Evil, here embodied in the two nations Fire Keep and Ice.

Many of the prejudices of pulp Sword & Sorcery are carried over into the movie – the equation of homosexuality with evil, the dark-skinned, moronic hordes versus the light-skinned intelligent good guys, etc. – and this brings a bitter taste to the mouth. To counter this in small part, Bakshi and Frazetta try to marry two quite different personalities in the character of Teegra, who is on the one hand a complete ninny, as would match her bimboesque appearance, and on the other brave, bright and resourceful. Those dark-skinned goons – Evil's cannon-fodder – are primarily of Neanderthal appearance (although their officers more resemble modern negroids); the movie can be read as depicting the hypothetical conflict, in dim prehistory, between the Neanderthal and Cro-Magnon strains of humankind, which the Cro-Magnons of course won. Thus *Fire & Ice* could be thought of as an example of prehistory being written by the winners. On occasion the actions of the Neanderthal goons are clearly and accurately modeled on higher-primate behavior.

Where the movie really triumphs is visually: certainly *Fire & Ice* is consistently the most beautiful of Bakshi's movies – it is hard to think of a lovelier commercial animated feature from a Western moviemaker, with the exception of the very much later and far bigger-budgeted Disney *Tarzan* (1999). Indeed, there's a feeling that in making *Tarzan* – not to mention parts of *Mulan* (1998) – the Disney animators studied *Fire & Ice*; although the movies are visually very different and although the earlier movie could not benefit from such technological bonuses as Deep Canvas, they have a similar visual affect.

Fire & Ice marked the end, for about a decade, of Bakshi's cinematic career; indeed, his later screen activities can be regarded as hiatuses in his newfound career – newfound, thanks to Frazetta – as a fine artist. This is not to say that Bakshi's canvases, certainly the later ones, remotely resemble Frazetta's: they don't. They possess the same "eye" as Bakshi's animations – the same sense of beauty in the grotesque, the same ability to distort beyond reason and yet retain the illusion of the mimetic – and they have a tremendous presence, often emphasized physically by the intensity, vigor, and sheer thickness with which the paints are applied.

There was still another major animated feature to come, but aside from that there has since been only television work. One tv series is of considerable relevance here, representing as it did a breakthrough in children's animated Saturday-morning television: *Mighty Mouse: The New Adventures*. Way back in his Terrytoons days Bakshi had been involved in *The Mighty Mouse Playhouse*, the Terrytoons tv show that, in its heyday, could eclipse even *The Mickey Mouse Club* in the ratings. Its first incarnation ran from 1955 to 1966, and there were countless episodes, some of which Bakshi directed. When *The Mighty Heroes* went into syndication in 1967, it was as a segment of *The Mighty Mouse Playhouse*. Filmation, nearly a decade and a half later, attempted to revive the character, along with the Terrytoon duo Heckle &

Cool World (1992)

🌀 color / animated/live-action ⏱ 101 minutes

Frank Harris, returned from World War II, sees his mother killed in an accident; his grief and a device called the Spike transport him to the Cool World, a parallel universe populated by grotesque Doodles (animated comic-strip creatures). Greeted by ol' Doc Whiskers, inventor of the Spike, he finds himself a solitary Noid (flesh-and-blood human) in what could be described as the urban wilderness of human nightmare. Decades later, back in the Real World of 1989, convicted *crime-passionnel* murderer Jack Deebs has finished his prison sentence; while imprisoned he has gained fame through his comic-book creation (as he thinks), the Cool World, and its population of bizarre characters, notably the sumptuous, blonde, nymphomaniacal nightclub singer Holli, who seeks desperately to make the transition to the Real World and sees him as a means to that end. Seized into the Cool World, Deebs is warned off by Harris, now a brutalized police detective (although un-aged): the one law in the Cool World is that there should be no sex between Noids and Doodles – a cause of great frustration, as it happens, to the stern-willed Harris and his Doodle girlfriend Lonette. But Holli seduces Deebs, and thereby becomes a real woman. Returned to the Real World with Deebs, she sets off in relentless pursuit of hedonism, a course which he proves unable to stay – especially when both of them show frequent flash symptoms of reversion (or, in his case, *con*version) to Doodlehood. Before kicking him out of her life, Holli confesses that her real goal is the Spike of Power. Back in the Cool World, Harris conjures up his past anguish over his mother's death to effect his own transition in pursuit. Aided by Deebs's nice-girl neighbor Jennifer, he and Deebs chase Holli, who succeeds in extracting the cork-like Spike of Power. Her doing so has the effect of opening a Pandora's Box, releasing all the nightmares of the Cool World into our own. Deebs, transformed into a Doodle wimpish superman, succeeds at last in gaining and replacing the Spike; all Doodles are sucked back into the Cool World.

Jeckle, in *The New Adventures of Mighty Mouse and Heckle and Jeckle*, but this didn't have the flair of the original and lasted only a single season, 1979–80 (with reruns for a further two seasons).

Enter Bakshi as producer and John Kricfalusi (later to attain independent fame through creating *Ren & Stimpy* and others) as director. It seems that at the outset Bakshi was determined to supply the CBS executives with what they thought they wanted – essentially, a retread of the original series. But as soon as he saw what the animators were coming up with he followed his natural instincts and backed them to the hilt: the wilder, the more outrageous and the more surreal, the better. In their excellent book *Saturday Morning Fever: Growing Up with Cartoon Culture* (1999), Timothy Burke and Kevin Burke cite one of the series' animators, Eddie Fitzgerald, as saying that the CBS execs "would ask for changes in the material and Ralph would just nod and agree and afterward totally ignore their requests." Constantly fighting off the execs took its toll on Bakshi in terms of strain, however; by all accounts he was not an easy man to work with during this time.

Mighty Mouse: The New Adventures premiered on September 19, 1987, and it was instantly apparent that here was something new in children's animated television – for one thing, it was quite deliberately designed to appeal to adults as well.

It is hard to describe the ambience of the Bakshi/Kricfalusi show. Some have likened it to the cartoons of Tex Avery and the Golden Age of Warners, and there's certainly a lot of truth in this; Bakshi has always been very public about the respect in which he holds the relevant animators and the deep love he has for their work. But more pertinent, perhaps, is the show's conceptual sophistication. Especially in the second series, even the episode titles mostly betray an ideative level not normally associated with kiddie fodder: "Anatomy of a Milquetoast," "Mouse and Super Mouse," "Mighty's Tone Poem," "Mundane Voyage" . . . There was also the introduction of Mighty's Clark Kent-like *alter ego*, plain Mike the Mouse, a factory assembly-line worker (the original Mighty Mouse dwelt on the moon, and had no mundane persona), and various of the episodes referred to this duality, with titles like "Still Oily After All These Years" and "Snow White and the Motor City Dwarfs." Another introduction was Mighty's sidekick Scrappy. Recursive elements included appearances by such Terrytoons stalwarts as Deputy Dawg and Oil Can Harry, and in particular the episode "The Ice Goose Cometh" explored a very refined recursive-fantasy trope in resuscitating an animated character from a past era into the real modern world.

What made the show notorious, however, was an episode in the first season in which Mighty sniffs a flower and seems to regain strength from it. This, trumpeted the American Family Association's religious-right leader, the Reverend Donald Wildmon, was clearly symbolic of cocaine-sniffing. Since Bakshi's public attitude toward drug-taking had not been entirely censorious over the years, one can follow Wildmon's reasoning . . . but only barely. The sequence was cut before transmission. Popular legend has it that this incident is what killed the series; this seems improbable, because it endured for a further season and a half before being axed. The other explanation seems equally unlikely: that advertisers couldn't see the point of putting ads for kids' products on what was largely an adults' show. Whatever the reason, it does seem strange that such a popular show was killed after only two seasons.

Bakshi Productions subsequently created various minor pieces. There was a live-action/animated music video for the Rolling Stones, *Harlem Shuffle* (1986). *Tattertown: A Christmas Special* followed in 1988 on Nickelodeon; this half-hour show, the pilot for a series that never materialized, was set in a town made entirely of junk, a concept Bakshi had first come up with decades earlier. In 1989 came *Dr. Seuss' The Butter Battle Book*, done in conjunction with Ted S. Geisel (Dr. Seuss), a parable of the Arms Race, the Yooks and the Zooks being at Swiftian loggerheads over which side of bread should be buttered. There were some live-action tv shorts. But overall there was a sense that Bakshi was withdrawing from screen work to concentrate on what was now the main love of his artistic life: painting.

Bakshi has claimed to me that the motive for his return to the big screen with the live-action/animated feature *Cool World* (1991) was that "Hell, I needed the money." Certainly he has publicly voiced on many occasions his bitterness over the final shape this movie took. Originally intended as a fairly low-budget, small-scale, horror-oriented movie, it was progressively mutated by committee decisions at Paramount into a big-budget production with stars Gabriel Byrne, Brad Pitt and Kim Basinger. Hugely puffed by Paramount before its release – one stunt was to drape a 75-foot image of the hyper-promiscuous protagonist Holli Would across the famous Hollywood sign (the irony of this gesture was lost on many) – the movie was excoriated by the critics and has been generally reviled ever since . . . except by a few. Writing in *The Encyclopedia of Fantasy* (1997), I summarized:

> [*Cool World*] stands as one of the fantastic cinema's most significant achievements, an instauration fantasy that reveals greater depths with each viewing. It is also something of a landmark in animated movies: while the live-action/animation junction is less surely handled than in the comparable *Who Framed Roger Rabbit* (1988), the manic creativity of *Cool World*'s animation probably has no peer, with visual grotesqueries and inventiveness – often totally irrelevant to the plot – seemingly threatening to spill out of the screen and into our laps: the climactic scenes of the Doodles pouring into our world are merely confirmation of what has been happening throughout the movie. Many of these nonce-creations are recursive, with characters differing from their originals by only the width of a breach-of-copyright suit. Plus there are the parodies: of "That's All Folks" in the movie's finale, of *Ghostbusters* (1984) as the Doodles stream out from the Spike of Power, and, perhaps rather spitefully, of the opening sequence of Disney's *The Rescuers Down Under* (1990), culminating in a seedy jail rather than in the romantic shade of Ayer's Rock. The depiction of the Cool World itself is also of interest: from its bizarre architectures and constant thrum of frenetic activity arise a *different* world that is completely realized – almost claustrophobically so.

The reason for the howl of critical revulsion at *Cool World* is almost certainly the comparison – actively encouraged by Paramount's publicity whizzes – between it and Richard Williams's/Robert Zemeckis's *Who Framed Roger Rabbit*, released just three years earlier (and which had similarly been attacked by the critics, albeit with less vehemence – something those same critics conveniently forgot). *Cool World* can at first viewing seem to be Bakshi's answer to Disney, an attempt to do the same sort of thing but with smuttier jokes. With that tunnel vision, it is perfectly true that *Cool World* isn't as successful a movie as *Roger*. Bakshi was unable to achieve the technical near-perfection that

Williams had attained in *Roger*, and hence the same suspension of disbelief cannot be maintained.

But this is to judge the movie not on its own grounds but on someone else's – on *Roger's* – and that is a sure recipe for bad verdicts. If one watches *Cool World* on its *own* terms one begins to realize what an exceptional movie it in fact is. It is not perhaps a very *pretty* movie, but it successfully tackles a set of sophisticated fantasy themes and reveals greater depths with each fresh viewing. There is no hyperbole in the statement that *Cool World* is one of the most significant works of fantasy or science fiction that the cinema has seen; it has a conceptual sophistication that baffles most mainstream movie critics, not because they are incapable of understanding it but simply because they do not expect to find it in a. commercial "entertainment" movie and hence fail to realize it is there.

One of only two Doodles sufficiently human to make discussion of her characterization sensible is Holli (the other being Lonette, Frank Harris's girlfriend). Holli is an idealized sex image packing almost as much punch as Jessica Rabbit; in fact, one of *Cool World's* minor weaknesses is that Holli's personality doesn't quite survive the transition from animated dream to live Kim Basinger, for in the loss of Holli's comic-strip childishness – and hence fundamental innocence, whatever her ethical lack – there is also lost her empathic appeal. And it's the animated Holli who provides a critique of the escapist motive in our love of fantasy: challenging Harris, she argues that he remains in the Cool World only because he lacks the courage of soul to return to the Real World. Much later, justifying to Lonette his decision not to take her with him to the Real World, he not only confirms Holli's charge but also, in so doing, turns it around: "Let me tell you something about over there. It *hurts* over there. It's *lonely* over there. . . . They've got eight million ways for you to die over there, hon, and all of them are *permanent.*" The Cool World seems not such a nightmare in this light.

Overall, the movie examines in part the relationship between physical and created universes, and the dangers of allowing one to take over the other. Of related interest is the curious way in which the Doodle characters, when they come to the Real World and despite the fact that the script's thrust seems to be the opposite, have the quality of being somehow *realer* than the normal humans around them – as if they've been imbued with a greater quantity of whatever it is that registers our existence on the fabric of the universe. The message is that the folk of the universes we create are more *living* than the people we see around us. It is a notion that has on occasion been explored elsewhere in fantasy, but this is, if not its first, at least an early airing of it in the cinema. By the time of *Last Action Hero* (1993) and in particular *The Mask* (1994), the denser reality of the reified artifact over the normal being had become a premise in the movies.

It is clear that any brief summation of *Cool World* will be, through oversimplification, a false one, and the movie continues to be the least understood and most consistently vilified in Bakshi's portfolio. The fact that he himself is, as noted, one of the vilifiers, because of what was done to his original vision, affects the preceding arguments not one bit. And he was certainly stung by the hysteria of the response to the movie; he has shown no inclination since then to return to the big screen. He has, however, done some further work for the small screen. In 1994 there was the live-action feature-length tv movie *The Cool and the Crazy*. Two animated shorts for the Cartoon Network, both in 1995, were *Malcolm and Melvin* and *Babe, He Calls Me*; both were, however, savagely edited before airing and Bakshi largely disowns them.

What may have driven Bakshi out of animation altogether was his experience with HBO and its series *Spicy City*. This animated series, aimed at adults, was based in a William Gibsonish, noirish science-fictional, future world where technology, most especially biotechnology, has so degraded human existence – so divorced the soul from physical reality – that the word "inhumanity" has almost lost its meaning, in that the characters upon whom various brutalities are committed aren't really humans in any meaningful sense of the term. There's also some recursive parody aimed not so much at animation as at the comics, in particular the introduction of each episode by, rather than *Tales from the Crypt's* Crypt Keeper, a sexy female called Raven. Women are curvaceous and erupt from their garments at the slightest provocation, while the male heroes are rock-jawed hunks of the Superman variety, but with shorter hair and less intelligence. The quality of the animation is unfortunately patchy and the critical response was indubitably mixed (with the balance being unfavorable); but it was neither of these factors, nor indeed the respectable ratings (not sensational, though sometimes outgunning HBO's own *Spawn*, the series' direct rival and widely considered a success), that caused *Spicy City* to be plucked off the air after only one season – and after the second season had been given the go-ahead by HBO. Instead it seems to have been just a matter of internal HBO politicking.

Today Ralph Bakshi is content to live the life of a painter, gaining some additional income through selling his old animation cels over the Internet. Occasionally there is an exhibition of his fine art. Although a book on his life and work was announced a few years ago, it never appeared, and this doesn't seem to bother him much. All he ever wanted to do was draw and paint, he says, and now his wish has been fulfilled because he's free to do exactly that.

Or maybe he'll be back.

RAOUL BARRÉ (1874–1932)

The French-Canadian animator Raoul Barré started what is recognized as the first commercial animation studio. He also devised the system whereby the sheets on which animators draw have a set of holes at the edges and their drawing boards have pegs. By fitting the holes over the pegs, exactly the same positioning could be maintained from one sheet to the next, thereby eliminating the jumps and jerks that were characteristic of earlier animation. A further technique he developed was the slash system, whereby a hole was slashed in a single sheet of paper that contained the drawing of a background; anything that had to be animated was put into the hole. A third innovation that came from his studio was in fact the brainchild of his business and creative partner William C. Nolan: this was the idea of producing a background that was much longer or taller than the frame so that, by progressively moving the background, one could give the illusion of motion to an animated character who was in fact staying in the same place.

Barré was born in Montreal on January 29, 1874. He made his early career as a newspaper cartoonist, then decided to try his hand at animation. Between 1912 and 1913, he and Nolan produced several animated advertising movies, and in 1914 they set up an animation studio in the Bronx. They hired Gregory La Cava and Frank Moser as animators, and soon set to work producing their first series of shorts, the Animated Grouch Chasers. Appearing in 1915, these interspersed live-action and animated sequences, so that their format somewhat resembled a newsreel in format. The first was *The Animated Grouch Chaser* (1915). When they're viewed today, the surprising thing is how good they are – not only in technical terms but also because their animated sequences are actually properly constructed mini-shorts with a well told story.

The following year, William Randolph Hearst decided it would make economic sense to start up an animation studio in order to bring to the screen the various popular comic strips he was publishing. He looked around and saw that Barré was doing well. Accordingly, he lured away all of Barré's key staff, including La Cava, Moser, and – the unkindest cut of all – Nolan. It is probably not a coincidence, as La Cava had been made head of the new studio (grandiosely titled the International Film Service), that much of its work was subcontracted to Barré, including several of the shorts in the Phables series (based on print cartoons by Tom Powers). Again, these shorts are a lot better than one would expect of such an early date. In *Cooks vs Cooks: The Phable of Olaf and Louis* (1916), Olaf, who is merely a cook, ruins a turkey dinner, while Louis, who is a real *chef*, dammit, manufactures an exquisite meal out of a fire hose. In *Feet is Feet: A Phable* (1916), a fat woman vainly suffers while wearing a pair of shoes that is far too small before having the sense to confess her size and opt for something more fitting. In *The Phable of a Busted Romance* (1916), a workman finds and returns the purse of Miss Gotrox, which contains $10,000; his hankerings for her evaporate when she tips him just a Canadian dime for his honesty. It is likely because of their cozy homespun moralizing that the Phables have been largely forgotten.

Of considerably more note is the Mutt & Jeff series, based on the comic strip by Bud Fisher. Fisher is also credited with the long series of shorts even though they were in fact done by Barré and various others. Unlike most of the "directors" in similar situations, Fisher went to great lengths to maintain the fiction that he worked on the shorts. Among the animators Barré hired to help out were Burt Gillett, Ben Sharpsteen, Bill Tytla, Al Hurter, I. Klein and Dick Huemer. The series was brought to Barré by a promoter and cartoonist named Charles Bowers, who had managed to obtain the animation rights from Fisher.

Bowers appears to have been a bit of a crook. The reasons for Barré's abrupt departure from animation in 1918 are not fully

Drawing for *Felix the Cat Trumps the Ace* (1926).
© Collection La Cinémathèque Québecoise.

understood, but it seems that either he was maneuvered out by a greedy Bowers or he discovered that Bowers was cooking the books and wanted to put as much distance as possible between himself and any criminal charge. Either way, after Bowers took over the studio Barré lasted just a year before Fisher fired him for fiddling the accounts. Nevertheless, Bowers managed to persuade Fisher to sign up with him again in 1921 and yet again in 1924. This latter time his animators rose up en masse and negotiated a separate contract with Fisher for the Mutt & Jeff shorts. Bowers's later career in animation was largely devoted to stop-motion work, some of which he did for Walter Lantz's studio. This marked a reversal of sorts, as Lantz's first big break in animation had been when he was hired by Bowers to work on Mutt & Jeff shorts.

The first of the Mutt & Jeff shorts was, appropriately, called just *Mutt and Jeff* (1913). In these shorts Mutt is a tall, thin sophisticate while Jeff is a short, fat and supposedly stupid fellow who nevertheless always seems to get the better of Mutt. The Mutt & Jeff shorts of the Barré era are by no means classics – the studio was expected to turn out one per week, so quality was not a priority – but, yet again, they are better than one might expect. However, they were nowhere near as entertaining as the best of the Animated Grouch Chaser series, where the imagination of Barré and his team was given wider scope.

Barré later pursued a career as a fine-arts and advertising painter. He made one further foray into animation, doing some work on Pat Sullivan's/Otto Messmer's Felix the Cat series in the years 1925–27, before returning to Montreal, where he died on May 21, 1932. This, at least, is the standard story. The Social Security Death Index, however, reveals that a Raoul Barré born on June 5, 1878, died in Los Angeles in May 1969. There is so much that is enigmatic about this early master of animation that one wonders if he left us with yet one further piece of enigma to ponder.

The Hicks in Nightmareland (1915)

♭ b/w / animated/live-action silent ⊙ 13³/₄ minutes
Animated Grouch Chasers

In live action there are various scenes of people on the beach browsing in a book which contains the stories of this compilation. In animation there is a series of short stories. In the first section, *The Hicks in Nightmareland*, Hercule Hicks, asleep beside his wife on the beach, dreams he has died and become an angel among the clouds. Encountering an attractive lady angel, he borrows her telescope to spy on plain Ma Hicks doing the laundry, and begins to think unangel-like thoughts about his companion . . . but then to his chagrin wakes up back on the beach before she can reciprocate. In *Bunkum's Boarding House*, Silas Bunkum vets applicants on the grounds of appearance — a pretty girl gets a cheap rental, a fat man is rejected because he'll eat too much — but the skinny man accepted in the fat man's place proves voracious. In *The Kelly Kid's Bathing Adventure*, the Kid, swimming in the river, has his clothes eaten by a goat. He paints "trunks" on himself, courtesy of a freshly painted park bench, but fools no one. *A Sand Microbe Flirtation* has a pretty lady microbe who, after flirting with a microbe stranger, is pulverized by her wrathful microbe husband.

Cramps (1916)

♭ b/w / animated silent ⊙ 7¹/₄ minutes
Mutt & Jeff

Jeff wakes with cramps, and Mutt tries to help. After shenanigans with a too-hot hot-water bottle, Mutt goes to steal some medicine from the doctor's office downstairs. But he gets the proportions wrong and, after feeding it to Jeff, believes he has put him into a coma. In respooled animation Mutt fetches an antidote, but this gives Jeff "fiery" breath — which Mutt tackles with a fire extinguisher. In a third attempt to mix a cure for Jeff he accidentally substitutes nitroglycerine for glycerine in the formula . . . with predictable results.

DON BLUTH (1937–)

Setup for *Banjo the Woodpile Cat* (1979), showing Banjo with Crazy Legs. Photograph: S/R Laboratories.

Born on September 13, 1937, raised until the age of six in El Paso, Texas, and then on a farm in Payson, Utah, until his late teens, when the family moved to Santa Monica, California, Don Bluth has spent the bulk of his animating career attempting to recreate the dream he had of what Disney animation should be when, at the age of seven, he first saw a screening of *Snow White and the Seven Dwarfs* (1937). In his efforts to maintain what he sees as the great Disney tradition (perverted as it has been by the revisionists of that studio since at least the early 1970s), he has spent some two decades seeking his own voice. Along the way he has produced some beautifully animated movies that somehow, in most cases, fall short of being what a fully satisfying animated feature should be. Only in the year 2000, with the release of *Titan A.E.*, did he manage to break out of the Disney mold and fully realize himself as an animation director.

He was first hired by Disney in 1955 as an assistant animator under John Lounsbery, working on *Sleeping Beauty* (1959). It seems ironic in hindsight that he lasted in the job only a couple of years, becoming bored with the drudgery of animation on the lower rungs and packing it in to become, instead, a Mormon missionary in South America. The strength of his Mormon convictions was not just a youthful flash in the pan, but continues to this day. In his book *The Animated Films of Don Bluth* (1991), John Cawley quotes Bluth on the interaction between his religion and his movie work:

I'm not preachy. I'm not didactic and I don't think movies should do that. But I like movies that fill you with hope. I like things that free you from your ills, your prejudices, and all the other things that hold us in spiritual darkness. If you can make people believe that they have the power to help themselves

DON BLUTH

and help the world, then I think you've done a great deal of good. Movies have the power to do that.

At the end of the 1950s he was back in Los Angeles; although he did some piecework for Disney on *The Sword in the Stone* (1963), this was just a way of supplementing his income as he devoted his full creative energies to live theater. He and his brother Fred opened the Bluth Brothers Theater in an old supermarket in Culver City, to produce amateurish versions of classic musicals. This enterprise petered out, as such worthy but doomed enterprises inevitably must, and he went off to college to earn a degree in English Literature. It was only after this, in 1967, that his animation career truly began.

He took a job doing layouts at Filmation for series such as *The Archies* and *Sabrina, the Teenage Witch*. These Filmation programs were being churned out as Saturday-morning tv kiddie fodder, and their soullessness soon got to Bluth: the only reward to be derived from the job was the money. This time, however, he didn't ditch animation wholesale, as before; instead he looked around for a studio where there was at least a sense that animation was regarded as an artform, rather than merely a matter of creating – as quickly and as cheaply as possible – a piece of ''product'' that was just good enough to have a chance of renewal at the end of the season. His eye, naturally, fell upon Disney, and in 1971 he rejoined Disney as a trainee; his talent was instantly recognized, and within two months he was working as a full-grade animator on projects like *Robin Hood* (1973) and *Winnie the Pooh and Tigger Too* (1974). For *The Rescuers* (1977) he was a directing animator, and for *Pete's Dragon* (1977) he was animation director, no less. His next assignment was as producer-director of the high-prestige featurette Disney showcase *The Small One* (1978), about a boy in the Holy Land whose scrawny, unwanted donkey is selected by Joseph to carry the pregnant Mary to Bethlehem.

Bluth was clearly, in the minds of the powers that be, destined for the very top of the Disney tree. However, he and a couple of fellow animators, John Pomeroy and Gary Goldman, were growing increasingly dissatisfied with the Disney animated output. A measure of Bluth's frustration may – although he has never been proven the culprit – have emerged in a curious schoolboy prank that was played during the making of *The Rescuers*. In one scene, as Orville the albatross flies Bernard and Miss Bianca across the night-time cityscape of New York, there is visible through an open window, for just two frames, the torso of a naked model from *Playboy*. This is invisible during screenings of the movie – the image simply flashes by too swiftly to be seen. The two frames, on discovery, were excised for the video release. In 1999, however, a new, digitally remastered version of the movie was released on video, derived directly from the original prints, and in the interim the studio had forgotten about the prank. It wasn't long after the release that eager kids discovered, thumbs on the freeze-frame button, you could isolate

Banjo the Woodpile Cat (1979)

color / animated ○ 24 minutes
A cheeky little kitten, Banjo, always in trouble on the farm, stows away on a delivery truck to seek adventure in the city. Adventure he accordingly has, in the company of alley cat Crazy Legs and sexpot crooner cat Zasu, before deciding he must return to the farm and his rightful place.

The Secret of NIMH (1982)

(vt *Mrs. Brisby and the Rats of NIMH*)
color / animated ○ 82 minutes
A widowed fieldmouse, Mrs. Brisby (the name was changed from Frisby seemingly at the last moment), must move her children to a new locale before the onset of the ploughing season. Helped (or hindered) by the zany crow Jeremy, she is advised by the terrifying Great Owl to seek the aid of the superintelligent rats that live under the rosebush by the farmhouse. We discover that these rats are escapees from a research institution, NIMH (hence the enhanced intelligence); that they owe their salvation to Mrs. Brisby's dead husband; and that they are feuding among themselves over their future – the feud being between, on the one hand, wise old guru Nicodemus and his young protégé Justin and, on the other, the murderously scheming Jenner. Good triumphs and the Brisby family is saved. (Based on the book *Mrs Frisby and the Rats of NIMH* (1971) by Robert C. O'Brien.)

An American Tail (1986)

color / animated ○ 77 minutes
Shostka, Russia, 1885. Antisemitic pogroms threaten the Mousekewitz family. Papa decides they must go to America, even though Mama describes America as just a fairytale, like that of the Giant Mouse of Minsk, who frightened all the cats. They stow away aboard a transatlantic ship; young Fievel is washed overboard but eventually reaches New York on his own. Shyster Warren T. Rat (a cat in disguise) sells him into sweatshop slavery, abetted by corrupt politico Honest John at Tammany Hall. The mice of New York are being terrorized by the cats; only an escaped Fievel has a plan – to construct a fake Giant Mouse of Minsk. All cats but Tiger (a bumbling feline sidekick whom Fievel has picked up) are driven from New York, and Fievel is reunited with his family.

The Land Before Time (1988)

🎨 color / animated ⏱ 70 minutes

It is the twilight of the day of the dinosaurs. Some of the herbivorous dinosaur herds are questing to Great Valley, where the foliage is believed to still be lush; among them is a bunch of orphaned infants — the brontosaur Littlefoot and his pals: the triceratops Cera, the pterodactyl Petrie, the anatosaur Ducky, and, youngest of all, the stegosaur Spike. Frequently beset by marauding tyrannosaurs and intermittently inspired by Littlefoot's visions of his dead mother, they learn that cooperation is necessary for survival as they eventually achieve their quest.

All Dogs Go to Heaven (1989)

🎨 color / animated ⏱ 89 minutes

1930s New Orleans. Mobster mongrel Charlie B. Barkin is victim of a gangland killing at the hands of his erstwhile partner in crime, Carface. Unlike humans, all dogs go to Heaven, no matter their misdeeds; but Charlie can't stand it there and, although knowing Heaven is a one-time-only offer, returns to Earth to seek revenge. Carface has imprisoned orphan child Anne-Marie, who can talk with animals; he uses her to rig the nightly rat races run in his gambling den. Charlie and moronic sidekick Itchy kidnap the child in the hopes of profiting from her themselves. But in the process — after various adventures including a dream sojourn in an impressively apocalyptic Hell, a spell of captivity among the denizens of the New Orleans sewers, and a Twilight Barking-style mass rallying of the New Orleans dogs — Charlie finds his vengeance, his own heart of gold, new parents for Anne-Marie and his way back to Heaven.

Rock-A-Doodle (1991)

🎨 color / animated with some live action ⏱ 77 minutes

Silver-throated rooster Chanticleer believes (à la Chaucer) that the sun rises each morning only to hear him crow; when a minion of Grand Duke Owl, head of the Forces of Darkness, stops Chanticleer crowing one morning and the sun rises nevertheless, the rooster and the other farmyard beasts are disillusioned, and off Chanticleer goes to the city, where he becomes a singing star, The King. But thereafter darkness reigns over the farm. A storm one night sends a group of animals, headed by the dog Patou and (transformed into a kitten) the farmer's young son Edmond, into the city to bring Chanticleer home and the sunlight back to the farm.

the naughty picture. The spokespersons for the Moral Majority thundered that Disney was deliberately marketing porn at the little innocents, and all copies of the video had to be withdrawn and replaced, at hideous expense.

Bluth's name came to be associated very intimately with *The Rescuers*; this is curious, as *Pete's Dragon* (1977) is the Disney feature he did most to shape. This project was the brainchild of veteran Disney man Ken Anderson, the movie's animation art director. The movie itself is a lot better than its reputation; the Disney marketing team launched it as "the new *Mary Poppins*," thereby assuring it a venomously hostile reception from *Mary Poppins* fans everywhere. Since it is a far less ambitious effort with a wholly different ethos, it suffered from a comparison that should never have been made in the first place. What it does have in common with the earlier movie — and with Disney's previous failed attempt at "the new *Mary Poppins*," *Bedknobs and Broomsticks* (1971) – is the interaction between toon figures and live-action humans. It thus seems rather quaintly dated when we watch it today, as we're accustomed to the far more sophisticated means of attaining this illusion developed for *Who Framed Roger Rabbit* (1988) and its successors. Despite mediocre songs, it is a jolly enough minor movie.

Although *The Small One* received plaudits at the time and continues to do so, it was essentially put together as a sampler to show what the new breed of Disney moviemakers could do. It is an excellent featurette, though it lacks any innovation or sense of creative adventure: this is a display of traditional Disney animation at its best, rather than the artistic breakthrough one might have hoped for; a personal suspicion is that Bluth was determined not just to show his own abilities and those of his team members but also to demonstrate by example to the committees at Disney what it was the Disney animators as a whole should be doing — to wit, continuing to produce animations of the type they had been creating while Walt was still alive.

Be that as it may, already by 1973 Bluth, Pomeroy and Goldman were thinking of abandoning Disney and were planning their own studio, to be called Don Bluth Productions. Working in Bluth's converted garage, they labored in their spare time over the years to produce a showcase featurette of their own, *Banjo the Woodpile Cat*. As this neared completion in 1979 the trio resigned from Disney in one of the studio's more famous walkouts. Eleven other Disney animators resigned to join the trio, working on *The Secret of NIMH*, the new studio's first feature. Financial backing for the film was supplied by a group of ex-Disney execs trading as Aurora Productions. Disney reeled. Completion of its new feature, *The Fox and the Hound* (1981), had to be delayed as the cream of its young turks departed.

It was the stated intention of *Banjo the Woodpile Cat* (1979) to show the Disney studio how Disney animation should be done, and so it's hardly surprising that it's a first-rate Disney animated movie, with all of the strengths traditionally associated with that studio – except one: the storytelling. The tale of the mischievous kitten who runs away to find fame in the big city, where he learns better and whence he returns home to a rapturous welcome, is cute enough, but also just a trifle flaccid and trite; one is left at the movie's end with a feeling of "So what?" Thus, while of good entertainment value for children, it doesn't really engage the attentions of adult viewers. But the animation and characterization are charming, and the movie bounces along happily; most importantly, the featurette was good enough to gather interest in and investors for future Bluth creations. The studio was employed for the brief animated sequence in the Olivia Newton-John/Gene Kelly musical *Xanadu* (1980), regarded as the sole highlight of a poor movie. And it was as a direct result of *Banjo* that United Artists took on *The Secret of NIMH*, then still in production.

The Secret of NIMH (1982) was a far weightier enterprise, not just weightier than anything Bluth's team had attempted before but also than most of what Disney had recently been doing (with the ironic exception of *The Fox and the Hound*, which proved to be one of Disney animation's great classics). *The Secret of NIMH* is likewise one of the classics of American commercial animation. Based on Robert C. O'Brien's fine children's novel *Mrs Frisby and the Rats of NIMH* (1971), it manages to duplicate the book's feat of telling a ripping adventure story for the young at the same time as confronting one or two tricky moral issues about the way in which the life sciences treat animals. For the most part the animation is spectacularly good, and some of the action sequences must have made the Disney staffers drool with envy. Yet the movie falls away in its final sequences. The end result is rather like discovering someone has stolen the soft center out of one's chocolate. Such a failing would be enough to destroy a lesser movie; *The Secret of NIMH*, however, is not a lesser movie.

Great things were expected of *The Secret of NIMH* at the box office, but those expectations were confounded, for reasons that had nothing to do with the movie itself. In the first place, it had the misfortune to be released opposite the Steven Spielberg blockbuster *E.T. – The Extraterrestrial* (1982), which more or less wiped out any other family offering put on the market at the same time. Second, United Artists lost courage at the last moment and didn't give it the kind of blockbuster launch a comparable Disney movie certainly would have received; instead, it was nudged out into the public arena nervously and piecemeal, with regional rather than national distribution, as if apologizing that it was imitation Disney rather than being proud to be genuine Bluth. The movie was by no means a spectacular flop, but it was certainly unsuccessful enough that the suits at UA could congratulate themselves on fulfilling their own prophecy.

Bluth and his colleagues were, in essence, out on their collective ear; Aurora withdrew financial backing from their

feature-in-progress, *East of the Sun, West of the Moon*, and nobody else was immediately willing to take them on. Matters were not helped by the coincidence of a national strike in the animation business. Don Bluth Productions, having done everything that could be expected of it, was forced to file for bankruptcy. For several years that appeared to be the end of a very brave venture. The suits at Disney must have been joining their counterparts at UA in an orgy of faceless self-congratulation – Disney animation itself was in dire straits, with no new animated feature on the horizon, a situation which seems to have considerably pleased the very financial strategists who had engineered it. (When, in 1985, the next Disney feature, *The Black Cauldron*, appeared, it too had disappointing box office results.)

Still smarting, Bluth, Pomeroy and Goldman founded a new company, Bluth Group. If the cinema industry was willing to ignore a precious resource, the opposite was true of the burgeoning video-arcade games industry. Rick Dyer, who owned a small company called Advanced Micro Computers, approached the trio with an idea he'd had for an animated arcade game featuring a quasi-medieval knight and his adventures against Arthurian-style monsters and villains to save a fair princess. Funding was found for three pilot sequences. The games company StarCom, later renamed Magicom, stepped in, commissioning the team to produce what had come to be called *Dragon's Lair* (1983). Still available today, it was the first laserdisc arcade game and almost certainly the one most fondly remembered. Since the game's plot is not in itself especially inspired, it is reasonable to assume that the phenomenal success of *Dragon's Lair* was directly attributable to the quality of the animation. The game caught on and became a national craze; Ruby–Spears Enterprises produced for ABC a short-lived animated (not by Don Bluth) tv series based on it in 1984–85.

Bluth and his colleagues were back in the money again. Despite all their achievements in the cinema in the years since, they have never abandoned the games market. More immediately, in 1984, they followed *Dragon's Lair* with *Space Ace*. *Dragon's Lair* itself was followed up by 1991's *Dragon's Lair II: Time Warp* (a revised version of *Space Ace* was released roughly simultaneously). At the time of writing, Bluth was talking of a 2001 release for a 3D version of the game.

Although the 1980s was a decade in which it seemed that the bean counters were taking over the American movie industry, one or two figures emerged who scored such phenomenal individual triumphs that they could effectively write their own checks and do exactly what they wished to do, without seventy-five committee meetings and a radical dumbing-down of any plans. Obviously the most noteworthy of these was Steven Spielberg, who, during that decade – and well beyond – was responsible in one way or another for an astonishing series of hugely successful movies. He had noticed a considerable talent

A Troll in Central Park (1993)

(vt *Stanley's Magic Garden*)

color / animated 76 minutes

Gnorga, Queen of the Trolls, detests goodness and beauty, and has banned flowers from her realm. Cute little troll Stanley has been blessed with a green thumb; when his illicit garden is discovered, Gnorga banishes him to a "place of stone" where nothing will grow, and which hence ought to be Hell for him. However, that place of stone is Manhattan, and he lands in Central Park, where he continues his cultivational activities unabated — and assisted by truant tots Gus and Rosie. Gnorga, finding the punishment has misfired, comes to Central Park as a tornado to destroy Stanley, the children and everything he has achieved. However, after all seems lost (Stanley is turned to stone), good triumphs thanks to the faith of the children.

Thumbelina (1994)

(vt *Hans Christian Andersen's Thumbelina*; vt *Don Bluth's Thumbelina*)

color / animated 86 minutes

A woman asks a good witch for a child and is given a barleycorn seed. When this flowers, a tiny adolescent girl, christened Thumbelina for her size, emerges. Being on a different scale from everyone else, Thumbelina is lonely; she dreams of wedding the Fairy Prince described in the fairy-tale books she reads. In due course she is discovered by Cornelius, Prince of the Fairies, and the two fall in love — although a major hurdle is Thumbelina's lack of wings. After various complications and adventures they wed.
(Based on the story "Thumbelina" (1836) by Hans Christian Andersen.)

The Pebble and the Penguin (1995)

color / animated 74 minutes

Among certain penguins, the male presents the female of his choice with a pebble; if she accepts it, they mate for life. Shy, stammering penguin Hubie loves and is loved by glamour-bird Marina; his rival for her affections is loathsome, suave, hunkish superpenguin Drake. A meteor brings with it to Hubie's feet a glowing green gem, which he wishes to give to Marina. Thanks to Drake's vile machinations, Hubie is seized by a boat trapping Antarctic seabirds for zoos. He escapes with streetwise cynical penguin Rocko. After diverse adventures and song-and-dance routines the two return safely to Hubie's home, where Drake is cast down and the lovers united.

and probably also a kindred spirit in Bluth. Spielberg was prepared to put his money and his not inconsiderable industry clout behind Bluth's next theatrical feature, the story of a young refugee mouse whose family flees pogroms in Russia to try to make a new life in the raw, young United States. News of a Spielberg-Bluth teaming was electrifying. There are many comparisons that can be made between Spielberg and Walt Disney, but the most important in this context is that Spielberg is, as Walt was, a masterful storyteller. Since storytelling has always been Bluth's great difficulty, it would seem, and did seem, that Spielberg and Bluth together constituted a dream team, a marriage made in heaven between the great storyteller and the great animator.

In all fairness, *An American Tail* (1986) was pretty good — and was recognized as such at the time by the reviewers, who treated it as something of a milestone in commercial animation and, at least in the U.K., approached it as a movie for adults as well as children — one with something serious to say. Quite what that something *was* has been, on reflection, rather troublesome to establish, although certainly all the ingredients of a message are there: the antisemitic pogroms, the corruption fostered by big business or trade unionism or indeed any organization allowed to operate unfettered — in short, the persecution of the weak by the strong, whether the weak are Jews in Russia being massacred by the Cossacks, or immigrant mice in New York being murdered by cats or having the lives squeezed out of them by the crueller edge of capitalism. All in all, whatever message there is visible only through muddied waters, and it's perhaps because of this muddiness — not to mention a sudden plunge in the quality of storytelling in the last portions of the movie — that *An American Tail* has been judged more harshly by history than is truly justified. Even so, it is illuminating to compare it with the first of its direct-to-video sequels, *An American Tail II: Fievel Goes West* (1991), produced by Spielberg with Robert Watts and without the participation of Bluth, Pomeroy and Goldman. While there can be no doubt that the former is the *better* movie, the latter, which lacks any hifalutin pretensions and is merely a romp, is considerably more successful as a straightforward piece of entertainment and is indeed also, in places where it should be, more emotionally moving (something exceptionally uncommon in direct-to-video releases). The story is far more ephemeral, but it is better told.

An American Tail was perhaps not as successful as its makers might have hoped. The reviewers could discuss it as being worthy of consideration by adults, but the unimaginative distribution chains at the time knew better, classifying everything animated, sight unseen, as kiddie fodder — unless it was by Ralph Bakshi, in which case most of them wouldn't touch it with a ten-foot pole. *An American Tail* was thus generally stuffed into the movie schedules to accord with the timing of school holidays, and peremptorily removed from them once the kids had gone back. Despite this, there is no

Setup for *An American Tail* (1986) showing Fievel with Tanya and Papa Mousekewitz. Photograph: Howard Lowery.

question that the movie was very profitable for all concerned – it broke records for the first release of an animated feature, and has continued to enjoy strong video sales. On the strength of the movie, Bluth and business partner Morris Sullivan were able to move their company, now called Sullivan-Bluth Productions, to Ireland, a country which has the enlightened policy of offering tax breaks to creative individuals and enterprises. A further incentive to go to Ireland was to escape difficulties with the American unions. In order to complete *An American Tail* within a tight budget, the studio had been forced to offer its employees wages lower than union rates. Once in Ireland, Sullivan-Bluth began work on another potential blockbuster, *The Land Before Time* (1988).

In many ways, *The Land Before Time* can lay claim to being

Bluth's most satisfying, most fully rounded feature to date. All his famous – notorious – failings in the story department are absent, primarily because there is so very little here by way of story to be messed up. The movie offers a simple quest tale as a group of youthful herbivorous dinosaurs makes its way without adult assistance from a place of threat and danger to a place of safety and plenty, where they are reunited with their parents, along the route learning the value of cooperation. There are no real claims to greatness or to cinema-history glory in this modest and unassuming movie, but, like *Dumbo* (1941) – with which it can profitably be compared – it is laden with charm beyond all predictable measure and, through its very simplicity, touches a chord in almost every viewer.

It was quite a courageous venture for the fledgling studio to embark on: although dinosaurs are currently all the rage among kids and adults alike, they were not especially fashionable at the time – even Godzilla was going through a dry patch. In effect, Bluth and Sullivan were relying on Bluth's ability as a creator of animated characters to persuade audiences that creatures they were likely to think of as stupid, vicious, cold-blooded and extinct were really cute 'n' cuddly personalities they might like to have as pets. Littlefoot and his pals didn't even have the advantage of Dumbo, defined early within the movie as a pathetic object whose side everyone thereafter staunchly takes. It was a tall order, and it cannot be denied that Bluth fulfilled it magnificently. Although the movie was not an out-and-out blockbuster on first release, it became phenomenally profitable as time went on and the revenues began pouring in from merchandising and video and tv releases. A seemingly interminable string of direct-to-video sequels by other hands followed in due course, beginning with *Land Before Time II: The Great Valley Adventure* (1994) and still, at the time of writing, going strong, with *Land Before Time VII: The Stone of Cold Fire* (2000) the most recent. Perhaps, in a backhanded sort of a way, the ultimate critical accolade came in 2000, when Disney released its CGI (computer generated image) behemoth *Dinosaur*; not only can the strong similarities between the two movies be regarded as a tribute to *The Land Before Time* – although Disney dispensed with plausibility by having its dinosaurs interacting with primates – but, among the countless who compared the two movies, the huge majority did so to *Dinosaur*'s disfavor.

For their next feature, Sullivan–Bluth Studios signed up with Goldcrest. That movie was *All Dogs Go to Heaven* (1989), which is an interesting if not entirely original (think of 1941's *Here Comes Mr. Jordan*, just for starters) afterlife fantasy in which a gangster mutt, Charlie, escapes from Heaven, seeking revenge upon his murderer. Instead he finds himself changing the habit of a lifetime to perform good deeds, significantly finding adoptive parents for the telepathic (with animals) orphan moppet Anne-Marie. As always, there's some splendid animation – notably, at least, in terms of visualization, during Charlie's first sojourn in Heaven – but yet again there's a softness in the storytelling that makes the movie somehow unmemorable; the characters, despite some excellent voicing efforts, are likewise. The movie is amiable enough, however, and has been sufficiently popular over the years in the video market to spawn a much later, non-Bluth sequel, *All Dogs Go to Heaven 2* (1996).

Pausing only to make a 65-minute live-action video, *Glitch* (1991), drawn from various gigs by punk rockers Pigface, Bluth plunged straight into his next animated feature after a nasty falling out with Goldcrest. This was *Rock-A-Doodle* (1991), a movie whose history went back all the way to the time of *The Secret of NIMH*, when one of the projects under active development was a feature called *Chanticleer*, to be based on the vain rooster who, in Chaucer's "Nun's Priest's Tale," believed the sun rose each morning only to hear him crow. Quite a lot of the subsequent plot is reminiscent of *Banjo the Woodpile Cat*. The main problem is that, as with *All Dogs Go to Heaven*, it's all far too amiable and unexceptionable – and as a result unexceptional.

One cannot say that *Rock-A-Doodle* is a bad movie – Bluth has never made an outright *bad* movie – but it's extremely difficult to find any reason to call it a good one.

This was to become a continuing problem with Bluth's next three movies: they all have their charms and appeals, but, because their stories are so soft and ultimately coreless, it is hard to conceive of any motive to watch them rather than anything else available. *A Troll in Central Park* (1993) is an enjoyable urban fairy tale – and, as an aside, is an excellent New York movie – but has the feel of a half-hour television special stretched out to 76 minutes. Very much the same can be said of *The Pebble and the Penguin* (1995), although it is substantially brightened by the characterization (and voicing, by James Belushi) of Rocko, the ragamuffin, scratchy-edged penguin-about-town who befriends the bland main-protagonist penguin, Hubie. In between these two came *Thumbelina* (1994), loosely based on the Hans Christian Andersen tale: this movie is the nearest to shoddy that Bluth's work has ever come. There can be no harsher judgement of this movie than that, as one watches it, one has the recurring thought that, had it been made by Hanna–Barbera instead of Don Bluth, at least it would have been *funnier*.

All through this period there was the feeling about Bluth's career that a brilliantly talented animator – indeed, moviemaker – was going to waste. As flat movie after flat movie emerged, there was the constant urge to pick the man up and shake him; if ever his name came up in a discussion of commercial animation it would be with the feeling that duty insisted he be mentioned because he was still steadily plugging away, regularly producing movies that were sort of OK but that no one wanted to have to go and watch. What made this even sadder was that the mid-1990s were a time when the air was full of buzz about a great upsurge in animation's fortunes: Disney was being public about its increased commitment to the genre, alone and with Pixar, while Steven Spielberg and his cohorts were busily setting up DreamWorks.

The company Twentieth Century-Fox took heed of the buzz and determined it should not miss the boat. Accordingly it set up Fox Animation Studios in Phoenix, Arizona, and invested hugely in the most up-to-date and sophisticated animation equipment imaginable. *A Troll in Central Park*, *Thumbelina* and *The Pebble and the Penguin* were all done in conjunction with Warners, and represent a nadir in the Bluth/Goldman fortunes (Pomeroy had by this time gone back to Disney). When Fox gave the call, there was very little to make Bluth and Goldman wish to think twice. There was of course a fair amount of skepticism about the move – was Fox really wise to hire two men widely (if sadly) regarded as has-beens? But none of this was allowed to dim what were very bright hopes.

Optimism was rewarded. It took three long years to make *Anastasia* (1997), but it was worth it. The movie represents a triumphant return to form for Bluth – indeed, he was arguably

better than he had ever been. The movie had its fair share of detractors, most of whom were concerned with story weaknesses and illogics – apart from all the irrelevant comments that were made around the time of release about its historical inaccuracies, presumably by people who use John Wayne movies as source documents for the old American West. On the other hand, the *Chicago Sun–Times*'s Roger Ebert, not noticeably a friend to Bluth's endeavors over the years, in the course of a glowing review of the movie stated, "What won me over most of all, however, was the quality of the story." He had several other pertinent comments to make:

> *Anastasia* tells this story within what has become the almost rigid formula of the modern animated feature: the heroine and the hero both have sidekicks, the villain commands nasty little minions, and romance blooms, but doesn't get too soppy.
>
> Much depends on how colorful the villain is, and the mad monk Rasputin (Christopher Lloyd) is one of the best cartoon villains in a long time. . . .
>
> Animation is the road less traveled for the movies. Although it offers total freedom over the inconveniences of space, time, and gravity, it's so tricky and difficult that animated features have always been rare – and Disney has always known how to make them best. With *Anastasia*, there's another team on the field.

Disney was certainly aware of this last point. Over the years, Goldman in particular has muttered so frequently about the activities of the "Disney Dirty-Tricks Department" mounting spoilers against Bluth releases, that one's sole response must be to smile patronizingly – why should Disney stir itself to spoil, say, *Thumbelina* when the movie was so manifestly capable of doing this for itself? But in the case of *Anastasia* there is preponderant evidence that Disney was severely worried, and that, at least in Australia, there were heavy-handed attempts to coerce distributors. And, not having a new animated feature in the movie theaters with which to mount direct competition to *Anastasia*, Disney made a huge affair over re-releasing 1989's *The Little Mermaid*, stuffing the stores full of *Little Mermaid* merchandise in the hope of spiking *Anastasia*'s chances there as well. Whether or not this latter strategy worked is impossible to judge – the *Anastasia* characters are not especially merchandisable in any case – but certainly it does seem that, all over the world (not just Australia), the distribution of the Bluth movie was not as good as one would expect for a movie of this caliber and obvious popular attractiveness.

Anastasia was, nevertheless, a success; it must have been good for Bluth and Goldman to realize they were back on top of the animation world again. Ebert was only one of many to predict that Disney could look forward to having a real fight on its hands in future.

Anastasia (1997)

⬥ color / animated ○ 94 minutes

When you wish upon a Tsar . . . Taking as its starting-point the fact that eight-year-old Princess Anastasia went missing when the rest of the Romanovs were murdered in the Russian Revolution, this film has her escaping the assassins but arriving amnesic in an orphanage. Years later, having left the orphanage, she falls in with conmen Dimitri and Vladimir, who are seeking a fake Anastasia in order to claim a reward and her inheritance. Little realizing they've found the real thing, they take on "Anya" and head off with her to Paris and exiled Grand Duchess Marie, Anastasia's grandmother. Attempting to thwart them are the ghost of Rasputin and his idiot sidekick bat, Bartok. Along the way it emerges that it was Dimitri who, as a boy, saved the child Anastasia. The two fall in love. In the end, Anastasia, although acknowledged by her grandmother, prefers Dimitri's love in obscurity to celebrity and the reclamation of her rightful inheritance.

Bartok the Magnificent (1999)

⬥ color / animated ○ 68 minutes

A prequel to *Anastasia*. Prince Ivan of the Romanovs impulsively throws fairground performer Bartok a royal ring as a tribute, and that night is kidnapped, seemingly by the wicked witch Baba Yaga, a figure from Russian folklore who dwells in the creepy Iron Forest. Bartok and assistant Zozi, a suave performing bear, are commissioned by public acclaim and royal factotum Ludmilla to rescue the youth. Captured by the witch, Bartok is set three tasks by her. These completed, she tells him she is not the kidnapper: the prince is incarcerated back in Moscow. Ludmilla is revealed as the villain of the piece and Bartok as the hero he has always wanted to be.

Titan A.E. (2000)

⬥ color / animated ○ 94 minutes

The extraterrestrial species the Drej, who are made entirely of energy, destroy the Earth, believing humanity to be an emerging technological threat. Few humans survive, but one is the child Cale, son of the inventor of the worldship *Titan*; Cale's father succeeds in escaping, too, and in hiding the *Titan* somewhere in the Galaxy, but dies before he can rediscover his son. As a young man Cale falls in with the piratical spacefarer Korso, his beautiful young pilot Akima and their alien sidekicks – the smooth Preed, the kangaroo-like weapons mistress, Stith, and the molluscoid eccentric scientist, Gune. Pursued by the murderous Drej, the companions eventually track *Titan* to an interstellar icefield; but by that time it has emerged that Korso and Preed work for the Drej. Preed dies in the final shootout with the Drej; Korso has a change of heart and sacrifices himself for the good of humanity; and Cale activates the *Titan*, which evaginates to form a fresh planet, complete with flora and fauna: New Earth.

Still from *Thumbelina* (1994), showing Thumbelina and Prince
Cornelius. Copyright: Warners.

What makes the movie so good is its characterization. Most
critics have picked on Rasputin and his zany sidekick Bartok as
the characters who give the movie its appeal, but this is probably
a misguided opinion. Visually and in terms of his animation,
Rasputin owes a lot to various precursors – one who springs
immediately to mind is the evil vizier Zigzag in Richard Williams's
butchered 1995 release *The Princess and the Cobbler* – and in
terms of general affect Rasputin seems pretty similar to Merlock,
also voiced by Christopher Lloyd, in Disney's *Duck Tales: The
Movie – Treasure of the Lost Lamp* (1990). Bartok is not quite
indistinguishable, but only not quite, from Creeper in Disney's
The Black Cauldron (1985), Fidget in Disney's *The Great Mouse
Detective* (1986), or Batty Koda in Young Heart's *FernGully: The
Last Rainforest* (1992), among others.

No, the real triumph in *Anastasia*'s characterization is
Anastasia herself. Animation has always had great difficulty with
the characterization of young women. On the one hand it
realizes that sexually attractive females are good for the box

office; on the other it wants to ensure that the heroine is of an
age that the supposedly juvenile audience can identify with. Ever
since *Snow White and the Seven Dwarfs* (1937,) and most
extremely in the studio's late-1990s crop of features, such as
Pocahontas (1995) and especially *Mulan* (1998) – Esmeralda in
1996's *The Hunchback of Notre Dame* is a glorious exception
– the Disney approach has been to produce a heroine who has
many of the attributes of a beddable young woman, and has a
stated age accordingly, but who is, in most regards, a 14-year-old
girl. Other commercial studios have almost without exception
followed Disney's lead in this respect. This may not be confusing
for the kids in the audience, but it most certainly is for their dads.
The moviemakers are quite consciously using two different
channels through which to cast their heroines' spell over the
audience, and the two do not mesh well. (In lower-grade anime
the dichotomy is even more severe, as sexually active characters
rush around in schoolgirl attire.) In stark contrast to all this
confusion, there is no question but that Anastasia is a fully mature
young woman, rather than a woman-child in the Disney mold.
Moreover, she is very definitely the protagonist in her own story.
In more conventional movies the character of Dimitri, being

male, would take over as the romance blossomed; Anastasia would degenerate into a heroine whose plot function was merely to scream in all the appropriate places, to land herself in sufficient and sufficiently stupid jams for her male counterpart to come dashing gallantly to the rescue. But this is not what happens, not here. To be sure, Dimitri, assisted by Vladimir, *attempts* to dominate Anastasia, and she probably could not come through all her adventures without the pair's assistance, but in the end she is the one who makes all the decisions that matter to her.

It is for this reason that, when one thinks of *Anastasia* in retrospect, the character that immediately leaps to mind is not Bartok or Rasputin but, for once, the eponymous heroine. It's refreshing that this is the case.

The movie is of technical interest as well. Although Disney would soon unveil its new 2D technique, Deep Canvas, in *Tarzan* (1999), *Anastasia* offers some of the best examples of traditional 2D animation to come out of the latter years of the 20th century. Perhaps the greatest achievements are the two ballroom scenes, one early in the movie and the other acting as a sort of spectral reprise much later on. Because of the colossal advances in cinematic special effects over the last couple of decades or so, we have become used to the notion – blasé, even – that moviemakers can perform magic before our very eyes; a traditional animation must do something more if it is to impress us when it makes, say, ghosts drift out of walls. This Bluth magnificently managed this feat in the second of the ballroom scenes through a combination of composition, an almost painterly eye, and the application of sheer visual artistry – a fantasticator's vision. Even the most effects-toughened pre-adolescents can be at least momentarily silenced by this scene: it is not only magic up there on the screen, but *beautiful* magic.

In fact, the "traditional" animation of *Anastasia* wasn't quite as traditional as it might appear. Fox Animation's digital imagery supervisor, Thomas Miller, was quoted as saying, around the time of release, that *Anastasia* "contains the largest percentage of 3D computer elements of any traditionally animated film that I know of." The computer effects were present not just in crowd scenes and in various snowfalls but especially in such items as the music box that represents to Anastasia her heritage, and in the reliquary that symbolizes and epitomizes Rasputin's evil powers.

Throughout most of his career Bluth has always had a bewildering number of pots on the burner at any one moment. Among the projects that have never been made are *Hansel and Gretel*, *The Baby Blue Whale* (intended as an "underwater Bambi," according to author John Cawley). later the rather similar-sounding *A Song of the Ice Whale*, *Satyrday* (a fantasy tale of humankind's last times, based on the 1980 novel by Stephen Bauer), and the movie version of the game *Dragon's Lair* (more on this below). So it's surprising that, with the completion of *Anastasia*, there were not at least two or three new projects, in various stages of development, jostling in the queue for attention.

But apparently such was the case. Obedient to big-business mentality, Fox set about axing animators. Seeing that the writing could be on the wall for Fox Animation Studios after just one movie, Goldman and Bluth swiftly came up with a new idea: earlier Bluth features had spawned strings of direct-to-video sequels made by other hands, so why not keep the DTV (direct-to-video) business in-house this time? Thus was born *Bartok the Magnificent* (1999). Unlike most DTV sequels – including most of the Disney ones – this is a movie that could well have benefited from a theatrical release. Certainly the animation is far superior to the average DTV standard, and the story, while slight, is involving. The characterization of Bartok is actually more effective in the sequel than in the original. It is a minor movie, but there's nothing wrong with minor movies *per se*.

After *Bartok the Magnificent*, the expectations for Bluth's next feature were mounting. This was a project on which some of the preproduction work had been done under more than one other director with a view to making a live-action movie. Bluth was given it to examine as a possible CGI project, and in the end almost completely redesigned it as a 2D-animation project. In subject matter it represented a complete departure from anything he had done before: it was a space opera.

The schedule that Fox gave him and his team was bordering on the sadistic – it ended up being 19 months – and the haste shows in the form of obviously bandaged-together elements of plot. Nevertheless, *Titan A.E.* (2000) can be seen as Bluth's greatest achievement to date, and also as the most important animated movie he has ever made – because *at last* the comparison could not be made between it and any Disney animated feature. It is as if he had finally accepted that there was no future in trying to make more and more movies that Walt Disney might have made; from then on, he had to start making his *own* movies.

When news first came out that Bluth and Fox Animation were planning a CGI-rich animated space opera, many hearts sank. Ever since George Lucas released *Star Wars* in 1977, the science-fiction movie audience had been repeatedly patronized by second-rate space opera. The thought of Bluth offering his own – presumably (in terms of sf) amateurish – twist on this genre was enough to stir even the strongest stomach. Perhaps everyone except those who had seen preview material expected some kind of *All Dogs Go Faster Than Light*.

Instead we were given a fast-moving, knowing, and visually spectacular addition to the subgenre, an instant classic of screened space opera. Some of the advance reviewers screamed that the movie was derivative, and of course this is true: space opera, especially movie space opera, is by its very nature a derivative genre, with 90 percent of the ideas and events in any given example of the form being drawn from the common stockpot. So to accuse *Titan A.E.* of a lack of originality is to betray the accuser's ignorance of the form in which Bluth was working. (There have been rumors that our old friends the

Disney Dirty-Tricks Department may have orchestrated these accusations, in just the same way that it seemed curious that so many people should have made such a fuss about *Anastasia*'s lack of historical veracity. But in this instance there's no reason to believe the rumors: movie critics are, by and large, notoriously ignorant of sf or any of its subgenres. They can make fools of themselves unaided.)

Because of this initial outcry, however, *Titan A.E.* has gone down in the records as a badly received movie. A few months after its release, I conducted a survey on the World Wide Web of the reviews that it had received and discovered that, quite to the contrary, it had been extremely *well* received. A huge majority of the reviews proclaimed it to be a thoroughly enjoyable, excitingly entertaining, and oftentimes beautiful movie, well worth making a great effort to see. Similarly, at the 2000 World Science Fiction Convention in Chicago, where gatherings of sf purists might be expected to attack the movie, if anyone would, the talk was instead of how surprised everybody was that they'd enjoyed it so much.

As indicated, the plot is fairly ramshackle, and some of the characterization suffers as a result – in particular, Korso proves an ineffective villain because his motivation for villainy never seems plausible. But elsewhere the characterization is excellent. First, Bluth and his team succeeded in creating some genuinely believable aliens: the tripedally kangaroo-like yet somehow very definitely female, Stith, is the prime example here. More foregrounded than this, perhaps, is that for the second time in a row Bluth has succeeded in giving us an animated heroine who is, far from a simpering child, almost certainly the strongest and most appealing member of the cast. Although it is inevitable from the outset that Akima and our mighty-jawed hero, Cale, will fall in love – this is, after all, on page one of both the animated-movie and space-opera rulebooks – it is delightful to spend most of the time wondering why on earth Akima should think to saddle herself with Cale when she could get on so much better without him. This is an exact reversal of the situation in so many animated movies and space operas alike.

As for the visuals? Well, these left even the movie's most hostile critics at a loss for words. It is very hard indeed to think of any other sf movie that has attained such beauty in its backdrops. It is even hard to think of any astronomical artist who has achieved such majesty in his or her spacescapes – one can say with full confidence that, had Chesley Bonestell been alive to see *Titan A.E.*, he would have applauded those spacescapes, and enviously so. As more than one critic remarked, if animation can do this, why are Hollywood special-effects masters like Industrial Light & Magic still in business?

In any event, Fox badly botched the release – much as United Artists had doen with *The Secret of NIMH* nearly two decades earlier, and for much the same reason: a sudden loss of nerve at the last moment. Moreover, the movie faced more or less direct competition from the new Disney CGI-animated blockbuster *Dinosaur* and Nick Park's much-trumpeted *Chicken Run*. Even so, the general release of *Titan A.E.* outgrossed the general release of Disney's *Fantasia 2000*, with the movie debuting at 5 in the box-office charts. All of that hardly adds up to commercial failure. Yet this is precisely what Twentieth Century-Fox declared *Titan A.E.* to be. If the Fox execs were disappointed by *Titan A.E.*'s box-office performance, then that can only have been because they foolishly hyped themselves up to believe in the impossible. The company's response was depressingly predictable, however: within weeks of the movie's release, Fox Animation Studios was closed down, having produced just one DTV and two theatrical movies. Bluth and Goldman, along with all the rest of their team, were out of jobs. Shortly afterward, in an interview with Larry Lauria in *Animation World Magazine*, Bluth remarked that *Titan A.E.*'s performance was entirely irrelevant to the decision to close the studio down: Fox had begun laying off animators a full year before the movie was released.

Part of the original presentation Bluth and Goldman had made to Fox back in the mid-1990s was for a Dirk the Daring *Dragon's Lair* feature movie. Right up to the moment the decision was made to close the studio down, they assumed this project was very much in the works. In the weeks afterward, it became their number-one priority, but this time the two men were talking about the possibility of releasing it, not into the movie theaters via the standard distribution system, but instead through the Internet. This notion was based on the assumption that very soon – certainly by the time the movie would be completed – domestic technology would enable consumers to download movies and stream them through their television sets. Time will tell how realistic such ideas are. What is more important is that though Bluth has been counted down and out before, he has succeeded in pulling himself back into the fray.

Many of the other creators discussed in this book could be given the label "an animator's animator." Bluth, by contrast, because of his passionate devotion to his chosen artform and his generally dogged adherence to standards that others have too readily dismissed as passé, might better be termed "an animation fan's animator." He has also maintained a far higher degree of independence than other commercial animation directors. As he said in that interview with Larry Lauria:

> Lots of times at a studio, a film is made by committee, and the committee endeavor is not very good. . . .
> Animation will not go away – but you need to school yourself, educate yourself, and in educating yourself make sure you have something to say.

BRUNO BOZZETTO (1938–)

Like Ralph Bakshi – with whose work he shares a few stylistic similarities, although Bozzetto's humor is much gentler and quirkier – Bruno Bozzetto has played a leading role in establishing animation as an artform for adults rather than children. As far as the English-speaking world is concerned, he has done this almost exclusively through a single feature movie, *Allegro non Troppo* (1976). The film is something like an homage to Disney's *Fantasia* (1940), but in fact it is a much more original work than that description might imply.

Bozzetto was born in Milan on March 3, 1938. While still very young, he developed twin passions for drawing and, as a medium for storytelling, the movies. Animation was therefore an obvious destiny, and in this he was much encouraged by his father. At the outset, however, he was more pulled toward live-action moviemaking. But, as he has put it, "I soon discovered that animation was a medium that made it possible to tell beautiful stories without having to worry about actors, makeup, lighting, and all the other problems inherent to live-action films. Not until 1987 was he to realize his dream of making a live-action feature; this was the comic fantasy *Sotto il ristorante cinese* ('Under the Chinese Restaurant').

His earliest experiments in animation were at the age of 18 or 19 as a member of the Cine Club Milano. He produced his first short, *Tapum! La Storia delle Armi* ('Tapum! The Arms Story'; 1958), when he was only 20 years old. This wittily tells the short, short story of human weaponry, from caveman's club to nuclear bomb, its message being that if we use the latter, we'll soon be back to using the former. Two years later, in 1960, he founded Bruno Bozzetto Film; since then he has produced a steady stream of shorts as well as a plethora of tv commercials to finance the shorts. More recently he has farmed off the commercials to a separate company, Bozzetto srl, allowing him to concentrate on his own work.

He is an extremely prolific animator. He has produced about 120 educational cartoons for television, mainly for the Italian popular-science series *Quark*; a few are mere 30-second spots, but most are in the 8–12-minute range. Other work for television, aside from the *Sandwich* series (1984) – thirteen 6-minute live-action shorts – has been similarly extensive. His two notable series of animated shorts for tv have been *Lilliput-put* (1980) and *Gli Sport del Signor Rossi* ('Mr. Rossi's Sporting Feats'; 1975); these could be thought of as Bozzetto's equivalent of Disney's series of *How to . . .* theatrical sports cartoons featuring Goofy, although much shorter (2 minutes).

Signor Rossi is Bozzetto's major series creation, and has had numerous theatrical outings: the fussy little Signor Rossi is a sort of Everyman figure, complete with all the foibles and

Allegro non Troppo (1976)

♩ color and tinted b/w / animated/live-action ○ 85 minutes

In the live-action sequences, an MC (Maurizio Micheli) wishes to make a movie of musical pieces accompanied by animation, and assembles an orchestra of old women. The orchestra's conductor (Nestor Garay) develops a deep loathing for the downtrodden artist (Maurizio Nichetti) forced to provide the animation, but it is the animator who gets the girl — i.e., the extremely lovely stagehand (Maria Luisa Giovannini). The animated sequences comprise an homage to Disney's *Fantasia* (see page 66).

In the *Prelude à l'Après-midi d'un Faun* sequence (music by Debussy), set in an Arcadian paradise, an ageing satyr attempts unsuccessfully to relive his youth among the nymphs. The *Slavonic Dance #7* sequence (music by Dvořák) portrays the rise of militarism through the human need to mimic. The sequence done to Ravel's *Bolero* parodies *Fantasia's Rite of Spring* sequence, depicting the marching, rhythmic evolution of life from lowly origins as a Coca-Cola spill. Sibelius's *Valse Triste* accompanies the tale of a half-starved stray cat who sees the ghosts of a house's occupants before fading to become a ghost itself. Vivaldi's *Concerto in C Minor* accompanies a simple tale about an epicurean bee trying to pollinate in a field where a couple are making love. The sequence set to an extract from Stravinsky's *Firebird* suite revamps the Eden legend, with the Serpent being the one to eat the apple; his resulting indigestion gives him apocalyptic visions of a technological future.

neuroses the rest of us try to hide. A German hip-hop band is named Signor Rossi in the character's honor. He made his first appearance in 1960 in the short *Un Oscar per il Signor Rossi* (*An Award for Mr. Rossi*); this was followed by the shorts *Il Sig. Rossi Va a Sciare* ('Mr. Rossi Goes Skiing'; 1963), *Il Sig. Rossi al Mare* (*Mr. Rossi on the Beach*; 1964), *Il Sig. Rossi Compra l'Automobile* (*Mr. Rossi Buys a Car*; 1966), *Il Sig. Rossi al Camping* ('Mr. Rossi Goes Camping'; 1970), *Il Sig. Rossi al Safari Fotografico* ('Mr. Rossi on Photo-Safari'; 1972) and *Il Sig. Rossi a Venezia* ('Mr Rossi in Venice'; 1974). The first of these is fairly typical: Mr. Rossi is fast-talked into buying a movie camera and, to the despair of his long-suffering wife, becomes a home-movie junkie. His finished movie, a small spool representing the salvageable bits of thousands of meters of exposed film, is so bad that it is enormously funny, and he receives an Oscar. *Il Signor Rossi Compra l'Automobile* is generally regarded as the best of a very good series: our diminutive hero is seduced by car mania, buys not the svelte roadster of his dreams but instead a little bubble car, is subjected to widespread road rage, and then, having souped up his car with a rocket motor, subjects others to it to devastating effect — rather like the car-crazy Mr. Toad of your worst nightmares.

There have also been three feature movies starring the character. In *Il Signor Rossi cerca la felicità* (*Mr. Rossi Looks for Happiness*; 1976) a fairy gives our hero a magic whistle. By

blowing this he can travel through time and space; accordingly he visits the Stone Age, Ancient Rome, Ancient Egypt, the Middle Ages, a desert island, Fairyland, and so on, before realizing that happiness is born from within, not through magical gadgets. *I Sogni del Signor Rossi* (*Mr. Rossi's Dreams*; 1977) shows him in Walter Mitty guise: after watching a Tarzan movie he fantasizes about himself as the apeman, Sherlock Holmes, Zorro, Aladdin, and others. *Le Vacanze del Sig. Rossi* ('Mr. Rossi's Vacation'; 1977) is less fantasticated; here he goes on an endlessly thwarted quest for relaxation and quiet, first at the seaside, then on a farm, and finally in the mountains.

Bozzetto's shorts in general make up an impressive *corpus*; only a few can be treated here. *Drop* (1993) deals with a perpetual domestic problem: doing household repairs does not mean that things *stay* fixed. *Self Service* (1974) offers an analog of the corruption of human civilization, with the discovery by mosquitoes of the succulent toe of a sleeping man leading inevitably and swiftly to a crime- and church-ridden mosquito society. *Baeus* (1987) tells of a bug's love for a human female, a love eventually requited only through the use of magic. *Una vita in Scatola* (*A Life in a Tin*; 1967) portrays the entire life of a human in six minutes — a life of utter pointlessness, since only his grave is ever located in the paradisiac land of his dreams, his living existence being marked by ceaseless travel between home and school, home and the factory, etc. *Baby Story* (1978) could be regarded as the funniest sex-education movie ever made, telling the story from before conception through birth, all from the viewpoint of the uterus's interior. *Ego* (1969) contrasts the near-monochromatic life of a factory-line worker with the vividly colored, extravagantly imagined world of his dreams, in which he fantasizes about sex and ultimate power (the two are intertwined), and shows that Bozzetto is a master of experimental animation as well as of more conventional forms. *Sottaceti* (*Pickles*; 1971) is made up of a series of short segments, some only a few seconds long, satirizing in scattershot fashion various targets concerned with the human condition (war, peace, religion, democracy, electric light, advertising, television, life itself). It concludes when a newborn baby, seeing the horrors of the world, demands to be returned to the womb, a demand its mother repeats to *her* mother and so on all the way back to Eve — and even beyond, for Eve kicks away the apple. *Mister Tao* (1988) embodies in a single serene character all our philosophical quests for enlightenment, for the meaning of the universe, and for understanding of the human condition. *Cavallette* (*Grasshoppers*; 1990) zooms through the entire history of man the warmonger, contrasting the transience of these disputes with the undisturbed permanence of the grasshoppers swarming in and around a clump of grass. In *Point of View* (1998) we watch arboreal happenings "through the eyes" of a mushroom.

Very few of these have any human dialogue at all, and what there is of this is a highly entertaining, highly expressive gibberish — making the shorts truly international in appeal. The soundtracks

Still from the *Valse Triste* section of *Allegro non Troppo* (1976).
© Bruno Bozzetto/Italtoons.

Still from *Vip, Mio Fratello Superuomo* ('Vip: My Brother Superman'; 1968) showing Supervip.
© Bruno Bozzetto/Italtoons.

— which, in the absence of dialogue, must bear the burden of that aspect of the storytelling — are quite exceptional in their wit and their ability to communicate a great deal through apparently very little. To take just a single example, the "democracy" segment of *Pickles* shows nothing but an animated chess game, yet the soundtrack (grunts and gasps and ·snickers from the chessmen against a background of crowds baying, interrupted only by a burst of gunfire) tells the whole story and very effectively makes the segment's satiric point.

Bozzetto's first feature movie came along as early as 1965: *West and Soda*, an animated parody of the John Wayne-style Western. Lonesome cowboy Johnny loves beautiful Clementine, a virgin with a heart of gold, but their love comes close to being thwarted forever by the machinations of vile local bigwig Cattivissimo. Naturally, love triumphs in the end. Constantly inventive and somewhat confused — no major criticism of this sort of movie — *West and Soda* was the first Italian animated feature to be made since 1949, the year that had seen the release of Nino Pagot's *I Fratelli Dinamite* ('The Dynamite Brothers') and Anton Gino Domeneghini's *La Rosa di Bagdad* ('The Rose of Baghdad').

Bozzetto followed up just three years later with his second feature, *Vip, Mio Fratello Superuomo* (*Vip: My Brother Superman*; 1968). This again is a genre parody, the genre now being superhero stories as featured in the comics. In the Bozzetto movie, the theory is that there was once a whole race of superheroes, of whom only two now survive: Supervip, who is all you might expect of a superhero, and Minivip, who is small and myopic and whose superpowers are limited. Naturally, this being a Bozzetto movie, it is Minivip, the underdog, who actually saves the day — and humanity — when the two come across, on a remote island, the megalomaniacal Happy Betty; she plans world conquest by use of destructive Brain Missiles, which indoctrinate and subjugate to her will those unlucky enough to suffer their fallout.

His first two features were both parodies. There is a sense that, however clever, parodies can never be genuinely creative works. This seems an odd remark to be making about an artist so very manifestly creative as Bozzetto, but it nevertheless has truth. Indeed, it could be inferred that he is not truly happy with the feature-length movie, because his genuine triumph in this format, his third feature, *Allegro non Troppo* (1976), consists not of a single story but of an assemblage of unlinked shorts held together by live-action framing pieces (starring and largely scripted by Maurizio Nichetti, later to become a fine movie director and responsible for the animated/live-action near-masterpiece *Volere Volare* [1991]). It is often said that *Allegro non Troppo* is yet another parody, this time of Disney's *Fantasia*. But this is not strictly true, and certainly Bozzetto himself maintains otherwise: he borrowed the blueprint from the Disney movie, but the intention was homage. The live-action sequences, by contrast, are definitely parodic: in place of prestigious Leopold Stokowski and the Philadelphia Orchestra we have overpompous Nestor Garay and crazed animator Nichetti attempting to tame an elderly army of wannabe musicians as they aim to produce something very like another *Fantasia*. And one of the movie's sequences, done to Ravel's *Bolero*, is such a close homage to *Fantasia*'s *Rite of Spring* segment that it is difficult to see it as anything other than parody.

The animated sequences themselves are superb overall, and very much Bozzetto's – in general they represent the pinnacle of his work. All of the animator's preoccupations are in evidence here, from his revulsion towards militarism (in this instance satirized with Swiftian venom as born from the infantile need of men to mimic each other); to misgivings about the advance of technology (the Serpent in Eden eats the apple and his resultant indigestion rewards him with visions of a hideous, technology-dominated future); to a touching and rather earthy faith in the power of love, especially when physically expressed. He shows his ability to project true poignancy as well, in the sequence done to Sibelius's *Valse Triste*; this simple ghost story about an abandoned cat brings tears to most eyes. The sequence concerning Eden is the most ambitious, and also the one most open to analysis, especially since it reveals another of Bozzetto's characteristics: his deep humanism and humanity, which permeate virtually every movie he makes. Here, after the serpent has seen his visions of the technological Apocalypse, he advises Eve to leave the apple well alone, for through eating it she will start the process that will inevitably lead to humankind's

grim doom. This philanthropic gesture is, of course, not what one anticipates from the epitome of evil. The overt subtext of the sequence, then, is that, although the serpent is evil, his is mischievous rather than malevolent evil. One could go further and describe it as *innocent* evil, despite the contradiction in terms; the eating of the apple, as for Eve in the tale's standard version, destroys the serpent's innocence. This recasting thus involves a very revisionist view of the nature of primordial evil, or, to use the Christian term, original sin; it can thus be read as a veiled attack also on the Roman Catholic Church and organized Christianity in general – another of Bozzetto's frequently encountered *bêtes noires*.

Since the release of *Allegro non Troppo* in 1976, Bozzetto has been silent on the features front, with the exception of the three episodic movies starring Signor Rossi and 1987's live-action *Sotto il ristorante cinese*. One might easily gain the impression that Bozzetto has been resting on his laurels these past couple of decades. His long list of shorts belies this conclusion, of course. The truth of the matter is that he earned the freedom to concentrate on what brought him into animated movies in the first place – to wit, animation itself, rather than the quest for ever bigger and bigger bucks. As a result, he is one of the most *appealing* of all the great animators: he has all the fantasticating inventiveness, surreal humor, and satiric bite of someone like Ralph Bakshi or Bill Plympton, but he lacks the brashness which can so often lead his American counterparts into straightforward crudity (and even more so the animation directors of what might loosely be called the MTV stable, such as Mike Judge); a short like *Baby Story*, with its reasonably graphic depiction of the messier aspects of the sexual act, could have been gross in their hands, but in Bozzetto's it is utterly charming. His prevailing pessimism about the human future is in general conveyed with lightness and wit, and all through his work one is conscious of the genuine warmth of his heart and his profound empathy toward his fellow human beings. Although he is one of those who has ushered in the adulthood of animation, one would feel that the human future would be rosier if his movies became prescribed viewing for every child.

JOHN RANDOLPH BRAY

(1879–1978)

Where Winsor McCay is regarded as the creative father of animation, John Randolph Bray – born on August 25, 1879, in Addison, Michigan – can be regarded as its technological father. He also made a considerable deal of money out of it, not least because he had the foresight to patent the advances he made and then license them for a fee to other producers of animation. Because Bray and his business partner, Earl Hurd (1880–1940), held the rights to various integral parts of the basic animation process, it was impossible for any animated venture to proceed in the U.S. without those fees being paid, from 1914 until the most important among these patents began to expire in 1932.

Bray was a successful New York newspaper cartoonist before his interest turned to animation in about 1910; more specifically, it turned to the financial promise of the medium, which he believed would soon become the rage. But, if a good profit were to be made from animation, it was essential that the process be simplified as much as possible, because the method then employed by McCay and others – whereby each of thousands of frames had to be drawn in its entirety – was hopelessly time-consuming and therefore far too expensive to be used on any sensible commercial scale. The first measure Bray devised – and with hindsight it's startling that no one had thought of this before – was to print multiple copies of backgrounds on sheets of translucent paper; different sections could be blocked out so that when the sheet was placed over another sheet, you could see through it to what was on the first sheet – which was the animation. The crucial point was that only the animation had to be redrawn each time.

He filed a patent for this process in January 1914. He followed this up with patent applications for a means of applying tones to drawings (July 1914) and for a forerunner of the cel process (July 1915), whereby multiple layers of an animated scene could be done on translucent paper through which a light could be shone to reveal the whole. Again, this cut down the work because only the moving parts of any particular frame had to be redrawn each time. Independently, Earl Hurd came up with a very much better variant of this last process at about the same time (the patent application was dated December 1914, so it's possible he had seen Bray's patent, which had been granted in November): to put the animation on celluloid sheets placed over a single painted background. This became the basis for all cel animation. Probably realizing the importance of Hurd's invention and certainly recognizing him as a serious potential rival, Bray promptly formed a partnership with him, the Bray–Hurd Patent Company, which thereafter raked in the royalties on the two men's various inventions.

By this time Bray had made his first animated movie, the short *The Artist's Dream* (vt *The Dachshund and the Sausage*; 1913). Charles Pathé was at the time visiting New York, and Bray took the opportunity to show him his work. Pathé was sufficiently impressed to offer him a six-movie distribution contract. The first movie Bray did under this contract is widely regarded as the world's first commercial animated short, in that it wasn't a gimmick or a one-off but the first in a series, complete with a series character, destined for movie theaters and produced for financial gain as part of the recognized cinema industry. *Colonel Heeza Liar in Africa* (November 1913) is not a particularly fine piece of animation, but neither is it particularly bad. Certainly the central character – based on a mixture of Baron Munchhausen and Theodore Roosevelt – proved appealing enough to endure for scores of shorts over a decade or more, until finally the series terminated in November 1924 with *Colonel Heeza Liar's Romance*. The Colonel, a little man with a huge and bullying wife, told tall tales of his brave adventures in far-off lands (a formula Ub Iwerks was to repeat, unsuccessfully, in his Willie Whopper series twenty years later, with a small boy as fabulator in place of the Colonel).

Bray was the first – although Raoul Barré was soon behind him – to divide up the animation process so that cartoons could be produced on an assembly-line, mass-production basis. He himself gave up animating in favor of being a businessman at the earliest opportunity, but animated shorts continued to pour out of the Bray Company. Among these was the long series created by Hurd, inspired by R.F. Outcault's strip character Buster Brown, starring Bobby Bumps, who with his faithful dog Fido rather charmingly clowned his way through all manner of boyish scrapes, from *Bobby Bumps Gets Pa's Goat* (1915) to *Bobby Bumps and Company* (1925). Much shorter-lived was the Otto Luck series, directed by Wallace A. Carlson, about a somewhat wacky young romantic: there were four shorts in 1915, begun with *Otto Luck in the Movies*, and then nothing more. Even earlier were the seven-short-strong Police Dog series, drawn and directed by Carl Anderson and featuring a dog who befriends a beat policeman; one can only speculate about the contents of the second of these cartoons, which was called *The Police Dog Gets Piffles in Bad* (1915).

A pattern emerges as we look at the diverse shorts series introduced by the Bray Company hereafter, mainly as one component of the Paramount-Bray Pictograph, a weekly package delivered to movie theaters: most of them didn't last very long. Bray was an astonishingly successful businessman and an animation inventor of great note, but he seems to have been incapable of the other part of the equation that could have made

Frame from *Colonel Heeza Liar's African Hunt* (1914).
Private Collection.

his an empire that, in later decades, might have rivaled or even eclipsed Walt Disney's: that of understanding what made good entertainment. In 1916, for example, he began a liaison with the Fleischers, during which time the first Out of the Inkwell shorts were released. But largely because of his penny-pinching, the Fleischers soon went their own very successful way. Had Bray had Walt's knack for knowing what the people wanted, he would never have let them escape.

Instead, Bray backed losers — at least, losers for him. Paul Terry was employed for a short while at the studio, which released the first eleven of his Farmer Al Falfa shorts, all in 1916. Terry was then drafted into the Army, and further shorts in his lengthy series were done elsewhere. The Trick Kids, who were animated dolls and toys, lasted for ten cartoons during 1916, but were then abandoned. Much the most interesting shorts Bray released in this year were the Silhouette Fantasies, done by Bray himself in collaboration with C. Allan Gilbert. Of all animation's forms, silhouette animation is one of the rarest, despite the efforts of animation pioneers such as Lotte Reiniger. It is very much to be regretted that Gilbert stayed with the Bray

Bobby Bumps Puts a Beanery on the Bum (1918)

🎵 b/w / animated silent ⏱ 6¹/₂ minutes
Bobby Bumps
Earl Hurd created Bobby, based on the comic-strip character Buster Brown, and animated the longish series of cartoons featuring him and his bulldog Fido. Introduced as usual — through being drawn by Hurd's live-action hands — the pair become employed in the kitchen of a Quick Lunch Beanery. There are predictable japes when the cook has Bobby sub for him during his lunch-break. Having been told that when called he must drop whatever he's doing and come at once, Bobby is later called while carrying a towering stack of plates. Only through the intervention of Hurd's hands do Bobby and Fido escape the cook's wrath.

J O H N   R A N D O L P H   B R A y

Company for such a short time – his departure led to the abandonment of the series – for Bray had plans for a silhouette-animated feature movie. Now *there* would have been a movie worth watching!

The year 1917 saw the debut of Pat Sullivan's series star Hardrock Dome, a nutty detective, in *Hardrock Dome, the Great Detective*; but the series didn't last long: just four cartoons. Six cartoons were released in that same year starring Quacky Doodles, mother of a sprightly duck family. The series was created by Johnny B. Gruelle, best known as the creator of the Raggedy Ann comic strip. Again, Quacky Doodles didn't survive into 1918. Milt Gross, a successful strip artist who decided to have a go at animation, created a brief series of five cartoons for Bray in 1920, while the Technical Romances series, begun with *The Mystery Box* (1922), lasted just six cartoons in 1922–23.

In 1920–21 Bray released a dozen Krazy Kat cartoons, despite the fact that he didn't own the rights to the comic-strip characters, created by George Herriman. A long string of Krazy Kat cartoons had already been released by the Hearst Corporation, who did own the relevant rights, but Bray discovered that the Hearst studios were violating Bray's patent rights extensively. Instead of suing Hearst International Film Service, a process that Hearst's lawyers could drag out for an expensive decade or more, Bray chose to retaliate in kind. Hearst never did sue, and the only reason Bray gave up the Krazy Kat series was that he found the cartoons didn't do very well for him. The irony is that the Bray Krazy Kats (those few that have survived) are nowadays regarded as the best, the official Hearst productions being dogged by miserly budgeting. Herriman, the titular supervisor of the Hearst series, in fact distanced himself from it as much as possible, having seen the frightful travesty the Hearst team was perpetrating on his characters and scenarios; one wonders if he was, perhaps, copyright infringement or no, behind the scenes, cheering on Bray's short-lived efforts.

And then there was Walter Lantz. Not long before he had joined Bray as animator on the Colonel Heeza Liar shorts, Lantz became the human star of the live-action/animated Dinky Doodle cartoons, which he also wrote and directed; Dinky Doodle and his dog Weakheart were the regular animated stars. Some of the early shorts in the series were based on classic tales. It ran from *The Magic Lamp* (1924) to *Dinky Doodle in the Army* (1926). Lantz's other major contributions to the studio were the Un-Natural History series of shorts, begun in 1925 with *How the Elephant Got his Trunk* and running for fifteen or so shorts until 1927, and the Pete the Pup series – also known as the Hot Dog Cartoons – which, like the Dinky Doodle shorts, featured animated characters interacting with a live-action animator, Lantz himself.

Other series came and rapidly went (mainly rapidly). It is as if Bray reckoned his audience would know no better than to accept the mediocre, which he pumped out remorselessly. He issued the first color animated short as early as 1920, with *The Debut of Thomas Cat*. There had been earlier animated shorts shot in black-and-white film and then hand-colored, frame by frame, but this was the first one genuinely made in color using color film – supplied by Brewster Color, an unsuccessful precursor of Technicolor. Bray found Brewster Color technically deficient – the film scratched too easily – and abandoned the idea; as before, had he had the patience to persevere, he might later have outrivaled Walt Disney, who in 1932 successfully backed Technicolor, starting with the short *Flowers and Trees*.

In 1927 Bray abruptly closed his studio. For some years he had been doing well because of a distribution deal with Goldwyn, but Goldwyn had decided not to renew. Had Bray realized that the final frontier, sound, was just a couple of years around the corner, he might have stayed on. As it was, there seemed no reason to bother: he had got from animation exactly what he had wanted in the first place: a lot of money. Although he continued to produce some educational animated shorts, he was content to depart animation and live on the proceeds of his patents. Like so many other animators he lived to a ripe old age, dying just a few months short of his hundredth birthday, on October 10, 1978, in Bridgeport, Connecticut.

JOHN CANEMAKER (1943-)

Setup for *Bottom's Dream* (1983). Private collection.
© John Canemaker.

Born in Waverly, New York, on May 28, 1943, John Canemaker is a central figure to any study of the animation world from the last quarter of the 20th century onward, not just for his own animation – which is interesting enough – but for his writings on animation and animators. He is among the very few significant scholars/ historians the medium has ever had. His major books (there are some minor ones) – *The Animated Raggedy Ann & Andy* (1977), *Winsor McCay: His Life and Art* (1987), *Felix: The Twisted Tale of the World's Most Famous Cat* (1993), *Before the Animation Begins: The Art and Lives of Disney Inspirational Sketch Artists* (1996), *Paper Dreams: The Art and Artists of Disney Storyboards* (1999), and *Walt Disney's Nine Old Men* (2001) – are only a part of it; the reference literature of animation is crowded with his essays, interviews and articles. There is also a third strand to his career: teaching. He is a professor and director of the animation program (which he co-founded) at New York University's Tisch School of the Arts.

His earliest work as a professional animator included a couple of segments for *Sesame Street* in 1974 and 1975 and

seven spots for the CBS show *Captain Kangaroo* in 1975. It might have seemed that he was gearing himself up for a career in television, since he also wrote and presented two excellent documentaries: *The Boys from Termite Terrace* (1975), about the classic Warners animators, and *The Art of Oskar Fischinger* (1977), about that great abstract animator. However, at the same time he was creating personal works in the form of animated shorts. The first of these that he regards as having any significance is *Greed* (1974), in which cavorting beasts epitomize that particular Deadly Sin; it was done in a somewhat Disneyish style, totally alien to his later work. In that same year came two shorts more connected to popular culture: *Street Freaks* (1974), a tale set among street musicians, in which a youngster must discover how to live and let live; and *The '40s* (1974), a brief, collaged portrait of that decade done to the tune of "Boogie Woogie Bugle Boy."

For the next few years he did little animation outside of television, although he produced two theatrical interview-documentaries that are of considerable interest: *Remembering Winsor McCay* (1976), gravitating around an interview with McCay's one-time film assistant, John FitzSimmons; and, based on an interview with Messmer himself, *Otto Messmer and Felix the Cat* (1977), one of the key works that, decades later, brought Felix's creator out of the shadow of Pat Sullivan and into the limelight at last.

Canemaker's career as a creator of personal animated works really got started in 1978, with the short *Confessions of a Stardreamer*. The actress Diane Gardner provided the witty voicetrack, done in quasi-interview style, of a wannabe actress musing about her dreams and aspirations. As she does so, her words are realized literally in a caricaturish, cartoonish line and (seemingly) watercolor style. For example, when she talks of her old acting teacher as looking like a penguin, he becomes a penguin; then, when she talks of him demonstrating as Romeo, there is a series of quick interchanges as the teacher switches back and forth between Romeo, himself, the penguin, and the actress herself. All this is done with considerable brio.

This simplified drawing style, accompanied by constant, bewildering metamorphoses, is characteristic of Canemaker's subsequent work – even his commercial work. While he is perfectly capable of animating in the Disney/Warners mode – as shown in his short *The Wizard's Son* (1981), which is something of a homage to the Disney Silly Symphonies – he has generally preferred to concentrate on the pure strength of line and drawing rather than aim at "the illusion of life." For example, in the animated segment he contributed to *The World According to Garp* (1982), a crayon drawing done by Garp as a little boy suddenly comes to life, though still retaining its childish-seeming crayon style. The effect is that we see the simple tale (of the boy with his father, both of them airplanes, and of the father saving the boy from danger) as if through the child's own imaginings, so that it becomes very much more vivid, intimate, and *real* to us than could be managed through a more orthodox animated treatment. In *Bottom's Dream* (1983), widely regarded as Canemaker's masterpiece to date, the bewildering, exhilaratingly swift metamorphoses are accompanied by myriad shifts between this simpler style and something approaching conventional animation. Giannalberto Bendazzi, in his book *Cartoons* (1994), describes the effect of

Bottom's Dream as "a summary of the lessons of Disney and the post-Disney age." After a decade's gap Canemaker returned to personal moviemaking with *Confessions of a Stand-Up* (1993), which has thematic similarities to *Confessions of a Stardreamer* but is this time centered on comedian Dennis Blair. Following this was *Bridgehampton* (1998), which has a jazz score by Fred Hersch and uses Canemaker's paintings of his Long Island garden to depict the turning of the seasons.

Alongside his personal work, Canemaker has done some excellent commercial work. This has been mainly for television. One exception is the short *John Lennon Sketchbook* (1986), commissioned by Yoko Ono and based on the drawings by her late husband. Canemaker admirably tailors his own free-form fluidity of line to match Lennon's autographic style, so that it is as if one were watching the animated movie Lennon himself would have made had he lived. Of Canemaker's Home Box Office special *You Don't Have to Die* (1988), the *New York Post* commented:

> John Canemaker . . . takes the book illustrations by Tim and Adam Gaes and expands upon them, adhering to the visual style by incorporating new ideas while fleshing out old ones. Consequently, the animated image of Jason's heaven is even more reassuring in the TV show than in the book. His self-image as a future doctor is much less formal. Even the concept of chemotherapy is helped greatly by Canemaker's witty techniques.

You Don't Have to Die, about a young boy's experience with pediatric cancer, won an Oscar as Best Achievement in Documentary Short Subject. Canemaker has won a plethora of other awards at animation festivals.

What is significant about Canemaker's animation is that it brilliantly marries a sensibility of line and color more typical of the independent animators, with an immediate appeal born out of its sheer visual inventiveness using images that are individually instantly recognizable. The net result is that his work is intensely commercial: at the same time as being challenging, it is also just plain, downright fun to watch – there is none of the sense of duty one sometimes feels when confronted by "art for art's sake." This is no mean achievement; it is only to be regretted that, because of the contributions he has made to animation in other contexts, he hasn't created more of his vivid, memorable animations.

BOB CLAMPETT (1913–1984)

Still from *The Great Piggy Bank Robbery* (1946), showing Daffy
Duck and an anonymous detective. © Warner Bros.

In his love of the absurd and the surrealistic, Bob Clampett
appears to have been second only to Tex Avery in
animation's history. Some have even suggested that it was his
influence rather than Avery's that guided the Warners animated
shorts in this direction, thereby giving them their distinguishing
characteristics of rapid-fire action and conceptual fecundity. Be
that as it may, Clampett was certainly one of the formative
influences on the Warners cartoons, and as such his influence on
modern U.S. commercial animation has been profound.

Bob Clampett was born in San Diego, California, on May 8,
1913. While he was still an infant, the family moved to
Hollywood, and consequently he was fully aware of the movies
from a very early age: sometimes he could see filming going on
in the streets near his home. He attended the Theodore
Roosevelt Junior High School, for whose magazine he created a
cartoon character called Teddy the Roosevelt Bear. He also, while
only 12, had a number of cartoons published in the *Los Angeles
Times*; these attracted the attention of William Randolph Hearst,
who was sufficiently impressed to offer the child a job contract
for when he finished school. As a consequence, the young
Clampett spent much of his spare time working in the art
department of the *Los Angeles Examiner*, one of Hearst's
newspapers. The head of the art department, George Parmenter,
was responsible for Clampett's formal art training, sending him to
the Otis Art Institute.

A further important event in his childhood occurred when
he was still only 12: he made his first movie, using the family
camera. The silent comedy required title cards, so Clampett
approached a local company that specialized in movie title cards
to inquire about the cost of having these professionally
produced. That company was Pacific Title and Art Studio, whose
owner was Leon Schlesinger. According to Clampett's later
recollections, Schlesinger ended up having his company do the
job for free, but this is hard to believe.

Wabbit Twouble (1941)

📽 color / animated ⏱ 8¹/₄ minutes
Merrie Melodies/Bugs Bunny & Elmer Fudd
Elmer comes to Jellostone National Park for a restful vacation and encounters Bugs Bunny. Bugs induces him to camp right over the rabbithole, then, by painting over his spectacles, gets him utterly confused as to whether it's day or night. Elmer encounters a grizzly bear and plays dead; the bear sniffs his socks and departs. Elmer still playing dead, Bugs mimics the bear and commits all sorts of indignities on Elmer's motionless form. Elmer realizes the ruse and, trying to bash Bugs, bashes the bear instead. Exit tourist, pursued by bear. The ensuing chase through the forest produces some interesting visual gags among the trees based on the mechanics of cel animation itself — in specific, the way that the artists (obviously) need animate only the visible portions of their characters. At length all three find rest and relaxation in prison, having been arrested by a park ranger.

Bugs Bunny Gets the Boid (1942)

📽 color / animated ⏱ 7¹/₄ minutes
Merrie Melodies/Bugs Bunny/Beaky Buzzard
The first appearance of Beaky Buzzard, here called Killer. Mama Buzzard tells her four chicks to go and get food — a moose, a cow, etc. — but one of them, the dopey Killer, declines. She tells him at least to get a rabbit and boots him from the nest. Having learned how to fly, he spots rabbit tracks in the desert, at the end of which Bugs lounges. "Sh," Killer tells the audience, "I'm a-stalkin' a victim" — and he nosedives. After much trickstering, and some sight gags with an animal skeleton lying on the desert, Mama Buzzard arrives to rescue her little darling, and with a smacking kiss proclaims Bugs her hero for having saved him.

A Tale of Two Kitties (1942)

📽 color / animated ⏱ 6¹/₂ minutes
Merrie Melodies/Tweety
The first appearance of Tweety. The movie was intended to be a star vehicle for caricatured Abbott and Costello in alley cat form (Babbitt and Catstello), but the bird they were trying to snatch from his high nest stole the show and rapidly became a series star in his own right. The routines are fast-moving and hilarious. Tweety comes out with his catchphrase for the first time: "I tawt I taw a puddy tat. I *did!* I *taw* a puddy tat!"

At both Harvard High School, in Glendale, and then Hoover High School, Clampett contributed much cartoon work to the school yearbooks. But something much more exciting happened during these years. His aunt Charlotte Clark made novelty items for department stores and thought there might be a market for a stuffed doll of the new cartoon superstar Mickey Mouse. She turned to her nephew for the design, and, once the doll was completed, he and his father took it to show to Walt and Roy Disney. The Disneys were delighted, and soon had rented a house near the studio where Clark and her team could produce lots of these dolls for distribution to studio visitors. Clampett spent a fair amount of time on the Disney lot, and so it is hardly surprising that he became determined to follow a career as an animator.

On graduating from high school in 1931, he approached, oddly, not Disney but Leon Schlesinger, who by now had just started working in tandem with Harman-Ising to produce animated shorts for Warners. Schlesinger sent the lad over to Harman–Ising, who promptly hired him and soon had him working as an inbetweener (see page 83). He also attended story sessions, and very early on was producing ideas for sequences that were taken up by his principals — including, it is said, one sequence in only the second of the Merrie Melodies, *Smile, Darn Ya, Smile* (1931), starring the short-lived series character Foxy. Most of Clampett's early work for the studio, however, was on the Bosko cartoons: Bosko, a little black boy, was at the time the only series star of any note that the Schlesinger/Harman–Ising partnership had been able to produce for Warners.

In 1933 Harman–Ising and Schlesinger fell out, and the two animators took their services, and Bosko, to (eventually) MGM. Suddenly Schlesinger found himself with a contract to produce animated shorts for Warners and the copyright to the Looney Tunes and Merrie Melodies series, but no animation directors and no series star. Some of the Harman–Ising staff had, however, elected to remain with him. These included Clampett — who got his first screen credit in the Friz Freleng-directed *Shake Your Powder Puff* (1937) — and two other young men who were to play an important role in the future of the Warners cartoons, Robert McKimson and, especially, Freleng. Freleng was promoted to director of the two series, and the team set out to find a new series star. As part of this effort Schlesinger set them to produce, under Freleng's direction, a short that could act as a sort of talent contest for possible series characters. This short became *I Haven't Got a Hat* (1935), and it took the form of one of those ghastly classroom occasions when the kids are called up to perform their party pieces. Clampett proposed a pair of characters to be called Porky & Beans, the former a pig and the latter a kitten, his inspiration coming from a can of Campbell's Pork & Beans. Although the latter was regarded as the more likely series star, in fact it was Porky — trying frustratedly to get through a recitation of "Paul Revere" despite a desperate stutter

— who (surprisingly) caught the fancy of the audiences. Beans went on to appear in a few Looney Tunes, starting with *A Cartoonist's Nightmare* (1935), but failed to survive; whereas Porky, of course, became the first Warners animated star to have much by way of permanence, soon being promoted to serve as the studio's mascot and featuring in scores of shorts. No Warners cartoon seemed complete without, at its end, Porky appearing onscreen to stammer, "Th-th-th-that's all, folks."

Also in 1935, Tex Avery arrived at the Schlesinger studio, and Clampett was appointed as the new director's principal animator and key gag man. An inbetweener who worked with them was Chuck Jones. Clampett and Jones assisted Avery in the creation of Daffy Duck and later in the remodeling of Bugs Bunny, making him the character we know today. Something certainly sparked between Avery and Clampett: although Avery is credited with bringing to Warners the new wild style and surrealistic mode of humor, with nothing that would gain a laugh being regarded as unfit for use in a cartoon, there can be no question that his inspiration was fully supported and indeed supplemented by his animator; and later, after Avery's departure, it was Clampett more than any of the other Warners directors who carried on in the same spirit – if not more so. This fearlessness in deciding what was suitable material for treatment in animation would give Clampett a reputation for sick and black humor that brought him some condemnation at the time; today this very quality is part of the reason why his cartoons are held in such high esteem. (As an aside, Avery gave Clampett a friendly little tribute in the 1940 short *Circus Today*, which features a minor character called Captain Clampett, the Human Cannonball.)

Even while animating with Avery, however, Clampett had another idea, one that could not be realized within the Schlesinger context. He got in touch with Edgar Rice Burroughs and put forward a proposal for an animated series based on the author's adventures of John Carter of Mars. Burroughs was excited at the prospect, and, with the author's active cooperation, Clampett made a pilot which they took to MGM, who was then having a major success with the live-action Tarzan movies. The initial response from MGM was highly favorable. But then the executives there decided that, if they were going to take on an animated Burroughs series, it must be of the adventures of Tarzan, not John Carter. Somewhere in the midst of this Clampett lost interest, and neither Tarzan nor the John Carter series was ever made.

Another reason for abandoning the putative Burroughs series was that Schlesinger got wind of Clampett's intentions and, worried that he might lose this valued staff member, offered him a deal he could hardly refuse: a new contract that included a substantial pay hike and the promise that he would very soon be made a full animation director in his own right. In fact, Schlesinger later reneged on the latter part of the deal, bringing in Ub Iwerks, who had just found himself out of a job

thanks to the collapse of Celebrity Pictures. Again Clampett threatened to leave. Schlesinger told Clampett the master plan now was that he should work out of house under Iwerks, who maintained his own studio while working for Warners, and then take over from him as director whenever Iwerks should leave. Surprisingly, Clampett accepted this rather lame explanation. In fact, this time Schlesinger did keep his promise, promoting Clampett to full director on Iwerks's departure to Columbia after just a couple of Porky Pig cartoons, *Porky and Gabby* (1937) and *Porky's Super Service* (1937).

In 1937, then, Clampett achieved his goal. The first cartoon that he directed was a Porky item, *Porky's Badtime Story* (1937), in which Porky and Gabby have the titular "badtime" as they try to get to sleep in order to be at work in *good* time the following day, but are constantly frustrated by wilder and wilder mishaps and disturbances. The short is actually rather more irritating than funny: patterned along the lines of an anxiety dream, it has something of the qualities of that experience. However, Schlesinger liked it enough that Clampett was made primarily responsible for future Porky movies. His assistant director for the first few movies was Chuck Jones, and it is from this period that the celebrated ill will between the two men seems to have sprung.

Even before *Porky's Badtime Story*, Schlesinger had given Clampett his first directing assignment. This was to do the animated titles for the live-action Joe E. Brown feature movie *When's Your Birthday?* (1937). It was obviously an assignment that bore considerable responsibility, and hence prestige: either Schlesinger was expressing great faith in the abilities of his newest animation director or he was suffering from a guilty conscience about his earlier broken promise – or both.

One of Clampett's early Porky cartoons was the classic *Porky in Wackyland* (1938). Porky is on the trail of the valuable Do-Do, a bird capable of bending the laws of cartoon logic in myriad ways in his evasion of the pursuer; for example, he can draw a door in empty space and flee through it, slamming it behind him. More interesting than the chase, though, is the territory through which it largely runs: based on the idea of Lewis Carroll's Wonderland, Wackyland is a place of surrealistic topographies and creatures, like the man who has three heads because his mother was scared during pregnancy by a pawnbroker's sign. This short, in its cumulative effect, is more wildly inventive than anything even Avery had produced for Warners; it is seen today far less frequently than it should be because of one short, incidental piece of perceived – in fact, harmless – racial stereotyping, a common feature of cartoons of the era.

The same problem has bedeviled another of Clampett's classics, which has become notorious: *Coal Black and de Sebben Dwarfs* (1943), a translocation of the Snow White tale into a black environment – a World War II environment, too, so an insulting reference to the Japanese has been added to the list of *Coal Black*'s crimes (as if every WWII movie made in the United States for decades didn't do much the same). The Wicked Queen

Publicity cel for *Beany and Cecil*, dating from 1988.
Photograph: S/R Laboratories.
© Bob Clampett Productions.

("Queenie") is hoarding goods. She asks the Magic Mirror to send her a handsome prince, and up turns Prince Chawmin' – who, alas, fancies the Wicked Queen not one whit but falls instantly in lust with the curvaceous So White (the project was initially titled *So White and de Sebben Dwarfs*; the retitling took no account of the fact that she is named in the short). The Wicked Queen hires Murder Inc. to do away with the girl, but their operatives spare her life, leaving her in the forest. So White's pals, the Seven Dwarfs, have now joined the Army, and she goes to their base. Soon after, the Wicked Queen arrives, selling, according to her own advertising, "Poisoned Apples on a Stick." So White accepts one of the toffee apples and falls into a coma from which even Prince Chawmin's very best kiss can't raise her. Only the Dopey-equivalent among the Dwarfs can achieve that; when asked what he puts into his kiss to have such a "dynomite" effect, he responds that it's a military secret. The whole is done in affectionate parody of Disney's *Snow White and the Seven Dwarfs* (1937), with a frame of an old woman telling a child the story, and it's conceivable that part of the reason for the cartoon's evil reputation is that Disney has not felt it in its interest to rehabilitate it.

Whether or not *Coal Black* is racist is a very moot point. Certainly Clampett himself was not. He was a great fan of black jazz and believed it embodied the spirit that would see the United States – united racially as well as in name – prevail over fascism. It was at his insistence that black performers were used on the soundtrack, whereas prevalent Hollywood custom would have suggested he use white studio voice-actors and musicians; those black performers had no trouble working on the movie, which they saw as portraying a positive image. The message to the Nazis of this movie, which like most of the time had propagandistic elements, was that the black people of the United States, despised as subhuman by the Nazis because of their color, were as one with the whites in seeking to destroy fascism and would prevail. The import of the short runs exactly counter to that of a racist opus: while the aim of such would be to dehumanize, the thrust of *Coal Black* is – as in Ralph Bakshi's *Coonskin* (1974), which three decades later caused a very similar fuss for the same reasons – in fact to *humanize*. Its black characters may not be idealized human beings, but instead are (to use the adjective within the context of animation) *realistic* human beings, with human attributes that are largely, except in Queenie's case, appealing. Nevertheless, the stereotyping, although perfectly customary for Hollywood in the 1940s, is today unsettling for adults and potentially misleading for children.

Clampett did other Warners cartoons that were intended as wartime morale-raisers (aside from a number of the Private Snafu training shorts directed particularly toward the Army). He introduced the Gremlins in the 1943 Bugs Bunny short *Falling Hare*, and returned to them again in *Russian Rhapsody* (1944) – whose project title was *Gremlins from the Kremlin* – in which Russian Gremlins sabotage the efforts of Adolf Hitler. And there

Horton Hatches the Egg (1942)

♭color / animated ⏱ 9³/₄ minutes
Merrie Melodies
Based on the 1940 story by Dr. Seuss. The lazy blue bird Maisie cannot be bothered to hatch her own egg, so volunteers a passing elephant, Horton, to do it for her while she goes on vacation. Right through winter and on into spring Horton maintains his vigil; his friends laugh at him (one, in an amusing inversion of the partnership in *Dumbo* [1941], is a huge-eared mouse), but still Horton broods on. Three elephant hunters seize him and take him across the seas to a circus, but Horton remains on the egg: "I meant what I said and I said what I meant: an elephant's faithful one hundred per cent." Maisie comes to see the circus and finds the egg, after 51 weeks' hatching, at last about to open; it does so, and a little winged elephant – an "elephant-bird" – emerges. To her fury the infant chooses Horton as parent, and in due course the pair are released happily back to the jungle.

The animation and art styling in general throughout owe more to Seuss than to the Warners standard template, yet there is much of Clampett in the mix. Words and animation meshing perfectly, this is one of the classic Warners shorts.

The Hep Cat (1942)

♭color / animated ⏱ 6¹/₄ minutes
Looney Tunes
The first color Looney Tune. A streetwise cat, a self-proclaimed suave charmer and magnet for the ladies, receives a note saying: "Dear Gorgeous Hunk, If you would like to pitch some woo – Come back of the fence for a rendezvous. Love and kisses, Guess Who??" He obeys the summons and walks straight into the snarl of the dog who has been trying to catch him every night since time immemorial. A grand chase ensues, as it does after the dog employs a further amour-oriented strategy, using a hand puppet of a beautiful feline. In the end the cat settles for loving the discarded puppet.

A Corny Concerto (1943)

♭color / animated ⏱ 7³/₄ minutes
Merrie Melodies/Bugs Bunny & Elmer Fudd
A parody of Disney's *Fantasia* (1940). The venue is the Corny-Gie Hall, and the orchestra's conductor is a stubbled Elmer Fudd. The first item on the program is Strauss's *Tales from the Vienna Woods*, and luscious strings introduce a lushly Disneyesque pastoral background . . . into which come Elmer Fudd and his hound to hunt Bugs Bunny. They are as usual bamboozled, finally being tied up in a brassiere as Bugs dances away balletically in a tutu over the horizon. Next is *The Blue Danube Waltz*, to which is enacted a variant of "The Ugly Duckling."

Kitty Kornered (1946)

⌐color ╱animated ⏱ 7 minutes
Looney Tunes/Porky Pig & Sylvester
Everyone else manages to put their cats out at night, but Porky's quartet of cats (ringleader Sylvester) succeed in putting *him* out into the snow instead, and start a debauched party for four. When he gets back in, they wreck the house in fleeing his wrath. (A great visual gag has Sylvester clinging to a mounted moose's head. Porky pulls at him so hard that he hauls the entire moose out of the wall.) In the end the cats drive out Porky by persuading him there has been a Martian invasion and themselves dressing up as Martians.

The Great Piggy Bank Robbery (1946)

⌐color ╱animated ⏱ 7¹/₂ minutes
Looney Tunes/Daffy Duck
Daffy raids a mailbox for a Dick Tracy comic book. Reading it, he becomes so excited he knocks himself out, dreaming that he is private detective Duck Twacy. There is an epidemic of piggy-bank thefts, and Twacy's is one of those to go. Catching a trolley car labeled "To Gangster Hideout," he finds the neon-signed hideout and confronts a gang of Dick Tracy-style mobsters — Snake Eyes, Pumpkin Head, etc. He shoots them up and discovers their cache of piggy banks. Kissing his own in joy, he wakes to find himself smooching a barnyard pig.

The Big Snooze (1946)

⌐color ╱animated ⏱ 7¹/₄ minutes
Looney Tunes/Bugs Bunny & Elmer Fudd
After a spectacular chase, Elmer announces that he's had it: "I get the worst of it from that wabbit in evewy one of these cartoons." But: "Of course, there's the little matter of my contract with Mr. Warner . . ." He tears the contract up, and vows that in the future he'll stick to fishing. Bugs begs him, futilely, not to break up the act: this could be the end of both their careers. Coming across Elmer snoozing, Bugs takes a sleeping pill and joins him in Dreamland, which he immediately desecrates with paint, transforming it into a psychedelic nightmare of experimental-style animation. After many hijinks and indignities, Elmer wakes from the nightmare deciding that even being Bugs's perpetual victim in the cartoons is better than what he's just been through, and the performance partnership is reforged.

were new characters he brought to the screen who had nothing to do with wartime: Beaky Buzzard, in *Bugs Bunny Gets the Boid* (1942), and — fanfare of trumpets here — the immortal Tweety, in *A Tale of Two Kitties* (1942). The voice of Tweety was based on a baby voice that Clampett often adopted while fooling around in the studio. In later shorts, Clampett had to add more feathers to Tweety since Schlesinger became agitated over audiences being upset by the bird's rampant nudity. Much has been made of how it really was the action of Freleng in teaming up Tweety with his own character Sylvester as a partnership that made the two characters into such major stars, but it is worth noting that the early Tweety shorts, *sans* Sylvester, are brilliantly effective in their own right; in other words, while Sylvester probably could never have become a star without Tweety, Tweety might very well have — and looked well set to — become a star as a solo act.

A breakthrough cartoon featuring characters from outside the Warners stable was *Horton Hatches the Egg* (1942), based on the Dr. Seuss story. Fellow Warners animation directors Chuck Jones and Friz Freleng would much later benefit considerably from this example in their production of various television specials done with Dr. Seuss (Theodore Geisel), to the extent that it's often forgotten that Clampett got there first.

In 1946, having created many of the classic shorts using all the major Warners characters, Clampett left the studio to go off on his own. Robert McKimson was promoted to take his place as the third in the triumvirate of animation directors, alongside Freleng and Jones. For some time earlier, Clampett had in fact maintained a studio of his own near the Warners lot, where he could moonlight — as did some of his colleagues — on other jobs. At the same time he was in discussion with Schlesinger, who in 1944 had sold the studio that bore his name to Warners so that they could manage it directly, about cooperation on new, non-Warners activities concerned with television. Clampett helped Ray Katz, Schlesinger's brother-in-law, try to get the animation studio at Columbia, Screen Gems, back on its feet, and initiated a few shorts there, though he did not stay long enough to see them through to fruition. Screen Gems in fact closed down soon afterwards, in 1949. For Republic, who had just acquired the TruColor process (a rival to Technicolor), Clampett did the short *It's a Grand Old Nag* (1947), starring a character named Charlie Horse. Unfortunately, though they liked the short, Republic found it impossible to market it, not possessing a cinema chain of its own and being unable to persuade the other studios to buy it for *their* cinema chains.

But by now Clampett was keeping an eye on the possibilities of the new medium of television. Since his school days, when he had put on puppet shows for the entertainment of his friends, he had maintained a fascination for puppetry, which can, in a way, be thought of as a far less time-consuming form of animation. His first foray into television was a puppet show, *Time for Beany*, which was first screened in February 1949 on the local Hollywood station Channel 5 and soon went national. A short daily program, *Time for Beany* starred a little boy wearing, appropriately enough, a propeller beanie, along with others that included the lovable rogue, Dishonest John – supposedly based on Schlesinger – and especially the lonely sea serpent, Cecil. The program picked up three Emmy Awards. In 1950 Clampett created, co-wrote, and was the puppeteer for *The Buffalo Billy Show*, which ran for a season on CBS. But it was in 1962 that his biggest breakthrough came, when the animated version of what was now called *Beany and Cecil* started as a segment of the Sunday evening program *Matty's Funday Funnies*, renamed *Matty's Funnies with Beany and Cecil* to acknowledge the new arrivals. The new series from Clampett proved overwhelmingly more popular than the old Paramount theatrical shorts that made up the bulk of the show, and within three months the show was renamed again, this time becoming just *Beany and Cecil* and moving to Saturday mornings. *Beany and Cecil* rapidly built up a huge cult following that still survives today, and ran until 1967 (with a very short-lived revival in 1988 done without Clampett, who had by then died). All told, it featured 78 original cartoons, with four adventures per show; all were produced by Clampett. In one fondly remembered adventure, the heroes – who sailed aboard the ship the *Leakin' Lena*, skippered by Captain Huffenpuff – met up with Davy Crickett in a parody of Disney's live-action *Davy Crockett* series. Davy's most enduring piece of advice was: "Remember the Alimony." Elsewhere, a much-loved gag concerned an island shaped like a bathing belle and lasciviously named No Bikini Atoll.

After *Beany and Cecil*, Clampett more or less retired, although he and his wife, Sody, maintained a studio in Hollywood making commercials for television, while also exploiting the old *Beany and Cecil* cartoons on world wide television. In the mid-1970s, however, the arrival of a new scholarship in studies of animation history revealed quite how huge his contribution had been during the Termite Terrace era at Schlesinger's studio – a

contribution whose scale becomes all the more impressive when one realizes that Clampett was there for only 15 years, unlike Freleng, Jones and McKimson, who each clocked about three decades. Accordingly, Clampett was thereafter widely fêted in live and tv appearances and in the press. He proved generous in giving interviews – perhaps over generous, for it was now that Jones's long-term dislike of him came ablaze, the sparking point being claims that Clampett was taking credit for achievements that in fact belonged to others. In fact, all the Warners directors have done this from time to time, and there has been nothing sinister involved: in distant memories of what was a group enterprise, it can be hard to recall precisely who did what, and of course one's own contribution tends to loom largest in the mind. The feud is best forgotten.

Leaving aside all the gags and hilarity, what shines through in any consideration of Clampett's animation oeuvre is *freedom*. He could probably, with his multiple talents, have attained eminence in just about any field of the fine or applied arts, but he was wise to choose animation in that it gave him a freedom of exploration that probably wouldn't have been possible in any other medium. And that sense of freedom is transferred to the audience, who experiences the mental stimulation and exuberant exhilaration of wild rides through the hinterland of Clampett's ever-fertile imagination. He once summed it up himself:

> An [animator] can take pencil and brush in one hand and on a piece of paper can create a setting, be it an ancient city or a strange planet, and then animate figures doing anything at all that comes to his imagination. No other medium allows the creator to control every detail on every frame so completely.

Robert Clampett died on May 2, 1984, in Detroit.

WALT DISNEY (1901–1966)

Animator's drawing of Goofy. Private collection.
© Disney Enterprises, Inc.

Walter Elias Disney was born in Chicago on December 5, 1901, the fourth son of Elias and Flora Disney. He went on to found a media empire – although the term was of course unknown at the time – that today still holds a dominant position in the world's entertainment industry. He is widely regarded as being many things that, in fact, he was not; most notably, he is popularly thought of as an animator, although in fact he never animated after 1924. He was nonetheless a towering figure in the history of animation, not just as a director and producer of animated movies and as an entrepreneur who pushed commercial animation into areas where no one else dared go, but also as a genius in the art of storytelling through the medium of animation. In that sense, although he was no animator, there can be no disputing that he was a master of animation.

Throughout this book, Walt Disney is generally referred to as Walt rather than Disney to avoid creating constant confusion between Disney the man and Disney the company.)

It can frequently be difficult, in writing about Walt, to separate fact from the vast body of myth and legend that has been created concerning him, both by himself – his attitude toward autobiography was much like that of one of his heroes, Mark Twain – and by the Disney publicists over the decades. Matters have not been helped by his biographers, whose accounts are almost universally unreliable, being partisan in one way or another: they tend to be either beatifications or hatchet jobs.

We know of his first drawing activities from when he was about five or six, by which time the family had moved to a farm in Marceline, Missouri. Walt and his younger sister Ruth got hold of some tar and, using sticks, drew with it on the family home's whitewashed wall. His father's response to this creative endeavor might have put the young Walt off drawing for life, but his Aunt Margaret encouraged his artistic leanings with gifts of crayons and sketchbooks.

A few years later, after his two eldest brothers had run away from home to escape their father's harshly disciplinarian rule, the family moved to Kansas City. Walt, outside school hours, served as unpaid delivery boy for the newspaper distribution company his father had bought. He also, from 1915, began to attend children's art classes at the Kansas City Art Institute. At some stage or another he made flipbooks – as most children do – but a more significant childhood influence that was to mold the later man was his friendship with schoolmate Walter Pfeiffer. The Pfeiffers, in strict contrast with the dour household headed by Elias Disney, were fans of light entertainment such as vaudeville, and before long the two boys were putting on a comic double act for amateur nights at the local theaters, school shows, and so on. These theatrical experiences were to stand Walt in good stead later on; there are countless comments by his staff that one of his great powers as a live storyteller was that he not so much told his stories as *performed* them, so that in effect an important part of the animation task had been done before the first pencil was sharpened.

By the time the family moved back to Chicago in 1917 – with Walt remaining a few months after the others because he waited in Kansas City until graduation – he was regularly cartooning. Once there he started a correspondence course in art, which his father paid for, although he also insisted that Walt work to help the family finances. When not at school, therefore, Walt was either working as a guard on the El or washing bottles at the Jell-O factory where his father worked; there was not a huge amount of time left over for drawing, but he fitted it in somehow, as he also attended night classes at the Art Institute of Chicago. His sights were set on being a cartoonist, especially since at the Institute he came across the work of the comic-strip artist Carey Orr, progenitor of the *Tiny Tribune* strip in the *Chicago Tribune*.

In 1918, Walt, with his mother's silent compliance, faked his date of birth in order to enlist in the American Ambulance Corps. He was shipped to France and spent a year there, playing his part in mopping up after the war and drawing posters and cartoons, both for his comrades and to submit for publication. By the time he got back to Kansas City – joining elder brother Roy, who lived there, rather than going back to the family home – he was utterly determined that his future lay in cartooning. There were no vacancies at the two Kansas City newspapers, but the Pesmen–Rubin Commercial Art Studio had space for him during the pre-Christmas rush, and he began work drawing ads and letterheads. The most important thing he did at this company, however, was meet one of the other new employees, Ubbe

Iwwerks (a name soon shortened to Ub Iwerks). They worked together on a number of projects, but were both made redundant once the seasonal rush died down.

They decided to set up in business together as Iwerks–Disney Commercial Artists, a venture that lasted only a few weeks – though they did get some business. Walt, left Iwerks to carry on running the business and applied for a regular job at the Kansas City Slide Company (shortly renamed the Kansas City Film Ad Company), a firm that produced primitive stop-motion animated commercials to be shown in movie theaters. Walt became interested in the prospect of better animation than this and began studying the subject; he also persuaded the firm's cameraman to give him instruction. In addition, he persuaded his bosses to hire Iwerks who, no salesman, had been running Iwerks–Disney Commercial Artists steadily into the ground.

Walt was really gripped by animation fever. He was allowed to borrow a camera from work, and, in the garage of the home of elder brother Herbert and his wife (where Walt and Roy were now living), he made a short animated movie picking on those responsible for the poor road maintenance in Kansas City. He showed this to Milton Feld, manager of the local cinema chain, the Newman Theater Company, and Feld commissioned further movies in the series, each seizing on a group of topical local issues. These Newman Laugh-O-grams – as distinct from the succeeding *non-Newman* Laugh-O-grams – were done as newsreels, with Walt apparently drawing at lightning speed a series of topical cartoons. They proved popular, and Walt set his sights on greater things. In order to do so, he knew he would have to quit his job at the Kansas City Film Ad Company. He had to delay his departure for a while, until the Disney family sorted out various adversities that suddenly hit it: Herbert's job was transferred to Portland, Oregon; Elias was thrown out of work by the closure of the Jell-O factory and took his wife and daughter back to Kansas City, but, failing to find work there, he went to live with Herbert in Portland; Roy contracted tuberculosis and had to be moved to a hospital in Santa Fe, New Mexico. In April or May 1922, however, Walt gave up his job and incorporated a new company, Laugh-O-gram Films. In due course he was able to persuade Iwerks to quit the Kansas City Film Ad Company as well, and other young animators he hired included some who would become very famous names in animation's story, including Rudolf Ising and Hugh Harman.

They began to produce a series of animated 7½-minute shorts, eventually totalling six in all, based on revamping traditional tales: *Little Red Riding Hood*, *The Four Musicians of Bremen*, *Jack and the Beanstalk*, *Goldie Locks and the Three Bears*, *Puss in Boots*, and *Cinderella*. For bread and butter and also to experiment in styles – even trying clay stop-motion animation on occasion – they made a series of short shorts called the Lafflets. They had difficulty, however, in finding a distributor for these, and the eventual distribution deal they obtained – with Pictorial Clubs of Tennessee – was so disastrously one-sided that it marked the demise of the fledgling studio, which was even reduced to starting a sideline in

The Four Musicians of Bremen (1922)

🎵 b/w / animated silent ⏱ 7¼ minutes
Laugh-O-grams

One of the series of six Laugh-O-grams released in this year, the first animated movies made by Disney Studios aside from the brief, one-gag Lafflets released in 1920. All six were modernized versions of classic fairy/folk tales. In this one, the central character of the four musicians is a little black cat; the other three are a dog, a chicken, and a donkey. Blamed for all the ills of the town, the four are chased out. They rest by a pool, and the cat suggests they could charm a fish out of the water by their playing. The fish that emerges grabs the cat and drags him underwater. A swordfish chases him around and then, with the other three, up a tree, which the swordfish proceeds to saw down. Falling down the chimney of a house filed with crooks, the musicians drive out the crooks, who then bombard the house with cannon. The cat hitches a ride on a cannonball but falls off; all nine of his lives depart him, but he's able to grab the last of them in the nick of time so the four musicians can live happily ever after. A lot of incident in a very short space.

Alice's Wonderland (made 1923 but not released)

🎵 b/w / live-action/animated silent ⏱ 12 minutes
Alice Comedy

The pilot for the series of 56 live-action/animated shorts, the Alice Comedies, released between 1924 and 1927. Alice, played by Virginia Davis, visits the Disney studio and sees some animated creatures perform on the drawing board; in live action we see Hugh Harman, Rudolf Ising, Ub Iwerks and Walt himself, among other staff. That night she dreams she goes to Cartoonland, where she takes part in a parade with various animated animals and then dances with them; later she is chased by some lions that have escaped from the zoo.

Trolley Troubles (1927)

🎵 b/w / animated silent ⏱ 7 minutes
Oswald the Lucky Rabbit

The first to be released of the 26 Oswald the Lucky Rabbit shorts Disney made; the pilot, *Poor Papa* (1927), was canned. Here Oswald drives a trolley car which can perform shapeshifting tricks — swelling, shrinking, and stretching as the occasion arises.

child portrait photography in a desperate attempt to make ends meet. A temporary reprieve came in late 1922 with a commission from local dentist Thomas B. McCrum to make a live-action educational film, *Tommy Tucker's Tooth*, in which good Tommy looks after his teeth like a proper little gentleman while bad Jimmie Jones lets his teeth go all to hell, the slob, and pays dearly for it; a few brief animated sections showed the ghastly things decay was doing to

Jimmie's teeth. (Much later, after Walt had moved to Hollywood, he made a sequel for McCrum: *Clara Cleans her Teeth* [1926].) Another reprieve came in the spring of 1923, when a local businessman invested in the company against expected incomes, while Roy sent Walt occasional checks; but it was obvious the writing was on the wall, and the staff left for other jobs. In a desperate effort to drum up money, Walt planned with Carl Stalling, organist at the local Isis Theater, a set of live-action shorts to accompany popular songs. One of these Song-O-Reels, *Martha*, was made, but it was too late to save Laugh-O-grams. (In the longer run, of course, Stalling's association with young, broke Walt Disney proved to be an excellent career move: he became composer/arranger of choice for many of the early animators and later the big studios, while he was largely responsible for the genesis of Disney's Silly Symphonies series of shorts.)

In July 1923, Walt headed for Hollywood with $40, a change of clothes, and the pilot, called *Alice's Wonderland*, for a new series of animated/live-action shorts. In California he first stayed with his uncle Robert, who lived in Los Angeles; Roy was in the hospital nearby, another good reason for Walt to make the move, and on occasion helped out Walt with the $5 weekly rent he had to pay his uncle. There were, at the time, no animation studios in Hollywood, however; the animation industry was then based in New York. Walt approached various studios in the hope of being offered work as a live-action director, without success. He therefore decided to repeat his Kansas City tactics, and set up his Uncle Robert's garage as a primitive animation studio.

The only real asset he had was *Alice's Wonderland*. Before the final collapse of Laugh-O-gram Films (from whose creditors he had had some difficulty keeping the reel of film) he had sent a few potential distributors advance information about the proposed series. Now he reapproached one of these, the New York distributor Margaret Winkler. Her response was extremely enthusiastic; not only that, but she was, unlike Pictorial Clubs with the Laugh-O-grams, prepared to pay Walt sensibly, with the full advance to be given to him on delivery of each movie. Walt borrowed $200 from Roy and $500 from Uncle Robert and set himself up in business once more. His biggest expense was the employment of Virginia Davis, the girl who had played Alice in the pilot. Winkler liked Davis in the part so much that the deal was contingent upon it, so Walt had to lure Virginia and her family to California with a $100-a-month contract for the girl.

Walt did all the animation himself for the first of the Alice Comedies, *Alice's Day at Sea* (1924). Winkler was pleased with it and, true to her word, paid up quickly. At the turn of the year 1923–24, Walt knew that his fledgling studio was a going concern.

Winkler was a stickler for quality, however, and demanded that Walt give his best. This meant that the Alice Comedies proved not nearly as profitable as might have been expected; at the same time, this probably was responsible for the obsessive perfectionism that remained a part of Walt's makeup almost consistently for the rest of his life, an attribute that pretty directly led to his phenomenal success later on. He was also man enough to recognize that he himself was not an animator of sufficiently high caliber to continue the series. Casting about for someone he could employ for that part of the enterprise, he thought of his old pal Ub Iwerks. Iwerks had now been a part of two failed Walt Disney enterprises, and it took some blandishment to persuade him to move to California from his steady job at (again) the Kansas City Film Ad Company. In due course, however, Iwerks agreed, and from *Alice Gets in Dutch* (1924) onward, his more skillful hand is evident. Walt never animated again.

There then occurred one of those unpredictable tragedies that at first sight looked like a pleasing enough turn of events. Winkler had been associated professionally with the distributor Charles Mintz; now she married him, and he took over much of her business. Where Winkler had paid quickly and in full, Mintz began to delay payments and then to issue only partial payments. When Walt understandably raised hell, Mintz claimed financial hard times as an excuse. But nevertheless, as crooks do, Mintz insisted Walt keep up both schedules and standards, as if financial hard times were not something that might affect Walt as well. Even so, after the dust had settled, Mintz issued a contract for a further 18 Alice Comedies with an increased advance, and, on the strength of this seeming security, Walt hired more animators (including his old Kansas City employees Harman and Ising), both Walt and Roy married, and the brothers put down a deposit on a lot on Burbank's Hyperion Avenue, where they planned to build a new studio.

It hardly needs saying that Mintz soon began delaying payments again, and economizing in other ways, no matter what his contract might have said. Luckily, this time around, the Disney Bros. Studio was in a generally better financial shape, and indeed was able to move into the new building on Hyperion Avenue. Still, the wrangles continued with Mintz, who was now also complaining – perhaps with justification – that the series was becoming a little lackluster. Walt was casting around for new clients when, again through the good offices of Margaret Winkler (now, of course, Margaret Mintz), a promising deal came his way. Carl Laemmle of Universal approached Mintz looking for a new cartoon series featuring a rabbit, and Winkler proposed Disney Bros. Studio. Producing cartoons for Universal seemed like a good idea to Walt, and so he (or Iwerks, in conjunction with him) roughed up some sketches for a character; it was Mintz who named the character Oswald the Lucky Rabbit. Walt and his crew swiftly produced a pilot, *Poor Papa* (not released until 1928), with an Oswald who was old, fat, lecherous, and disreputable – the sort of rabbit you wouldn't like to meet in a back alley – and Mintz's staff rejected it; their other criticisms were that the humor was labored, the animation poor, and the story shoddily constructed. Perhaps surprisingly, Walt was given another chance, and this time he struck gold with *Trolley Troubles* (1927).

The new, trimmer and leaner Oswald bore a certain resemblance to an already popular character whose movies Winkler was distributing (in conjunction with Pathé), Pat

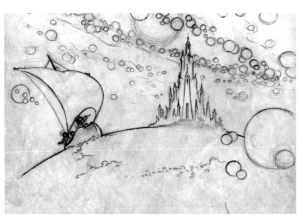

Animator's drawing for a sequence of *Snow White and the Seven Dwarfs* (1937) that was later cut. © Disney Enterprises, Inc.

Steamboat Willie (1928)

🎵 b/w / animated ⏱ 7 minutes

Generally credited as the first animated movie to have sound (in fact, there had been earlier forays by others – including Paul Terry's *Dinner Time*, released just beforehand), this launched Disney's career and that of his co-creation, Mickey Mouse; the third Mickey Mouse short to be made, it was the first to be released. The plot is minimal. Mickey is helmsman of a paddle-steamer skippered by a tyrannical Peg Leg Pete: with Minnie as an adoring onlooker, Mickey cavorts around, having fun and performing various acts of indignity and torment upon other animals.

Flowers and Trees (1932)

🎵 color / animated ⏱ 8 minutes
Silly Symphonies

The first color cartoon ever made, and the winner of Disney's first Academy Award. A male sapling and a glamorous sycamore fall in love. However, a lecherous old oak tries to poach the sycamore for himself, and the two males fight it out. The oak sets the forest on fire, but all are saved through the courage of the sapling.

Three Little Pigs (1933)

🎵 color / animated ⏱ 8 minutes
Silly Symphonies

Probably the most famous animated short of all time, this won an Academy Award, gave the world the song "Who's Afraid of the Big Bad Wolf?" and put the hitherto ailing Technicolor on the map. Fiddler Pig, Fifer Pig, and Practical Pig (all three named only in later years) each build houses, only Practical Pig's being sensibly built of brick. The Big Bad Wolf blows the first two down, but is thwarted by the third; then Practical Pig outwits him to save the two feckless pigs.

Snow White and the Seven Dwarfs (1937)

color / animated ◷ 83 minutes

A wicked (and vain) Queen asks her Magic Mirror who is the fairest of them all, and to her fury it tells her it's not her: there's a prettier gal in the land, Snow White. Swiftly locating the culprit, the Queen orders a Huntsman to kill her; he, however, sets her free in the forest. Fleeing, she comes to the Dwarfs' cottage. The Magic Mirror reveals to the Queen that Snow White still lives; the next morning, transformed into a hideous old hag, the Queen successfully tempts Snow White with a poisoned apple. The Dwarfs chase the villainess to her death, but the poisoned Snow White also seems dead. As they prepare to bury her, however, a handsome Prince she met earlier in the forest arrives to deliver True Love's First Kiss and thereby resuscitate her. (Based on the version told in *Kinder- und Hausmärchen* (1812–15) by Jakob and Wilhelm Grimm.)

Pinocchio (1940)

color / animated ◷ 88 minutes

An episodic tale. Geppetto makes clocks, toys, and automata. He christens his new and most realistic marionette Pinocchio, and prays the puppet might become a "real boy." This prayer is heard by the Wishing Star, which sends the Blue Fairy to give the marionette life – although, if he is to be a real boy, he must discover the principles of bravery, truth, and unselfishness. The Blue Fairy enlists Jiminy Cricket as Pinocchio's Conscience. Trickster fox J. Worthington Foulfellow (aka Honest John) and inept cat sidekick Gideon sell Pinocchio to evil puppeteer Stromboli, who imprisons his new found star. The Blue Fairy releases Pinocchio, but not until after the famous sequence in which his lies cause his nose to elongate ridiculously. Next Foulfellow sells Pinocchio to the Coachman, who takes him and hundreds of other boys to Pleasure Island, where boys are turned into donkeys. Jiminy saves Pinocchio, but not before the marionette has become part donkey. Discovering that Geppetto and his pets have been swallowed by the giant whale Monstro, the friends join them inside Monstro and light a fire to make the whale sneeze. A tremendous chase leaves the rest safe but Pinocchio apparently drowned. However, the Blue Fairy revives the marionette – and this time as a real boy. (Based on *The Adventures of Pinocchio* (1882) by Carlo Collodi.)

Sullivan's/Otto Messmer's Felix the Cat. However, the resemblance the modern viewer notices most immediately is to the early Mickey Mouse, whose birth still lay a little time away: change the ears and tail, and the Rabbit becomes the Mouse. Several of Oswald's adventures, too, were to be rehashed as Mickey shorts. Moreover, the villain created for Oswald to be pitted against, Peg Leg Pete, continued on into the Mickey shorts, although in due course his peg leg was politically corrected out of existence.

But that all still lay in the future. For the moment, with advances increased from those for the Alice Comedies, Disney was contracted to produce a new Oswald cartoon every fortnight, an arrangement that in the end lasted exactly a year. Before that year was up, Ub Iwerks reported to Walt – who thought Iwerks was just being paranoid – that George Winkler, Mintz's brother-in-law and Hollywood agent, seemed to be becoming as thick as thieves with some of Walt's top animators. All made sense a little while later when Walt and his wife, Lillian, took a trip to New York to negotiate with Mintz the contract for a new series of Oswald cartoons. Mintz first offered Walt a much lower per-movie advance, and, when that was refused, announced blithely that, under the existing contract, all rights in Oswald belonged to Universal, not Walt, and that Mintz was going to hire all Walt's main staff out from under him to continue producing Oswald shorts *sans* Walt. Walt phoned Roy in California, and Roy confirmed this was exactly what George Winkler had been setting up; of the top animators, only Ub Iwerks had remained steadfast. (In fact, Mintz's plans went awry. After he had set up his new studio to continue the Oswald shorts, and indeed after he had animated the first six of the new series, Carl Laemmle's Universal – whose ownership of the character was the pretext Mintz had used to deprive Walt of, as he thought, his livelihood – stepped in and awarded the continuation of the series instead to Walter Lantz, who was employed directly. This move put Mintz out of business.)

One of the most muddled episodes in animation's history now follows. The official Disney version until quite recently was that, on the train back to California, Walt and Lillian between them dreamed up a new cartoon character, to be called Mickey Mouse – Walt initially called him Mortimer, but Lillian insisted he should have a popular, down-to-earth name rather than a snobby one. The revisionist-history version, which is better supported by extant documentation, is that in a crisis meeting with Roy and Iwerks on Walt's return from New York, the three of them thrashed out the idea of a mouse star, and that Iwerks then did the artistic rendition. The Occam's Razor version is that one of the three, probably Iwerks, said something like, "Look, for Chrissake, all you've gotta do is take the ears off, *so*, and give him a long tail, *so*, and he's a *mouse*, not a rabbit – see? – so those [expletives deleted] can't sue us." The official Disney version these days accepts that Iwerks created the *form* of Mickey, but maintains that Walt created his *personality*. This is only slightly disingenuous: Mickey's character was initially indistinguishable from the silent Oswald's, but, as Walt explored the potential opened up by the advent of sound cartoons, Mickey did indeed develop a personality of his own, in a large part based on Walt himself, both his natural self and the performances he put on to demonstrate/tell each new story or story element.

Whatever the minutiae of Mickey's genesis, there was a practical difficulty for Walt and Iwerks as they worked up their ideas on the new character: the animators who were deserting to join Mintz still had three months' notice to work out, and Walt couldn't afford to just let them go as he still had to complete three Oswald shorts under his contract with Mintz; neither did he wish them to take all the information about the new series star with them to their new boss – even the hitherto astonishingly trusting Walt realized that could be a very bad idea. Everything therefore had to be done in secret. As for a plot? Well, Charles Lindbergh had made the first non-stop solo flight the previous year, an achievement that had engendered the Oswald the Lucky Rabbit short *The Ocean Hop* (1927) and which surely had more mileage left in it. Thus was born the first Mickey Mouse movie, *Plane Crazy* (1928), animated entirely by Iwerks, a barnyard fable in which Mickey reads about "Lindy" and is inspired to build, with the help of assorted farmyard animals, his own airplane, in which he flies around the sky with his willing-yet-unwilling girlfriend Minnie. Iwerks is reputed to have done over 600 drawings a day at the office; inking and painting were done at Walt's home by Lillian, her sister Hazel, and Roy's wife Edna; Walt would then bring the cels into the office to be photographed by a cameraman who had declined the Mintz shilling. The short – which was, remember, silent – was previewed in the middle of May 1928.

The same subterfuges were not required for the second Mickey short, *Gallopin' Gaucho* (1928), because by this time the Mintz animators had left. Moreover, Iwerks could call for help on the services of those who remained. (Mintz had poached all the senior animators except Iwerks, regarding the rest as beneath his notice. Two of those who remained, Les Clark and Wilfred Jackson, became among the most senior and respected figures in Disney animation history.) Once *Gallopin' Gaucho* was done, the search was on for a distributor.

And here Walt ran into a wall: the distributors weren't interested. They agreed that *Plane Crazy* and *Gallopin' Gaucho* were fine cartoons, but there was nothing particularly individual about them. Although Walt was convinced he was onto a winner with his mouse hero, to anyone else Mickey was just another funny animal. Out of discussions between Walt, Roy, and Iwerks as to what could be done to make Mickey different from other cartoon heroes of the time emerged an idea that birthed an empire: sound. There had been some experiments with sound movies already, but Hollywood was dragging its feet, with many senior figures convinced that the talkies were just a gimmick. There had even been · some experiments with *animated* sound movies, but nothing very serious. Give Mickey sound as his distinguishing characteristic, the three men reasoned, and audiences would come flocking – and, more immediately, distributors likewise.

It wasn't just a matter of adding sound to *Plane Crazy* or *Gallopin' Gaucho*, because both had been made as silent cartoons and would require drastic alteration if they were to use sound properly. Much better, even though the studio could barely afford it, was to make a third Mickey cartoon especially for the purpose: *Steamboat Willie* (1928), which drew its thematic inspiration from – and obviously hoped to piggyback on the popularity of – the recent Buster Keaton hit (silent) movie, *Steamboat Bill, Jr.* (1928). Carl Stalling was roped in to compose a musical soundtrack based on two songs Walt had chosen, "Steamboat Bill" and "Turkey in the

Straw." A more difficult matter was synchronizing the sound effects and the music with the animation; essentially the Disney principals and staffers worked this one out from scratch, with a key element being Wilfred Jackson's suggestion that they use a metronome.

Then there was the matter of finding a suitable sound system. RCA had a good one, but it was too expensive for the struggling studio to contemplate. However, Walt met up with the charismatic crook Pat Powers, who had on offer the Cinephone, a sound system that was much cheaper than RCA's and every bit as good – unsurprising, since it was essentially a pirated version of the RCA one. Powers actually offered Walt a very good deal for the use of his system, agreeing with Walt that sound cartoons were the wave of the future and wanting to be in on the ground floor; he also offered to hawk the series around the distributors for him. Walt must have begun to suspect that Powers was not entirely above-board when various peculiar complications arose thereafter. The worst was an expensive and disastrous recording session that had to be paid for despite having to be instantly canned. Not only the studio but also its individual principals were very nearly bankrupted by the time a good recording was obtained, with Walt himself voicing the characters on top of the musical score. ("Voicing" is a slightly euphemistic term here: the vocal parts are really just squeaks and yelps.)

But still the distributors did not bite, and the financial crisis was growing worse daily – not least because Walt had instructed Iwerks to get started on the fourth Mickey short, *The Barn Dance* (1928). In the end Walt had to go out looking for individual movie-theater proprietors, and here he got lucky: the independent promoter for the Colony Theater near New York's Broadway, Harry Reichenbach, was another who realized that sound cartoons were going to be phenomenally popular, and he not only agreed to give *Steamboat Willie* its first run but also offered good money for the privilege – $500 per week for a minimum two-week run. Accordingly, *Steamboat Willie* was given a Broadway premiere – on November 18, 1928. It proved hugely more popular than the main attraction, thereby emphatically confirming the faith held by all at the Disney studio and by Reichenbach himself.

Now, of course, the distributors suddenly became a lot more interested; however, all of them wanted to buy the character as well as the movies, and this Walt refused to contemplate – he had lost Oswald to one unscrupulous distributor; no way was he going to run the risk of the same happening to Mickey. Luckily it was in Powers's interests to promote Mickey, because in so doing he would be promoting his Cinephone system. He therefore offered to give Walt advances on the future Mickey shorts and, for a very reasonable percentage, to handle distribution matters, in return for a ten-year license, at a not so reasonable sum, for use of the Cinephone. It was an offer with catches, but Walt grabbed it – in hindsight, wisely, although Roy was horrified at the time.

The relationship with Powers did not last long. In January 1930 Walt and Roy confronted him with the claim that he had defrauded them out of a whopping $150,000 in royalties, and a few weeks

Fantasia (1940)

♪color / animated (with just a moment of live action)
⏱ 120 minutes

The first of Disney's anthology features. Johann Sebastian Bach's *Toccata & Fugue in D Minor* accompanies an almost abstract piece of animation suggesting an orchestral performance. Fairies of various kinds, mushrooms, flowers, goldfish, thistles, orchids, and milkweed dance balletically to selections from Peter Ilich Tchaikovsky's *Nutcracker Suite*. Mickey Mouse has the title role in an enactment of the story behind Paul Dukas's *The Sorcerer's Apprentice*. Igor Stravinsky's *The Rite of Spring* is the musical backdrop for a fantasia on evolution up to the end of the Age of Dinosaurs. An arcadian fantasia, with characters from classical mythology, accompanies Ludwig van Beethoven's *Pastoral Symphony*. Animals perform oafish ballet to Amilcare Ponchielli's *Dance of the Hours*. Modeste Moussorgsky's *Night on Bald Mountain* inspires a diabolical nightmare (reminiscent of parts of Hector Berlioz's program notes to his *Symphonie Fantastique*), with the vast figure of Chernabog in command of proceedings. The movie concludes with a parade of the devout to the strains of Franz Schubert's *Ave Maria*.

The Reluctant Dragon (1941)

♪color and b/w / live-action/animated ⏱ 72 minutes

A minor anthology feature whose live-action component follows Robert Benchley on a tour around the Disney lot. Into this are embedded a couple of animated fragments (featuring Casey Jr. and Donald Duck, respectively) and three shorts: *Baby Weems* tells of an infant prodigy who solves many of the world's problems before a juvenile illness robs him of his intellectual powers; *How to Ride a Horse* is the first of the *How to* series starring Goofy; and *The Reluctant Dragon* (based on the 1898 story of that name by Kenneth Grahame), more a feature-in-miniature than a short, tells how a dragon who is reluctant to terrorize and a knight who is reluctant to slay come to an accommodation.

later they paid him $100,000 (because Powers admitted to $50,000 of the filched royalties) to get back the rights to the cartoons and to cancel the contract for use of the Cinephone. But the fact that such huge — for the time — sums were involved indicates how much money was so swiftly surrounding the Mouse, a situation that could not have arisen without that initial deal with Powers. A new deal was struck, thanks to Frank Capra, with Columbia Pictures whereby, from February 1930, Columbia paid Disney an advance of $7000 per cartoon, nearly three times what Powers had been paying. This deal in turn lasted only a couple of years, with Walt going to United Artists in 1932 for a doubling of Columbia's advance.

Walt was wise enough to realize that mere novelty value would not be enough to sustain Mickey for long: within a couple of months other, bigger studios were coming out with their own sound cartoons. Disney animations would have to be *better* than those of their competitors. He thus began hiring additional animators — not a difficult task, because the impact of that Broadway premiere had been considerable, so there was a sense in the air that Disney was the place to be — and also looking around for ways to diversify. Carl Stalling, by now officially installed as the studio's Musical Director, suggested a second series of cartoons, these to tell a story through the combination of music and animation … and also be cheaper to produce, since there would be no need for such niceties as accurate lip synch (another novel idea). It was a bold proposition: a series without a central series character as a peg upon which to hang popular acceptance. But Walt was understandably in a bold mood, and so the Silly Symphonies came into being, the first of them, *The Skeleton Dance* (1929), animated entirely by Iwerks, proving a popular hit.

But all was not as well as it seemed at the studio. Ub Iwerks had had occasional contretemps with Walt over the years, not least because of Walt's lifelong habit of wandering around the studio after hours snooping through his animators' work and on occasion making changes. Iwerks's accumulating annoyance had come to a head over *The Skeleton Dance*. As noted, he had felt it necessary to animate this entirely himself, subscribing to Walt's own theory that quality was ultimately important because only through quality would profits in due course be maximized, even if in the shorter term the profits were all but wiped out. In this instance, however, Walt was fully aware that Iwerks was his most expensive animator and that there were younger and cheaper animators on the lot who could have been helping out, leaving Iwerks to do only the key drawings. The two men had fought over this; though Iwerks had won the fight, it was just one piece of creative interference too many for the animator, and in January 1930 he signed up with Powers to start his own studio independent of Walt. Moreover, Carl Stalling, believing — wrongly — that Iwerks was Disney's essential sparking genius, went too, firstly to Paul Terry's studio for a brief and unsatisfactory period and then to work with a number of studios, notably Iwerks's.

Sometime before 1933, Walt and his team — possibly Walt himself in conjunction with storyman Webb Smith, as Walt would later claim, but more likely just as a gradual evolution in the studio — made one of the most significant introductions in the history of animation: the storyboard. Before this, the stories for the vast majority of cartoons were more or less made up by the animators as they went along, although a few (not at Disney) were more formally scripted. Neither method was entirely satisfactory — and certainly, had the former remained the standard practice, there'd have been no possibility for animated features to be made — and so the storyboard swiftly became a vital animation tool. (It was not a new invention, as is often claimed. Back at the turn of the century, Georges Méliès had storyboarded parts of his movies, while live-action director William Cameron Menzies was storyboarding in the 1920s. Alfred Hitchcock was another live-action director to make early use of the storyboard, possibly beating Walt to it.)

Dumbo (1941)

Lobby card for *Dumbo* (1941) showing Dumbo with Timothy Mouse. Private Collection. © Disney Enterprises, Inc.

🎨 color / animated ⏱ 74 minutes

The stork delivers a child to Mrs. Jumbo aboard the circus train, but the newborn, Dumbo, is soon mocked by all the other elephants for his enormous ears. When Mrs. Jumbo retaliates against a tormenting youth, she is caged as a rogue elephant. Only a mouse, Timothy, befriends young Dumbo. Forced to take a painful and humiliating pratfall in a highly successful routine put on by the clowns, Dumbo and Timothy get drunk, and, in a classic piece of animation, Dumbo has hallucinations of pink elephants. On waking, the two friends discover themselves in the treetops: Dumbo unknowingly had flown there, using his ears as wings. Doubtful at first, Dumbo repeats the feat; the next day he takes flight in the circus ring, and soon his fame spreads all across the land. Based on *Dumbo, the Flying Elephant* (not published until 1978) by Helen Aberson and Harold Pearl.)

Bambi (1942)

🎨 color / animated ⏱ 69½ minutes

A baby deer named Bambi, a baby rabbit named Thumper, and a baby skunk named Flower learn as they mature of the beauties and harshnesses of the Cycle of Life — including the stringencies of the first winter, the amorousness of the first spring and, with fall, the cruelty of man, the intruder, as Bambi's mother meets her death in one of animation's most celebrated sequences. But such tragedies can all be survived, and the miracle of life is celebrated the following spring as each of the three pals becomes a parent. (Based on the book *Bambi* (1929) by Felix Salten.)

Song of the South (1946)

🔊 color ⁄ live-action/animated ⏲ 94 minutes

A tale of growing up in the American South is interspersed with animated exemplary fables told by the live-action character Uncle Remus (played by James Baskett) and drawn from Joel Chandler Harris's *Uncle Remus* (1880) and *Nights with Uncle Remus* (1883).

So Dear To My Heart (1949)

🔊 color ⁄ live-action/animated ⏲ 82 minutes

A live-action tale of rural childhood interspersed with a few brief exemplary tales done in animation. Wise Old Owl relates for their inspirational value the stories of David and Goliath, Joshua and the walls of Jericho, and, because of their "stick-to-it-ivity," Christopher Columbus and Robert the Bruce. (Based on the book *Midnight and Jeremiah* (1943) by Sterling North.)

The Adventures of Ichabod and Mr. Toad (1949)

🔊 color ⁄ animated ⏲ 68 minutes

Anthology comprising animated renditions of two classic tales. The *Mr. Toad* section is a reasonably close adaptation of Kenneth Grahame's *The Wind in the Willows* (1908); the second section, *The Legend of Sleepy Hollow*, is based slightly more freely on the Washington Irving story of that name in *The Sketchbook of Geoffrey Crayon* (1819–20). Basil Rathbone narrates the first, Bing Crosby the second.

Cinderella (1950)

🔊 color ⁄ animated ⏲ 74 minutes

The king, worried that his son, Prince Charming, is showing no interest in the ladies of the court, throws a ball to which is invited every eligible maiden in the land. The ugly sisters do their best to make it impossible for Cinderella to attend, but, helped by her animal friends and in particular by the Fairy Godmother, she manages it – with transformed mice as horses, the dog as a footman, the horse as a coachman, and a pumpkin as a coach. Cinderella and Prince Charming dance and fall in love; but she, knowing the spell will wear off at midnight, flees just before then, leaving behind a glass slipper. The King, watching his son pine, sends out his Grand Duke to search the land for the woman whose foot will fit the slipper. Cinderella's stepmother, Lady Tremaine, locks Cinderella away; however, the girl's mice friends Gus and Jaq free her, and Cinders in due course weds the Prince. (Based on the version in *Histoires ou contes du temps passé* (1697) by Charles Perrault.)

A storyboard is a collection of drawings and sketches, looking almost like a comic strip, that traces the course of the movie from beginning to end. These sketches might be seen as the key moments in the animation, giving the clue to what will be the significant action in the finished movie. The great advantage of the storyboard is that sections of it can be pulled out to be repositioned, reworked, or discarded entirely, while new sections can easily be inserted. As many or as few people as desired can make individual or group contributions to the storyboard until finally a schema for the final movie is settled upon. From the storyboard is derived a document that looks very much like a script but is more accurately termed a cutting continuity, in that it in effect reports the storyboard rather than defines it. Most animators regard this teaming of minds as a considerable benefit of the system, although one can see how this judgment by committee could also work to the movie's detriment. This indeed happened resoundingly at Disney during the later 1930s: the fabulous abstract conceptuals done by the experimental animator Oskar Fischinger – very briefly a Disney employee – for the *Toccata and Fugue* section of *Fantasia* (1940) were made more "accessible" (i.e., less interesting) and "blandified" by teams of Disney staffers, including Walt himself, who were frightened of taking the leap into purely abstract animation. Nevertheless, in the vast majority of cases the storyboard is an overwhelmingly constructive tool, and today it is hard to imagine animation being done without it or some (generally computer) equivalent.

Through the medium of the storyboard Walt was best able to capitalize on his own primary genius: as a storyman. What increasingly distinguished the Disney productions from those of the other studios was their strength of story, with depth of characterization an obvious and equally important corollary.

Another important development was color. Again, other animation studios had made primitive experiments with this – there was as yet no technique that allowed for live-action movies to be in color except via frame-by-frame tinting, which was ludicrously expensive and produced a lousy looking result. The stalwarts of Hollywood, just as with the advent of sound, were dubious as to whether color would ever be more than a ten-day wonder. Walt was the first animator to realize its enormous appeal and to push wholeheartedly for it. The young company Technicolor had what looked to him to be the best process, and he signed an exclusive contract in 1932 whereby his was the only animation studio to be allowed to use the process for the next two years. He chose the Silly Symphony *Flowers and Trees*, already in production in black and white, as his pilot project; soon the team was involved in inventing new types of paint that would neither chip nor peel off the acetate cels nor fade under the bright lights necessary for photography, as existing paints all too readily did. Sid Grauman, owner of Grauman's Chinese Theater in Hollywood, booked the short on the strength of an informal advance partial screening, and *Flowers and Trees* premiered there on July 30, 1932, to an enthusiastic reception.

Future Silly Symphonies were all in color, and their quality as movies steadily and rapidly improved so that they rivaled in popularity the studio's "traditional" output of shorts featuring Mickey and his pals. (The most important of those pals, Donald Duck, debuted in the Silly Symphony *The Wise Little Hen*, released on June 9, 1934.) The first Mickey Mouse short in color did not come along until February 23, 1935.

By then, though, Walt had conceived a new dream: the full-length animated feature movie. As late as November 1933 Ted Sears was writing from the Disney studio to fellow animator I. Klein that "having just completed *The Pied Piper* [Silly Symphony released 1933], we have come to the conclusion that our best screen values are in small cute animal characters, we haven't advanced far enough to handle humans properly and make them perform well enough to compete with real actors." Someone forgot to tell Walt this, because a year later he was plunging the studio into his latest venture, *Snow White and the Seven Dwarfs* (1937), with its two central characters being human beings and the remainder almost all at least humanoid.

There were a couple of logical reasons why Disney should be looking to make a feature. One was to be the first to do so, thereby gaining an obvious advantage over rival studios. The other was that the costs of making each new short were rising rapidly and the revenues to be derived from them much more slowly: at some point soon the two figures were going to meet in the middle, by which time the studio should have some alternative game plan. No one, not even Walt, has ever known quite how or why or even when he came to decide on the Grimms' tale "Snow White and the Seven Dwarfs" as a subject, but by late 1934 he was ready to talk his animators through his idea for the new project. The meeting he held for this rapidly became a performance by him of the full story as it could be animated, with him acting out and voicing all the parts; by all accounts this performance was mesmerizing, and it was to prove the basis for much of the movie's eventual animation.

Outside the studio, once news leaked of what soon became known in the industry as "Disney's Folly," the reaction from Hollywood was largely negative: nobody, maintained those same old stalwarts who'd thought sound and then color were mere gimmicks, would be prepared to sit through an hour and a half of uninterrupted animation. Animation was only for kids (heard that before?), and everybody knew kids couldn't sit still for more than a few minutes at a time. Adults might have the requisite attention span, but adults wouldn't want to go and see an animated movie. Within the studio there were negative reactions as well, notably from Roy and Lillian, who were understandably terrified of the budget Walt proposed: half a million dollars (in the end it was nearly one and a half million). But there was to be no stopping Walt. And there was to be no stopping his perfectionism, either: because of the constant revisions he dictated, *Snow White* cost about $200 a foot to make at a time when the shorts were costing at most about $75 a foot.

Alice in Wonderland (1951)

🎨 color / animated ⏱ 75 minutes

Alice pursues the White Rabbit down the rabbit hole to become enmeshed in a series of weird incidents. She encounters the Door Knob, whose advice to drink from a "Drink Me" bottle to become small eventually leads her to become a giantess. Thereafter, while all the time in general following the White Rabbit, she meets the Dodo, witnesses the endless Caucus Race, meets Tweedledum and Tweedledee (who tell her of the Walrus and the Carpenter), grows huge in the White Rabbit's house, is victimized by talking flowers, meets the Caterpillar, grows huger than ever, is accused by a nesting bird of being a serpent, reduces to normal size, meets the Cheshire Cat, attends the Mad Hatter's Tea Party, enters the nightmare world of Tulgey Woods, escapes thence into the palace gardens of the King and Queen of Hearts, plays croquet, is put on trial by the Queen of Hearts, berates the Queen for her tyranny and then, suddenly back to normal size, flees through her earlier nightmare adventures in reverse to emerge back in the garden where she started. (Based on *Alice's Adventures in Wonderland* (1865) by Lewis Carroll.)

Peter Pan (1953)

🎨 color / animated ⏱ 77 minutes

Wendy, Michael, and John Darling are left alone by their parents for the evening, their dog/nanny, Nana, having been kenneled outside by Mr. Darling as a punishment to Wendy for her "nonsense" about the flying boy Peter Pan. That night Peter visits the nursery again to recover his shadow, left on a previous visit, and the three children fly off with him and his fairy companion Tinker Bell to the island of Never Land to join the Lost Boys. There, pirate Captain Hook seeks vengeance on Peter for having long ago amputated his hand in a fight and fed it to a crocodile. With the help of the island's Indians, the Lost Boys defeat the pirates and in particular Peter defeats Hook. Adventures done, the children travel back home aboard Hook's ship, given the power of flight by a sprinkling of pixie dust from Tinker Bell. (Based on the play *Peter Pan* (first performed in 1904), the story "Peter Pan in Kensington Gardens" (1906), and various subsequent book versions, all by J.M. Barrie.)

What Walt realized was that the huge effort and expenditure were an investment not just in a single movie but in the whole of the studio's future career, because he and his team were in effect working out from scratch the art and science of making animated features in general. Those Hollywood diehards were right in one respect: no one could be expected to sit through an animated *"short"* that lasted 90 minutes, so an animated feature would have to be a beast of a somewhat different nature. Just as in a novel compared with a short story, there would have to be far more attention paid to such aspects as characterization and story complexity — in brief, the movie would need far greater psychological depth. This was more than just a matter of art: it was also one of technique.

At the premiere of *Snow White and the Seven Dwarfs* – held at the Carthay Circle Theater on December 21, 1937 – it was emphatically obvious that "Disney's Folly" was set to be a rampant and highly profitable success. A crowd of some thirty thousand gathered just to be outside the theater during the performance. The glitterati inside were applauding not just individual bits of animation and dialogue but even the layouts and backgrounds. Frank S. Nugent in the *New York Times* perhaps best summed up the reactions of the critics (although there were a few ultra-diehards who still stuck to their negativistic guns despite the evidence of their brains) when he wrote: "If you miss *Snow White and the Seven Dwarfs*, you'll be missing the ten best pictures of 1938." Later, famously, the Oscar Walt was awarded for the movie consisted not just of a single statuette but of one full-sized one and seven little ones, all mounted on the same stand.

As soon as the profitability of *Snow White* was assured, production went into full swing on Disney's second animated feature, *Pinocchio* (1940). Many would maintain that this is the best animated movie ever made; while this is obviously an indefensible statement (what is meant by "best"?), it could certainly be claimed, in terms of its animation alone, to be, as an ensemble, the finest piece of sustained traditional animation ever produced. It was also, on first release, a thumping loss-maker for the studio: in part this was because of the movie's very high cost (Walt had, with *Snow White*, proved his point that attention to quality was worth it, no matter the expense, and with *Pinocchio* he applied the principle again, this time in spades), but mainly it was because, with the advent of World War II, Disney's overseas markets virtually disappeared.

In technical terms the movie is of special note because of its extensive use of an adapted version of the multiplane camera, which Ub Iwerks, by now back with Disney (as a technical and effects wizard rather than an animator), had developed. Essentially the multiplane camera creates an enhanced illusion of depth through the use of multiple backgrounds (planes), each at a different distance from the lens, all except the rearmost plane having holes through which the camera's eye can probe; thus, if the main focus were to be on, say, an intermediate plane, the nearer and more distant planes would be slightly out of focus, just as our eyes see things naturally in the world around us. As the focus changes we seem to be moving through and into the scene; the illusion is astonishingly convincing, as best exemplified in *Pinocchio's* opening sequence. But use of the multiplane camera is expensive: rather than producing a single background for a sequence the artists must create many – in that opening sequence there were no fewer than twelve.

In the wake of *Snow White and the Seven Dwarfs*, Walt had resisted pressures to spin off series of shorts from the movie featuring its more popular characters, particularly Dopey – although the Dwarfs did later appear in a couple of shorts exhorting people to buy war bonds and in a commercial. But after *Pinocchio* he was less adamant, probably because he saw the

necessity of trying to quickly recoup some of the movie's losses. The kitten Figaro had a brief career in the shorts, in one instance alongside the goldfish Cleo, a clone of whom, renamed Bianca, also appeared in a few Mickey Mouse shorts as Mickey's pet goldfish; and Jiminy Cricket, after reappearing in 1947's compilation feature *Fun and Fancy Free* as a sort of master of ceremonies, went on to become an extremely successful television character.

Walt's next feature movie marked another departure. Shorts – even the most lavish of shorts – were far cheaper per foot to produce than feature movies, yet a feature movie was likely to bring in far greater revenues than an equivalent running time of shorts. What better way of earning some money quickly and relatively safely than to produce a feature movie that was essentially just an assemblage of shorts? This is not perhaps the most glamorous depiction of the genesis of *Fantasia* (1940), but certainly these considerations were a large part of it. The other origin of the movie was a chance meeting between Walt and the distinguished conductor Leopold Stokowski, probably in late 1937. Stokowski said, in the way one does, that at some point he'd like to collaborate with Disney on something. Walt replied that at the moment the studio was working on a Mickey Mouse short based on Dukas's *The Sorcerer's Apprentice*. Stokowski offered his services as conductor, and later offered the idea of a feature comprising a set of shorts, each done to a different extract from classical music. From then on Stokowski's involvement in the project, as both arranger and conductor, was enormous. Deems Taylor was hired as linkman, being a suitably prestigious narrator to keep the musical purists happy yet at the same time having a good vocal presence to assure more general audiences that what they were watching, while it was culture, need not in fact be actively painful. (At the insistence of distributor RKO, who felt that the movie's running time was "way too long" at a full two hours, most of Deems Taylor's contribution was in fact cut out for the movie's first, 81-minute general release.)

The critical reception was much more mixed than for Disney's two previous features. Some reviewers rejoiced in the movie's wit, intelligence, and brilliant animation; others regarded it as a butchery of the classics and criticized the animation for schmaltz. Both camps were right – in part. Stokowski's adaptations were not especially gentle, and in particular that of Stravinsky's *The Rite of Spring* was pretty objectionable (and, boy, did Stravinsky himself object!); but listened to as a movie soundtrack, which is the way they ought to be listened to, they are fine in general, and the performances – by the Philadelphia Orchestra under Stokowski's baton – are superb. The animation *does* show some ghastly lapses in taste; it takes a strong stomach to endure the dreadful tweeness of the section based on Beethoven's Pastoral Symphony, for example. But the movie has countless good points as well, and much of the animation is genuinely stunning, as in the *Toccata and Fugue*, *Rite of Spring*, *Night on Bald Mountain* and *Ave Maria* segments, while the original (longish) short from which the whole enterprise had sprung, *The Sorcerer's Apprentice*, is not only a brilliant example of quite how good an animated short can be – it's hard to think of how it could be bettered – but also has an iconographic power that has rendered the depiction of Mickey in his wizardly attire one of the most immediately recognizable in the world and one that conveys meaning far beyond the mere image.

The real problem that Disney had with the movie had nothing to do with the critics, however. Walt's obsessive perfectionism had turned a potentially inexpensive project into a monumentally expensive one – it cost nearly as much as *Pinocchio* – and the expenses mounted yet further because, in order to screen the movie properly, theaters required a sophisticated sound system ("Fantasound") in which few were prepared to invest without financial inducement. Moreover, the public didn't fancy the idea of exposure to all this culture stuff, Deems Taylor or no Deems Taylor; while it wasn't quite a matter of their staying away in droves, certainly the box-office figures were far below the minimum that could have made sense. For once Walt's idealistic ambition, his grand dreams, seemed to have teetered over the edge into a form of megalomania, an impression enhanced by reports of his comment on viewing the rushes of the *Pastoral* section: "Gee, this'll make Beethoven." A re-release in 1946 brought inadequate revenues to shift the movie into the black, and really it wasn't until the Flower Power culture of the 1960s, with its focus on marijuana and LSD, embraced *Fantasia* as "the ultimate trip" that the profits finally started rolling in; Disney, being a family-oriented studio eager to disassociate itself from anything concerning illicit substances, was embarrassed all the way to the bank.

A genuinely cheap feature movie was required, and this came in the form of *The Reluctant Dragon* (1941). It's a somewhat half-hearted compilation feature that takes the form of a documentary about Disney animation, fronted by Robert Benchley, illustrated with animated fragments plus two very different but good animated shorts, *Baby Weems* and *How to Ride a Horse*, the latter featuring Goofy, and an adequate longer (12 minute) short, *The Reluctant Dragon*, which is presented as the movie's climax. It is not a satisfying movie – even less so in later releases, which omit *How to Ride a Horse* – and is deservedly rarely seen today. The audiences of the time agreed, and the box office results were poor; however, the movie had been cheap to make, so it did manage to make a profit.

By the time *The Reluctant Dragon* reached the cinemas, Walt had problems much closer to home. The expansion of the studio with the onset of feature production had led to unrest, and Walt was temperamentally incapable of understanding his staff's resentments. Although he was financially generous with his employees when the studio enjoyed prosperity and even when it didn't, he was unable to realize that what really troubled his staff was an increasing feeling of alienation from their creations – job descriptions had been introduced to replace the old happy-go-lucky system whereby everybody could do a bit of everything – and from their boss, Walt, who seemed to be turning into just another movie mogul. The situation was ripe for unionization of the animators (other divisions of the studio had already been unionized

without difficulty), a matter which was handled clumsily by Walt and appallingly by Herbert K. Sorrell of the Screen Cartoonists Guild, who adopted confrontational tactics that couldn't have been better designed to alienate Walt's. An impassioned plea by Walt to his staff, explaining the reasons for many of the petty and not so petty grievances the animators felt, staved off crisis for a while; but then he foolishly fired animator Art Babbitt as a troublemaker. Since Babbitt was unionizing for selfless reasons – he had become an active member of the Guild because he felt the junior staff was grossly underpaid – Walt had picked precisely the wrong victim to use as an example to the others. Sorrell called a strike and, although only about half the employees heeded the call – including some of the most senior animators – the disruption was intense, the bitterness severe, and the damage exceptional to the public image of a studio that liked to portray itself as just one big happy family. Walt, who genuinely believed that was what the studio had been before those nasty serpents had disrupted Paradise, acted like a betrayed lover, becoming vindictive – he did his best to persecute the strikers through the FBI and the California Un-American Activities Committee – also developing a streak of paranoia that would remain with him the rest of his life. He lost the ability to trust those around him fully, and the formerly generous Disney contracts began iniquitously to encroach on all sorts of areas of the employees' private activities in a way that defies belief.

In the meantime, there were movies to be finished; *Dumbo* (1941) and *Bambi* (1942) were in the full swing of production. The accelerator was pressed on the former – the studio desperately needed a profitable release. Because of the strike, fewer animators could be deployed on it; also because of the strike and the financial situation, Walt realized that the studio could not afford the constant revisions and tinkering that had slowed his earlier full-length features and bulged their budgets. The result is a short movie which, stripped to the bare bones of its brilliance, depends on sheer storytelling and artistry rather than lushness; where it can be claimed that *Pinocchio* represents an acme in the art of animation, equally *Dumbo* can be seen as the *purest* example of an animated feature that Disney has ever produced and of what an animated feature *can be*. The animators did take the opportunity to score a few points against their striking colleagues; some of the clowns who talk about "hitting the boss for a raise" bear a suspicious caricatured resemblance to some of the principal strikers. Be that as it may, *Dumbo* was a smash hit and has remained so ever since its release: it is probably the most loved of all the Disney animated features.

In the midst of the strike, Walt was approached by John Hay Whitney, director of the Motion Picture Division of the Co-Ordinator of Inter-American Affairs, an organization dedicated to countering fascism in South America through promoting good relations with the North. Whitney suggested that a goodwill tour to South America by Walt would advance the cause, and the two men agreed that Walt should take a crew of animators with him with a view to making a series of movies about the different countries of the South. Probably motivated by a desire simply to get

Lady and the Tramp (1955)

🎨 color / animated ⏱ 76 minutes

Young spaniel Lady's owners are expecting a baby, and street mongrel Tramp explains to her that it's the habit of humans, when a baby arrives, to get rid of their dogs. This proves not to be the case: the baby arrives and Lady is still a loved member of the family. However, shortly after, framed for a domestic crime, she is muzzled. She flees across town and falls in with Tramp. The two dogs raid a chicken coop and, caught, Lady is impounded; she is returned home but in disgrace. A rat assaults the baby; Tramp, who was passing, kills the rat, but Aunt Sarah assumes the two dogs have been attacking the infant. This time Tramp goes to the pound and Lady is locked in the cellar. Her owners return and soon understand the truth of the matter. Lady's doggy pals save Tramp from being put down by the dog-catcher in the nick of time, and Tramp is adopted into Lady's family.

Sleeping Beauty (1959)

🎨 color / animated ⏱ 75 minutes

King Stefan and his queen hold a party for the christening of their daughter Aurora; to it come the three good fairies, Flora, Fauna, and Merryweather, plus the bad fairy Maleficent, furious she wasn't invited. Maleficent puts a curse on Aurora: on the sunset of her 16th birthday she will prick her finger on a spindle and die. Merryweather is able to ameliorate but not nullify the curse — rather than dying, Aurora will fall asleep until woken by True Love's kiss — so instead the three try to keep her secure until after the fateful day. The three good fairies raise Aurora in secret (as Briar Rose) in the forest. On her 16th birthday Aurora encounters Prince Phillip and they fall in love. Aurora goes with the three fairies to the birthday party being thrown for her at the palace, but is magically lured by Maleficent to a tower where she pricks her finger. The good fairies put the whole castle under the same spell as Aurora and arm Phillip with the Shield of Virtue and the Sword of Truth. Maleficent casts a forest of thorns around the palace but Phillip fights through it, killing Maleficent with the Sword of Truth when she attacks him in the guise of a dragon. Her death cancels out her evil; Phillip wakes Aurora with True Love's kiss and all ends connubially. (Based on the version in *Histoires ou contes du temps passé* (1697) by Charles Perrault.)

away from the mess at the studio, Walt leapt into the project with full enthusiasm — an enthusiasm further kindled by financial guarantees from the U.S. Government. A party including Walt toured Brazil, Argentina, Chile, and Bolivia in the late summer of 1941. The fruits of their endeavors were the compilation movies *Saludos Amigos* (1943) and *The Three Caballeros* (1945).

In their absence the strike was settled; Walt grumbled that this had been done by simply agreeing to everything the Screen Cartoonists Guild demanded. Part of the deal was that the strikers,

including Walt's *bête noir*, Babbitt, be reinstated, although most of them soon left for better and happier jobs elsewhere. Walt never understood that he thereby lost some of his best and brightest, one of the foremost among them being the detested Babbitt.

Also awaiting the party on their return was the task of finishing *Bambi*. The genesis of this movie had been as early as 1935, when Walt had read Felix Salten's novel and decided that he wanted to make an animated feature of it. Discovering that the movie rights had already been bought by director Sidney A. Franklin, he did a deal with Franklin, who eventually became part of the project and is glowingly acknowledged in the opening credits. Where *Dumbo* had triumphed through its spareness, *Bambi* took exactly the opposite approach: the movie is as noteworthy for its visual richness as for its affecting story and its often highly accurate depictions of nature. This latter aspect caused some hostile critical comment: the realism offended some people's preconceived opinions as to what animated movies *were supposed to be* (fluffy little fantasies for the kiddies, as if Michelangelo should have stuck to cupids because that was what paintings were *for*). Others were upset because they thought that the portrayed animal world, in which the weak go to the wall, was in some way meant to be a prescription for human behavior. The public didn't pay too much attention to the critics: *Bambi* was a success, although less so than *Dumbo* (and, having been hugely more expensive to make, correspondingly far less profitable). Kids and their parents wept at the death of Bambi's mother and otherwise thoroughly enjoyed what is one of cinema's great weepies. *Bambi*, too, is today regarded as one of animation's masterpieces.

But then things started to go downhill. *Saludos Amigos* and *The Three Caballeros* were cheap and easy to make, and they turned in respectable profits. Pausing only to make the partially animated wartime propaganda movie *Victory Through Air Power* (1943), which recommended in essence that the only way to deal with Hitler was to bomb Germany to pieces, Walt took the lesson of the two South American movies to heart and produced a string of compilation features about which the best that can be said is that some of the shorts they contain are very juicy currants in an otherwise undercurranted pudding.

Naturally, he presented these to the public as, for example, attempts to do for popular music what *Fantasia* had done for the classics, but it was blazingly obvious that in reality they were rather cynical attempts to cash in on the well-earned Disney reputation. *Make Mine Music* (1946) has the shorts *Peter and the Wolf* and *The Whale Who Wanted to Sing at the Met* to its credit, but most of the rest is dross. *Fun and Fancy Free* (1947) tacks together two featurettes, of which the second, *Mickey and the Beanstalk*, holds some interest. *Melody Time* (1948) has *Little Toot* as well as the underrated foray into experimental animation *Bumble Boogie*. And *The Adventures of Ichabod and Mr. Toad* (1949) is another two-parter, although this time both the featurettes are strong: the first is a fast-moving rendition of Kenneth Grahame's *The Wind in the Willows* (1908), a book that had long been on Walt's hit list for a full-length feature of its own; and the second is a dramatization of Washington Irving's story "The Legend of Sleepy Hollow" (c 1819).

Walt's interests had by now drifted away from animation. Live-action movies were cheaper per foot to make and consequently more profitable, and in his early days he had rather fancied himself as a live-action director. Paradoxically, therefore, the two most interesting features he made during these years, from an animation point of view, were actually live-action movies that incorporated some animation. Ub Iwerks was the key figure in enabling Walt to mix the two genres on screen; and Iwerks must have been quietly smug when, on the release of *Song of the South* (1946), the critics generally hailed the relatively short animated sequences while dismissing the live-action elements as being merely standard stuff.

Set in the Reconstruction South, the movie is very much a product of its times in its romanticized view of an era when everyone was happy because the blacks knew their place; this attitude is indeed pretty jarring to the modern viewer, white or black, and must have been so to many at the time, even though the movie's view was actually pretty progressive for its era. Some of the worst of the movie's sentimentalisms have been cut from later releases, which may or may not be a good thing. The live-action story is simplicity itself. Little Johnny (Bobby Driscoll) is sent to live on his grandmother's good ol' plantation. Unhappy with the situation there, he runs away and encounters ex-slave Uncle Remus (James Baskett), who uses three of Joel Chandler Harris's Brer Rabbit tales as parables in persuading the boy that he must go back to his grandmother's home and face things. The animated sequences are much more interesting, starring Brer Rabbit and his foes and being based on the tales about the Briar Patch, the Tar Baby, and the Laughing Place; in a final piece of animation, Brer Rabbit appears amid the live-action to join Uncle Remus, Johnny, and a couple of their friends in a last song. Not surprisingly, the animated sequences are often shown separately as independent shorts. The list of directing animators on the movie reads like a roll call of Disney greats: Milt Kahl, Eric Larson, Ollie Johnston, Les Clark, Marc Davis, and John Lounsbery.

So Dear to My Heart (1949) is a lesser movie in a similar vein, and the animated sequences are shorter and scrappier. Once again, animation is used as a way of conveying moral lessons to a youthful hero played by Bobby Driscoll. An animated Wise Old Owl retells the (animated) tales of David and Goliath, Robert the Bruce and the Spider, Joshua and the walls of Jericho, etc. These little sections in a predominantly live-action movie probably represent Walt's nervousness about the public's reaction to his studio producing a feature movie without any animation at all; he was to conquer that nervousness in 1950 with *Treasure Island*.

Also in 1950 came a long overdue return by Disney to the business of making full-length animated features. It was almost as if Walt were consciously reprising the start of the studio's career in feature movies, for *Cinderella* (1950) was, like *Snow White and the Seven Dwarfs*, based on a classic fairy tale. It was a movie Walt had

Mary Poppins (1964)

color / live-action/animated ⊙ 134 minutes

London, 1910. The Banks children, Jane and Michael, are so naughty that no nanny will tolerate them. When their father advertises for yet another replacement, they devise a "better" advertisement; he throws this on the fire and the scraps of paper fly heavenward to reach the magical Mary Poppins. Once installed, she magically transforms even the dullest chores into games. The main animation comes when they meet her friend Bert, a sidewalk artist and chimneysweep, and leap into a picture he has chalked on the sidewalk; all four romp among animated creatures until rain both ends the idyll and washes the picture from the sidewalk. A second, much shorter, piece of animation occurs in accompaniment to the song "Feed the Birds (Tuppence a Bag)." (Based on the series of books by P.L. Travers that began with *Mary Poppins* (1934).)

The Jungle Book (1967)

color / animated ⊙ 78 minutes

An infant, Mowgli, is abandoned in the jungle. The old panther Bagheera has the child adopted by a wolf family. A few years go by, but then the tiger Shere Khan, who obsessively hates humans, returns to the region; the wolves decide Mowgli will be safe from him only if escorted to a man-village, a chore Bagheera volunteers to undertake. En route they have adventures, making friends with the herd of elephants led by Colonel Hathi, with a bumblingly ne'er-do-well bear called Baloo, and with the apes of the quasi-kingdom ruled by the orang-utan King Louie, but also having to resist the hypnotic attentions of the boa constrictor Kaa and then beat off assaults by Kaa and Shere Khan. Finally they reach the village, and for the first time Mowgli sees a human female; from that moment he is lost to his jungle friends. (Based loosely on tales from *The Jungle Book* (1894) by Rudyard Kipling.)

been wanting to make for decades – perhaps ever since that early Laugh-O-gram version of the story back in 1922 – and had been working on, here and there, since before *Snow White* was made. In this movie it's as if he had learned all the lessons there were to be learned from the best of his previous animated features: *Snow White* had shown him the continuing power of classic fairy tales as plots for animated movies; *Pinocchio* and *Bambi* had taught him the value of using background art that was beautiful in its own right; *Dumbo* had demonstrated that there was no need to maintain that level of detail and attention throughout, because if the story and the animation were good enough the movie actually benefited from having the art stripped down to its essentials where this was sensible; and *Fantasia* . . . well, *Fantasia* had taught him not to make another *Fantasia*.

There is also an element of demythologizing in the movie. For example, although there are many direct parallels between the witch in *Snow White* and the villainess here, Lady Tremaine,

One Hundred and One Dalmatians (1961)

♪ color / animated ⏱ 79 minutes

Songwriter Roger Radcliff marries Anita, and his Dalmatian, Pongo, marries her Dalmatian, Perdita; soon Pongo and Perdita have fifteen puppies. Anita's old schoolmate Cruella De Vil is collecting Dalmatian puppies to make coats out of their fur and, when Roger and Anita refuse to sell the litter, hires a pair of bumbling crooks to steal them. Pongo and Perdita go off in search of their brood. They release not just their own puppies but a total of 99 and, after a hazardous chase, return home with them to Roger and Anita, who decide to adopt all of them. (Based on the book *The Hundred and One Dalmatians* (1956) by Dodie Smith.)

The Sword in the Stone (1963)

♪ color / animated ⏱ 79 minutes

Young Wart is out hunting with his bullying older foster brother, Kay, when he stumbles across the wizard Merlin and his owl, Archimedes. Merlin sets out to educate the callow youth, putting him through a series of lessons involving their both being transformed into animals; the last of these culminates in a spectacular shape-shifting magical battle between Merlin and the witch Madam Mim. Returned home, Wart is deputed to act as squire to his foster brother at the tourney in London whose victor — as denoted by his ability to pull a magic sword from its lodging in an anvil — will be proclaimed king of England. Wart leaves Kay's sword behind in their tent at a crucial moment and, in desperation and knowing nothing of the significance of the sword in the anvil, yanks it out to give to his foster-brother as a substitute weapon. And so Wart is crowned as King Arthur. (Based loosely on the three volumes of *The Once and Future King* by T.H. White, primarily *The Sword in the Stone* (1938) but with elements from *The Witch in the Wood* (1939) and *The Ill-Made Knight* (1940).)

who is a witch in all but name and sorcerous abilities (and even has a familiar in the shape of the cat Lucifer), the latter seems to be an individual not out of fantasy but all too credibly from real life. Similarly, the Fairy Godmother here is a bumbling, plump character instead of the wholly magical and thereby transcendently incomprehensible Blue Fairy of *Pinocchio*. This demythologizing works very well in *Cinderella*, where it actually adds to the magic; but carried to a further extreme it was utterly to destroy the magic of some of the later animated features Walt produced – *The Sword in the Stone* (1963) and *The Jungle Book* (1967) in particular are travesties of their originals.

The same has often been said of Disney's next animated feature, *Alice in Wonderland* (1951), although here Walt's critics are being in part a little unfair: the primary reason why it is a bad movie – and it is – lies in the fact that it is probably impossible to successfully bring Lewis Carroll's great fantasy to the screen. Others who have tried it have generally failed even more miserably; perhaps the only three versions that have achieved even partial success have been Lou Bunin's live-action/stop-motion movie, *Alice au pays des merveilles* (*Alice in Wonderland*; 1951) – a movie that the Disney studio, fearful of competition, criminally attempted to expunge from the pages of cinematic history, very nearly succeeding – Jan Švankmajer's live-action/animated/puppet version, *Neco z Alenky* (*Alice*; 1988), and Jonathan Miller's live-action movie for BBC Television, *Alice in Wonderland* (1966). What all three versions do is take the original on its own terms and attempt to convey its dreamy, sometimes nightmarish, logical illogicality and surrealism – in short, they try to make the movie that Lewis Carroll himself might have made. What Walt did, seemingly incapable of understanding either Carroll's humor or the fact that it was totally unlike and immiscible with his own, was splash his own brand of zaniness slap in the face of the original. The effect was disastrous: everything that makes Carroll's original such a joy was annihilated by the onslaught of wackiness and pizazz. It is significant that probably the most successful character in the movie – to take it on *its* own terms – is the Door Knob, which is the new character Walt introduced himself.

Disney in general had trouble adapting classic British tales to the screen. Much later, in 1966, Walt released *Winnie the Pooh and the Honey Tree* as the first in a series of shorts based on the A.A. Milne stories. These were met with great acclaim in the United States, but were extensively reviled in Britain as complete travesties, with all the subtle amiability of Milne's original humor shredded in an orgy of wackiness; it is entirely depressing that, on both sides of the Atlantic, most kids today regard the Disney desecration as the definitive version of Pooh, having never encountered the superbly written originals. (To be fair, Disney did at least make a good attempt at adapting its visual style to the originals' highly sympathetic E.H. Shepard illustrations.) Here, too, Walt was moved to add a new character to the tales: the Gopher. This intruder does at least confess his trespass by announcing, "I'm not in the book, you know!" at frequent intervals, but that doesn't make the trespass any less of a crime. Walt was clearly sensitive on the subject, because the studio created a piece of mythology to make the inclusion of the Gopher seem somehow more justifiable. To quote from my *Encyclopedia of Walt Disney's Animated Characters*:

> In 1966 the Hartford (Connecticut) *Times* produced an interesting article in this respect: the reporter claimed that Milne's niece Angela had said that Milne himself had originally planned to put a gopher in the books, because he and Christopher Robin had seen one near their home, but that his publisher had insisted that the character be removed. By an astonishing coincidence, Walt had unknowingly insisted that a gopher be put into the story because he felt it needed one. This is a very good tale, but it suffers from the embarrassing disadvantage that gophers do not exist in the United Kingdom...

Walt had much greater success, with qualifications, in his next stab, after *Alice in Wonderland*, at adapting a British classic tale: *Peter Pan* (1953). Although the process of Disneyfication failed to capture the affect of J.M. Barrie's various book versions of the tale, Barrie himself was more satisfied with his own stage adaptation, which bears many of the characteristics of a pantomime. Wittingly or otherwise – probably wittingly – it was the spirit of the stage adaptation that Walt managed to capture on screen. The movie is tremendous entertainment – a great pantomime, really – although it is marred in one small respect by the tendency noted earlier to demythologize. Part of the magic of the stage Tinker Bell is that the audience never sees her as more than a rapidly moving dot of light, and the strength of the story can be gathered from the way that grown-ups and children alike can be induced, toward the end, to clap their hands fervently, often with tears in their eyes, to bring back to life what everyone *knows* is just some jerk at the back with a flashlight – it's a perfection of the art of suspension of disbelief. Walt, by contrast, decided to show us Tinker Bell as a distinct little human being (years later, in his live-action homage to both versions, *Hook* [1991], Steven Spielberg went so far as to cast Julia Roberts in the role). In fact, Walt's was quite a successful bit of character creation, and Tinker Bell has been used ever since as a symbol of the "Magic of Disney"; but the gambit lost something from the story that perhaps Walt didn't know was there in the first place.

Two developments marked Disney's next animated feature, *Lady and the Tramp* (1955). First, it was made in CinemaScope; second, it was based on an original story rather than on an existing novel or other printed source. The use of CinemaScope, with its wider screen, had an unexpected beneficial effect on the animation, essentially increasing the range of what the animators could do. The main point is that they were given a much bigger background to work against. The first consequence of this was that, as Ward Kimball put it, it was the animated characters who moved around rather than the backgrounds; that is, there was more space for a character to move in without, as it were, running off the edge of the background. A more important consequence, perhaps, was that there was room for a greater number of characters to interact meaningfully with each other in any particular frame; and this also meant that there was less of a necessity to cut backward and forward from one character to another during, say, dialogue. There were – and still are – some who felt this was a bad thing, in that it made *Lady and the Tramp* more like a live-action movie. The general consensus aside from this is that *Lady and the Tramp* is an extremely satisfying movie, with a good story, good characters, and even good songs. It is also unusual for a Disney animated feature in that it largely eschews extended episodes of wham-bam slapstick humor. It's interesting that Walt had the confidence to release a movie which, like *Bambi* long before, did not need to lean on out-and-out laughter to ensure its popular appeal.

Walt was devoting increasing amounts of time to the Disney tv shows and to Disneyland, the theme park he had opened in 1955 and which went on to confound the prophets of doom by

Animator's drawing of Minnie Mouse. Private Collection.
© Disney Enterprises, Inc.

racking up profits. Indeed, without Disneyland it's possible Disney would have gone under around this time. Matters weren't helped by the poor reception given to *Sleeping Beauty* (1959), the new animated feature. The main complaints of the critics seemed to fall into two camps: (a) *Sleeping Beauty* is just *Snow White* rehashed, and (b) *Sleeping Beauty* isn't like *Snow White*. Apologists for Walt have written that the trouble with the movie was his lack of involvement; those same apologists fall abruptly silent in the face of modern reassessments, many of which claim that, quite to the contrary, it's likely the finest fairy tale feature that Disney has produced. Without a doubt it's the most beautiful: the exquisitely detailed backgrounds by Eyvind Earle alone are worth the price of admission, and the often slightly stylized animation and drawing work perfectly with the movie's unusual, rather pastellish color values. In addition, there's Disney's most astonishing villainess in the shape of Maleficent – shapes, rather, because toward the end of the movie she shape-shifts into the most spectacular dragon, the better to fight Prince Phillip. That fight scene, as he battles his way through the briars around the castle and against the fire-breathing Maleficent, is one of the finest action sequences in all of cinema. Nevertheless, as noted, the movie was poorly received, and it lost money heavily on first release.

The response of the Disney studio to an expensive flop had always been, where possible, to follow up with something much more cheaply produced in the hope of raking back some of the losses in a hurry. This had not always been a constructive habit, yet at the same time it is true that at least one of Disney's cheap-and-cheerful numbers, *Dumbo*, had proved a classic. The same can be said of the follow-up to *Sleeping Beauty*, 1961's *One Hundred and One Dalmatians*. One reason for the movie's relative cheapness was a technical development — yet another brainchild of Ub Iwerks — that would probably have come along anyway, even though Walt personally did not much care for the results. One of the most time-consuming — and therefore expensive — parts of the animation process had always been the business of tracing the animators' pencil drawings in ink onto the animation cels. In the old days of black-and-white this hadn't been too bad, because there was only the one color to think about, but nowadays the inkers might be asked to use ten or fifteen different ink colors on a single cel. What Iwerks had done was devise an adaptation of the Xerox process whereby — to simplify a bit — the drawings could be photocopied directly onto the cel. The only drawback was that the process involved the animated shapes and details having a firm black line; this not only created an artificiality about the depictions but also meant that all the finer points and subtleties were lost.

In *One Hundred and One Dalmatians* the animators did what all the best artists do: turn a failing into a strength. In particular, for the movie's human characters they didn't strive for what would have been an unattainable realism but instead opted for a caricature-like style which was still perfectly acceptable as a representation of reality; you have to look closely at a still of Roger, Anita, or (with one or two quite consciously drawn exceptions) Cruella to realize that the depiction is in effect symbolic rather than naturalistic. Coupled with a fast-moving story that was packed with humor and good characterization, this simpler style of animation, as with *Dumbo*, worked very well. *One Hundred and One Dalmatians* was unsurprisingly a popular hit, remaining a perennial favorite.

What, then, persuaded Walt to go on to make 1963's *The Sword in the Stone*? What persuaded him, having made it, to release it? The kindest of its critics say that it is forgettable; everyone else only wishes this were the case. The big trouble is that T.H. White's *The Once and Future King* was the wrong Arthurian book on which to base a Disney animated feature. The movie's nadir is probably the moment when Merlin, clad in Bermuda shorts, arrives back in the Dark Ages still water skiing from a holiday in the 20th century. The most irritating running crassness is that the Dark Ages are throughout described as "medieval."

Fortunately, Walt had a surer touch when he stayed in his own territory. One night back in the early 1950s he had been tucking his daughter Diane into bed when he picked up the book lying by her bedside, one of the Mary Poppins adventures by P.L. Travers. Was it any good? he asked. Yes, she replied, it was very, very, very good, and could Daddy make a cartoon of it, please? Walt obediently asked about the movie rights but was told there were several other

Hollywood studios already after them; the only reason they remained unsold was that Travers was "difficult." Travers must have felt a bit more confident about Walt than about the others, however, because in 1960 she gave her permission for the movie rights to be sold to him — although even then she insisted that the movie be live-action, not animated, and that she be permitted to vet the script. In the end there was a slight compromise in that the movie *Mary Poppins* (1964) is indeed live-action, but contains an extended live-action/animated sequence. By today's standards the interaction of the live-action and the animated characters seems a little primitive, but at the time it was a state-of-the-art marvel — thanks to Ub Iwerks. In fact, Iwerks did not receive the Oscar awarded to the movie for special visual effects (one of five Oscars it won, having been nominated for thirteen in all) — which went to Peter Ellenshaw, Eustace Lycett, and Hamilton Luske — but was instead that year given a share of an award in the Scientific or Technical Class for "the conception and perfection of techniques for Color Traveling Matte Composite Cinematography."

The movie was an absolute blockbuster, of course. The animation tends to be somewhat forgotten, however, being overshadowed by the indubitable fact that it was a triumph for Julie Andrews in her first movie role. But it was a triumph also for Iwerks and the rest, and perhaps especially for Walt, who had kept faith in the project when others had said that the Mary Poppins books were old hat and that he was heading for a spectacular disaster.

It was a good note on which Walt could exit. He would supervise one more animated movie, *The Jungle Book* (1967), but would not live to see it released. The record-breaking *Mary Poppins* can be regarded as the last of his animated features, even though the bulk of its screen time is devoted to live action. A little over two years after its release, a cancerous spot was detected in Walt's left lung. When the lung was removed a few days later, it was discovered to be full of tumors. On the last day of November 1966 he collapsed at home and was rushed to the hospital. On December 15 he died of acute circulatory collapse brought on by the lung cancer.

He had turned commercial animation from a gimmick with 7-minute shorts featuring funny animals into a medium capable of producing full-length movies of both economic and artistic significance. The animated feature movie, confidently dismissed as "Disney's Folly" 65 years ago, is now a small but extremely important part of the movie industry, with major animated releases regularly topping the box-office charts. He had done much else as well — he had built an enormous entertainment multinational, he had done extensive work in television, produced a string of successful live-action movies, and he had more or less invented the theme park and seen Disneyland, Disney World and the Epcot Center become financial successes. He had developed movie merchandising to an undreamt-of extent, he had won 48 Oscars, seven Emmys and about *nine hundred* other awards and citations around the world — but it will be for his contributions to animation that this non-animator will always be best remembered.

GEORGE DUNNING (1920–1979)

Sericel for *Yellow Submarine* (1968). Private Collection.
© Subafilms Ltd.

Born in Toronto, George Dunning made his popular name in the U.K., primarily through his feature movie based on Beatles songs, *Yellow Submarine* (1968). Although the general consensus is that this is a marred movie, it nevertheless served to point commercial animation as a whole toward the idea that there was an alternative to the Disney "realist" approach in the making of popular feature animations. The reissue in 2000 of a remastered edition of the movie, complete with a remastered version of its soundtrack album with all the attendant publicity, has brought Dunning's name and work back into the limelight.

Long before he came to popular attention, however, he was recognized within the industry as a highly talented creative animator. His career proper started in 1942 when he joined the National Film Board of Canada, where he worked with another little-known (at least to the public) but highly influential animator, Norman McLaren. At the NFBC he made a number of shorts, some educational and some experimental, including such items as *Chants populaires no. 2* (1943) and *Les Animaux malades de la faim* (1944). He first began to attract attention with *Grim Pastures* (1944) and *Cadet Rousselle* (1946), the latter based on a well-known folk song and done in conjunction with Colin Low; these were animated in silhouette, a style of animation pioneered by Lotte Reiniger earlier in the century but not frequently used since, except for effect in the midst of other animation. Also of interest

among his shorts during this early period are *The Three Blind Mice* (1945) and *Family Tree* (1950).

After a trip to Paris in 1948, when he met distinguished European animators including Paul Grimault, he founded a production company, Graphic Associates, in Toronto, with a former NFBC colleague, Jim McKay. In 1955 he moved on to join UPA in New York, where he worked for a few months on the animated series featuring Gerald McBoing-Boing. In 1956 UPA sent Dunning to London to open a U.K. branch, but by the following year, when UPA changed owners, he had opened his own production company there, TV Cartoons, employing some former UPA staff.

TVC did commercial work for television – both programs and advertisements – as well as some prestigious shorts, but its first widely acclaimed movie, which Dunning directed, was *The Flying Man* (1962), based on a story by Stan Hayward, who was later to become extremely well known as the co-creator with Bob Godfrey of Henry's Cat. The style of animation offered a complete break from the general Disney or Hanna–Barbera formats then on display: in effect, *The Flying Man* is an animated watercolor, done on glass, with the brushstrokes not so much left visible as reveled in; the flight of the man is spiritually symbolic, so the animation

Yellow Submarine (1968)

🎨 color / animated with brief live-action ⏱ 87 minutes
Pepperland comes under the tyranny of the Blue Meanies, who deploy a monstrous flying creature called The Glove and a variety of missiles, including bright green apples that leach color from the land and its people, petrifying the latter. Old Fred — who could be either a retired military gentleman of uncertain provenance or a hotel commissionaire — takes the ancestral Yellow Submarine in search of help and finds the Beatles in Liverpool. He brings them back with him to Pepperland; en route they pick up the Nowhere Man as an ally. In Pepperland they impersonate Sergeant Pepper's Lonely Hearts Club Band, restore color to the domain, and beat the Blue Meanies into submission with a barrage of hippy sentiments and Beatles numbers.

perfectly matches the theme. The short won the Grand Prix at the Annecy Festival in the year of its release.

In 1964 or 1965 King Features was approached by ABC with the idea of producing an animated series based on the Beatles, using Beatles songs and the kind of zany Liverpudlian humor displayed in the band's own movies *A Hard Day's Night* (1964) and *Help!* (1965). Although the Beatles themselves were not much interested in the project, being engrossed in those movies and their other concerns, they allowed their names, personalities and recorded songs to be used; the voices of the Fab Four were supplied by actors Paul Frees and Lance Percival, and the financing was supplied by toy manufacturer A.C. Gilmer, who had an eye on a huge merchandising market. King Features farmed out the animation to two production companies, Astransa in Australia and primarily Dunning's TVC in London. This was the first time real people had been the basis for a regular cartoon on network television. The animation of the series and indeed the series itself are not of any particular merit — essentially the episodes were excuses to play a couple of Beatles songs, complete with words at the bottom of the screen to assist viewers who wanted to sing along — but the show was phenomenally popular in its first season (1965–66) before fading in its second and entering rerun limbo (although retitled *The New Beatles* from 1967).

King Features's producer Al Brodax, who had set up the original deal, was convinced that the way was open for an animated Beatles feature, and so *Yellow Submarine* (1968) took shape, with Dunning as director and TVC doing the animation. Once again, the band themselves, presumably expecting more of the same after the mediocre tv series, did not want too much direct involvement, though this time it was a joint production between King Features and the Beatles' own company, Apple. According to George Martin, responsible for the musical soundtrack, in a 1995 interview:

When the film was first mooted, The Beatles didn't like the idea at all. In fact they wouldn't have any part in it. And when Brian [Epstein] had committed them, it was part of a deal he did with United Artists, I think. But when Brian committed them

to the picture and he said that they would provide new songs, they said, "Well, we're not going to write any decent songs, we'll give them all the rejects we didn't really want."

In any event, the four musicians did agree to be filmed for a brief live-action coda, but otherwise their lack of interest was fairly profound; actors played their characters' voice parts in the movie (Lance Percival, who had voiced Paul and Ringo for the tv series, this time around played Old Fred, the plot's linchpin).

Dunning had more radical ideas about the animation of *Yellow Submarine* than simply an extended rehash of the tv series. Heinz Edelmann was brought in for the character and other design, and his mixture of Pop Art and psychedelia was so powerful that stills from the movie today serve as iconic representations of that hippy era. The surrealism of the script Brodax produced along with Lee Minoff, Jack Mendelsohn, and best-selling novelist Erich Segal gave the animation surrealism as well, so that the brightly colored terrain of Pepperland is populated by creatures who seem to have been spawned by the joint imagination of Salvador Dalí and Hieronymous Bosch.

To the popular press, the tag line for the result of these efforts was obvious: along with the same year's *2001: A Space Odyssey* (1968), and with perhaps more edge to the double entendre, *Yellow Submarine* was "the ultimate trip." Psychedelic animation's most ostentatious outpouring, to a backing of old Beatles songs, might seem a grim prospect, but the movie is in fact surprisingly enjoyable, with a constant stream of visual and conceptual fantasy notions tripping from the screen. The "Lucy in the Sky with Diamonds" sequence, done in a far more Impressionistic style than the rest — although in the same garish colors — is especially striking. The movie was a commercial success, and it also caused a reappraisal of the modes in which commercial animated features could operate; for example, John Hubley's impressive opening sequences for Martin Rosen's *Watership Down* (1978), which is otherwise conventionally animated, probably owe a great debt to *Yellow Submarine* — not especially in their style but simply in that they were there at all. Even The Beatles became more interested in the movie after they'd seen it.

Thereafter, Dunning created three highly acclaimed shorts — (*Moon Rock* (1971), *Damon the Mower* (1971), and *The Maggot* (1972) – but, sadly, he left his second foray into feature movies lapse until it was too late in his short life. This was to be an adaptation of Shakespeare's *The Tempest*. The beautiful stills that survive from the few minutes that he had animated suggest that it would have been a landmark in animation, and indeed in cinema as a whole.

Dunning died in London in 1979. TVC, the company he founded, continued to make fine animations for tv, including *The Snowman* (1982), *When the Wind Blows* (1986), *Father Christmas* (1991), and *The Bear* (1998), all based on graphic novels by Raymond Briggs; *The Wind in the Willows* (1995) and *The Willows in Winter* (1996); and *Famous Fred* (1996), not to mention the delightful shorts *The World of Peter Rabbit and Friends* (from 1992).

THE FLEISCHERS

Max Fleischer (1883–1972)
Lou Fleischer (1891–1985)

Joe Fleischer (1889–1979)
Dave Fleischer (1894–1979)

Setup for *Gulliver's Travels* (1939). Photograph: Sotheby's.
© Warner Bros.

Born on July 19, 1883, in Vienna, Max Fleischer was the second of the seven children of Austrian tailor and amateur inventor William Fleischer and his wife, Amalia. Max's elder brother, Charles, and younger sister, Ethel, played little part in the story of the Fleischer studio, while the youngest child of the seven, Sol, died in infancy of typhoid. But the remaining four brothers together, each to a greater or lesser extent, created an animation business that for nearly three decades rivaled Disney and which, if circumstances were different, might today occupy the position in our world that Disney occupies.

The story of the Fleischer enterprise is largely the story of Max and Dave. Max was a young child when his parents emigrated to New York, fleeing anti-Semitism in their native land. Born in New York were Joe, on February 28, 1889, Louis, on July 16, 1891,

and Dave, on July 14, 1894. The children, as they grew up, all in one way or another inherited their father's inventing trait; Charles invented various devices that are well known to us today, such as the conveyor-belt system at supermarket checkouts and the first device for getting toothpaste into tubes. For Max, Joe, Lou, and Dave, however, their inventive flair was to take them into moviemaking, specifically into animation.

Max showed an artistic bent from an early age. He derived an education and training from the Mechanics and Tradesmens School, the Art Students League, and the Cooper Union. He had high hopes of getting a job in the art department of Brooklyn's

79

Poster for *Popeye the Sailor Meets Sinbad the Sailor* (1936).
Private Collection.

Modeling (1921)

🎞 b/w / animated/live-action/stop-motion silent ⏱ 9¼ minutes
Out of the Inkwell

The animator's hands play with a steel-nibbed pen, drawing circles which then go back into the nib, before one flock of shapes escapes and comes together to form the figure of Ko-Ko the Clown. A set of blobs coalesces to clothe him. Cut to the far end of the studio, where in live action a sculptor is completing a portrait bust for a customer. As sculptor and animator wrangle with the customer, Ko-Ko continues clowning on the drawing board, skating around over a frozen pond before drawing with his skate tracks a portrait of the customer on the ice. After further clowning, this time with a bear, Ko-Ko produces a head of the customer out of a giant snowball. The customer points out that the animated clown is doing a better job than the two artists, and annoyedly the animator hurls a blob of clay at Ko-Ko . . . which Ko-Ko shortly hurls back, hitting the customer in the eye. The clown then goes through a hole in the ice to emerge in the studio, and is soon climbing up the clay bust, and eventually inside it, manipulating the face from within to humorous effect. After further slapstick in the studio, Ko-Ko flees first back to the drawing board and then into the inkwell.

Daily Eagle newspaper, but when he applied in 1900 there were no vacancies; instead he had to take a job with the paper as an errand boy. Over the next four years, he was able to work himself up to become a staff artist, learning the techniques of that trade – most of them related to photography, although for a short while, he drew a comic strip for the paper called *Little Elmo*. Much more important in the long term was that he became friendly with John Randolph Bray, then working for the *Daily Eagle*, but soon to become a pioneer of the animation industry. Soon after Bray's departure from the *Eagle* to pursue a freelance career, Max got a job in Boston as a photo engraver and retoucher with a firm called the Electro-Light Engraving Company. In 1914, he took a job as a commercial artist at the Crouse–Hinds Corporation, and from there he moved on to become art editor of *Popular Science Monthly*. It was here that his long-standing interest in animation became a central focus: he had inherited his father's love of gadgetry and he was also in love with art and drawing. Animation seemed to offer an ideal combination of both worlds.

Nine years younger, Dave, who showed astonishing artistic flair from a very early age, had to curtail his rudimentary artistic training because the family ran out of money for the fees and because his penchant for cartooning rather than performing the prescribed exercises maddened his teachers. His father instead employed him to visit the windows of department stores, drawing the clothing he saw on display there, so that William could copy the patterns. His first job related to the movies was as an usher at the Palace Theater; the sole advantage, aside from the very modest pay, was that he was able to give himself an education in the techniques of performance art, such as timing, by watching the vaudeville shows. In due course, he moved on to become an errand boy at the Walker Engraving Company, eventually working his way up to become an assistant in the art department. When he was 18 he moved on again, this time getting a job as a film cutter at Pathé Films. It would seem that he and elder brother Max were following converging paths, with Dave having the artistic ability, now backed up by training on the job, to help realize Max's animation dreams.

In 1911 Winsor McCay caused a sensation with his stage presentations of his first animated movie, *Little Nemo*. Others flocked to imitate him, but most of the hopefuls lacked his peculiar artistic flair and his diligence, with the result that much of the animation offered to the public was pretty poor stuff. Pioneers like Earl Hurd (in partnership with Bray) and Raoul Barré made fundamental inventions to decrease the amount of work involved in animation and to tackle the problem of poor register, but Max's inventive mind took a different tack. If the problem was that artists had difficulty in adopting all the techniques required by animation, the solution might be to take much of the artistry out of the equation. He therefore dreamed up the idea of the rotoscope: the sequences to be animated would first be shot in live action; then frame-by-frame blow-ups could be traced, with details added to convert the drawing from one of a live-action scene to one of, well, whatever it was that the animator's imagination desired. (In fact, although Max was granted a patent to the rotoscope in 1917, it was years later discovered that a Pennsylvania company had a very similar device in operation before him. This is probably the only reason that Max did not sue Walt Disney over the use of a rotoscope in his 1937 feature *Snow White and the Seven Dwarfs*.) Brother Joe was enlisted to construct the device, which took the form of a drawing board into whose middle was fitted a sheet of frosted glass; from below, a movie projector, adapted to show one frame at a time, shone the picture up onto the frosted glass, upon which the animator could work using tracing paper. Brother Dave was enlisted to devise something that could be turned into a cartoon; he had had an early ambition to be a clown, and still had the clown suit he had made, so the three brothers set up a white sheet as backdrop and filmed Dave clowning.

Thereafter it was a matter of making the film into a cartoon. Working in their spare time, the three brothers took a full month to complete the pencil drawings and several further months to ink them in preparation for the camera. All in all, the production of the first Ko-Ko the Clown pilot movie, a mere 100 feet long, took them a year, much of this time being eaten up by the difficulties of keeping the drawings in register for the camera. The cartoon showed Ko-Ko (the clown was not actually named until 1923; the spelling of 'KoKo' varied over the years, being sometimes 'KoKo' or 'Koko') being drawn into existence by the animator's hands, then doing funny tricks before dissolving into drops of ink that flowed back into the inkwell, which neatly capped itself.

Thanks to Dave's old contacts at Pathé, Max took the movie there in the hopes of selling them on the idea. As soon as Max mentioned the kind of timeframe required to produce such movies, he was more or less laughed out of the office. He devised a means of further speeding up the process – making the movie partly in live action, with the animated and live-action components interacting some but not all of the time – and went back to Pathé with the news that he could produce for them one cartoon a month. This was more like it, and Pathé set the brothers up with a studio, commissioning from them a 15-minute animated movie on the exploits of Theodore Roosevelt.

Unfortunately, the results were disastrous, and the brothers were out on their collective ear. Max went back to the dreary business of hawking his pilot Ko-Ko short around the various film studios and collecting rejections, until the day that, waiting in the outer office at Paramount, he bumped into his old friend from the *Daily Eagle*, John Randolph Bray. Bray explained that Max was wasting his time by trying to sell a short to Paramount, because he, Bray, had the exclusive contract for that, producing for Paramount a weekly compilation called the Paramount–Bray Pictograph. However, one component of this film magazine was animated

shorts, so it was possible that the Fleischer brothers' experiment could be of interest to him. Max showed him the movie and Bray liked it enough to give it a try. Audience reaction to this short, called *Out of the Inkwell* (1916), was very positive. Bray commissioned Max and Dave – Joe had by now got a job at Pathé as an electrician – to produce further cartoons like it at the rate of one a month.

U.S. participation in World War I intervened. Bray shifted the emphasis of his studio to the production of training and propaganda films for the military, and hired Max to work on these. Dave was recruited by the U.S. Army and employed as a film-cutter. The brothers managed to produce one further commercial cartoon, despite their war duties: *Experiment No. 1*, released in June 1918. Immediately after the war was over, they resumed their contract with Bray, and new Out of the Inkwell live-action/animated shorts began to appear regularly (although not at a rate anything like once a month), first in the Paramount–Bray Pictograph and then, when Bray shifted allegiances, in the Goldwyn-Bray Pictograph. The cartoons were clever and witty, but what most captivated the audiences was their seeming realism and the combination of live action and animation. Because of the rotoscoping, there was little or nothing of the jerkiness or clunkiness of rival cartoons. In special-effects terms the shorts were spectacular, so it was easy to believe that the animated creations were genuinely existing in a live-action world. Bray valued Max enough to make him a stockholder in the company.

Dave had, since leaving the military at the end of the war, done some animation experimentation of his own. Dave's primary role in the Out of the Inkwell cartoons was as a director and storyman/scripter (and, of course, as the live-action model for Ko-Ko). Max was in charge of the actual animation and was accordingly being given the solo credit. The two brothers quarreled constantly over this; in about 1920 Dave looked at the results of his own animation experiments and wondered why he was playing second fiddle to his older brother. He accordingly left Bray to set up on his own. This was a short-lived split: their parents banged the two brothers' heads together, and in 1921 they started a company in partnership, Out of the Inkwell Films Inc. In conjunction with an animator who had worked with them at the Bray studio, Charles Shettler, and with brother Joe as their electrician and cameraman, they set up shop in a basement on East 45th Street and Lexington Avenue. Soon they were doing well enough to hire more animators to take over the vast bulk of the drawing, leaving Max free to concentrate on running the business and Dave free to work on story and direction.

They did not devote themselves exclusively to Out of the Inkwell shorts, in 1923 diversifying to produce the hour-long educational movie *The Einstein Theory of Relativity*, mixing live action with animation. They were advised by various distinguished scientists of the day and had as overall advisor Garrett P. Serviss, a scientific journalist who is best remembered now for his parallel career as a science-fiction writer. Albert Einstein reportedly

Recreated setup for *She Wronged Him Right* (1934) showing
Betty Boop. Photograph: S/R Laboratories.

commended the movie highly. Less successful was another movie
done in the same year in conjunction with New York's American
Museum of Natural History; this was *Darwin's Theory of Evolution*,
almost exclusively filmed in live action and comprising visually not
much more than evocative scenes of animals, so that the voice-
over could narrate the informative content of the movie. It was a
contentious movie to make at the time, when the United States
still had not decided if the teaching of evolution should be
permitted by law (a matter which is, incredibly, regarded as being
available for debate even now, in the 21st century). The Fleischers
got around the problem by making the sophist claim that the
movie was merely illustrating an hypothesis, not promulgating it.

More significant in the long term than the two educational
features was an idea brought to the studio by songwriter Charles
K. Harris. By its very nature, cinema was not much of a medium for
audience participation. What Harris suggested was a movie geared
to a particular popular song and showing the lyrics of that song, so

that the audience could sing along as the organist played it – this
was, remember, still the days of the silents, so every cinema needed
an organist. Either Max or Dave soon afterward invented the
famous bouncing ball, which skipped along the tops of the lines of
the lyrics, allowing both audience and, for that matter, the organist
to keep time. The bouncing ball was introduced in September
1925 for *My Bonnie (Lies Over the Ocean)*, by which time a number
of these Ko-Ko Song Car-Tunes had already been released without
it, starting with *Oh Mabel* (1924). Each movie typically had a small
amount of animation featuring Ko-Ko, and then it was into the
song; sometimes, for the last few lines of the song, the letters of
the lyric would become animated as well. Early on, the ball was
animated, but the Fleischers found that it was better and easier to
use a physical ball or white circle on the end of a thin black stick.
The series lasted well into 1927; and in 1929, after the advent of
sound, the Fleischers revived the idea as the Screen Songs, in most
of which a live-action singer or group would be introduced, with
some animation, so that the audience could then join in with the
performers' rendition of the song in question, still guided by the
bouncing ball.

The early Song Car-Tunes had an additional advantage, although this cannot have been apparent at first: timing was of the essence in their making — mess up the timing and the whole enterprise fell apart. The Fleischers thus had to consider and tackle the problems of synchronization long before any of the other studios. They were therefore in a good position when their financier, Hugo Riesenfeld, introduced them to Lee De Forest, the inventor and pioneer of radio, who had in 1906 invented the triode, and who in 1919 had patented the basic process still in use today whereby sound can be incorporated into a movie. At the time the movie industry hadn't been much interested, but De Forest and Riesenfeld reckoned — perfectly correctly, of course — that it could be only a matter of time before audiences would require all movies to be in sound. De Forest had actually made quite a number of sound movies, although of course only a few theaters were able to show them; now he and Riesenfeld had had the idea of sound cartoons. Accordingly, the Fleischers produced a few Song Car-Tunes which had rudimentary soundtracks in the form of musical backgrounds. One of these, however, is a contender for the first sound cartoon of all time: *My Old Kentucky Home*, released on May 13, 1926. A dog plays a trombone and then says: "Now let's all follow the bouncing ball and sing along!" Not, perhaps, the grandest of ways to introduce a revolutionary breakthrough in mass communications, but no worse than several others. Max, however, didn't really share the faith in the future of sound cartoons, so the Fleischers rather missed the steamboat, allowing Walt Disney, just a few years later, to gain the greatest benefit from the new medium.

Another invention from around this time, seemingly Max's alone, was a new job function: the inbetweener. Before this an animator would be expected to do all the drawings for a movie himself. The standard practice, then as now, was first to do the key drawings, then later to go back and fill in the ones in between these. It seems that Dick Huemer was the first animator who, acceding to a request from Max, permitted a humbler staff member to do these inbetween drawings. Soon it was standard practice throughout the animation industry to employ armies of inbetweeners so that the principal animators would have the time to do more of what they did best.

The Fleischers, Max in particular, were becoming increasingly impatient with their means of distribution, which was through Margaret Winkler. They found no fault with Winkler herself — she was probably the best in the field — but the system of distribution she had to use, "states rights," involved so many middlemen that a movie's original creators tended to see only an unacceptably low percentage of the revenues. Max therefore set up Red Seal Pictures in 1924 with the aim of competing directly with the big studios for the nationwide cinema block-bookings that Winkler was unable to obtain. At first everything flourished for the venture, which was run by Edwin Miles Fadiman. Unfortunately, Fadiman quarreled with Max, and after his departure the finances of the company, which had made sense only because of Fadiman's skills, fell into disarray, with losses far exceeding

KoKo's Earth Control (1927)

♭ b/w / animated silent ⏱ 5³/₄ minutes
Out of the Inkwell
The animator's hands draw Ko-Ko and his dog on the surface of the globe; cleverly, Ko-Ko is fully animated during the whole time he is being drawn. The two come to a building marked "Control of Earth." Inside, as Ko-Ko plays with such innocuous switches as the ones that control rain or shine and day or night, the dog becomes captivated by the one labeled:

DANGER
BEWARE
DO NOT TOUCH
EARTH CONTROL
IF THIS HANDLE IS PULLED THE WORLD WILL COME TO AN END

Despite Ko-Ko's efforts to stop him, the dog pulls the lever: the Sun destroys the Moon, and Ko-Ko and the dog find themselves in a near-barren wasteland where strange things can happen, such as Ko-Ko swapping heads with a Chinese demon and the dog being thumped by an angry tree. The short ends with a lengthy sequence of live action and animation depicting the world indeed falling apart.

income. Red Seal Pictures collapsed in 1926. Although the Out of the Inkwell studio continued to produce new Ko-Ko cartoons, the Fleischers were so short of money that they were having difficulty getting their film developed.

A speculator named Alfred Weiss approached the Fleischers and proposed the setting up of a new corporation, with himself as president, to continue making the Fleischer movies. This came about in 1927, and was marked by the Out of the Inkwell series changing its name to The Inkwell Imps, prefaced by three words that cannot have pleased the ever credit-greedy Max: "Alfred Weiss presents." Weiss arranged for the movies to be distributed by Paramount, a relationship that continued even after Dave discovered Weiss was a crook, successfully sued him, and thereby got rid of him. The new corporation the Fleischers established with Paramount was called Fleischer Studios Inc., but in effect it was merely a subsidiary of the major studio, which held the copyright on the cartoons and their characters.

Then came 1928 and the release by Walt Disney of *Steamboat Willie*, and suddenly audiences and the movie industry were demanding sound with everything. The Fleischers were now not slow to take the plunge, releasing the first of their Screen Songs — the replacements for the Song Car-Tunes — *The Sidewalks of New York*, in February 1929 and, in October that year, *Noah's Lark*, the first of their Talkartoons (which initially were more like rivals to Disney's Silly Symphonies). As with other early sound animations, the initial Talkartoons were animated first and had the music and dialogue added afterward. It was obviously a tedious business,

Dizzy Dishes (1930)

♭ b/w / animated ◷ 6 minutes
Bimbo/Betty Boop

The first appearance of Betty Boop. Bimbo the Dog is a waiter at a restaurant. A huge customer orders roast duck, and Bimbo neglects the other customers in order to prepare this dish. His attentions are diverted by the restaurant's sexy cabaret singer, who, despite having floppy canine ears, is almost identical to the fully formed Betty. Filled with passion, Bimbo dances with the roast duck, plays it like a banjo, etc., while the customer who ordered it is reduced to eating the crockery and table. The short ends with the customer wrathfully chasing Bimbo, who carves himself a model train and escapes on it. Primitively animated (by Grim Natwick and Ted Sears, under Dave Fleischer's direction), this is of interest only because of Betty.

Bimbo's Initiation (1931)

♭ b/w / animated ◷ 6¼ minutes
Bimbo/Betty Boop

Our hero falls into a manhole and down a long ramp to where the members of a "mystic order" await him, intending to force him to join up. Various surrealistic techniques of mental torture are used in an attempt to brainwash him into joining, but still he resists. Betty Boop appears in a doorway, saying, "Come inside, big boy." Bimbo's response to her appearance is "What a pippin!" But the door through which she alluringly goes proves, when he reaches it himself, to be just the outermost of a series of progressively smaller doors, the last of which extrudes a duct that swallows him. Finally, one of the indoctrinators pulls off "his" robe and hood to reveal "himself" as Betty Boop. As she dances seductively, Bimbo decides that he does want to join the society after all. It is then revealed that all the other members are Betty Boops in disguise.

Poor Cinderella (1934)

♭ color / animated ◷ 10½ minutes
Betty Boop

The color debut of Betty Boop. Although theoretically Betty's act had been cleaned up by now, in fact redhead Betty is in very sexy form in this fairly standard, song-driven rendition of the tale. It is also something of a technological triumph for the Fleischers in that a sort of 3D effect is maintained throughout; this was achieved by use of a built set rather than the customary drawn one. The transformations of mice into horses, etc., are especially impressively done. Cupid works his magic on Prince Charming with not an arrow but a mallet! There are little quasi-erotic triggers throughout the movie: the stick of dogsbody Cinders's broom is startlingly phallic, the palace clock is borne by two nude female sculptures, and Betty's garter is well in evidence during the ball.

getting the lip-synch accurate, and so the Fleischers kept dialogue to a minimum, relying on popular songs (usually supplied by Paramount) to hold the audience's ears. Brother Lou, who had carved out for himself a successful career in music before being dragged by his wife's family into their jewelry business, was now recruited to assist with the synchronization of the music; he was as close to a musical director as the Fleischers had for some years.

Unlike the Silly Symphonies and more like the very much later Looney Tunes, the Talkartoons early on introduced a series star: this was Ko-Ko's dog, from the now defunct Out of the Inkwell series (the last Ko-Ko movie had been 1927's *Koko Needles the Boss*). Originally called Fitz, the dog was renamed Bimbo and became less identifiable as a dog. It seemed as if the public rather schizophrenically wanted their animated stars to be funny talking animals but, at the same time, to be as humanized as possible. Bimbo's status as a series star was not, however, helped by the fact that different animators portrayed him sufficiently differently that it can actually be rather hard, looking at the earliest Talkartoons, to work out which of them is intended to be a Bimbo vehicle and which isn't.

One of the early Bimbo cartoons, *Dizzy Dishes* (1930), had the character working as a waiter in an establishment also employing a canine singer. From Bimbo's reactions to her, it is evident that she is extremely attractive to male dogs; and yet at the same time, despite her doggy ears and, on occasion, a rather repulsive pseudo-canine way of moving her mouth, there can be no doubt that there is something archetypally sexy for human males as well. Created by the great animator Grim Natwick – lore has it that, at first, Natwick was the only person at Fleischers capable of animating her – this character was Betty Boop, and she was an immediate smash hit with the audiences. Obviously, the Fleischers couldn't immediately capitalize on Betty's instant popularity; but from May 1931's *Silly Scandals* until the middle of 1939, new Betty Boop cartoons were appearing at a rate considerably greater than one a month.

Although she had her "boop-boop-a-doop" catchphrase from the outset, she did not acquire the name Betty Boop until August 1932, with the release of *Stopping the Show*. Before then she had been completely redesigned by Dave Fleischer, retaining enough of her appearance to still be recognizable as Natwick's original but losing all her canine attributes. Quite deliberately, Dave made her as sexy as was possible without alarming the censors – in a split second of *Betty Boop's Rise to Fame* (1934) she even shows a naked breast. It cannot be denied that she is one of the very few animated characters who, like Jessica Rabbit in *Who Framed Roger Rabbit* (1988), carries a definite sexual charge. Bimbo was demoted to be her sidekick, and Ko-Ko was resurrected to become another. With her tiny mouth, big, big eyes, hugely oversized head, plunging décolletage, ever-shorter dress, and titillating garters, Betty was a conscious mixture of child and woman, so that, however outrageous the goings-on, she preserved at the same time an aura of complete, childish innocence. It is very difficult to find offense in a Betty Boop short, although sure enough in due course there would be those who could.

Natwick had modeled the character originally on singer and actress Helen Kane (1904–66), who as a Paramount star was regarded as fair game, and Betty's voice was likewise imitative of Kane's, although in fact supplied by other actresses, notably May Questel. Kane appeared in a number of movies, beginning with *Pointed Heels* (1929), and was the original "boop-boop-a-doop" girl, but she would almost certainly be completely forgotten today were it not for the fact that in 1934 she sued the Fleischers for plagiarism in the matter of Betty Boop, also stating that her own popularity had been damaged by the fact that audiences now thought she was being merely imitative of Betty. This was a tricky case for the Fleischers to defend because they'd never thought there was any real secret about Betty's origins. Nevertheless, defend it they did, producing the voice actresses who had played the part of Betty and making sure their appearances resembled Kane's as much as possible. In fact, or so claimed Max in court, he had himself dreamed up Betty – a blatant lie. Also, the Fleischers were able to prove – although dishonestly so, Lou having to doctor a perfectly genuine but insufficiently convincing 1928 Paramount film of the singer Baby Esther – that usage of the phrase "boop-boop-a-doop" predated Kane's adoption of it. In a complete travesty of the truth, the court declared that the Fleischers had no case to answer.

In the first few years of the 1930s, the vocal protests of the moral minority about bad language and smut in the movies began to rise to a shriek. Cinema owners started complaining to the studios about the objections they were receiving from customers concerning the screen activities and personas of stars like Paramount's very own Mae West. In 1934 a new production code was drawn up by the movie industry to counter the uproar, and animations were affected as much as live-action movies. For the Fleischers and, particularly, Betty Boop this was very bad news. In hindsight one might say that it was the Fleischers' own fault: they had in part been responsible for the outcry in the first place, having packed many of the Betty Boop cartoons with sexual innuendo and having taken every opportunity visually to emphasize her feminine allure. After about 1935 Betty had to be toned down, until she became little more than an attractive but clean-living, all-American, middle-class housewife (albeit without the husband). The subject matter of her cartoons had to become similarly anodyne. Although she managed to hold onto a good deal of her popularity, her days were numbered. In 1939, despite a few further cameo appearances by Betty, this phenomenally successful series ended – in fact, Betty herself did not appear in the last cartoon billed as a Betty Boop short, *Yip, Yip, Yippy* (1939). It is an irony that, had she survived just a little longer, she would undoubtedly, with the outbreak of war, have enjoyed a new lease on life as a forces' darling, in which case she might, like Mickey Mouse, be still extant.

Aside from Bimbo and Ko-Ko, Betty had a number of other supporting cohorts. Included among these were the usual fairly

Be Human (1936)

🎞 b/w / animated ⏱ 6¼ minutes
Grampy/Betty Boop

Betty Boop is appalled at the cruelty with which a brutish local farmer treats his animals, and phones Prof. Grampy's Animal Aid Society. Grampy drives in, seizes the farmer, and puts him on a treadmill where an automatic whip gives him the same sort of lashing that he has been giving some of the animals. The treadmill powers various gadgets for the pleasure of the animals at the Aid Center – for example, shaking an apple tree so that pigs can gorge on the apples.

Popeye the Sailor Meets Ali Baba's Forty Thieves (1937)

🎞 color / animated ⏱ 13½ minutes
Popeye

Bluto plays the part of Abu Hassan, leader of the Forty Thieves. Popeye and Olive are on holiday in Arabia and hear the emergency radio warnings about Abu. The Forty Thieves raid the café where the lovers are eating, and Popeye has a mainly symbolic fight with Abu that results in him finding himself intimately entwined with a candelabrum. The Thieves steal everything movable from the town, including Olive. Popeye pursues to the Open Sesame cave but arrives at the door just as it shuts; he uses his pipe as a blowtorch to burn an entrance through the stone. After being much bashed, Popeye produces a spinach can and tells it: "Open, sez me." Spinach imbibed, he is more than a match for Abu and the Thieves.

uninspired characters typical of animation at the time, such as Gus Gorilla – whose equivalent, probably with the same name, could be found on any animation lot. Rather more substantial was Grampy, a bearded, somewhat scatty inventor not dissimilar in personality from Norman Hunter's roughly contemporaneous book character Professor Branestawm, though different in appearance. The general view is that Grampy provided a sort of vicarious outlet for the inventive cravings of the brothers Fleischer, and there were certainly hopes that he might become a series star in his own right. However, he never graduated beyond co-starring with Betty in a number of her weaker cartoons.

Another co-star was earmarked for greater things. This was the spinach-swilling Popeye, whose first screen appearance was in the Betty Boop short (with Betty playing only a small role) appropriately called *Popeye the Sailor* (1933). Max, having bought the screen rights to the character, wanted to try him out in a sure-fire Betty Boop cartoon before committing himself to a full-blown Popeye series. Popeye had been created in 1929 by E.C. Segar for his comic strip *Thimble Theatre*; much earlier, in 1919, Olive Oyl had been born, her heart belonging at that time to a character called

Superman (1941)

(vt *The Mad Scientist*)

color / animated ⏱ 9 minutes

Superman

The first of the series produced by the Fleischers and mainly directed by Dave Fleischer. After a rapid account of why Superman is here on Earth, the story starts at the *Daily Planet* with the receipt of "another letter" from the Mad Scientist: "Beware — you fools! My electrothanasia ray strikes tonight at 12. Total destruction will come to those who laughed at me and failed to heed my warnings. Beware — I strike at midnight!" Lois Lane flies off to find the lair of the Mad Scientist and his sidekick crow; on arrival she is immediately overpowered and bound. Only when the Mad Scientist begins to use his ray does Clark Kent say: "This looks like a job for Superman." After righting a toppling skyscraper, the superhero flies up the path of the ray, all the while deflecting its fury with his own body, then causes the mechanism to backfire so that it is destroyed. Lois is saved and the Mad Scientist jailed. The short was nominated for an Oscar.

Raggedy Ann and Raggedy Andy (1941)

color / animated ⏱ 17½ minutes

Adapted from the stories by Johnny Gruelle, this featurette sees a little girl try to buy Raggedy Ann from the toy shop, only to discover that Ann and Andy must be sold as a pair, for a dollar rather than the fifty cents that she has. In flashback, the toy shop owner explains why the two are inseparable. Long ago, back in Ragland, where the two dolls were made, Andy jilted Ann, who had to be hospitalized, her heart broken; his declaration of renewed love brought about her complete recovery. To seal their togetherness, the hand of one was sewn to the hand of the other.

Back in the present, the soft-hearted toy shop owner gives the child the pair of dolls for free.

Harold "Ham" Gravy. Despite his mirror-shattering appearance and his unprepossessing personal habits and attributes, Popeye soon became both the man in Olive's life and the focus of the comic strip. Other associated characters were born in the comic strip, such as the W.C. Fields-like J. Wellington Wimpy and Popeye's "adoptid inkink" Swee-pea. But Bluto, Popeye's perpetual would-be nemesis and often enough Olive's abductor, was original to the cartoons, being especially designed by Segar at the Fleischers' behest. Also original to the cartoons was the intensity of Popeye's spinach dependency; although he indulged in his habit frequently enough in the comic strip to have markedly affected spinach sales for the better, in no sense did he resort to the ever-ready can at each and every turn. Another running joke introduced in the cartoons was the immediate and huge bulge the imbibing of

spinach produced in the sailor man's right biceps; this could take the form of an anvil, a mighty mallet, or, in later and more elaborate versions, an express locomotive at full charge. Whatever the symbolic shape the Fleischer animators gave it, the biceps was almost immediately put to devastating use against the villain or villains, usually Bluto, with or without henchmen.

Previous Fleischer cartoons had been marked by their constant inventiveness, a quality generally ascribed to Dave's influence and his propensity toward stuffing his animations with countless gags. It is therefore possible to watch a whole string of, say, Betty Boop cartoons without the interest flagging: each is different from the other and has its individual appeal, so it matters little that the star is always the same. This cannot be said of the Popeye cartoons, which are substantially less imaginative than was their comic-strip counterpart. Essentially, there's only one plot in the Popeye cartoons: Bluto commits a crime (often, as noted, the abduction of Olive); Popeye sets out to rectify things; it looks black for our hero until he plucks the can of spinach from his clothing; now endowed with phenomenal strength, he beats the living daylights out of his foe. The Fleischers did try to introduce some variations on this, but only half-heartedly. Secondary characters like Wimpy were relegated to the sidelines, thus precluding most of the wit that had characterized the comic strip. The result is that the prospect of watching a dozen Popeye cartoons in a row is a nightmare. A single Popeye cartoon may entertain, but it goes a long way; there is no desire to watch another for at least a few months and preferably longer than that. The three extended Popeye movies that the Fleischers made – *Popeye the Sailor Meets Sindbad the Sailor* (1936), *Popeye the Sailor Meets Ali Baba's Forty Thieves* (1937), and *Aladdin and his Wonderful Lamp* (vt *Popeye Meets Aladdin*; vt *Popeye the Sailor Meets Aladdin and his Wonderful Lamp*; 1939) – are difficult to watch without suffering the onset of somnolence, even though the first of them somehow succeeded in being nominated for an Oscar: all that happens is that Popeye bashes up more villains and for a longer time. Since the character also lacks anything much by way of depth – indeed, he has no real personality other than being a collection of stereotyped attributes – it is unsurprising that, while everyone today knows of the Fleischer Popeye cartoons, it is actually quite hard to see one. The Popeye shows endlessly repeated in the deader hours of children's tv scheduling are drawn from *The All-New Popeye Hour*, created with some success (it ran for fivr years) in 1978 by King Features and based on the comic strips, of which King is the copyright owner, or occasionally the far less successful tv series *Popeye and Son*, which ran from 1987 to 1988 and had Popeye and Olive settled down in a nice cozy marriage.

All of these cavils aside, the Fleischer series of Popeye cartoons was probably the most popular in all of animation history. The Fleischers kept churning them out at a phenomenal rate until 1957, the series moving into Technicolor late in 1943 with *Her Honor the Mare*. There were hundreds of them, and audiences lapped them up, leaving the Fleischer studios with little time to do anything else.

But do other things they did. The longish series of Color Classics was begun in 1934 with Betty Boop's color debut, *Poor Cinderella*. This was a visually remarkable movie, in that it has an astonishingly realistic feel thanks to a 3D process with which the Fleischers were experimenting, whereby a miniature set was created and the animation shot in front of it. Other Color Classics were less ambitious; initially the series used Cinecolor, but very soon moved to Technicolor. Far less successful was the highly innovative series called Stone Age Cartoons, which, begun in 1940 with *Way Back when the Triangle Had Its Points*, can be regarded as precursors of Hanna–Barbera's hugely successful *Flintstones* tv series but probably flopped because of the lack of an identifiable series character. The Animated Antics cartoons were testing grounds for various characters from the Fleischers' first feature movie, *Gulliver's Travels* (1939), to see if any of them were capable of graduating to become a series star: the answer was no, except in the case of Gabby, a cheery little fellow who had been a town crier and general clown in the feature. Maybe even for Gabby the answer should have been no, because his series, started in 1940 with *King for a Day*, died in 1941 after only eight shorts.

The Fleischers were Disney's only real rivals as the 1930s wore on, and it was inevitable that, in the wake of Disney's *Snow White and the Seven Dwarfs* (1937), they should feel bound to respond. (They had actually tackled that story in 1933 with the Betty Boop cartoon *Snow-White*, one of the finest examples of Dave Fleischer's fertile inventiveness.) That response, *Gulliver's Travels*, received an astonishing amount of advance billing, so it was a crushing disappointment for all concerned, not least the Fleischers, when it proved on release to be just a little lackluster.

What there is of the plot is drawn approximately from the first part of Swift's original, covering Gulliver's time in Lilliput. Nowadays the movie is largely forgotten, although many of its images – especially that of the giant Gulliver surrounded by minuscule Lilliputians, and the sequence in which he tows the Blefuscan fleet – are surprisingly familiar, through their frequent appearance as stills; while the song "It's a Hap-Hap-Happy Day" has, thanks to being reprised frequently in Paramount animated shorts, the same quasi-traditional status as "Hi Ho, Hi Ho, It's Off to Work We Go." The reasons for its modern obscurity are not too hard to understand: although it enjoys a welter of often brilliant "business" – always Dave Fleischer's strength – it is singularly short of *event*, with perhaps the first three-quarters of the movie seeming to be prelude, and hardly a superfluity of action in the final quarter, which lacks any sense of climax. As for its dearth of accolade at the time of release, there is also the possibility that the movie's satire of two nations going to war over a complete trivium cut a little too deeply in 1939, when of course the cause of the looming war was anything *but* a trivium.

Hoppity Goes to Town (vt *Mr. Bug Goes to Town*; 1941), the Fleischers' second and final essay at a feature-length animation, is significantly better, and indeed is one of the great neglected masterpieces of animation's history. The plot is original to the

Gulliver's Travels (1939)

🎨color / animated ⏱ 74 minutes

Gulliver is stranded in Lilliput on the night before what should have been the wedding day of Lilliput's Princess Glory and Blefuscu's Prince David; however, a war has arisen between the two nations because Lilliput's King Little III and Blefuscu's King Bombo could not agree over the song to be sung at the ceremony. Gulliver, found on the beach by the excitable, irascible watchman Gabby, wakes just as Blefuscu mounts its first bombardment, and terrifies attackers and defenders alike. In due course he befriends the young royal lovers, declares the war is ridiculous and can be solved by singing the rival anthems simultaneously, tows away a newly attacking Blefuscan fleet, escapes assassination, and sails off into the sunset leaving behind two reconciled nations and a happy pair of lovers. (Based loosely on the first part of *Gulliver's Travels* (1726) by Jonathan Swift.)

Cel for *Hoppity Goes to Town* (1941), showing Smack the Mosquito. Photograph: S/R Laboratories.
© Republic Pictures.

Hoppity Goes to Town (1941)

(vt *Mr. Bug Goes to Tow*) ☙color / animated ◯ 78 minutes

The fence of a city garden is broken, so pedestrians on the sidewalk cut across the dilapidated lawn, endangering the bug community living there. The hub of the community is the bee Mr. Bumble's Honey Shop; his lovely daughter, Honey, is in love with the grasshopper Hoppity, due to soon return from his travels. But letching after Honey is vile capitalist C. Bagley Beetle, who has a home in the base of a monument above the garden; he tries to persuade Mr. Bumble to give him Honey's hand in marriage in return for the safety of a home on Beetle's estate. Hoppity returns, and love between him and Honey reignites, much to Beetle's fury; the latter and his inept sidekicks, Smack (a mosquito) and Swat (a fly), are determined to put an end to the romance, if necessary by putting an end to Hoppity.

The grasshopper proves to be a somewhat luckless do-gooder: soon after his return, he performs great heroics to put out a fire at the Honey Shop, only to inadvertently throw gasoline upon it instead of water. He is convinced the bugs can find a safe and lovely home in the house's upper garden, and leads them there; unfortunately, the householders — Mr. and Mrs. Dick Dickens — have an accident with a garden hose, and the bugs are all flooded back down to where they started from.

Hoppity overhears Dick Dickens perform a song he has written and the Dickenses discussing how the music publishers may pay a fat advance for it, allowing the Dickenses to repair the garden fence. He reports this to the other bugs. The Dickenses wait, but the check from the publishers doesn't come; this is not for the usual reason that checks from publishers don't come, but because Beetle and his henchmen have waylaid it and hidden it in a crevice. Hoppity is blamed by all the other bugs for the lack of fence-mending.

Because of the missing check, the Dickenses are forced to give up the house, and developers plan a skyscraper on the land. Beetle, learning of this, realizes that both the lower garden and his own property will soon be built over. He decides to tell Mr. Bumble only part of this, and to promise that *all* the bugs can come and live on his estate if Honey will marry him. Hoppity overhears Beetle scheming with his henchmen; to stop him from blabbing they seal him up in the envelope with the check and stuff it back in the crevice, leaving him to die. But he doesn't die: the envelope is freed as construction starts, just moments before Honey's marriage to Beetle would have been finalized.

Hoppity overhears the Dickenses, who have returned to the site for one last nostalgic look, talking about how they could build their dream house and garden atop the skyscraper if only the publisher's money ever turned up. Hoppity succeeds in getting the envelope with the check back into the mail, and in due course it reaches the Dickenses. Meanwhile, ever the optimist, he has persuaded the other bugs that their salvation and paradise lie at the top of the skyscraper under construction, and he leads them on a weeks-long, heroic and hair-raising ascent through the bricks and girders. Dick's song is released as a record, is a smash hit, and makes his fortune. By the time the bugs reach the top, the dream cottage and garden are indeed in place. All live happily ever after — except the three crooks, who are barred from Paradise.

movie, something which until recently has always been a rarity among animated features, and also has far more complexity and depth than one expects from an animated movie. It is actually a far more *mature* animated movie than anything Walt Disney managed to produce during his lifetime. This statement demands explanation. Walt's animated movies were always supremely conscious of the fact that they were *animated* movies, and thus subject to rules different from those for live-action movies. This is one of the great strengths of his animated features — if a movie could be made in live action, then it's almost by definition a poor animated movie, because animation is capable of so much more. Yet the majority of animated features would seem woefully simplistic as live-action movies for adults, their characters acting on the most puerile of motivations in plots that have little capacity to grip. This is in no way a criticism: a primary component of the fascination of an animated feature is this very self-consciousness, this joy in animation itself. What distinguishes *Hoppity Goes to Town* from its contemporaries, and indeed from most other animated features (although there are many counter examples in Japanese anime, as exemplified by most of the movies of Hayao Miyazaki), is that *it takes the medium of animation for granted*. Yes, this is an animated movie, but, if the technology of special effects were up to it, *Hoppity* could work equally well as a live-action movie. For an analogy, consider the Moog synthesizer. When this instrument first burst onto the scene, there were plenty of recordings whose purpose was to show off the tricks this technological marvel could perform — rather like most of the early animated movies, in fact. Only some while later did people start issuing recordings of the Moog being used for its true purpose: as a musical instrument. Likewise there is the sense all through *Hoppity* that this is a story being told via the medium of animation because the maker considered animation the most appropriate medium for telling this particular story, rather than the customary sense that the story has been tailored to fit the animated medium.

This characteristic is also one of the reasons why *Hoppity* is timeless. Yes, there are some details that mark it as a period piece — the style of the cars, or of the trousers worn by incidental human characters — but apart from these it could be the brand new release from Disney or DreamWorks. It is also quite brilliantly directed by Dave Fleischer. The "business" is fast and furious where it needs to be, the characterization is superb without necessarily being ostentatious, and the atmospheric big-scale shots are exquisite. The only human characters to have other than incidental parts, the Dickenses, never actually appear on screen; yet it is difficult to remember afterward that this is the case, so real have they been made by their dialogue, actions, and voice characterizations. Walt Disney was obviously aware of this movie when he made his *One Hundred and One Dalmatians* (1961), and of the parallels between the two; more to the point, the makers of *Antz* (1998) and *A Bug's Life* (1998) must have been thunderingly aware of it, because both movies, stripped to their very essentials, are variant riffs upon it.

There was to be one more major event before the spectacular demise of the Fleischer studios. Max bought the screen rights to the immensely popular *Superman* comic strip created by Jerry Siegel and Joe Shuster. The first of the resultant animated shorts was released just three months before *Hoppity*, after a massive promotional blitz aimed at portraying these to be the most spectacular shorts ever made. Viewing these movies today – they started with *Superman* (1941) – it is easy to see why they were so highly regarded at the time, and also, unfortunately, easy to see why they have so drastically dated. Rotoscoping was extensively used in an effort to make the characters as believable as possible, but at the same time, during the many action sequences, the speed of the characters' movements was accelerated with the aim of keeping the audience's pulses racing. Unfortunately, the overall effect is to make the characters very obviously artifacts of ink and celluloid, and there is also the uneasy sense that the film is being run through the projector too fast.

Even before the last of the Superman cartoons was released, the Fleischer studio was a thing of the past. The end came very suddenly, and various reasons, some less plausible than others, have been put forward for this. At the heart of the dissolution is certainly the fact that Max and Dave couldn't stand each other, and indeed went through long periods when they refused even to speak to each other; the blame for this must be put firmly at Max's door. All through their association he had sought to claim complete credit for everything they had done, and to Dave, the more talented of the two in matters of art, storytelling, and animation but not in matters of business management, this was intolerable: he regarded it as theft – which of course it was. Somewhere deep inside Max's subconscious there must have been the realization that Dave, had he been equipped with something so simple as a good business manager, was capable of being one of animation's brightest lights on his own, an option not open to Max himself. This must have fueled Max's resentment of his younger brother. Furthermore, it was beginning to be publicly realized that Dave, not Max, was the important member of the Fleischer setup. Even so, Max's arrogant conscious ignored or drowned out any messages from his subconscious when, late in 1941, around the time that *Hoppity* was undergoing its final edit, he sent a telegram to Paramount saying that under no circumstances would he ever consider working with Dave again, an ultimatum that was intended to signal the end for Dave. Big studios may often be stupid, but Paramount wasn't quite that stupid; knowing full well that Max by this time represented little more than an unnecessary paycheck, they descended on the Fleischer operation, and demanded early repayment of a hefty loan they had made to the studio. When

that repayment failed to materialize instantly, Paramount used this as a pretext to shut the operation down, hiring the key members of Max's staff out from under him – including even his son-in-law, animation director Seymour Kneitel – in order to set up Paramount's own animation division, Famous Studios, to continue where the Fleischers had left off.

After the demise of the Fleischer organization, Dave was snapped up almost immediately by Columbia to head the animation unit there, Screen Gems. He worked on the series *The Fox and the Crow*, which had been started by Frank Tashlin in 1941 with *The Fox and the Grapes*. Dave was instrumental in launching the Li'l Abner series of shorts, based on the Al Capp comic-strip character and begun with *Amoozin but Confoozin* (1944); the series flopped after only five shorts, by which time Dave, believing that office politics prohibited anything good ever coming out of Columbia's animation unit, had departed for Universal, this time to work not as an animator but as a general troubleshooter, writing gags, doing some special effects, and employing his expertise in the improvement of movies through adjustment of their timing and pacing. He remained with Universal until his retirement in 1967, his name turning up in the credits of some of the most unexpected movies, such as Alfred Hitchcock's *The Birds* (1963) and the Julie Andrews/Mary Tyler Moore vehicle *Thoroughly Modern Millie* (1967). He died in June 1979 in Los Angeles.

Max unsuccessfully tried to set up on his own. Then, with a few colleagues, he joined the James Handy organization to produce animated training movies. Other members of that organization were surprised by how poor the animations of Max and his friends were. He produced *Rudolph the Red-Nosed Reindeer* (1944), which has frequently been broadcast on television; he also put his name to (and may even have written) a book called *Noah's Shoes* (1944), which can be read as an allegorical attack on his brothers, particularly Dave. In 1955 he sued Paramount when they tried to televise the Fleischer shorts with adulterated credits; it seems the case was settled out of court. In 1958 he was appointed head of the art department at the old J.R. Bray studio. In 1961 he was involved in a half-hearted attempt to create a new Out of the Inkwell series. On September 11, 1972, he died in Woodland Hills, California, in the sheltered accommodation where he and his wife, Essie, had lived for the previous several years.

Joe Fleischer did some work for Famous Studios before quitting to become an electrical contractor. He died in Hollywood, Florida (not to be confused with the California Hollywood), in January 1979. Lou became a lens grinder, and in bitter irony found himself working in a menial position for the Ware Lens Grinding Company in the last of the buildings the Fleischer studio had occupied. Later he made a number of bouncing-ball training movies for the Army, then moved to California to become a piano teacher and tuner. In November 1985 he died in Woodland Hills.

FRIZ FRELENG (1904–1995)

Setup for *The Hare-Brained Hypnotist* (1942) showing Bugs
Bunny and Elmer Fudd. Photograph: Howard Lowery.
© Warner Bros.

Throughout his long career, Isadore Freleng called himself by
that name or as I. Freleng, but he is best known as Friz. He
was born on August 21, 1904, in Kansas City, Missouri, also
famous as the home of Walt Disney and Ub Iwerks. (Sources are
confused as to his year of birth, often giving 1905 or usually
1906; but, according to the Social Security Index, it was 1904.) In
1919 he went to Westport High School in Kansas City, there
drawing cartoons for school publications. He had no particular
art training aside from what he received in high school, but it was
obvious he had a great flair for cartooning. Among the part-time
jobs he took while still in high school were as a caddy at the
Kansas City Country Club and as an office boy at the Armour
Packing Company, in whose in-house magazine he also published
some cartoons.

Shortly after graduating from high school in 1923 he got a
job with the Kansas City Film Ad Company – which produced
commercials for cinemas – where he found himself working with
Ub Iwerks and Hugh Harman. Walt Disney, a recent employee,

had not long before left for California, and shortly afterward
Iwerks followed. Harman went to join Walt a year later, but not
before gaining a very favorable impression of the young Freleng,
whom he had trained in animation. For some time Freleng bore
the entire burden of the Kansas City Film Ad Company's
animation, doing every aspect of the job from animation through
inking and painting, and sometimes even having to operate the
camera himself. Not surprisingly, Harman strongly recommended
his protegé to Walt, and in 1927, when animator Ham Hamilton
quit Disney because of ill feelings between himself and Walt, the
summons came.

It was a heck of a jump for Freleng – not in terms of salary,
because it seems he took a pay cut, but of status and job interest:
he had gone from the fairly mindless and rudimentary animation

required by the Kansas City Film Ad Company to working on Oswald the Lucky Rabbit shorts and the Alice Comedies alongside fellow-animators Iwerks, Harman, and Rudolf Ising in a four-strong team. Here it was Iwerks rather than Harman who apparently took the young Freleng under his wing. But Freleng found it impossible to work with Walt and, after a while, quit, returning briefly to Kansas City and the Film Ad Company.

Shortly afterward, in 1928, Charles Mintz lured away most of Walt's best animators to a new studio he had set up, and at Harman's and Ising's suggestion Freleng was recruited to join them. Mintz's new studio did not last long. Founded on the basis that Oswald the Lucky Rabbit could with impunity be stolen away from Disney because the character had been copyrighted to Universal, it foundered when Universal's boss, Carl Laemmle, decided that Universal could animate its own character and took Oswald away from Mintz, hiring Walter Lantz to open the Universal animation studio. Freleng did some work on the Krazy Kat series before being recruited in 1929, again by Harman and Ising, to join them in a new venture they had set up with Leon Schlesinger to supply animated shorts to Warners.

Freleng had helped Harman and Ising on *Bosko the Talk-Ink Kid*, the pilot movie they had done for their Bosko series and the *raison d'être* for the business venture with Schlesinger. Bosko, an early sound animation star, was a black boy (black characters being quicker to animate than white ones because there was less need for lines in the drawing of the figure) of indeterminate age who enjoyed various fairly amiable adventures. Freleng animated a whole slew of the Bosko shorts, being credited on them as early as the first, *Sinkin' in the Bathtub* (1930). In *Bosko's Big Race* (1932), his presence is acknowledged through one of the dogs in the race being called Frizby. In addition, he animated other Harman–Ising series characters, including Foxy & Roxy, Piggy & Fluffy and Goopy Geer. Beginning in 1933 with *Bosko in Dutch*, he also directed (uncredited) two or three of the Bosko shorts.

But 1933 was a year containing a development for Freleng even more momentous than directing his first cartoons. Harman and Ising fell out with Schlesinger over money and departed, taking Bosko with them. Schlesinger was left with an animation studio, a contract with Warners to produce cartoons, and the copyright to two animated series – the Looney Tunes and the Merrie Melodies – but no one to direct his animation. Accordingly, he promoted Freleng to animation director of both Looney Tunes and Merrie Melodies. This was an enormous responsibility for a relatively inexperienced animator; leaving aside the responsibility, the pressure of work must have been intimidating on its own. Luckily, the situation didn't last long. Rapidly Schlesinger brought in others, raiding Disney to recruit Jack King and Tom Palmer. The latter proved incapable of producing what Warners wanted, and so Freleng brought in Ben Hardaway and Tubby Millar, two men who had worked with him back in the Kansas City Film Ad Company days.

ain't Nature Grand? (1930)

🎞 b/w / animated ⏱ 6³/₄ minutes
Looney Tunes/Bosko
Animated by Freleng with Norm Blackburn, this has various gags strung around a fishing expedition: a bird chases one of Bosko's worms, Bosko himself chases a butterfly, a pair of bees improvise a plane and a Gatling gun to chase Bosko, etc. Plotless, this relies fully on the fascination audiences of the day had toward sound cartoons, although, aside from a few words from Bosko, there is only a musical soundtrack.

I Haven't Got a Hat (1935)

🎞 color / animated ⏱ 7 minutes
Merrie Melodies/Porky Pig
The first appearance of Porky Pig, in what seems to have been intended as a talent show to find a new Warners series star; the others here to make an impression, but only in a small way, were the scampish little black cat, Beans, and the two cute puppies, Ham & Ex. The pretext is a classroom musicale. It was not actually a particularly auspicious debut for Porky; the short would doubtless have been wisely forgotten were it not for the fact that it was his first.

Rhapsody in Rivets (1941)

🎞 color / animated ⏱ 7¹/₂ minutes
Merrie Melodies
At a building site the foreman, complete with a Stokowski-style mane of hair, conducts the workers as they construct a building to the strains of adapted excerpts from Liszt's Hungarian Rhapsody #2; thus a deep phrase on the cello accords with a man sawing through an upright beam, etc. The animation is splendidly rich, and the surreal sight gags plentiful. One of the workers is a near ringer for MGM's/Tex Avery's Droopy; at quitting time, as he closes the door of the skyscraper they have just finished building, it collapses in a heap of rubble.

Pigs in a Polka (1943)

🎞 color / animated ⏱ 7³/₄ minutes
Merrie Melodies
The story of the Three Little Pigs done to extracts from, mainly, Brahms's Hungarian Dances. The Big Bad Wolf makes use of disguises — a sexy female gypsy dancer, an old violinist in the snow (provided by talcum powder) — and these fool Fiddler and Fifer Pig. Their straw and matchstick houses destroyed in turn, they seek refuge in Practical Pig's stone house, which though only two stories high has by the end of the short developed an elevator shaft, into which the Wolf is lured.

Daffy – The Commando (1943)

♮color / animated ⏱ 7¼ minutes
Looney Tunes/Daffy Duck
In his bunker somewhere on the front, Uberlieutenant Von Vulture receives a telegram from the Gestapo telling him on no account must he let one more Allied commando get through. Moments later he hears a plane overhead, and he and his diminutive sidekick turn a searchlight to the sky, where they pick up a parachuting Daffy Duck. After standard frolics, the duck flies as a human cannonball all the way to the Fatherland, alighting beside a rotoscoped Hitler, who is addressing a rally. Daffy bops him on the head with a mallet. One of the Warners wartime propaganda efforts, this was afterward, curiously, considered too provocative to be shown on U.S. television.

Life With Feathers (1945)

♮color / animated ⏱ 7¾ minutes
Merrie Melodies/Sylvester
The first appearance of Sylvester. A little blue lovebird whose wife no longer loves him decides to end it all by offering himself up to a cat, and chooses Sylvester. But Sylvester is too suspicious of the bird's motives to accept the sacrifice, and the short becomes an interesting converse of the traditional cat-chasing-bird scenario, with the bird trying all kinds of inventive stratagems to get himself eaten.

Hare Trigger (1945)

♮color / animated with brief line action ⏱ 7½ minutes
Merrie Melodies/Bugs Bunny/Yosemite Sam
In the Wild West, Yosemite Sam is a noted robber of mail trains: Bugs is a passenger aboard a mail train who disrupts a holdup using sight-gags: a contest to see who can draw a gun quickest requires pencil and paper, etc. At one point Bugs opens the door on the club car to reveal a live-action Western saloon in full swing; when he returns later, the scene has been transformed into an almighty punch-up, into the midst of which he bamboozles Sam.

Tweetie Pie (1947)

♮color / animated ⏱ 7 minutes
Merrie Melodies/Tweety & Sylvester
The first time Tweety (his name misspelled) and Sylvester (although here called Thomas) teamed up, and Warners's first Oscar-winning animated movie. A householder rescues Tweety from Sylvester's clutches and installs him in a luxurious cage. That night Sylvester tries everything to steal the bird from the high cage, in between being roundly beaten by his mistress as she is drawn downstairs by the racket.

Schlesinger had another problem. While the Merrie Melodies were independent of each other, the Looney Tunes had traditionally had a series star. Since Bosko was no longer available, Schlesinger had to cast around, eventually coming up with the notion of Buddy, who was much the same as Bosko, but white. The great criticism of Bosko had always been that he had no personality; the same was true twicefold of Buddy. But somehow, though the animation team despised them even as they worked on them, the Buddy shorts trundled on for a couple of years and helped Schlesinger's studio out of a deep hole.

Freleng directed many of the Buddy cartoons, but it had already become evident that he had a particular flair for handling musical shorts. From *Goin' to Heaven on a Mule*, released in May 1934, to *The Cat Came Back*, released in February 1936, Freleng directed all but one of the Merrie Melodies (the exception was 1935's *Rhythm in Bow*, done by Hardaway). Thereafter, he continued to do the vast majority of them, despite occasional contributions from Tex Avery, until 1937, when Freleng left for MGM. During his brief absence – he returned to the Schlesinger fold in 1939 – the load was taken on by, aside from Avery and Hardaway, Frank Tashlin and Chuck Jones. One of Freleng's 1935 Merrie Melodies, *I Haven't Got a Hat*, had been responsible for producing the new series star that Schlesinger had been searching for: Porky Pig.

Freleng's stay at MGM was not only short but also not especially happy. He had been lured away from Schlesinger by MGM's Fred Quimby with the promise of more money, bigger budgets, and artistic freedom. Quimby kept his promise about the first two, but on arrival at MGM Freleng discovered that Quimby had bought the screen rights in Rudolph Dirks's strip cartoon *The Katzenjammer Kids* for a series to be called Captain and the Kids, and that he, Freleng, was expected to direct on this. Freleng's immediate reaction was that the series was doomed from the outset – at the time the public wanted talking animals, not cartoon humans – and he was proven correct: despite those bigger budgets and the fact that the cartoons (with one color exception, they were done in sepia tone) were in fact quite good, the series died in early 1939 after only fifteen releases. Nevertheless, the short relationship with MGM was beneficial to both parties: Freleng was an early influence on one of his co-directors, William Hanna, who would remain with MGM and eventually, with Joseph Barbera, create the Tom & Jerry series; and Freleng himself benefited from the greater animating discipline required for the more complex task of working with the Captain and the Kids shorts: on his return to the Schlesinger studio his style and technique had noticeably improved.

Although Freleng participated in the early development of the character Bugs Bunny – his first Bugs cartoon was *Hiawatha's Rabbit Hunt* (1941) – it was really as a director of animated musicals that he continued to thrive. His *Rhapsody in Rivets* (1941) was nominated for an Oscar, as was *Hiawatha's Rabbit Hunt*: both lost out to Disney's *Lend a Paw*, and comparing the three one can't

Still from *Roman Legion Hare* (1955) showing Yosemite Sam.
© Warner Bros.

help but feel that *Rhapsody in Rivets* was robbed. Two further musicals of Freleng's were nominated for Oscars in subsequent years; *Pigs in a Polka* (1943) and *Rhapsody Rabbit* (1946). The tale goes that Freleng rather more literally *was* robbed in the latter instance. According to the story, the processing labs at Technicolor accidentally delivered *Rhapsody Rabbit* to MGM, where Hanna and Barbera were working on the similar *The Cat Concerto* (1947). (The Warners cartoon has Bugs in concert trying to play Liszt piano music but hampered by the antics of a mouse; in the MGM cartoon Tom is doing much the same and is bedeviled by Jerry.) Screening the Warners movie out of curiosity, the team at MGM recognized both the similarity and that their cartoon was likely to be regarded as an imitation of Freleng's. They therefore rushed work on *The Cat Concerto*. Although they did not succeed in having it released ahead of *Rhapsody Rabbit*, the two were eligible for Oscars in the same year. During the judging for nominees, the cartoons were shown in alphabetical order, so the impression given was that *Rhapsody Rabbit* was imitating *The Cat Concerto*! In the end, the MGM cartoon was not only nominated but won.

In terms of character creation, Freleng is renowned more for his genius in developing other directors' characters than for his ability to create new ones himself. This is not to say that he did

Back Alley Oproar (1948)

🎨 color / animated ⏱ 7¹/₂ minutes
Merrie Melodies/Sylvester/Elmer Fudd
Alleycat Sylvester gives a vocal recital outside the window where Elmer is trying to sleep, and Elmer's stratagems to get him to shut up escalate exponentially from the traditional thrown boots, and Sylvester's musical retaliations likewise. Finally Elmer resorts to dynamite, blows himself up and goes to Heaven; on finding the Heavenly Chorus consists of cats, he opts instead for The Other Place.

This is an elaborated color remake of *Notes to You* (1941), also directed by Freleng, which featured Porky Pig and an anonymous cat in place of Elmer and Sylvester.

Speedy Gonzales (1955)

🔊 color / animated ⏱ 6½ minutes
Merrie Melodies/Speedy Gonzales/Sylvester

An Oscar-winning short. Across the border from Mexico is the Ajax Cheese Company, and Mexican mice gather at the fence to sniff, but dare not cross because of gringo border guard Sylvester. One mouse proclaims that the only mouse who could get the cheese is Speedy Gonzales, and comments: "I know Speedy Gonzales. He's a friend of my seester." Another retorts: "Speedy Gonzales, he's a friend of *everybody's* seester!" (The joke was to reappear in other Speedy shorts.) So Speedy is summoned and commences to ferry cheese from the factory back through the fence to the waiting mice. Sylvester deploys a fishing net, mousetraps, landmines, etc., in his attempts to stop the raids, each time being hoist by his own petard. Finally he blows up the cheese so Speedy can't get it, but the fragments of cheese rain down on the delighted mice on the far side of the fence.

Birds Anonymous (1957)

🔊 color / animated ⏱ 6¾ minutes
Merrie Melodies/Tweety & Sylvester

An Oscar-winning short. Sylvester is, as usual, after Tweety when he is interrupted by a pompous cat from Birds Anonymous, Sam, who explains how eating "just one" bird leads to two, and then to lots and finally the end of the road. Sylvester obediently attends a meeting at Birds Anonymous HQ in Halligan's Alley. Of course, the first thing he sees on tv when he gets home is a cooking program extolling the delights of roast turkey, but still his self-control holds. He switches on the radio: "Bye, Bye Blackbird" has just finished and the next song is to be "When the Red, Red Robin Comes Bob, Bob, Bobbin' Along." He handcuffs himself to a radiator, but in a fit of weakness pulls it from the floor and is about to devour Tweety when Sam intervenes . . . only to find himself likewise relapsing into bird addiction.

Knighty Knight Bugs (1958)

🔊 color / animated ⏱ 6½ minutes
Looney Tunes/Bugs Bunny/Yosemite Sam

An Oscar-winning short. "Ever since the accursed Black Knight captured our Singing Sword," says Arthur to the Knights of the Round Table, "evil times hath befallen us." Court Jester Bugs is sent under threat of death to tackle Black Knight Yosemite Sam and his dragon. Bugs steals the sword, despite its propensity to indeed sing at inopportune moments, and succeeds also in taking possession of the Black Knight's castle. The siege to get the castle back is predictably accident-prone, though the sightgags are excellent and superbly timed. In the end, the Black Knight and dragon are confined in the arsenal, the dragon sneezes, and the tower is blasted off spaceship-style into space.

not contribute major new characters to the Warners stable. The short that introduced Porky Pig to the world – *I Haven't Got a Hat* – featured a lineup of other potential Warners stars: taking the form of one of those gruesome classroom exercises whereby each kid has to present an "act" of some kind, it was, in effect, a testing ground for them. Of Porky, Freleng later wrote:

> When I was a kid, I had two playmates – a little fat kid called Piggy and his younger brother who was called Porky. I always wanted to do a comic strip with two kids with those names. But in animation, everything is animals, so when I had this classroom cartoon, I thought of Porky.

Of course, "Porky Pig" is not the most original of names, but *this* Porky is special not just because he went on to star and co-star in many Warners shorts – almost as many as Bugs Bunny, in fact – but also because he became the emblem of the studio some years before Bugs appeared on the scene, and, although overshadowed by Bugs, has to an extent remained so. For a long time, few Warners cartoons seemed complete without Porky's sign-off (voiced by Mel Blanc), "Th-th-th-that's all, folks!"

Another series character introduced in *I Haven't Got a Hat* was Beans, a cheeky little black cat. He had a couple of cartoons of his own, both done in 1935 by Jack King – *A Cartoonist's Nightmare* and *Hollywood Capers* – and thereafter made a number of others in supporting roles with Porky. Beans also made a couple of shorts with Ham & Ex, a pair of impudent puppies who likewise debuted in *I Haven't Got a Hat*.

Later on, in *Golden Yeggs* (1950), Freleng created another supporting actor, the diminutive gangster Rocky. Though Rocky is actually a very funny character, he appeared in only four more cartoons: *Catty Cornered* (1953) with Tweety & Sylvester, in which Rocky's hulking lamebrain sidekick, Mugsy, was introduced, and the remainder with Bugs. Hugely more important was a character Freleng created much later. By his own account, he had become bored with Elmer Fudd as a constant adversary of Bugs Bunny. Yosemite Sam first appeared in rather different form (and unnamed) in *Stage Door Cartoon* (1944), but his real debut was in *Hare Trigger* (1945). He didn't actually change much thereafter, there being little scope for personality development in a character whose sole attributes, aside from his red moustache and his Lone Ranger mask, were his diminutive size, his roar of a voice, and the fact that he was in a constant fury, but that doesn't matter: he was (and is) funny enough just like that. He was the perfect foil for the intellectual, trickster-ish Bugs, even more so than Daffy who, while perfectly capable of throwing a tantrum of his own, was actually hindered by the fact that he too had more than a shred of intelligence, however perverted. What personality Sam does have has been attributed to various sources, but the most important one is Freleng himself: Freleng was a small man with a red moustache (although nothing like as magnificent as Sam's), a loud voice, and an explosive temper. He was obviously loved by his

Still from *The Three Little Bops* (1957).
© Warner Bros.

fellow directors, much as Sam was loved by the public, although in Freleng's case there was more than just these attributes to love. Chuck Jones summed it up after Freleng's death: "He was a giant, in my best estimation, and it is hard to recognize a giant in your midst when he is only five foot four."

Yosemite Sam is a perennial favorite but, as noted, it was really in the development of existing characters that Freleng flourished. His version of Bugs Bunny is generally less cerebral than Jones's but is far less of a manic zany than either Avery's or Robert McKimson's. In a short like *Knighty Knight Bugs* (1958), for which Freleng won one of his Oscars, we see his treatment of the rabbit in both guises. Initially Bugs is the Court Fool – and anyone who knows their Shakespeare will tell you that the zaniness of such a character conceals intellect and wisdom. Through much of the short Bugs is a quick-witted zany, and perhaps too confident in his quickness of wit for his own good: he is surprised at the ease with which he performs the set task of stealing back the Singing Sword from Yosemite Sam and the dragon, whereas a wiser individual would be suspicious that this task, which has already claimed the lives of some of the Knights of the Round Table, had been *too* easy. In the finale, Bugs's overconfidence is shown, at least to him, to have been justified after all as, himself unscathed and his foes confounded, he strolls off languidly homeward.

Sylvester the cat was another creation of Freleng's but, "Sufferin' succotash!" and all, he looked to be destined for the same scrapheap as Beans and Ham & Ex before Freleng, in conjunction with Robert Clampett, developed him in a direction that today seems obvious but at the time may have seemed anything but. Over at MGM, Hanna and Barbera had been going great guns with their Tom & Jerry series, whose mainspring is Tom's obsession with catching Jerry, not as a mouse which he might eat but as *that particular mouse* – which is to say that there is an established relationship between them. Sylvester, while an appealing enough character in his early shorts – begun with Freleng's *Life with Feathers* (1945) – had nothing especially distinctive about him: he didn't seem a strong enough character to assume the burden of series star. In short, he was a Tom without the Jerry.

Somewhat earlier, in 1942's *A Tale of Two Kitties*, Clampett had introduced the little canary Tweety, who obviously had considerable potential for further use but nevertheless was disqualified from series-star status because his appeal – which was huge – was derived primarily from his wide-eyed, naïf helplessness.

Shocking Pink (1965)

↳color /animated ⏱ 6¹/₂ minutes
Pink Panther
The Panther is lazing in his hammock when a pompous voice-over goads him into embarking on some home improvements. There is a running gag with a basement lightbulb that goes off each time the Panther is halfway down to fetch his tools and then he tumbles. His attempts at carpentry lead to the back of the house falling off. His attempts to fix a dripping shower cause floods. In the end he digs out and loads a blunderbuss, to the voice-over's rising panic; but in fact the Panther blasts the lightbulb.

Friz Freleng's Looney Looney Looney Bugs Bunny Movie (1981)

(vt Looney Looney Looney Bugs Bunny Movie)
↳color /animated with some live-action clips
⏱ 76 minutes
Knighty Knight Bugs (1958) serves as a prologue to this celebration of Freleng's work at Warners, primarily his work with Bugs.

Act I, Satan's Waitin', initially sees Yosemite Sam planning evilly to marry and thereafter fleece a rich widow, a plot which Bugs thwarts by disguising himself as the widow and causing confusion and mayhem. One final prank lands Sam in Hell, where the Devil offers him a deal: he may go back to Earth so long as he sends someone (and Sam immediately decides on Bugs) to Hell in his place. Sam is restored successively as a Roman guard, as a traveler in the Sahara Desert and as a Wild West outlaw, but each time Bugs bests him and Sam finds himself back in Hell. The Devil offers him one last chance to return to Earth, but Sam prefers to stay in Hell rather than face the Rabbit again. Shorts extracted or adapted are Hare Trimmed (1953), Roman Legion Hare (1955), Sahara Hare (1955), Wild and Wooly Hare (1959), and Devil's Feud Cake (1963).

Act II, The Unmentionables, has as its frame a parody of The Untouchables , with Bugs as Elegant Ness battling the gang led by minuscule mobster chief Rocky. Shorts extracted or adapted are Golden Yeggs (1950), Catty Cornered (1953) and The Unmentionables (1963).

In Act III, The Oswald Awards, there are brief cameos from Pepe Le Pew, Porky, the Three Little Pigs, the Big Bad Wolf, Foghorn Leghorn, Yosemite Sam, Tweety Pie, Sylvester, and Daffy, before Bugs appears to act as host for the awards ceremony. The ceremony is an excuse to show clips from old shorts: extracted or adapted are The Three Little Bops (1957), Birds Anonymous (1957), High Diving Hare (1949), and Show Biz Bugs (1957).

A series star has to be a doer in some way and, if you turned Tweety into a doer, he'd become a different personality and in the process lose most of his appeal.

It was Clampett who spotted that a solution to the dual problem might be to pair the two characters, and he actually mapped out the short Tweetie Pie (1947) before leaving Warners. However, it was Freleng who so magnificently put the pairing into practice: he picked up a well deserved Oscar for that initial short and went on to direct the vast majority of the long string of further Tweety & Sylvester cartoons, picking up another Oscar for what is probably the best of them all, Birds Anonymous (1957). Again, although Clampett initiated the catchline "I tawt I taw a puddy tat. I did! I did tee a puddy tat!," it was Freleng who elevated it to the status of universal catchphrase: there was even, in 1950, a hit record based on it. What Freleng had done was produce a pairing of characters from which both characters benefited. Although Sylvester starred in many further shorts without the canary – some of them with McKimson's creation Hippety Hopper – it was as a vastly strengthened screen personality due to the "Tweety experience." (Interestingly, it is almost unimaginable that Tom could pursue a solo career; he needs Jerry.)

The other major character that Freleng took over was Speedy Gonzales, created by Robert McKimson in Cat-Tails for Two (1953). Freleng seems to have been convinced that Speedy had little interest in his own right, and after both men had done a few shorts with him – the best is probably McKimson's Tabasco Road (1957) – paired him up with Sylvester, presumably with the idea in mind of creating another cat-and-mouse team. The Speedy & Sylvester shorts that both men created thereafter are, with the exception of the Oscar-winning first, Freleng's Speedy Gonzales (1955), good enough cartoons but have nothing especially memorable about them. Later team-ups with Daffy Duck under the DePatie–Freleng umbrella, mainly done by McKimson, suffer the same difficulty – not least because the budgets had by then been slashed and Daffy turned into something of a mindless villain. It is conceivable that Freleng's initial judgment of Speedy Gonzales was wrong, and that the character would have been best left as a solo performer. He was another Warners star to receive the accolade of a hit record.

Warners closed its animation studio in 1962 (some work trickled on into 1963), although the writing had been on the wall for some while before that: limited animation, earlier used for effect, had now become the norm for reasons of cost, and there is a sense of fatigue in many of the later Warners shorts. Chuck Jones departed for a stint at MGM directing Tom & Jerry cartoons. Freleng did some further work for Warners on the live-action/animated feature The Incredible Mr. Limpet (1964), although he left the project after the storyboarding stage, leaving the animation direction to others, among them Bill Tytla. He did a little work for Hanna–Barbera, notably as an animator on the feature Hey There It's Yogi Bear (1964), but this was obviously a bit of a step down for the man who had been Warners' longest-serving and most prolific director, and his heart appears not to have been in it.

Much more exciting was an idea hatched by the Warners executive David DePatie: to open a new animation company using the facilities that Warners no longer required. He and Freleng were able to lease the old studio from Warners and so establish DePatie–Freleng Enterprises to continue producing animation. An irony came just a matter of months later when the Warners bosses decided they had been hasty in ceasing production of animated shorts, and found that, in order to produce any more, they had to contract with DePatie–Freleng. This agreement gave Freleng further opportunity to work with all his old favorites among the Warners stars except Bugs and Porky, but the budget allowed for each short was something like half what it had been, and the inspiration seems to have flagged to match the budget.

Besides, there was something much more important to think about. One of DePatie–Freleng's first commissions was from Blake Edwards, to produce animated titles for his forthcoming live-action movie *The Pink Panther* (1963). There is at least some truth in the occasional bitchy comment that this movie owed its success less to the live action than to the credits, which immediately established the animated Pink Panther (who has no counterpart in the movie proper beyond the name) as a star – indeed, an icon. Accordingly United Artists/Mirisch commissioned from DePatie–Freleng a series of theatrical shorts featuring the character. That series continued virtually unabated until 1977, with Freleng gaining an Oscar for the first of them, *The Pink Phink* (1964). In 1978–79, ABC screened *The All New Pink Panther Show*, which did indeed feature fresh animation; over thirty of the shorts produced for it were later given a theatrical outing. Starring alongside the Panther in many of these was a character called The Inspector, clearly based on Peter Sellers's portrayal of Clouseau but for copyright reasons not identified by that name. Earlier tv appearances for the Panther had been in *The Pink Panther Show*, which ran on NBC in various forms under that title and as *The New Pink Panther Show* and *The Pink Panther Laugh and a Half Hour and a Half Show* from 1969 to 1979. Later on, Hanna–Barbera tried with limited success to revive the character in *Pink Panther and Sons*, which ran on NBC and then ABC during 1984–86.

The essence of the Pink Panther shorts is that they are, for all intents and purposes, silent movies, aside from sound effects and Henry Mancini's addictive theme. In a few, there are voice-overs or even elementary dialogue, and in a couple the Panther himself actually speaks, but the principle holds true: such stories as the Pink Panther shorts – usually a series of gag variations on a theme – are told visually rather than verbally. Running gags are another characteristic, allowing for a fair amount of repeated animation; and there are further economies through the use of extremely stark, stylized backgrounds, limited animation, and a highly restricted cast of characters – often the Panther himself is the sole character of any note throughout a short. Part of the humor is Mancini's theme, which continues unperturbed no matter what the mayhem being shown on-screen. But there is perhaps even more to Mancini's contribution than that. There is something very Gallic and understated, very *French*, about the humor of the series as a whole (these are the kind of shorts Jacques Tati, the French comic and moviemaker, might have made) – far from the frenetic activity of the Warners cartoons at their peak – and it is at least arguable that the jaunty theme contributed to this, insofar as it inhibited the animators from the glorious excesses of action more typical of the *American* commercial animated short.

Other DePatie–Freleng series included The Tijuana Toads, Blue Racer, Roland Ratfink, The Dogfather, The Barkleys, The Ant & the Aardvark, and Hoot Kloot. None achieved anything like the success of the Pink Panther.

In 1969, Warners abandoned the distribution of animated shorts, and that meant the end of the DePatie–Freleng Looney Tunes and Merrie Melodies. In 1980, David DePatie announced he was leaving the partnership to run a new animation division of Marvel Comics. Freleng, for his part, returned yet again to Warners to direct animated television specials as well as a couple of feature-length quasi-compilations, *Friz Freleng's Looney Looney Looney Bugs Bunny Movie* (vt *Looney Looney Looney Bugs Bunny Movie*; 1981) and *Daffy Duck's Movie: Fantastic Island* (vt *Daffy Duck's Fantastic Island*; 1983). He also produced and co-directed the feature-length *Bugs Bunny's 3rd Movie: 1001 Rabbit Tales* (1982).

Friz Freleng died in Los Angeles on May 26, 1995. In addition to his five Oscars, he had won three Emmy Awards, for the Dr. Seuss tv specials *Hallowe'en Is Grinch Night* (1977) and *The Grinch Grinches the Cat in the Hat* (1982), and for the live-action/animated educational ABC After School Special *My Mom's Having a Baby* (1977). But – by sufferin' succotash – more valuable surely than any award must be the laughter and delight accorded to his work by untold millions of viewers all over the world.

TERRY GILLIAM (1940–)

Born in Medicine Lake, near Minneapolis, Minnesota, on November 22, 1940, into a strictly Presbyterian family, Terrence Vance Gilliam has earned an international reputation as a director of live-action feature movies, including *Time Bandits* (1981), *Brazil* (1985), *The Adventures of Baron Munchausen* (1989), *The Fisher King* (1991), *Twelve Monkeys* (1995), and, most recently, *Fear and Loathing in Las Vegas* (1998), with *Good Omens*, based on the novel by Terry Pratchett and Neil Gaiman, reportedly on the way for 2002. It is easy to forget that he first made his name as an animator, and that his brief spell working in the field has been disproportionately influential on other practitioners of the art. His animation once led to him being described as the "Fred Astaire of modern Surrealism," a description that (appropriately for discussion of Surrealism?) makes no sense on closer examination, but which nonetheless somehow seems to fit perfectly.

Fairy tales formed an important part of his life from early childhood onward. Moreover, he began to draw from an early age. After the family moved to Panorama City, California, in 1951, he began to absorb the movies in great quantity, allying his enthusiasm for them with that for his drawing. He therefore was particularly entranced by animation, especially the Disney movies *Snow White and the Seven Dwarfs* (1937) and, most of all, *Pinocchio* (1940). After graduating from Birmingham High School he moved on to Occidental College, initially to read physics but after a few weeks switching to art, then to political science and finally to architecture. Away from his studies he was developing his cartooning, not least to the benefit of the college magazine, *Fang*, which he began to fill with cartoons heavily influenced by *Mad* magazine.

A few months after graduating from Occidental College he went to New York, where in 1962 he got a job as assistant editor on the humor magazine *Help!*, a job that lasted until *Help!* folded three years later. In the evenings he worked for free at menial tasks in a stop-motion studio; during the day he was handling the work of cartoonists like Gilbert Shelton and Robert Crumb. He was also directing comedy photostrips, *fumetti* (like comic strips, but using photographs), often with friends and acquaintances as actors – one friend-of-a-friend proved on arrival to be Woody Allen. More to the point, it was through the *fumetti* that he met John Cleese, then playing alongside various members of what would later be the Goodies and the Pythons in *Cambridge Circus*, a revue mounted by the Cambridge Footlights. Gilliam was also experimenting in an amateur way with animation, using the method pioneered by Norman McLaren of drawing directly onto blank film stock.

After *Help!* folded, he hitchhiked around Europe for a few months, in passing doing a little work for René Goscinny, co-creator of Asterix the Gaul, at *Pilote* magazine in Paris. On return to New York he survived very briefly in children's illustration before heading back to California, where he and Joel Siegel produced a graphic book, *The Cocktail People* (1966), for which

Still (detail) from *Monty Python and the Holy Grail* (1975). © Python (Monty) Pictures Ltd.

Gilliam supplied the illustrations. Thereafter they both worked for an advertising agency, Gilliam as art director and copywriter. He didn't last long before a combination of race riots, the Vietnam War, police brutality, a British girlfriend, the threat of the draft and the fact that a number of major movie directors had recently moved to Britain convinced Gilliam that he should do likewise, even though his involvement in the movies was as yet only a dream.

On arrival in London he contacted Cleese, who put him in touch with tv producer Humphrey Barclay, then working on the satirical children's comedy program *Do Not Adjust Your Set*. Among others involved with the show in one way or another were Eric Idle, Terry Jones, and Michael Palin. Barclay bought some of Gilliam's sketch scripts and also got him a job as resident caricaturist on the comedy chat show *We Have Ways of Making You Laugh*, hosted by Frank Muir. While working on the show he got the chance to do his first professional animating. Radio DJ Jimmy Young specialized in links full of deliberately groan-worthy humor, and one of the staff writers had compiled a tape of this. Gilliam suggested the way to use it on television was to allow him to make an accompanying animated movie. Given minimal budget and a tight deadline, the only form of animation he could choose was the mode that later became his hallmark, cutting out photographs, his own drawings, and other materials and filming them in what was essentially stop-motion.

The result got an extremely good audience reaction. Gilliam was commissioned to do further animation for *We Have Ways of Making You Laugh* and also for Barclay's *Do Not Adjust Your Set*. A few commissions from other tv shows followed, as did the job of producing animated titles for the Vincent Price movie *Cry of the Banshee* (1970). He was also asked to join a group – comprising Cleese, Idle, Jones, Palin, and Graham Chapman – that was then, at the behest of BBC comedy consultant Barry Took, doing preliminary work on a new series, eventually called *Monty Python's Flying Circus*. This ran 1969–70 and 1972–74, in its 1974 season being called simply *Monty Python*.

It is often little realized how fundamentally important a component Gilliam's animation was to this iconoclastic, groundbreaking show. Before it there had been plenty of shows made up of comedy sketches, but in those each sketch had been in effect a short movie, building up to a punchline that acted almost as the permission to move on to the next discrete sketch. The Pythons were eager to get away from the punchline mentality, but simply stringing together unpunchlined sketches would have led to an unsatisfying chaos. One stratagem the Pythons used to avoid this was the "And now for something completely different" link, but what really held the whole enterprise together were Gilliam's animated sequences. These started with the opening titles, animated to John Philip Sousa's march *The Liberty Bell*. The art was drawn from a mixture of artistic styles – not surprisingly, since often enough what were being used were cutouts from the Old Masters and the like, combined with airbrushed backgrounds and additional details. Elsewhere Gilliam's sound effects were usually indefinably obscene grunts, squeaks, and so on that somehow perfectly complemented the rather clunking movements on-screen. For reasons that are not easy to pin down the whole effect was on occasion excruciatingly funny but, more than that, it gave the show a visual style and coherence that emphatically declared its differentness from other tv offerings.

Gilliam's animations, some re-filmed, reappeared in the first of the Monty Python movies, *And Now for Something Completely Different* (1971), which is essentially a compilation of re-made highlights from the tv show. He was also commissioned for some 25 minutes of animation for the U.S. tv show *The Marty Feldman Comedy Machine*, a half-hour sketch show that aired on ABC for a few months in 1972 and starred, apart from Feldman himself, such luminaries as Spike Milligan and Orson Welles.

Immediately afterward it was back to work with the Pythons, this time on their first "real" movie, *Monty Python and the Holy Grail* (1975). Here the animation serves a more important function, often taking over the storytelling. The reason may have been partly financial: the movie's budget was under $500,000, so there wasn't much left over for special effects.

All of this time Gilliam had been somewhat discontented with being cast in the role of animator. His appetite for animation had been further soured by some particularly asinine censorship that ABC had imposed upon him during his stint for *The Marty Feldman Comedy Machine*. He had certainly had a long-time interest in animation, and he largely enjoyed doing it, but the movies' real attraction for him was and always had been the prospect of directing live action. Accordingly, when the Pythons were trying to work out who should direct *Monty Python and the Holy Grail*, he leaped at the opportunity of codirecting with Terry Jones. From there on he never looked back. He did some more animation for *Monty Python's Life of Brian* (1979) and *Monty Python's The Meaning of Life* (1983), but essentially his career has since then been as a live-action director – and a brilliant one at that.

Reflections of the animations that Gilliam did while with the Pythons can be found in much modern work, not so much in terms of the Surrealism as in the finding of beauty in the ugly. Gilliam has often explained that, working under hectic pressure as he almost always was, he didn't have the time for beauty: he had to settle for the crude, the rough and ready. Yet time and again in his animation we find something exceptionally lovely in grotesque figures that lumber jerkily in movements that should lack grace altogether but somehow are possessed of *great* grace.

PAUL GRIMAULT (1905–1994)

Born in Neuilly-sur-Seine, near Paris, on March 23, 1905, Paul Grimault was an animator who managed to produce work that was at one and the same time highly commercial in its appearance and yet, in its affect, often more like fine art. For this he may have had to thank the influence of his early association with German Surrealist painter Max Ernst; another early associate was the great French comic and moviemaker Jacques Tati.

Trained as a graphic designer at the School of Applied Arts in Paris, he worked for a while as a store designer. Friends, including Jean Anouilh, advised him to turn his hand to animation, and in 1936 he and André Sarrut founded a production company, Les Gémeaux, to produce short animated films for advertising. Grimault's first solo attempt at a movie outside this was never completed at all – it was to be called *Monsieur Pipe* – but in 1941, under German Occupation, he took scraps from an advertising short done for Air France and reconstituted them as the short *Les passagers de la Grande Ourse* ('Passengers of Ursa Major'). Although the Occupation obviously inhibited further progress, this can be seen as one of the first of a new wave in French animation. Before World War II the work of

French animators had been rather like that of their Hollywood counterparts a few years earlier, generally being just extensions of comics art, made to move and put up on screen. Immediately after the Occupation was over, however, Grimault was one of a group of French animators who eagerly pushed out the edges of the envelope, incorporating the disciplines of the graphic arts and bringing a new richness to the screen; another noteworthy characteristic of Grimault's own animation is that his direction owes more to the traditions of live-action movies than to those of animated cinema.

Among the shorts that he produced in the postwar years are *Le marchand de notes* ('The Note Seller'; 1942), *L'épouvantail* ('The Scarecrow'; 1943), *Le voleur de paratonnerres* ('The Stealer of Lightning Conductors'; 1945) and *La flûte magique* ('The Magic Flute'; 1946); the latter two feature a series character called Niglo, as does *Les passagers de la Grande Ourse*. *Le petit soldat* ('The Little Soldier'; 1947) is based on the Hans Christian Andersen story about the doll falling in love with the brave little toy soldier.

Les Gémeaux had employed for the design on *Le petit soldat* an old friend of Grimault's, Jacques Prévert, and immediately after they'd finished that movie, in 1946, the two men together started work on a feature, *La bergère et le ramoneur* (*The Shepherdess and the Chimneysweep*; 1953), again based on an Andersen story. Those familiar with the saga of Richard Williams's *The Thief and the Cobbler* (1995) will have an uneasy sense of recognition about what happened next. The years went by and still *La bergère et le ramoneur* remained unfinished. Finally, with the movie still only three-quarters done and money seeming just to vanish into the project with no perceptible benefit, Sarrut, Grimault's partner in Les Gémeaux, tired of the constant delays, and in 1953 pushed out onto the marketplace an unfinished version of the movie, which both Grimault and Prévert disowned. Widely anticipated to be the great breakthrough for French animation, *La bergère et le ramoneur* did only modestly on the home market and less well than that abroad. The movie is nevertheless of interest. The setting in which the two lovers struggle for happiness is a world in which the proles are forced to lead a troglodytic existence underground while the aristocrats idle away their days in the sunshine above.

The experience with *La bergère et le ramoneur* shattered Grimault, and for nearly fifteen years he steered clear of animation, except for the 1958 educational short *La faim du monde* ('The World's Hunger'). But in 1967 he managed to obtain the original negative of *La bergère et le ramoneur* and realized that he had the opportunity to finish it. The task involved not just completing the missing sections but also doing extensive redesign, modernization of the style and story reconstruction, and it would take him well over a decade; in the interim he released the shorts *Le diamant* ('The Diamond'; 1970) and *Le chien mélomane* ('The Dog who Loved Music'; 1973), the latter concerning nuclear warfare.

Finally, in 1980, his revised and expanded version of *La bergère et le ramoneur* was ready for release. The emphasis of the story had changed quite a bit so that the central figure was now a big black bird that befriended the lovers. Accordingly the title

Le roi et l'oiseaux (1980)

(vt *The King and Mr. Bird*)

🕭 color / animated ⏱ 87 minutes

The kingdom of Takicardie is ruled by "King Charles V & III is VIII and VIII is XVI." He commissions a painter for a portrait; despite being advised to draw a cage around the central figure before he starts work, the painter neglects to do so, with the result that the painted king — Charles's damned soul — escapes from the picture, destroys the real king, and takes his place to institute a tyranny. Also painted were a shepherdess and a chimneysweep, and they too come alive; they love each other, but the tyrant has conceived a passion for the shepherdess, and so the two lovers must flee, pursued by the king's police and aided only by a mockingbird who has made his nest on a turret of the King's palace and who befriends them. In the end, the common folk are freed from the tyrant and the lovers live happily ever after.

was changed as well. *Le roi et l'oiseau* (*The King and Mr. Bird*), as it was now called, premiered in 1980, and was at once acclaimed as the great breakthrough in French animation that it had been anticipated to be over a quarter of a century earlier.

Grimault's only other feature movie, *La Table Tournante* ('The Turning Table'; 1988), uses a frame which is largely live-action as a means of bringing together re-edited versions of his main animated shorts.

Grimault has more than once been described as France's Walt Disney, although he was never an entrepreneur or mogul in the sense that Walt was. By contrast, he seems to have maintained throughout his life the feeling that animation was a personalized matter, more suitable for cottage industry than big business. Countless young animators came to him for advice and have since written warmly of his open-hearted generosity in helping them, among them such figures as Andreas Déja, George Dunning, Jean-François Laguionie and Ihab Shakir.

Paul Grimault, a great animator and perhaps an even greater man, died in Paris on March 29, 1994.

HALAS & BATCHELOR

John Halas (1912–1995)   Joy Batchelor (1914–1991)

Setup for *Hamilton in the Music Festival* (1962).
Photograph: S/R Laboratories. © Halas & Batchelor.

John Halas was born Janos Halász on April 16, 1912, in Budapest, Hungary. As a young man he moved to Paris and was apprenticed to George Pal. Having learned the techniques of animation, he came to Britain in 1936, meeting Joy Batchelor in that year; after a brief return to Hungary, Halas settled in his new country, marrying Batchelor, just before the outbreak of World War II. Joy Batchelor was born in Watford, Hertfordshire, on May 12, 1914, and attended the local art college. She became a commercial artist and screenwriter; it was while she was working on *Music Man* (1938) that she met Halas. The two formed a graphic-design team at the start of the war and did advertising work for the J. Walter Thompson agency before being employed by the Ministry of Information to make propaganda and informational movies, which they did for the remainder of the war and even after. Their animation company, Halas & Batchelor Animation Ltd, was founded in 1940; it soon became the largest animation studio in Britain, and for some decades represented the sole British riposte to the U.S.A's Disney, producing seven animated features and about 2000 shorts. Much of this work was excellent; but most of it has been largely forgotten and is certainly poorly documented.

Typical of their wartime and postwar production was *Handling Ships* (1945), done for the Admiralty, and the Charley series of shorts, done for the Central Office of Information: Charley was a typical bloke used as a mouthpiece for the COI's messages about postwar legislation – *Charley's New Town* (1947) is an example. Other officially sponsored movies by Halas & Batchelor included such gems as *Dustbin Parade* (1942) and *Water for Firefighting*

(1948). But there were some lighter titles mixed in, including *Carnival in the Clothes Cupboard* (1941). For the Poet and Painter series, done for the Festival of Britain in 1951, work was specially commissioned from artists like Henry Moore and Mervyn Peake. Halas & Batchelor's full-scale return – almost a fresh entry – to civilian moviemaking is probably best dated back to *The Owl and the Pussycat* (1952), an experimental stereoscopic short based on the Edward Lear poem. *The Figurehead* (1953) was an affecting stop-motion puppet animation based on a Crosbie Garstin poem about a pining mermaid.

They first really came to public attention with *Animal Farm* (1955), the first animated feature movie ever made in Britain. Based on George Orwell's "fairy story," this is often misclassified as a movie exclusively for children; there must have been a lot of very bemused kids in Saturday-morning movie theaters. In this the movie resembles the book: just as Orwell took the *form* of the conventional talking-animal tale – traditionally a genre associated with children's literature – in order to present his satire more effectively, so Halas & Batchelor exploited the fact that animation is often considered merely a juvenile mode of cinema to make the satire of their own version more biting.

As with the book, it's a popular misconception that the movie is an attack on socialism/communism. In fact, it is nothing of the sort

– far from it, the socialist society set up by Snowball and the other animals in the aftermath of Jones's expulsion is presented as an ideal, not just as an improvement on the debased, exploitative capitalism it has replaced but as a paragon of social behavior. What is being savagely attacked by the fable is the corruption of that theoretically attainable ideal by greed and moral dishonesty, and its eventual degeneration into exactly the same kind of rotten capitalism that should have been extinguished with the revolution. Orwell's targets, and likewise this faithful interpretation's, were not socialism or even communism but tyranny and exploitation; that his depressed conclusion was that the baseness of human nature will forever make those triumph over and trample upon our ideals is no endorsement of capitalism – rather, it is a lament for what we could be were it not for the flaws within ourselves that are not so much tolerated as actively encouraged in capitalistic societies. If there is an anti-socialist or -communist message here it is this fatalistic one: the only trouble with communism is that, like the teaching of Jesus Christ, it doesn't work.

The movie was widely acclaimed on its release as a masterpiece; that this should be so in Britain was predictable for patriotic reasons, but U.S. critics were, if anything, even more enthusiastic. Viewed today, it is less than a masterpiece in terms of its animation – often somewhat primitive and not quite stylish enough for that to be an artistic strength – but it is still a significant (and highly enjoyable) piece of sophisticated moviemaking, showing that the Disney approach need not be limited to fairy tales or heartwarming stories.

Batchelor on her own was the director of the short (55-minute) feature *Ruddigore* (1967), based on a highly compressed version of the Gilbert & Sullivan operetta as performed by the D'Oyly Carte Opera Company and the Royal Philharmonic Orchestra; the character Robin Oakapple (played by John Reed) was called upon to give narration to cover up the compressions necessitated by D'Oyly Carte protectiveness. Despite the cuts in the libretto, *Ruddigore* is a charmingly done movie, with the animation reminiscent more of book illustration than the screen, and it is a great pity that it is rarely seen today.

There were other highlights during the 1960s and 1970s. *The Tales of Hoffnung* (1964) was a seven-part tv series animated by Halas and based on the tales and drawings of the great raconteur Gerard Hoffnung; it was amalgamated in 1965 as *The Hoffnung Symphony Orchestra*. Halas very much adhered to Hoffnung's own drawing style in these elegantly witty pieces. *The Butterfly Ball* (1974) was based on the best-selling illustrated book by Alan Aldridge and William Plomer, *The Butterfly Ball and the Grasshopper's Feast* (1973); very stylishly done, this can be seen as in the tradition of George Dunning's *Yellow Submarine* (1968). *Automania 2000* (1963) was a satire on Western Man's addiction to the car.

In the mid-1970s, Batchelor gave up any active participation in the studio's production, but Halas continued working well into the 1980s. Also in the mid-1970s the studio became one of the first to experiment with the then-futuristic technique of computer

Animal Farm (1955)

🎨 color / animated ⏱ 75 minutes

Manor Farm has fallen on hard times and its farmer, Jones, has turned to drink. Elderly prize pig Major, just before dying, prescribes a socialist utopia: "All animals are equal." Next morning, led by the pigs, the animals revolt, drive Jones off the farm, and, inspired by the genius pig Snowball and Major's precepts, take it over, renaming it Animal Farm. All goes well until Winter. Even then Snowball has a plan to cope; but the pig Napoleon, greedy for power and luxury, has him murdered and thereafter vilified as a traitor to the revolution. The new dictatorship the pigs establish systematically corrupts the tenets upon which Animal Farm was founded. Even when the loyal farmhorse Boxer, the inspiration of whose brawn and industry has done much to keep the revolution alive, is traded by the pigs to a glue factory, the other animals tolerate the tyranny. Only years later, when the identification of the pig tyrants with the previous human one is complete, do the animals once more rise up to cast out the oppressors. (Based on *Animal Farm: A Fairy Story* (1945) by George Orwell.)

animation, with shorts such as *Autobahn* (1979) and *Dilemma* (1981). But, in general, the later 1960s and the years thereafter were marked for the studio less by high-quality theatrical production and more by work for television, much of which was not of any great merit. The 78 five-minute shorts in the series *DoDo: The Kid from Outer Space* (1964) were at least the studio's own. The style of *DoDo* was akin to that of early Japanese anime such as *Astroboy*. But other, and generally mightily less distinguished, series were done for Rankin-Bass – *The Jackson 5ive* (1971–73) – *The Osmonds* (1972–74) – and Hanna–Barbera – *The Addams Family* (1973–75; better than most), *The Partridge Family: 2200AD* (1974–75). Although one kept reminding oneself that this commercial hackwork was financing higher things, it was nevertheless depressing to see the animators of *Animal Farm* and the rest reduced to such straits.

A later tv project of Halas's was the 1987 BBC series called (embarrassingly for the author of the current book) *Masters of Animation*; it and the book he wrote to accompany it are invaluable in casting light on a truly international lineup of animators, many of them undeservedly obscure at least insofar as mass appreciation of their work is concerned. At the time of writing, the videos of the tv series are still available.

Halas was also of note as an educator in animation, and he served as a director of ASIFA (Association Internationale du Film d'Animation, the international body promoting animation and animators); he was awarded an OBE in 1972. He died on the night of January 20, 1995, in London. His wife and long-time collaborator, Joy Batchelor, predeceased him, dying in London on May 14, 1991. In late 2000 a retrospective of their short work was released on video and DVD, and it is to be hoped this heralds an overdue revival of interest in this highly talented duo.

Hanna & Barbera

William Hanna (1910–2001)   Joseph Barbera (1911–)

Setup for *Jerry and Jumbo* (1953).
Photograph: S/R Laboratories. © MGM, Warner Bros.

William Denby Hanna was born on July 14, 1910, in Melrose, New Mexico, and less than a year later, on March 24, 1911, Joseph Roland Barbera was born in New York City. Between them the two men can be said to have founded television animation as . . . well, not so much an art as a science. For years, their company, Hanna–Barbera, had the field of tv animation – especially for children but with a strong adult audience – more or less to itself, and even today an astonishingly high proportion of tv animation bears the Hanna–Barbera logo. This dominance of the industry came about through a streamlining of the animation process at every level such that this

expensive and labor-intensive technique could make economic and scheduling sense in the television context. This inevitably led to a sharp decline in animation and story standards, even though the quality of character creation and gag-writing has on (increasingly rare) occasion been extremely high. It is hard, on being confronted by the enormous mountain of Hanna–Barbera tv series, often virtually indistinguishable from one another, to reconcile this with the fact that, earlier in their careers, the two men created some of the finest, funniest, and most lovingly crafted theatrical animated shorts of all time.

The Hanna family moved to Los Angeles in 1919. Hanna's father was a construction engineer, and it was while working with his father on the building of the Pantages Theater in Hollywood in 1929 that Hanna learned of the new animation studio Harman–Ising; this company had a contract with Leon Schlesinger, who in turn had just gained a contract with Warners to produce animated shorts. Although Hanna had no training in art, the notion sounded interesting. He applied for a lowly job with Harman–Ising and was taken on. In the youth of American commercial animation, there was always the opportunity for someone eager and industrious to make good, and it wasn't long before Hanna had risen to become head of the Harman–Ising ink-and-paint department. He also became recognized as a gagman and in due course storyman.

In 1933, Harman and Ising fell out with Schlesinger over budgets, and their company severed its connection with him. Although given the chance of joining the new organization that Schlesinger had rapidly put in place, Hanna chose to stick with Harman–Ising, even though the studio's future looked uncertain. After a short hiatus, in 1934 Harman–Ising landed a contract with MGM to continue producing shorts, now in a new series called Happy Harmonies. One of these, released in June 1936 and called *To Spring*, is of note in that it represents William Hanna's first short as a director. The honeymoon between Harman–Ising and MGM did not last long, however, and in 1937 the studio was once more out of employment as MGM decided it would establish its own in-house animation facility. Hanna, once bitten so twice shy, this time took up the offer of a position with the larger company – as a director of animation.

Barbera's road to MGM was more circuitous. Born in New York's Little Italy but brought up in Brooklyn, Barbera discovered his talent for drawing while still at school. After school he went to New York University and the American Institute of Banking, eventually getting a job with the Irving Trust Company. He looked set for a career on Wall Street. However, he was also taking art classes in his spare time, and he got into the habit of taking piles of his cartoons from one New York-based magazine to another during his lunch hours. His break into the market was a long time coming, but when it did it came from a prestigious quarter: *Collier's* magazine. Once the dam of editorial indifference had been breached, that first drop became a trickle and then a flow, and he was able to abandon his financial career to be a freelance sketch artist.

His real ideal was animation, though; aside from anything else, it offered higher pay and better job security. He had by now honed his drawing skills so that he could produce cartoons extremely quickly and fluidly, with the minimum number of strokes of the pen – an ideal qualification for any artist who seeks to become an animator. When Disney's *The Skeleton Dance* had come to New York in 1929, Barbera had been enthralled by it, and indeed had written to Walt Disney offering his services in any

Puss Gets the Boot (1940)

🎨 color / animated ⏱ 9 minutes
Tom & Jerry
The first Tom & Jerry cartoon, with Tom here called Jasper. Setting the pattern for the series, it has Tom/Jasper toying sadistically with Jerry prior to scarfing him. After smashing an ornament, Tom/Jasper is told by broom-wielding householder Mammy that, if he breaks one more item, he's going to be booted out. The game then becomes one of Jerry trying to break things so Tom/Jasper will get the blame, while the cat tries to stop them from being broken. It is a game Jerry emphatically wins.

Life with Tom (1953)

🎨 color / animated ⏱ 7³/₄ minutes
Tom & Jerry
Jerry has written a bestselling book, *Life with Tom*, and to Tom's fury all the neighborhood is laughing at Jerry's accounts of how he has constantly outsmarted the cat. This gives an excuse for the short to contain excerpts from various earlier Tom & Jerry shorts: *Cat Fishin'* (1947), *The Little Orphan* (1947), and *Kitty Foiled* (1948). Tom catches up with Jerry and prepares to exact awful revenge before Jerry shows him a check from the publisher for $25,000 in royalties, with half to go to Tom.

Hey There It's Yogi Bear (1964)

🎨 color / animated ⏱ 89 minutes
Spring springs and the bears of Jellystone Park emerge from hibernation, the cue for various quests to begin: that of Yogi to purloin the picnickers' food, that of Ranger Smith to stop him, and that of cutesy Cindy Bear to romantically ensnare Yogi. When one of Yogi's "sicklekological" tricks fails, Smith arranges for him to be shipped off to the San Diego Zoo. Yogi fools dimwit bear Corn Pone into going in his place, and adopts a new role as the dread Brown Phantom, stealing the trippers' food like never before. Cindy, pining, tricks Smith into also sending her to the zoo — but unknown to her he sends her to the St. Louis Zoo. Partway there, her cage bounces off the train and she is kidnapped by Chizzling Bros Circus and press-ganged into a high-wire act. Yogi emerges from pseudonymity just in time to discover this, and the rest of the movie follows his and buddy Boo Boo's quest to rescue Cindy from the circus and bring her home — via, improbably, New York — to Jellystone Park.

appropriate capacity. Walt actually replied to this letter, saying he would look Barbera up the next time he was in New York, but – not unnaturally for a man who at the time was being bombarded by applications from thousands of teenage hopefuls all over the country – forgot all about it. Meanwhile Barbera landed himself a job with the Fleischer studios in Manhattan, only

Cel for an unidentified short showing Dastardly and Muttley.
Private collection. © Hanna-Barbera, Warner Bros.

Oliver and the Artful Dodger
(1972) tvm

🎨 color / animated ⏱ 72 minutes

A sequel to Charles Dickens's *Oliver Twist* (1839). The Artful Dodger has forsworn crime, and he and his gang now make their living as best they can by trading salvaged metal on the streets of London, as a sideline thwarting the efforts of Mr. Bumble to increase his income by seizing unwilling children for his orphanage. Oliver, in the meantime, has been living in comfort with Mr. Brownlow. Brownlow dies halfway through telling Oliver that he has left him everything in a will hidden in a secret drawer in his bedchamber. But Brownlow's disowned, crooked nephew, Sam Sniperly, arrives, takes over the establishment, and sells all the furniture (including the bedroom furniture), casting Oliver and housekeeper Mrs. Puddy out on the street. Oliver calls on his old pal Dodger to help him find the furniture, the secret drawer, and the will. Oliver and the Dodger trace the furniture to the establishment of Master Dreadly, in rural Dreadly-on-Thames, where they go — pursued by Sniperly, who hopes to find the will first and destroy it. At grim Dreadly House they discover Mistress Dreadly friendly to their cause, but not Master Dreadly; nevertheless, they find the will and, after many complications evading Sniperly, get it back to London. With his new wealth Oliver buys back the Brownlow house for an orphanage. Dodger, however, realizes a life of comfort is not for him and returns to the streets.

to discover that there was no real future for him there; he lasted just four days. Undeterred, he applied for and got a job at the Van Beuren studios, then operating out of the Bronx and releasing its generally rather mediocre product through RKO.

If history is anything to go by, the best place for a novice animator to start is with a second-rate studio, where there's scope for a meteoric rise through the ranks and then, often, a rapid departure for somewhere more prestigious. Barbera was no exception: within a few months of joining Van Beuren he was elevated to become an animator, with particular responsibilities as a storyman; a few months after that Van Beuren lost its contract with RKO and, in 1936, closed down.

Unceremoniously out on the street, Barbera decided to go to California to seek his fortune among the richer animation pickings there, specifically at Disney. However, the New York State-based animator Paul Terry, hearing of his plans, snapped him up for Terrytoons. According to Barbera in later life, this was because Terry had become infuriated by Disney's habit of hiring away from him all of his best animators, and so was keen to get one back wherever he could. What Terry could not have foreseen was that the next raid on his human resources would come not from Disney but from a wholly unexpected quarter: MGM's new animation studio, headed by long-serving and reportedly humorless MGM executive Fred C. Quimby. Quimby knew nothing about animation but a good deal about the ruthless exercise of big-corporation power. He promptly hired most of the Harman–Ising staff, including Hanna, out from under Harman and Ising, then called an old friend in New York, Jack Zander, now working at Terrytoons, and told him to do the same to Paul Terry. Lured by bright prospects and higher salaries, Terry's staff, Barbera included, complied. Quimby also hired Friz Freleng from Schlesinger, although Freleng's stay was brief.

Quimby's regime at MGM began disastrously. The same mentality that had plundered other studios for staff now assumed that simply bringing a hugely popular comic strip to the screen would inevitably produce a hugely popular animated series, and so he bought the rights in Rudolf Dirks's *The Katzenjammer Kids* without any thought as to whether or not it was a suitable subject for animation. In the end, the team Quimby had thrown together made a pretty good attempt at it, but the cartoons flopped nevertheless: what the public wanted at the time was funny animals. Moreover, adequately animating the strip's human characters required considerably more time and effort than animating funny animals, so the cartoons were expensive. Quimby, floundering, turned to another newspaper cartoonist, Milt Gross, and then to another, Harry Hershfield, both times without success. He finally was reduced to begging Harman and Ising to return.

Legends abound of the miseries of working at the MGM animation studio around this time. Factionalism was rife, the main factional split being between those animators whose roots were on the West Coast and those who had been imported from the East Coast. Hanna was demoted from his position as an animation director to a storyman; Barbera, who had joined up as a member of Friz Freleng's team, had to watch as the great man first was frustrated by Quimby's stubborn foolishness and then departed. It was obvious to both of them that the studio could not last long as it was. One day Hanna and Barbera, who up until that time had worked little together but who had become friends, for want of anything better to do sat down and fooled around with some ideas for a cartoon of their own.

That cartoon was eventually made and was released as *Puss Gets the Boot* (1940). It featured a cat called Jasper and a mouse called Jerry, and, although Hanna and Barbera were not mentioned in the credits (just Rudolf Ising as producer), it was their movie. Soon the cat would be renamed Tom. A legend had been born.

In the eye of memory, the Tom & Jerry cartoons might seem like just an endless collection of chase movies, inventively constructed and brilliantly timed, but essentially all much of the same. They are actually considerably more than that. Leaving aside those shorts that diverged wildly from the series format, what was so strong about them was that, from the very outset, there was a *relationship* established between Tom and Jerry; in order for there to be a relationship, the two had to have *characters*. There was also an interesting piece of psychological inversion involved: although Jerry, the mouse, is the character we want to triumph over the much larger and often sadistic Tom, and we cheer him on as he does so, in fact it is *Tom* with whom we generally identify. The obsessed cat has all the foibles that we associate with ourselves, and caricatures on the screen our own reactions to life's many frustrations, to the clever plans of our own that go awry. It is Tom's cringe that you are likely to see people mimic, not Jerry's tiny strut. If Tom were an idiot this identification would not take place, but Tom is not: although ever outwitted by the mouse, he is himself intelligent – albeit frequently guilty of the stupidities that intelligence brings with it, notably through overconfidence in his own abilities. Moreover, although we always know that Jerry will win the contest in the end, in strictly logical terms this is by no means a foregone conclusion: Jerry has no special powers (like, say, Speedy Gonzales's speed) that might make his victory inevitable, but instead is just a plucky little mouse who must rely on quick wits and happenstance, often the latter, to pull him out of each new scrape. Thus there is a dramatic tension in each of the Tom & Jerry shorts *despite* our foreknowledge of the conclusion.

There was also great inventiveness on the part of Hanna and Barbera, and a lightning sense of pace and timing, which became even more pronounced after Tex Avery joined the MGM unit in 1941. This showed the rest of the animators there just how fast-moving an animated short could be. Unlike most animated series, which tend to reach their heights after the first few years and then begin to taper off in terms of quality and inventiveness as their creators get bored, run out of ideas, or become desperate – most often all three – the average standard of the Hanna & Barbera Tom & Jerry shorts actually continued to improve as time went on. And what a standard it was! Between

Charlotte's Web (1973)

♭color / animated ◷ 96 minutes
Farmer's daughter Fern saves the runt of a pig litter from being put down and keeps him as a pet, naming him Wilbur. When Wilbur is older he is sold to Fern's Uncle Homer on the neighboring farm, but she comes to visit every day and soon learns to understand the animals there. Wilbur discovers he is merely being fattened up for slaughter. The spider who lives in the corner of the barn door, Charlotte, takes pity on him and plots to save his life. This she does by weaving words into her web so that he comes to be regarded as a miraculous pig. Uncle Homer and family take him to the fair, where he is awarded a special prize; in accepting it, Uncle Homer swears he shall never slaughter Wilbur. (Based on the book *Charlotte's Web* (1952) by E.B. White.)

The Jetsons Meet the Flintstones (1987) tvm

♭color / animated ◷ 95 minutes
Elroy Jetson invents a time machine and catapults himself and his family into the remote past, where they arrive near Bedrock City and encounter the Flintstones and the Rubbles. But then a further mishap sends the two prehistoric families into the future, where they find themselves taking over the Jetsons' roles. Both sets of stranded "temponauts" must cobble together new time machines to restore the *status quo*.

Yogi Bear and the Magical Flight of the Spruce Goose (1987) tvm

♭color / animated (with brief live-action section in b/w) ◷ 92 minutes
Various Hanna–Barbera stock characters — Yogi Bear, Boo Boo, Huckleberry Hound, Quick Draw McGraw, Snagglepuss, Augie Doggie, and Doggie Daddy — visit an exhibit containing the "largest plane ever built" (by Howard Hughes), the *Spruce Goose*, and get locked inside it together with an unwitting stowaway, feisty fem-libber tot Bernice. Fiddling with the controls, Yogi achieves a magical takeoff, and soon all are bound for the South Pole (also called the Arctic). Adventures are had with invading aliens, sharks, a latter-day Noah's Ark, and the Dread Baron and his dog Mumbly (essentially Dastardly and Muttley). Finally, just as magically as it left, the *Spruce Goose* arrives back in its bay . . . and the characters wake from a deep sleep. It has all been a dream — or has it?

Yogi's Great Escape (1987) tvm

♭color / animated ◷ 94 minutes

Three bear-cub orphans are dumped on Yogi's doorstep as spring starts. Ranger Smith gets news Jellystone Park is to close and the bears to be distributed to zoos. Yogi, Boo Boo, and the orphans flee in a car Yogi has made from junk. The Ranger, with the incompetent Snapper the Trapper and his dog Yapper, pursues. Gangs of kids befriend and aid the fugitives, who do a sort of U.S. Grand Tour in search of a new home. After they've had adventures with Quick Draw McGraw, Wally Gator, Snagglepuss, etc., Jellystone Park is reprieved by the president and the pals return home.

Yogi and the Invasion of the Space Bears (1988) tvm

♭color / animated ◷ 90 minutes

UFOnauts abduct Yogi and Boo Boo from Jellystone Park — having seen the bears trick picnickers out of food, they assume bears are Earth's most intelligent species. They duplicate Yogi and Boo Boo and put an army of duplicates ("duploids") back into the park, their eventual plan being to take over Earth. Naturally Cindy Bear, Yogi's heartthrob, sees the difference immediately, and the rangers aren't far behind when they see duploid Yogis and Boo Boos — in triplicate — passing up free eats. After much space chasing, the two bears get home and the duploids are deactivated; they're finally disposed of through Yogi and Boo Boo selling them to the tourists as souvenirs.

Jetsons: The Movie (1990)

♭color / animated ◷ 82 minutes

The new asteroid mining operation run by Spacely Sprockets is bedeviled by sabotage, and boss Mr. Spacely sends confirmed loser George Jetson out to take over. Jetson arrives accompanied by wife Jane, teen daughter Judy, small son Elroy, dog Astro, and robot Rosie. With the help of a child alien and a child robot, Elroy discovers that the saboteurs are cuddly Ewok-style aliens whose underground civilization is being destroyed by the mining. The Jetsons persuade Mr. Spacely to enter a partnership with the aliens for the future environment-friendly running of the mine. In the midst of this lies a good piece of semi-abstract animation done by Kurtz & Friends to accompany the song "You and Me," one of several performed by chanteuse Tiffany, who also voices Judy.

1940 and 1952 no fewer than 13 Tom & Jerry shorts were nominated for Oscars, of which seven won: *Yankee Doodle Mouse* in 1943, *Mouse Trouble* in 1944, *Quiet Please* in 1945, *The Cat Concerto* in 1946, *The Little Orphan* in 1948, *The Two Mouseketeers* in 1951, and *Johann Mouse* in 1952. In all the history of animation there has never been anything quite like that run of success. (Although it was not a Tom & Jerry movie, the two men also directed the 1955 nominee *Good Will to Men*.)

The mid-1950s saw television begin to erode more and more the need for the animated theatrical short — indeed, for the theatrical short in general. Animated shorts, being relatively expensive to produce, were the hardest hit as the studios cut back their costs in response to the general decline of cinema audiences. MGM decided to bow out of the contest in 1957, even though its animation unit could be considered among the most flourishing of all. Hanna and Barbera could have chosen to take their talents to one of the other studios — there would have been no shortage of takers, even though of course Tom & Jerry wouldn't have been part of the package, being MGM's property. Instead the two men opted neither to fight nor to retreat from the powerful new medium but instead to embrace it — indeed, to do so wholeheartedly. They set up the company Hanna–Barbera with the specific purpose of producing animated programing for television.

The first series they prepared (for NBC) was *The Ruff and Reddy Show*. This was a half-hour show and consisted mainly of old Columbia theatrical shorts; however, each week's presentation featured an original 5-minute short starring the dog and cat team of Ruff and Reddy as they fought the denizens of Evil in the form of characters like Captain Greedy and Scary Harry Safari. Although the show was broadcast in black-and-white until 1959, Hanna and Barbera had the foresight to make the cartoons in color from the outset, even though this cost more — not at all a typical Hanna–Barbera trait! This of course paid dividends in the long and even not so long term, as further royalties accrued from re-screenings.

To a great extent the story of William Hanna and Joseph Barbera as masters of animation really ends here, because very little they did hereafter has much merit as animation. With every possible corner cut in the animation process in order to produce screen fodder at the prices the tv networks were prepared to offer, the countless Hanna–Barbera series offer very few moments of visual splendor and a plethora of moments of visual banality, with pieces of animation being recycled in a further attempt to save time and costs. Moreover, Hanna and Barbera themselves rapidly retreated from being animation directors, becoming instead producers. It was a contest between commerce and art, and from the very outset Hanna and Barbera assumed that commerce would win and acted accordingly.

Yet to dismiss their efforts quite so abruptly would be to ignore the many strengths the Hanna-Barbera series displayed for some further decades. We recall that both Hanna and Barbera rose to animation directorship through the story

Setup for *The Creation* (1984) showing Adam and Eve in the Garden. Private collection. © Hanna–Barbera, Warner Bros.

Arabian Nights (1994) tvm

(vt *Scooby-Doo's Arabian Nights*; vt *Scooby-Doo in Arabian Nights*)

♫color /animated ⏱ 69 minutes

Scooby-Doo and Shaggy get a job as the Caliph's food tasters but, misunderstanding, devour all his lunch. Under sentence of death they hide in the harem, where the shortsighted Caliph determines to take a disguised Shaggy as his bride. To stall, Shaggy, Scheherezade-style, tells stories. First up is that of Aliyah-Din and the Magic Lamp, featuring Yogi Bear and Boo Boo as the Genie and his apprentice and based on the Aladdin tale (plus a dash of the Douglas Fairbanks *Thief of Bagdad* [1924]) but with a Cinderella-style female protagonist who eventually marries the Sultan's heir. In the second tale, which has a tenuous connection with the original, Magilla Gorilla stars as Sinbad the Sailor. The conclusion has Scooby and Shaggy spared execution and hired as the Caliph's official storytellers.

Jonny Quest Versus the Cyber Insects (1995) tvm

♫color /animated ⏱ 90 minutes

Unknown foes are threatening Earth via climatic changes, swarms of insects, armies of armed, man-size, carnivorous insects, and various murderous mechanical insects. In the vanguard of the defense is Quest Team — Jonny; Jonny's father, Dr. Benton Quest; Roger "Race" Bannon; Race's daughter, Jessie; Hadji, an Indian pal; Dr. Eve Belage, a medical scientist aboard the Quests' space station; Bandit, Jonny's dog; 4DAC, their robot. The arch-villain, set on global domination, proves to be the psychopathic Dr. Zin, based in an "asteroid fortress." Zin seizes samples of a lethal prehistoric bug Bellage has regenerated from fossil DNA and clones a gigantic, near indestructible variant, which can recreate itself manifold, like a Hydra's head, from its own exploded body fragments. Jonny and Jessie lead the fighting and outwitting to destroy the assassins and thwart Zin. Having saved Earth, the gang escapes just as Zin's asteroid stronghold explodes . . . but Zin escapes, too, to scheme another day.

department, with both men — especially Barbera — being noteworthy as gag writers. It is therefore not surprising that some of the dialogue within the series verges on brilliance — complete with genuinely catchy catchphrases plus many great one-liners — or that some of the material put out by the company during what one might think of as the Golden Age of Hanna–Barbera stands among the funniest cartoons of all time. Moreover, Hanna and Barbera showed that the genius in character creation they had displayed with Tom & Jerry was no fluke: characters such as Yogi Bear and The Flintstones are brilliantly realized, even if the brushstrokes are often broad.

There was one further achievement that often goes unnoticed. With a running time of perhaps 22 minutes, each episode of *The Flintstones* or *Yogi Bear* is, in theatrical terms, a featurette. Many studios have tried to make featurettes and some of these efforts have been truly excellent, yet it is exceedingly rare to find a featurette that is consistently funny throughout. But this was what Hanna–Barbera attained on our television screens repeatedly through these series.

Creations of note in the Hanna–Barbera series have been (with their dates of first airing) *The Huckleberry Hound Show* (1958), *Quick Draw McGraw* (1959), *The Flintstones* (1960), *Top Cat* (1961), *The Yogi Bear Show* (1961), *The Jetsons* (1962), *The Adventures of Jonny Quest* (1964), *Shazzan!* (1967), *The New Adventures of Huck Finn* (1968), *Dastardly and Muttley and their Flying Machines* (1969), *Scooby-Doo, Where Are You?* (1969), *Wacky Races* (1970), *The Addams Family* (1973), and *Hong Kong Phooey* (1974). There have been literally scores of others, many of them short-lived and all too many of them dire; a few were done in conjunction with Halas & Batchelor. There has also been a scattering of feature movies, some theatrical and some for television, but mostly spun off from the tv series. Of special note is the hour-long tv special *Alice in Wonderland, or What's a Nice Kid Like You Doing in a Place Like This*, which aired on ABC on March 30, 1966, with a voice cast including Sammy Davis Jr. (Cheshire Cat) and Zsa Zsa Gabor (Queen of Hearts), plus Mel Blanc and Alan Reed voicing a two-headed caterpillar as per Barney and Fred from *The Flintstones*.

The studio's first venture into theatrical features was *Hey There It's Yogi Bear* (1964), a charming movie that is difficult to reconcile with so much of the lackluster, grudging material they produced for television. The animation is, for the most part, reasonably simple, but this is a matter of Hanna–Barbera playing to their strengths, for it is generally superb within that context. Moreover, when greater complexity is called for, the studio is not found wanting: enormous care is expended on, particularly, the backgrounds of Jellystone Park. There is, too, excellent characterization: the two circus owners, Snively and Grifter Chizzling (voiced by J. Pat O'Malley and Mel Blanc respectively), and their dog, Mugger (Muttley, of Dastardly and Muttley, in another guise), are wonderfully funny villains, while Julie Bennett's voice characterization of Cindy Bear is a virtual showstopper. All through the movie there's a genuine affection on display for the characters, and this gives what should, on the face of it, be an ephemeral, completely lighthearted movie a significant emotional affect. Most of the song routines are very funny, generally being parodies of the Disney song routines. All in all, this is Hanna–Barbera at their best, and it compares favorably with some of the best produced by the other commercial studios.

Charlotte's Web, done in 1973 and released theatrically, is another worthwhile effort, this time quite different in style from the usual rapid-gag Hanna–Barbera product; although the animation is not sophisticated, the retelling of E.B. White's classic children's story is pleasant and fairly sensitive to the mood of the original. Done for television the previous year, *Oliver and the Artful Dodger* (1972 tvm)

is another movie cast from other than the standard Hanna–Barbera mold, being an extension of Dickens's story. The animation is somewhat rudimentary and, in particular, the lip-sync is sometimes appalling, but the overall effect is pretty enough. There's an integrity to the production – as if writers, directors, animators, songwriters, and voice actors alike were at least *attempting* to produce the best movie they could. In short, although far from a classic, it doesn't have the mass-produced, cynical aspect of so many of the other Hanna–Barbera productions. Unfortunately, the same cannot be said of exercises like *The Jetsons Meet the Flintstones* (1987 tvm) and *Jetsons: The Movie* (1990).

In the late 1980s, there appeared a group of Yogi Bear television movies about which the best that can be said is that they're not as bad as might have been expected. Perhaps the foremost of this little flurry is *Yogi and the Invasion of the Space Bears* (1988 tvm), which has variable animation but some pretty backgrounds – although the recycling of various bits of "business" from *Hey There It's Yogi Bear* is tiresome. There has also been the still continuing series of Scooby-Doo television movies: *Scooby-Doo Meets the Boo Brothers* (1987 tvm), *Scooby-Doo and the Ghoul School* (1988 tvm), *Scooby-Doo and the Reluctant Werewolf* (1989 tvm), *Scooby-Doo on Zombie Island* (1998 tvm), *Scooby-Doo and the Witch's Ghost* (1999 tvm) and *Scooby-Doo and the Alien Invaders* (2000 tvm), with the theatrical movie *Scooby-Doo* scheduled for a 2001 release. To the list must be added *Arabian Nights* (1994; vt *Scooby-Doo's Arabian Nights*; vt *Scooby-Doo in Arabian Nights*), although it also features a diversity of other Hanna–Barbera characters. In the latter the animation is so limited as to be outright simplistic and often seems out of focus; despite this the direction, characterization, and screenplay of the first of its two tales are quite good, although the influence of Disney's *Aladdin* (1992) is rather too obvious in parts of the animation. Jonny Quest has spawned a couple of tv movies – *Jonny's Golden Quest* (1993 tvm) and *Jonny Quest Versus the Cyber Insects* (1995 tvm) – which are marginally better than the Scooby-Doo movies.

Nestling like a jewel among this stuff are the thirteen featurette-length movies in the series Greatest Adventure Stories from the Bible, released in 1984 direct to video and containing some of the best of Hanna–Barbera's later animation: *The Creation, Noah's Ark, Moses, Jonah, David and Goliath, Joshua and the Battle of Jericho, Daniel and the Lion's Den, Joseph and His Brothers, Queen Esther, Samson and Delilah, The Nativity, The Miracle of Jesus*, and *The Easter Story*. This series represents, of course, a tremendously shrewd piece of commercial moviemaking – the videos have sold consistently well ever since their release – but the movies do not *feel* cynically produced: they are surprisingly enjoyable, even for non-Christians.

Such is the paradox of William Hanna and Joseph Barbera, who achieved great heights in their animation . . . and then chose to abandon them.

William Hanna died on March 22, 2001, at his home in North Hollywood, California.

HARMAN & ISING

Hugh Harman (1903–1982)   Rudolf Ising (1903–1992)

Still from *Peace on Earth* (1939). © MGM, Warner Bros.

Hugh Harman and Rudolf Ising played a very important pioneering role in the early days of American commercial animation. They were among the core group of animators Walt Disney gathered around him as he made his initial steps toward revolutionizing commercial animation, and they played a major part in the inauguration of two other great animation studios: those of Warners and MGM.

Hugh N. Harman was born on August 31, 1903, in Pagosa Springs, Colorado, and died on November 25, 1982, in Beverly Hills, California. Rudolf Ising was born on August 7, 1903, in Kansas City, Missouri, and died of cancer on July 18, 1992, in Newport Beach,

California. Both men were more than once nominated for Oscars, and in 1941 Rudolf Ising won one with *The Milky Way* (1940).

Both of them worked at the Kansas City Film Ad Company in the early 1920s, alongside Walt Disney and Ub Iwerks, and also animated on Walt's Laugh-O-grams. They were early emigrants to California to join Walt in the animation of his Alice Comedies and then the Oswald the Lucky Rabbit shorts. Their time with Walt

Smile, Darn Ya, Smile (1931)

color / animated ⏱ 7 minutes
Merrie Melodies/Foxy

Owing a lot to Disney's first Oswald the Lucky Rabbit short, *Trolley Troubles* (1927), this sees Foxy having various scrapes and japes as a trolley-car conductor. His favorite passenger is his girlfriend, Roxy, a lady fox. At the end, after a nightmarish rollercoaster ride along the trolley tracks, Foxy awakens in his own bed: it has all been a dream. The title song was much later reused to great effect in *Who Framed Roger Rabbit* (1988). Foxy appeared in two other shorts: *Lady, Play Your Mandolin!* (1931) and *One More Time* (1931).

Shuffle Off to Buffalo (1933)

b/w / animated ⏱ 6¹⁄₂ minutes
Merrie Melodies

Somewhere in the skies is the place where babies are made, then given to the storks to deliver. The elderly man who runs the establishment receives requests from would-be mothers: Mrs. Nanook of the North asks for twins, so off go twin Eskimos, etc. Much fun is had with the factory-line preparation of babies for consignment (the workers are reminiscent of Santa's elves). There's a certain amount of racial stereotyping, and one or two popular entertainers of the day — e.g., Maurice Chevalier, Eddie Cantor — are caricatured in infant form.

appears to have been not entirely happy, so when George Winkler, brother-in-law of the distributor Charles Mintz, came trawling around the Disney studio in 1927–28 with the aim of luring away Walt's best animators to set up a new studio, *sans* Walt, for the creation of further Oswald shorts, Harman and Ising seem to have been early recruits. That venture proved rapidly abortive, Universal taking over Oswald for itself not long after Mintz had opened his studio and thereby throwing all the defectors from Disney out of a job. But already Harman and Ising had produced, with Friz Freleng's help, a pilot for a possible new series of animated shorts. This pilot was the 4-minute 51-second live-action/animated *Bosko the Talk-Ink Kid*, in whose live-action component Ising appears briefly. Bosko was a little black boy (black for no other reason than that black characters are quicker to animate, the figures requiring fewer internal "construction" lines) who underwent various merry adventures, much in the manner of Mickey Mouse and indeed Oswald the Lucky Rabbit, both of whom he somewhat resembled.

Harman and Ising hawked *Bosko the Talk-Ink Kid* around various studios and distributors, without success. However, the independent producer Leon Schlesinger, president of the grandiosely titled Pacific Arts and Titles, had dreamed up a commercial idea for animated shorts. In those days the bigger studios were also distributors who owned or (in effect) franchised

movie chains, to whom they were obliged each week to supply a package containing not just the new feature movie but also a newsreel, a short, and other ancillary items. Furthermore, most of the big players not only distributed movies but also published sheet music, especially the music associated with their feature movies but also other songs. Schlesinger's idea was that it would be at least doubly in such companies' interests to distribute animated shorts that plugged the music they were publishing and the features they were making. He approached Warners with this concept, and they saw the sense of it. Thus was born the Looney Tunes series, the first of which was also the first Bosko cartoon to be released, *Sinkin' in the Bathtub* (1930), based around the song "Singin' in the Bathtub," which had been a highlight of the early Warners color musical feature *Show of Shows* (1929). The animated short received much praise, even though it seems primitive by the standards Disney had already attained, and Bosko and the Looney Tunes were well set on their way.

All told, nearly forty Bosko shorts were released by Warners, the early ones being directed by Harman and Ising together and the later ones being mainly Harman's solo work, with a few done by Friz Freleng. Bosko's girlfriend, Honey, appeared in many of these shorts, including the first. The Bosko shorts are little seen today because of perceived racial stereotyping; this is a shame because, crude though they are, they have frequent flashes of wit and only rarely contain anything approaching an overtly racist attitude.

In 1931, Ising was moved over to concentrate on the second of the great Warners animated series, the Merrie Melodies, leaving Harman to work almost exclusively on the Looney Tunes. (It is not known how much the two moonlighted on each others' series, but, bearing in mind how much they worked in tandem throughout their careers, we must assume it happened fairly often.) The first of the Merrie Melodies was either *Lady, Play Your Mandolin!* (1931) or *Smile, Darn Ya, Smile* (1931), the former probably being released first and being supervised (i.e., directed) by Frank Marsales, the latter probably being supervised by Ising, although the credited animators are Friz Freleng and Max Maxwell. Both shorts featured a new series star, Foxy, whose appearance was astonishingly like that of Mickey Mouse and who, with girlfriend Roxy, starred in just three shorts – the third being *One More Time* (1931). Another short-lived Merrie Melodies star, presumably generated by Ising, was Goopy Geer, a performing dog whose first appearance (of three) was in *Goopy Geer* (1932).

In 1933, Harman and Ising quarreled with Schlesinger over money – they wanted bigger budgets for the shorts, whereas he was constantly trying to pull the costs down – and the two animation directors departed together, taking Bosko with them. After a brief pause, they were welcomed by MGM, which had been thinking of setting up an animation studio and was only too glad to recruit an outside contractor, in the shape of Harman–Ising Productions, to do this for them. The main series Harman–Ising produced for MGM, made in Technicolor at double the budget Schlesinger had been prepared to afford, was Happy

Harmonies, conscious imitations of Disney's Silly Symphonies, with an influence from Warner's Merrie Melodies. The Happy Harmonies were, at their best, serious rivals to the Disney series in terms of animation and general visual appeal. Both men were interested in character animation, and this too is generally a strong point of the series. However, where the shorts generally fall down is in terms of character creation – too many of the characters are in effect the same, despite visual differences – and, even more importantly, story; this latter failing became especially obvious because, as their own producers without any editorial control, Harman and Ising could let their cartoons run on as long as they liked, often exceeding 10 or 11 minutes when the industry standard was more like 7 or 8.

The overrun in duration had an impact on the series' budgets, which likewise tended to overrun. MGM grew impatient with this and in 1937 dispensed with Harman–Ising, who determined to do what they perhaps should have done in the first place: start their own animation studio. They installed Fred Quimby, an MGM executive with no knowledge whatsoever of animation, to head this new studio, and his first act was to lure most of the Harman–Ising staff away from the principals. Among these men was William Hanna who, with Joseph Barbera, would in due course put MGM's animation studio on the map with the Tom & Jerry cartoons. Another recruit was Friz Freleng, from the Schlesinger stable, but he didn't last long at MGM.

Harman and Ising were once more out of work. Walt Disney, perhaps for nostalgic reasons, commissioned them as freelancers to create the Silly Symphony *Merbabies* (1938); it fits very well into that series and is a charming short. They also took on other, less glamorous bits of commercial piecework.

However, under Quimby the new MGM animation studio was rapidly in difficulties, mainly because he had no idea what he was doing. He found himself with little choice but to eat crow and hire back Harman and Ising; by the same token, so far as one can deduce, pickings for them as independents had been thin enough that they had no choice but to eat crow and agree to be hired. The two men were in fact exactly what MGM needed, and almost immediately they began to prove it. Ising created the first MGM series character, Barney the Bear, in part based on himself; like Barney, Ising was renowned for his fondness for sleep. In the first cartoon of the series, *The Bear that Couldn't Sleep* (1939), the main joke is that a string of events thwarts Barney's attempts to hibernate. Barney was too amiable ever to become a front-line series star, but his series continued for a remarkably long time, the last Barney short being *Bird-Brain Bird Dog* (1954).

Far more important was a singleton short that Harman created, *Peace on Earth* (1939). Released just a few months after the start of World War II, this begins with a family of squirrels singing Christmas carols. One of the youngsters asks what the expression "Peace on Earth, good will to all men" could mean, for none of the children know what a "man" is. An older squirrel explains to them, with phenomenally impressive flashbacks to scenes of warfare, that

once upon a time the world was populated by monsters who fought each other, with ever greater powers at their disposal, until only two of these man creatures were left, and they killed each other – bringing peace on Earth.

This pacifistic short was enormously admired at the time, in a way that maybe it wouldn't have been a couple of years later, after the United States had entered the conflict. Perhaps rather shamefully it was beaten for that year's Oscar by the charming, beautifully done, but otherwise unexceptional Disney Silly Symphony *The Ugly Duckling* (1939), actually a remake of a 1931 black-and-white original. Part of the mythology of animation history is that *Peace on Earth* was also nominated for the Nobel Peace Prize; as there is no such thing as a nomination list for the Nobel Prizes, which are judged entirely by international committee, this is obvious nonsense. (Presumably, as happens thousands of times each year, somebody sent the committee a wasted letter.) Ising, not to be outdone, directed *The Milky Way* (1940), a fairly standard cartoon taking talking animals into space, which nevertheless is distinguished as the first non-Disney animated short to win an Oscar; before it, Disney had been the winner eight years running.

In strictly pragmatic terms, the most significant thing either of the two men did for MGM – and the greatest mark they made on animation history – came in 1940, when the short *Puss Gets the Boot* was released, with Ising credited as the director. In fact, the movie was directed by William Hanna and Joe Barbera, and it introduced for the first time the characters Tom & Jerry.

Over at Warners, Tex Avery had fallen out with Leon Schlesinger in connection with *The Heckling Hare* (1941) and had been fired (see page 11). He was almost immediately snapped up by Quimby for MGM, and soon was bringing to the MGM animation division all the rapid pace and surrealistic inventiveness that would thereafter distinguish it. With Hanna and Barbera heading up another unit for the production of Tom & Jerry shorts, all of the sudden Harman and Ising began to look like yesterday's men. It was probably welcomed by all when, around the end of 1942, Ising was recruited by the U.S. government to become officer in charge of animation at the Hal Roach studios, renamed Fort Roach for the duration of World War II. Harman went with him, and thereafter the two men devoted the war years to producing animations for training and the like.

After the end of the war, Harman and Ising never really returned to the mainstream of animation, although they made occasional contributions later – such as some story work for Walter Lantz. Their studio lived on for some years making technical and promotional movies; one example is *Good Wrinkles: The Story of a Remarkable Fruit* (1951). Done for the California Prune and Apricot Growers Association's division Sunsweet, it featured a cast of prunish characters who might be regarded as the forerunners of Will Vinton's California Raisins (see page 194). By the time Harman died in 1982 and Ising in 1992 their role in the early history of animation had been largely forgotten, yet animation's story would have been quite different without them.

JIM HENSON (1936–1990)

Born on September 24, 1936, in Greenville, Mississippi, James Maury Henson became primarily noted for his adaptation of puppetry to the screen – he can be regarded as a sort of Walt Disney of puppetry. But, as his television shows and movies became increasingly ambitious, he also added some animation, primarily stop-motion, into the mix.

Pulled toward the world of the imagination primarily by his grandfather, he was a child of the first television generation, so it's not surprising that in his later career he put the two together. In 1954, he got his first television break when a local station, WTOP, advertised for students to act as puppeteers on one of its children's shows. Jim and a friend built some puppets and were hired. The show was short-lived, but the exposure was enough to persuade NBC to give the teenage Henson small slots in other local shows on its Washington subsidiary, WRC-TV. At the time, however, he didn't see any particular future in puppetry as a career; he was set to become a commercial artist.

In May 1955, WRC-TV decided to up his profile, giving his puppets a 5-minute show of their own – called *Sam and Friends* – in a prime slot. The show ran for over six years, winning the Hensons (he was working with his wife, Jane) a local Emmy. But, more significantly, it saw the debut of various character creations, including Kermit – although at the time Kermit wasn't a frog but a lizard. The term "Muppets" came to be used as a generic description of these characters. Most important of all, it saw the Hensons devising new techniques of televising puppets, so that the actions screened were produced not just by puppetry but by a mixture of puppetry and simple forms of animation using camera tricks. A trip to Europe to see the work of the classical puppeteers there fired Henson's ambition to achieve more in the medium. At the same time, his supposedly modest little show was beginning to attract network attention, and he and the puppets were booked for various guest slots on networked shows; they became almost a regular fixture on *The Today Show*. The Muppets' main income, however, was derived from their use in commercials, and this would remain the case for some years.

It was through the 1960 and 1961 conventions of the Puppeteers of America that Henson met Frank Oz, son of the established puppeteers Mike and Frances Oznowicz. Jane Henson, now a mother, had decided to give up performing, so Henson was looking for a new collaborator. Oz was, unfortunately, at the time too young to join him, so Henson instead hired Jerry Juhl, another who would become an important element in the Henson organization. Oz eventually joined Henson a couple of years later, after the operation had moved to New York. A short time earlier Don Sahlin joined as well; he became the organization's technical genius, although he would also be responsible for creating many of the puppets used for *Sesame Street*.

The next big break came in 1963 when one of the characters, the dog Rowlf, one of Sahlin's creations, was booked as a regular on ABC's networked *The Jimmy Dean Show*, performing in tandem

Detail of still from *The Dark Crystal* (1982), showing Jen.
© Jim Henson Productions.

with the country singer. For this, Henson had to train himself to become a live performer; hitherto all the voicing for the characters, which at this stage he did himself, had been prerecorded, but clearly this wasn't feasible when the puppet was interacting with a live artist. Rowlf went on to have his own show, *Our Place*, for a few months on CBS in 1967; in this summer replacement for *The Smothers Brothers Comedy Hour*, Rowlf emceed for what was essentially a live-action variety show.

In 1968, the Children's Television Workshop was set up in response to a Carnegie Institute report which had discovered – *mirabile dictu* – that most of the supposedly educational tv being aimed at U.S. kids was essentially a waste of screen time. One of the programs suggested in the plans to correct this situation was a preschoolers' educational show, and part of the proposal was that puppets might play a part. The show's producers approached

Henson, and after some considerable deliberation – he was in the business of entertaining grown-ups, not preschoolers – he accepted the offer. Thus was born *Sesame Street*, which premiered on November 10, 1969, the "Sesame" coming from "Open Sesame." At first, his involvement was only with the sections of the show using puppets, but soon he was responsible for many of the animated parts as well. He and his team created new puppet characters, including Big Bird and the Cookie Monster; Kermit, by now a frog, was developed as one of the central figures. Henson and Oz provided much of the script, based on the curriculum given to the program's makers by the Children's Television Workshop, and between them also supplied the puppets' voices. The program was instantly successful; Big Bird even appeared on the cover of *Time*.

Henson's early doubts about the wisdom of participating in *Sesame Street* were, however, being realized. The Muppets and he were now famous – as entertainment solely for children. He didn't want them to be typecast in this way; he regarded them as entertainment for adults as well as children – which was, of course, why *Sesame Street* was so successful: adults were watching alongside kids and for their own amusement.

A spinoff from *Sesame Street* was 1974's *The Muppet Valentine Special*, which with hindsight can be seen as a pilot for *The Muppet Show*, although that was not the intention at the time; in it, the Muppets interacted with actress Mia Farrow. The real pilot came a year later, with *The Muppet Show: Sex and Violence*, which was screened by ABC. Although the title did not really reflect the content of the pilot, which was innocuous enough, it did emphasize that Henson was looking to appeal to a non-juvenile audience. There was no human guest star, however, and Kermit barely appeared. A prototype Miss Piggy was present as one of the cast of the parody *Return to Beneath the Planet of the Pigs*. The Swedish Chef made his debut, as did various other characters who would later be important to the series, which ABC, however, chose not to pick up. CBS likewise passed on it, and it was left to ITC – the U.S. division of the U.K. company Associated Communications Corporation – to make the show and sell it to national syndication; ironically, the CBS stations were first in line to buy it. The filming of 24 episodes of this ITC/Henson Associates co-production started in London in January 1976. In the end the show ran for five seasons and was phenomenally popular.

One consequence of the filming in London was that it was natural for Henson Associates to establish a division there. This has developed into the main headquarters of Jim Henson's Creature Shop, the world's leading center for what has come to be called animatronics. Among the many movies for which the Creature Shop provided animatronics, with Henson himself involved to a greater or lesser degree, were: *An American Werewolf in London* (1981), in which Henson also had a small role; *Dreamchild* (1985), a fantasy on the life of Alice Liddell, the original Alice in Wonderland; *The Witches* (1989), based on Roald Dahl's children's novel; and *Teenage Mutant Ninja Turtles* (1990).

The Dark Crystal (1982)

♮color /puppetry/animatronics/stop-motion animated
◷ 94 minutes

For 1000 years, the cruel Skeksis have ruled the world. Now there are only ten left – soon to be nine, for their Emperor is dying. Far off in the forest, their benign counterparts, the shambling Mystics, are likewise waiting for their master to die. Long ago, the Skeksis sent their army of huge and chitinous Garthim to slaughter the world's elfin race, the Gelfling. Now, as the Mystic sage dies, he charges the (seemingly) last Gelfling, Jen, with finding and returning to its place a lost shard of the once shattered Dark Crystal that reposes in the Skeksis' castle; otherwise, according to prophecy, the Skeksis will rule forever. The seer Aughra gives Jen the shard and explains that at the forthcoming conjunction of the three suns the world as it is now will end. Considerably aided through many adventures by a girl Gelfling, Kira, Jen is at last able to ram the shard into the crystal just as the three suns come together. The surviving Mystics and Skeksis fuse, one-to-one, and become transcendent creatures; reunited, they leave the world and the Dark Crystal – now the Crystal of Truth – to Jen, Kira, and their descendants.

Labyrinth (1986)

♮color /live-action/puppetry/animatronics/stop-motion animated ◷ 101 minutes

Fantasy-obsessed teenager Sarah, left by her stepmother in charge of baby half-brother Toby, inadvertently uses the correct magic words to call on the king of the Goblins to take the child away forever. She changes her mind, and the king, Jareth, appears to her, offering her a contract: she may have Toby if, within the next thirteen hours, she can reach him through the labyrinth that lies between her home and the castle where Toby is being held – otherwise Toby will become a goblin. In this quest, Sarah eventually succeeds, though not before encountering fairies that appear cute but are spiteful and biting, the untrustworthy dwarf Hoggle, the friendly monster Ludo, and much else. In the end, all that saves her and Toby from Jareth's duplicities is her ritual incantation of the words "You have no power over me," which enables her to perceive that he and his kingdom have been only an illusion.

Ever since the late 1950s, Henson had been experimenting with moviemaking, both live-action and animated; his live-action short *Timepiece* (1964) was nominated for an Oscar. It was therefore inevitable, even had the popularity of *The Muppet Show* not dictated it, that Henson and the Muppets would be transported to the big screen. *The Muppet Movie* came in 1979, *The Great Muppet Caper* in 1981 and *The Muppets Take Manhattan* in 1984. These movies were not especially successful, however, and it was generally deemed that the Muppets were

best kept to tv. (Nearly a decade later, after Henson's death, times had changed: *The Muppet Christmas Carol* (1992), *Muppet Treasure Island* (1996) and *Muppets from Space* (1999) did much better, not just in cinemas but on video, where their predecessors were now also making strong showings.) Aside from Muppetish activities, however, there was an important meeting in 1977 between Henson and the prominent fantasy artist Brian Froud at Froud's home in Chudleigh, Devon, U.K., during which were laid the foundations for what would become *The Dark Crystal* (1982), Henson's first foray into the mainstream of fantasy moviemaking.

The Dark Crystal is a movie whose reputation has grown since its release. What Henson asked Froud to do was create a world for him, a world which Henson and his team could then bring to life using every means at their disposal, including puppetry, animatronics and stop-motion animation. There was no question of any kind of script or even story being worked out beforehand: those would come later, out of both Froud's own imaginings and the inspirations engendered in the rest of the team by his artworks. In the end, the bones of the story were worked out a few months later by Henson and his daughter Cheryl. That story is essentially very simple; what detracts from the movie is that Henson and the others saw fit to complicate it with plot embellishments that sometimes contribute little. But the puppetry, animatronics and characterization are excellent, as are the puppets themselves: the lugubrious Mystics could be figures of fun but are soon seen to have a ponderous dignity; the androgynous-looking Gelfling (the difference between male and female is that females have wings) stay just to the right side of cuteness; and the Garthim are impressively scary. Also of interest is the music: the soundtrack proper (performed by the London Symphony Orchestra) is standard, but the music performed by the characters – as for example at a feast held by the Podlings, the earthy people who raised Kira – belongs to much earlier folk traditions and is strikingly apt. Although *The Dark Crystal* cannot be described as an unalloyed triumph, it is in its unabashed (albeit often derivative) mythopoeia perhaps the most successful attempt to bring this variety of high fantasy to the screen.

Although again the puppetry and animatronics are excellent, Henson's second major movie outing, *Labyrinth* (1986), is a less successful piece, despite having a screenplay by Terry Jones that deploys some very sophisticated fantasy ideas. It is a movie whose virtues are eclipsed by its many flaws, not least of which is that it stars, as Jareth, king of the Goblins, David Bowie, upon whose uncertain acting abilities far too much has to depend. Several dull songs are rendered as rock videos; the effect of the visually and conceptually highly impressive last battle of wits between Sarah and Jareth in an Escheresque stairwell is thereby destroyed. And the fine performance of Jennifer Connelly as the questing teenager Sarah, portraying her as a confident, positive evocation of virtue, points up the flat portrayal of Jareth by Bowie, so that the contest between Good and Evil becomes one sided. The net effect is that one begins to feel as if, as it were, not only does the Devil not have

all the best songs but, when given many of the best lines, he can't deliver them very well. Thus, while sequence after sequence individually dazzles and amazes, the movie becomes rather boring.

During this time, Henson had been creating tv's *Fraggle Rock*, which ran from 1983 to 1988. This never achieved anything like the popularity of *The Muppet Show*, although it was not an inconsiderable work of fantasy; the main writer was Jerry Juhl. The Fraggles themselves – called Woozles early on in the project – are, rather like the Borrowers, a wainscot society dwelling beneath the workshop of a handyman named Doc (played by a live actor), who is unaware of their existence. His dog, Sprocket, knows they're there and makes determined but ever unsuccessful efforts to catch one to show to his master. As spiritual leader the Fraggles have an oracle, the Trash Heap, which dispenses dubious wisdom to those who ask. Two other wainscot societies share territory with the Fraggles: the vast (in Fraggle terms) and dreaded Gorgs, of whom there is but a single family left, and who aim to enslave the Fraggles; and the small Doozers, who are inventors and builders and whose structures are generally eaten by the Fraggles as snacks. The location of Fraggle Rock was changed according to the country in which the series was being broadcast, and, consequently, different live actors were called upon to play the role of Doc, whose precise trade also changed. Thus he was a baker (played by Michel Robin) in France and a lighthouse-keeper called The Captain (played by Fulton Mackay) in the U.K.

In straightforward 2D animation, there were two main spinoffs from Henson's puppeteering. *The Muppet Babies* ran in various formats for eight years from 1984 on CBS. As might be guessed from the title, it featured infant versions of the Muppets. Far less successful was a cartoon version of *Fraggle Rock*, which lasted just a single season, 1987–88, on NBC. Similarly short-lived was *The Jim Henson Hour*, which ran just a few months on NBC in 1989 and is primarily of interest for its second half, *The Storyteller*. Some earlier episodes of *The Storyteller* had been seen as specials on NBC and all episodes have since been screened separately; in these an old man tells his faithful dog tales of magic and mystery. Before his death, Henson had begun work on another tv series that enjoyed a certain amount of success – *Dinosaurs*, which ran on ABC from 1991 to 1993, with a few extra episodes added in 1994 – and had nearly completed a 14-minute 3D movie, *Jim Henson's Muppet*Vision 3D*, for Walt Disney World. The latter production features, among the usual cast of Muppets, Waldo, who is a digitally animated puppet, the digital animation of which is in fact driven by hand puppetry. There were also, during Henson's lifetime, countless tv specials and short movies, as well as regular Muppet appearances in the early days of *Saturday Night Live* (on NBC from 1975).

Henson died in the hospital on May 16, 1990, of a severe streptococcal infection that destroyed his lungs within a few days; he had admitted himself to the hospital just hours beforehand, not realizing how ill he had actually become. His premature death – he was only 53 – was mourned worldwide.

JOHN HUBLEY (1914–1977)

Still from *Everybody Rides the Carousel* (1976).
© Hubley Studios.

John Hubley was born in Marinette, Wisconsin, on May 21, 1914, and was in his teens when the family moved to Michigan. With the onset of the Depression he was sent to live with an uncle in Los Angeles who saw him through high school and college. A talented artist from an early age, Hubley applied in 1935 to Disney for a job, and soon found himself working as a background and layout artist on *Snow White and the Seven Dwarfs* (1937). He worked also on *Pinocchio* (1940) and *Dumbo* (1941) and on the early stages of *Bambi* (1942), but, although enjoying himself at Disney, became gradually disillusioned with Walt's quest for "realism" in animation and with the notion that animated stories required gags to pull them along. The strike at Disney in 1941 brought things to a head for Hubley; although he did not actively participate, as a man of leftish politics he naturally sympathized with the strikers, and soon afterward he left. The animation career of John Hubley can really be thought of as beginning at this time, because along with

this physical departure from Disney there was a parallel departure from the philosophy of Disney animation: Hubley was on a mission to make animation a genre in its own right rather than an offshoot of mainstream cinema.

He went initially to Screen Gems, the studio formed by Charles Mintz to produce animation for Columbia; Columbia had taken the studio away from Mintz in 1939 and he died in 1940. Recently appointed as production supervisor at Screen Gems was Frank Tashlin, an ex-Disney man who was only too happy to employ the malcontents who left Disney as a consequence of the strike. At Screen Gems under Tashlin, the animators were encouraged to try out new ideas, which most of them enthusiastically did, mainly in a desire to break the template that

Box illustration for *Ragtime Bear* (1949) in its
8mm home-movie release.

The Hole (1962)

color / animated ⏱ 15¼ minutes
John and Faith Hubley

An Oscar-winning short. Dizzy Gillespie and George Mathews improvise the dialogue of two workmen in a hole under Third Avenue in New York as they discuss the nature and consequences of accidents. One maintains, despite the other's jeers, that the only way to stop a nuclear war happening by accident is to get rid of the weapons that make it possible in the first place. At the end an accident — a piece of heavy equipment falls — persuades the skeptic.

Of Men and Demons (1969)

color / animated ⏱ 9¼ minutes
John and Faith Hubley

Every day is much the same for a simple subsistence farmer/fisherman until the demons of Rain, Fire, and Storm descend from their mountain home to disrupt his life for reasons of sheer capricious sadism. Almost despairing, he is joined by a mate, and together they rebuild an existence. By the time the demons next look, the two humans have built themselves an agricultural technology such that whatever weaponry the demons throw at them can actually be put to constructive use. Now the demons transform themselves into pollution, transportation, and heavy machinery, so that the world the humans have created for themselves becomes a toxic hell. But the versatile humans devise computers and with them create a new, high-tech, and clean world. The demons, in their mountain fastness, plot their next scheme.

Disney was imposing on the industry. Some of these ideas flourished; most did not. Hubley worked on several of the Screen Gems series of Color Rhapsodies — by now rather like a mixture of the Silly Symphonies and Looney Tunes — and directed movies like *Wolf Chases Pig* (1942) and *The Dumbconscious Mind* (1942). Perhaps most notable in terms of his later career was *Professor Small and Mr. Tall* (1943), in which the tall Professor Small and the small Mr. Tall, both drawn without any attempt at rounded coziness, debunk superstitions amid a world depicted with the utmost simplicity; the short thereby prefigured two of the trends of Hubley's later work: the thrust toward simplicity and a-realism in animation, and the tendency toward didacticism.

Tashlin was fired by Columbia in 1942 for talking back to its anonymous suits just once too often, and shortly afterward — the spirit having gone from the studio with Tashlin's departure — Hubley joined the Army to work at the Army Air Force First Motion Picture Unit (FMPU), run by Rudolf Ising. Ising didn't care very much what the cartoons the FMPU churned out looked like as long as the military was happy with them. The military, in turn, didn't care what the cartoons looked like as long as the message was conveyed with full clarity. This allowed the animators to experiment with different styles and techniques in a way that almost certainly wouldn't have been permitted by a commercial studio. The experience at the FMPU fueled those same two urges of Hubley: to experiment visually and to teach through his animations. A further bonus was that at this studio everybody was expected to do a bit of everything, from washing cels one moment to directing the next, with inbetweening (see page 83), camera work, etc., thrown in. It was ideal training for those who wanted to become the compleat animator.

In the early 1940s, Zachary Schwartz and Dave Hilberman, both of whom had been at Disney but were then working at Screen Gems and Graphic Films, decided to rent a studio together so they could moonlight in their spare time. Steve Bosustow, yet another ex-Disney worker, was now employed by Hughes Aircraft. He persuaded Hughes that the company needed a safety film and offered the commission to Graphic Films, but Graphic didn't want to do it. Hilberman intervened and got the job for Schwartz and himself. Thus was born the studio that was initially called Industrial Films and Poster Service. Their next significant commission came in 1944 from a trade union, the United Auto Workers (UAW), who wanted to produce a film promoting Franklin Roosevelt's reelection. By a circuitous route they had approached John Hubley, still at the FMPU, who, with the help of FMPU colleagues Bill Hurtz and Phil Eastman, storyboarded what was to be called *Hell Bent for Election* (1944). At first it looked as if the film would be produced by Leon Schlesinger, who had contributed studio space to an earlier animated movie for the union, but Schlesinger didn't want to get involved in party politics and so the UAW approached the Industrial Films and Poster Service. The movie was a great success, and the little company, changing its name to United Film

Production, started avidly prospecting for further commissions. Another name change came pretty swiftly, this time to United Productions of America, or UPA.

Hubley joined UPA full-time in 1945, having started to work for them on a freelance basis before then as a consequence of *Hell Bent for Election*. For some little while the output of the studio continued to be cartoons done for businesses, the unions (especially the UAW), or the government. Some of these movies attracted interest far outside their designated target areas, such as *Brotherhood of Man* (1945), which Hubley co-wrote and produced. This had been commissioned by the UAW in an effort to improve its recruiting in the American South, where there were problems getting whites and blacks to join up alongside each other. The resulting movie presented a strong case for racial tolerance and harmony and was distributed by the U.S. Navy.

In 1946, Hilberman and Schwartz left UPA to open a studio of their own, Tempo. They sold their shares to Bosustow, who appointed Hubley the company's supervising director. In 1948, Bosustow approached Columbia with the suggestion that UPA could contract with them as a regular supplier of animated shorts, beginning with further movies in the Fox and the Crow series, which Columbia's own studio, Screen Gems, had been letting peter out. Columbia looked at Screen Gems's recent output, agreed that just about anything would be better than what the studio had recently been doing, and contracted with UPA, closing Screen Gems down. The first Fox and the Crow short done by UPA, *Robin Hoodlum* (1948), directed by Hubley, had the Fox as Robin Hood and the Crow as the Sheriff of Nottingham. Columbia didn't like it very much since it diverged radically from the standard Disney/Warners fare that was doing so well in the movie theaters. It was by then too late to stop the second UPA Fox and the Crow cartoon, *The Magic Fluke* (1949), again directed by Hubley. Columbia rather reluctantly released both and was surprised when both were extremely successful – indeed, both were nominated for Oscars.

Stylistically, Hubley had been much influenced for these movies by a short Chuck Jones had done for Warners, *The Dover Boys at Pimento University, or The Rivals of Roquefort Hall* (1942), which had used limited animation and stylized graphics to produce a cartoon that was immediately accessible to all audiences despite not being "realistic." Like Jones in that short, UPA made extensive use of limited animation; this was partly done for economy but also because there are effects to be gained with limited animation that are far more difficult in full animation. For example, limited animation, if properly handled, can give a smearing effect to movements – an effect that is actually very appealing, if one is not glued to Disneyesque pseudo-realism.

For Columbia, UPA created a new series, Jolly Frolics. The first of these shorts was a cartoon about a bear – or, at least, that's what Columbia thought, because in fact the central character was a human being. Hubley and others at UPA wanted to break the mold of commercial cartooning in more ways than

Everybody Rides the Carousel
(1976) tvm

⌕ color / animated ⏱ 73 minutes
John Hubley

Harlequin introduces us to the Carousel of Life, with its eight rides of eight different physical and emotional ages. First is *infancy*, characterized by the trust/mistrust dichotomy, the two emotions symbolized respectively by a cute little kitten and its spiky unhappy kitten counterpart. The second stage is *toddlerhood*, characterized by autonomy/doubt, symbolized by a lion and a neurotic rabbit. Stage Three, *childhood*, is one of initiative/guilt, symbolized by a goofy bird and a shame-faced snake, although the earlier creatures are still occasionally present. In Stage Four, *schooldays*, the senses of competence and inferiority vie, symbolized by the child's growing bigger and smaller as he struggles with reading, carpentry, etc. A nice touch here is the sight of the pages of a book through the boy's eyes: one word is starkly intelligible but the rest are meaningless squiggles. *Adolescence*, Stage Five, brings with it the search for identity and the threat of role confusion, symbolized by two humanoid line figures, the latter made up of jigsaw pieces. *Young adulthood*, Stage Six, brings the possibilities of both intimacy and isolation. The dichotomy is symbolized by the characters developing Janus faces, which they hide under masks. Stretches of animation repeated with variations show how life decisions can go either way depending almost on pure chance. Stage Seven is full *adulthood*, characterized by generativity (caring) but bringing with it the risk of stagnation (lack of caring), the latter symbolized by the development of a fish head in place of a human one. In addition, all the symbols of the earlier stages play their part in the emotional ballet of adulthood. Stage Eight, *old age*, brings integrity (in the sense of integration of all that has gone before, symbolized by an owl) and its counterpart, despair (symbolized by a caricatured ghost); also playing its part is the acceptance of death.

just the stylistic: why, they asked, should it be taken as axiomatic that popular cartoons should always be about funny animals? Columbia was unconvinced, even when UPA showed them the star whom Hubley and his colleagues had devised. So it was that the funny-animal movie *Ragtime Bear* (1949) came into being. Columbia was surprised when most audiences seeing this very successful short ignored the bear and focused instead on the human character at the heart of it all, Mr. Quincy Magoo. The plot of the movie has nearly 100 percent blind Magoo going on vacation with a banjo-playing nephew who habitually wears a fur coat. The nephew gets lost and a grizzly bear starts fooling with the banjo. Via touch, Mr. Magoo assumes the bear is his nephew. Of course, by concatenation of circumstances he survives unscathed, and this set the pattern for the running joke that underpinned the succeeding highly successful cartoon series, not to mention comic strips, tv incarnations, tv commercials, and feature movies. In fact, Hubley himself, after directing three out of the first six Mr. Magoo shorts – the other two were *Spellbound Hound* (1950) and *Fuddy Duddy Buddy* (1951) – left the series almost entirely to Pete Burness to direct. A large part of the character's appeal came from the fact that the voice part was performed with frequent hilarious ad-libbing by Jim Backus, another of the character's co-creators.

Hubley by this time had other concerns, since he was now acting as producer for the UPA output, with Bosustow being credited as executive producer. One of Hubley's greatest achievements in this guise was the Jolly Frolics short *Gerald McBoing-Boing* (1951), based on a story-record by Dr. Seuss, directed by Robert Cannon and written by Phil Eastman and Bill Scott. The tale is of a little boy who, try as he might, in his attempts to talk can produce only the sounds "Boing! Boing!" Again done in the stylized, exceptionally simplified graphics that UPA had by now more or less made its own, it was hugely praised by the critics and walked off with an Oscar. More importantly, from Columbia's and UPA's commercial point of view, it was also enormously popular with the paying public. A short series followed, all directed by Cannon. The fourth and last short, *Gerald McBoing-Boing on the Planet Moo* (1956), gained another Oscar.

With two successful series under way, it might have seemed UPA was doing well, but the quality of its output came at a price: all its cartoons were going over budget. Accordingly, this revered establishment was actually in economic difficulties almost throughout its existence. The fact that far fewer images were required in the limited-animation style in which the studio specialized might suggest that the cartoons could be produced far more cheaply. But UPA had always been an artist-led studio, so much more time and effort was being put into each image to make sure it was as good as it could be. By 1959 most of the best staff had left what was becoming a sinking ship (Hubley had left earlier – see below), and Bosustow finally had to sell out to Henry Saperstein, who promptly took UPA into – in this order – production for tv, artistic oblivion, and a greater commercial success.

Hubley's responsibilities as supervisor/producer meant that he actually *made* surprisingly few movies for UPA. One of those he did make (with Paul Julian), however, is regarded as a great classic of the art of the animated short: the Jolly Frolic cartoon *Rooty Toot Toot* (1952). This is an animated rendition of the old barroom ballad "Frankie and Johnny," set to a jazz rhythm by Phil Moore. It takes the move away from realism to a new extreme for the animated short, using as characters figures that go almost beyond even caricature; the use of color, too, is radical, with the coloring-in only approximating to the outlines. The short was nominated for an Oscar but, surprisingly, did not win it. Also for UPA, he and Julian collaborated on the animated bridges separating the various scenes of Columbia's live-action movie *The Four-Poster* (1952). The movie was not well received, the general opinion being that the animated links were the best bits but, in context, actually rebarbative for that very reason.

Hubley's reasons for leaving UPA had nothing to do with the studio's rocky finances. Instead, they are shameful – although not to any of the parties directly involved. By the mid-1950s the

McCarthyist witch-hunt in the motion-picture industry was at a frenzied level. Most of the large studios kowtowed without a murmur, and not only merrily fired on the spot employees who had given their best but also actively cooperated with the persecutors in adding names to the notorious blacklist – it was, after all, an easy way to get rid of troublemakers. UPA was not a big studio in industry terms, yet Bosustow to his very great credit resisted the witch-hunters, who were pressurizing him to dismiss two well known lefties in his employ, Phil Eastman and John Hubley. As the pressure on Bosustow increased, both men resigned rather than cause him any further difficulty and the possible demise of the company.

This period was not entirely gloomy for Hubley, however. In about 1946 he had met Faith Elliott; the two were married in 1955 (his second marriage) and thereafter until the end of Hubley's life would be creative collaborators. Faith Elliott Hubley was born on September 16, 1924, in New York City, and started in Hollywood as a messenger for Columbia. She went on to work as a sound-effects cutter, a music cutter, and film editor; she was a script supervisor for continuity on Jack Donahue's *Close-Up* (1948), a function she was to perform again later for the very much more distinguished *Twelve Angry Men* (1957), directed by Sidney Lumet and starring Henry Fonda, a movie nominated for three Oscars. At the time John and Faith met she was editing a sex-education movie called *Human Growth*. The two first worked together on an unfinished project, an animated version of *Finian's Rainbow*. As left-looking in her politics as her husband, she attended art school after their marriage in an attempt to match him also as an artist. To his work she was able to bring an international influence that had not been there before.

The two set up their own studio, Storyboard (later to become The Hubley Studio), in New York, a comfortable few thousand miles away from the primary heat of the witch-hunt. Faith ran the business side of the company, acted often enough as co-producer, and did some art and animation, while also contributing to John's design ideas. In a 1973 interview with John D. Ford she described her role:

> I think John makes the major aesthetic contribution. We both work on storyboard and concept. We both work on soundtrack. In most cases John is the director, and I'll help in any way that I can. I'll be production organizer and see that the work gets finished on time.

For a while the two made tv commercials and the like, their first "art" animation being an experimental piece commissioned by the Guggenheim Museum, Bilbao; much influenced by the work of Norman McLaren, this was *The Adventures of an ** (1957). What is startling about the movie is how much John now felt free to break away from the stylistic constraints placed upon animation by the commercial studios – even by UPA, which was

considered dangerously avant-garde by most of the others. In the interview with Ford, John Hubley went into this in more detail:

> We decided to do a film with music and no dialogue and to deal with abstract characters. We wanted to get a graphic look that had never been seen before. So we played with the wax-resist technique: drawing with wax and splashing it with watercolor to produce a resisted texture. We ended up waxing all the drawings and spraying them and double-exposing them. We did the backgrounds the same way. It photographed with a very rich waxy texture, which was a fresh look.

Also of interest in the other early Storyboard/Hubley Studio movies is the new approach to dialogue, which broke away from the formal patterns of Hollywood. This feature, of dialogue being either improvised or sounding very much like it, was to be maintained almost throughout the entire Hubley oeuvre from here on – and some of the voice actors involved were no mean improvisers: Dizzy Gillespie did a number of movies with the Hubleys, and other contributors included Maureen Stapleton and Dudley Moore. On occasion, the Hubleys also used recordings of the chatter of their two daughters, Emily, who was later to become an animator in her own right, and Georgia, later to become a rock singer. Also evident early on was a strong connection with jazz: not only do the movies more often than not have jazz soundtracks, but the personal contacts between the Hubleys and the jazz community were obviously strong, as evidenced by the participation of Gillespie and Moore as voice actors, as well as that of Oscar Peterson, Ella Fitzgerald, Benny Carter, Quincy Jones and other musicians and composers.

Their second movie was *The Tender Game* (1958), a love story, complete with jazz backing by Peterson and Fitzgerald, in which the characters are little more than assemblages of lines. *Harlem Wednesday* (1958) continued in the same adventurous vein and was followed by *Moonbird* (1959), the first independent animation to win an Oscar; it tells of the nighttime hunt of two brothers for a fabulous bird. A considerably greater undertaking was the short feature movie *Of Stars and Men* (1961), based on the philosophical monograph of the same name by astronomer Harlow Shapley. This movie was a major expression of Hubley's bent toward didactic exposition as a possible territory to be explored within animation's thematic playground.

Other movies appeared in reasonably rapid succession, although perhaps not as frequently as expected; the Hubleys were doing a lot of commissioned work for commercials and the like, to the extent that they had to make it a rule to do at least one of their "own" movies per year. Critical recognition was widespread and enthusiastic. The next Oscar after *Moonbird*'s was for *The Hole* (1962), a very simple movie comprising little more than a conversation between two workmen on the dangers of nuclear armaments; it could probably work equally

a Doonesbury Special (1977) tvm

🎨 color / animated ⏱ 25¹/₂ minutes
John and Faith Hubley, with Garry Trudeau
Based on Garry Trudeau's popular *Doonesbury* strip, this has the gang of the Walden Puddle Commune pondering their present and future through flashbacks to their past, with a couple of Jimmy Thudpucker songs, one from now and one from then, epitomizing the compromise of '60s radicalism into the blander liberalism of the '70s, a theme also addressed by Zonker Harris in his "4th Annual State of the Commune Address." Highlights are "The Huddle," in which B.D.'s dreamed conquests on the football field are shattered as a stoned Zonker reduces the players to a bunch of amateur philosophers; and a segment of the dress rehearsal of the local vicar's Rock Christmas Pageant, as performed by children. Although made as a tv special, the movie was also released theatrically.

well as a short radio play. The animation is almost childlike in form, though with an emphasis on textures that gives it some gravitas. *The Hat*, which followed in 1964, deals with rather similar subject matter, this time featuring two border guards, one on each side, who talk to each other all the time but do not permit each other to cross the line, not even for one of them to retrieve his fallen hat – hence the movie's title. A commercial short, *Herb Alpert and the Tijuana Brass Double Feature* (1966), picked up another Oscar. In *Windy Day* (1968) and *Cockaboody* (1973) the Hubleys used the burblings of their daughters, Emily and Georgia, as a soundtrack; the trouble with such a tactic is that the chattering of children is nowhere near as fascinating as their parents fondly think. *Of Men and Demons* (1969) was nominated for an Oscar against very stiff competition; the winner that year was Disney's *It's Tough to Be a Bird* (1969), directed by Ward Kimball and one of the most Hubley-influenced of all the Disney shorts. *Voyage to Next* (1974) was another Oscar nominee; it has Dizzy Gillespie and Maureen Stapleton as Father Time and Mother Earth conducting a semi-improvised conversation about humankind's past and future. It was largely regurgitated – along with much else – in what is today generally billed as Faith Hubley's own feature movie, *The Cosmic Eye* (1985).

John's last two movies of note were for television: *Everybody Rides the Carousel* (1976) and *A Doonesbury Special* (1977). The last movie released during John's lifetime, *Everybody Rides the Carousel*, commissioned by CBS, explores and popularizes the theories of the psychoanalyst Erik Erikson. Again this was an outlet for John's didactic yen. While it is hard to take Erikson's psychoanalytic modeling seriously, and while the rather too accurate renditions of life's more frustrating phases is almost as irritating as living through them, the movie is surprisingly enjoyable. Diverse styles of animation are used, and a surprisingly high percentage of screen time is occupied by (often excellent) still illustration rather than animation.

The final touches to John Hubley's very last film were completed by Faith after his death during open-heart surgery on February 21, 1977, in New York City. *A Doonesbury Special*, made for NBC, is so completely different in style from the rest of the Hubley Studio's output that it is hard to believe it came from there. It's good fun but hardly a masterpiece of animation; it was presumably for sympathetic reasons that it was nominated for a 1977 Oscar. Strange that the movie establishment, many of whose extant members had stood complaisantly by during, or even complicitly participated in, the witch-hunts that drove Hubley out of the mainstream of the animation industry should choose to honor his memory in this way.

After John's death, Faith Hubley continued to release animated movies of her own. In his book *Cartoons* (1994), Giannalberto Bendazzi is perhaps a trifle harsh when he notes: "The many films directed by Faith Hubley after her husband's death are more notable for the causes they embrace (peace, tolerance, spirituality) than for their artistic achievement." But at the heart of this statement is a valid point. If looked at as individual frames, these movies are often exquisitely beautiful, often reminiscent of the art of Paul Klee and his ilk. But beautiful still images are not what animation is all about.

John Hubley, in his solo career, forced the animation industry to rethink many of the rules it had made for itself and had elevated to the status of axioms; commercial animation is immeasurably the richer for it. In their joint career as independent moviemakers, John and Faith Hubley did a great deal to establish experimental animation as worthy of consideration by the mainstream – as evidenced by their impressive tally of Oscars and Oscar nominations. Again, commercial animation is immeasurably the richer for it.

Ub Iwerks (1901–1971)

Still from *The Skeleton Dance* (1929).
© Disney Enterprises, Inc.

Of Dutch descent, Ubbe Ert Iwwerks (he later dropped that second "w") was born in Kansas City, Missouri, in 1901, and graduated from Ashland Grammar School there in 1914 with few formal skills. In 1916, he dropped out of high school and spent a year working at the Bank Note Company. In October 1919, he was hired as an apprentice commercial artist by the Pesmen–Rubin Agency; another apprentice hired around the same time was a young man named Walt Disney, and the two soon became good friends. The job didn't last long for either of them: within just a few weeks they were laid off. The two had chatted about starting their own business together; the opportunity had come more suddenly than expected, but they seized it nevertheless and, using Walt's money, opened up a commercial-art studio. The business did not prosper, however, and at the end of January 1920 Walt was forced to take a job at the Kansas City Slide Company, which produced animated advertisements to be shown in movie theaters; Iwerks joined him at the Kansas City Slide Company a few weeks afterward, in March 1920. Later that year the company they had founded, Iwerks–Disney Commercial Artists, filed for bankruptcy.

What Walt saw in Iwerks, even in those earliest days, was, aside from friendship, the ability to draw with astonishing speed; it was an ability that meant he was tailor-made to be an animator. Walt himself was in those days an enthusiastic amateur animator, and during his spare time, with Iwerks's help, he produced an animated movie poking fun at the poor road conditions in Kansas City. This was bought by an executive of the Newman Theaters

chain, Milton Feld, and it proved enough of a success that Feld commissioned Walt to produce twelve more, to be called the Newman Laugh-O-grams. The pilot was screened on March 20, 1921, in the Kansas City Newman Theater. In May 1922 Walt incorporated Laugh-O-gram Films, and later in the year Iwerks left the Kansas City Film Ad Company (as the Slide Company was by then called) to join him. When Laugh-O-gram Films folded in 1923 and Walt went west to Los Angeles to be with his brother Roy, a tuberculosis sufferer, Iwerks remained behind, rejoining the Kansas City Film Ad Company. Doubtless he was not too keen on the notion of pinning his fortunes any further to the brash young entrepreneur who had already folded two companies.

Even before leaving Kansas City, Walt had begun working on a new series of shorts, the animated/live-action Alice Comedies. And this time he struck at least temporary gold, selling the series to New York distributor Margaret Winkler. In March 1924, Walt asked Iwerks to join him in California, an offer Iwerks initially refused but a month or two later accepted, starting work under Walt at a princely $40 per week. For a couple of years he animated on the long string of Alice Comedies that Disney Studios produced, first for Margaret Winkler and then for her cohort and husband Charles Mintz.

Sometime around the end of 1926, or in the early months of 1927, Walt and Iwerks together created a new cartoon character,

The Skeleton Dance (1929)

🎞 b/w / animated ⏲ 6 minutes
Silly Symphonies
The first of the Silly Symphonies produced by Disney; the title basically
tells the whole story. What plot the movie has is based on the program
of Saint-Saëns's *Danse Macabre*, although the musical accompaniment is in
fact an arrangement by Carl Stalling — whose idea the movie was — of
Grieg's *March of the Dwarfs*.

Fiddlesticks (1930)

🎞 color / animated ⏲ 8 minutes
Flip the Frog
The first of the Flip the Frog cartoons; there is hardly a plot to speak of,
and the color is rudimentary, being little more than two-color. In a forest
glade an insect orchestra plays while Flip dances on a stage fashioned
from a sawed-off tree trunk. Later, he plays piano for a violin soloist who
is a duplicate of Mickey Mouse (the ratlike Mickey current at the time),
but wearing what looks like a short red skirt (a tunic?) rather than short
red pants. There are various antics; the best visual gag occurs when, in
the slow, sorrowful section of their recital, "Mickey" has to pause to wring
out his violin.

What a Life (1932)

(vt *What a Life!*)
🎞 b/w / animated ⏲ 8 minutes
Flip the Frog
Flip and a little friend are street musicians; their efforts bring them
plenty of applause but no cash. Eventually, they pawn their instruments
for food. But before they can buy a meal they are moved to give the
money instead to a blind street musician — who promptly decamps in his
chauffeur-driven limo! The two pals run into a house, help themselves to
food, and start playing the musical instruments they find lying around
there. The housewife appears and sexily vamps them. Just then her
husband arrives home, and she stuffs them into the closet; the husband
proves to be a street cop they have been intermittently baiting
throughout the day. He cries: "Come out of there or I'll shoot" . . . and
not just Flip and his pal but the plumber, the chimneysweep, and a whole
procession of other tradesmen emerge from the closet.

Oswald the Lucky Rabbit. The pilot of the Oswald cartoons, *Poor
Papa*, was delivered to Mintz in New York in April of that year, but
Mintz and his colleagues were unimpressed: Oswald, they felt, was
too old and too fat. Nevertheless, the series went ahead, with
Oswald redesigned in younger and leaner mode. The first cartoon
to star this new character, *Trolley Troubles* (1927), premiered in June.

The Alice series had been moderately successful; the Oswald series
was if anything a little more so, although neither of them set the
house afire. Now Disney Studios began industriously to churn out
a whole string of Oswald movies.

In February 1928, Charles Mintz issued Walt an ultimatum:
either Walt, then visiting Mintz in New York, must agree to a cut in
the advance given for each Oswald cartoon or Mintz would take
over the series himself and move it to his own production
company, Snappy Comedies. Walt refused the former option and
was forced to relinquish all claim to the character. During the train
trip back from New York to Los Angeles, he and his wife, Lillian,
invented a new series character, Mickey Mouse — or, at least, that
is the story told in the official Disney hagiographies. In fact, it was
Ub Iwerks who *designed* the new character, who was at first
distinguishable from Oswald only by the shape of his ears, tail, and
perhaps face; there is therefore a very good case for saying that it
was not Walt who invented Mickey Mouse at all, but Iwerks. It has
been counterclaimed by the Disney establishment that, while
Iwerks may have designed the *form* of the new character, Walt was
responsible for creating Mickey's *personality*. Here we are beginning
to split hairs, because the early Mickey — like most of the cartoon
stars of the day — didn't really *have* much of a personality. Such
arguments could continue well into the night. What seems likely is
that Walt realized that, with just a few changes, his rabbit star could
become a mouse star, allowing him to continue producing his
shorts much as before while obeying the letter of his forced
agreement with Mintz, and that Iwerks, as his employee, would
effect those few changes.

Through April, the few of Disney's animators who had not
thrown in the towel to go and work for Mintz — primarily Iwerks
with apparently very little help, if any — sweated in secret (the
Mintz/Winkler recruits were still working out their notice at
Disney) to produce the first Mickey Mouse short, *Plane Crazy*. It
owed a great deal to the Oswald the Lucky Rabbit short *The
Ocean Hop* (1927) but was directly inspired by Charles
Lindbergh's first solo flight over the Atlantic. On May 15 they
tried it out in a local movie theater, and the following day Walt
applied for Mickey Mouse to be made a trademark; the movie
itself was copyrighted on May 26.

The rest, of course, is history. Walt's team, before *Plane Crazy*
could be released, worked to give another of the Mickey shorts
they had been preparing, *Steamboat Willie*, a primitive
soundtrack, with the music of "Steamboat Bill" and "Turkey in the
Straw" added. More or less from the moment *Steamboat Willie*
was given an advance screening at the Colony Theater in New
York, on November 18, 1928, Mickey Mouse was set to take the
world by storm. The reason was not the character — as noted,
this was simply Oswald revamped — or the animation, nor even
the quality of the vocal soundtrack, which consisted almost
exclusively of grunts and squeaks, but the fact that the cartoon
had sound *at all*, and that the sound was approximately
synchronized with the on-screen action.

Still from *The Office Boy* (1932) showing Flip the Frog.

Quite what Iwerks thought of all this is not known. Leaving aside all niceties, he must have felt that Mickey was a character he himself had created. He had animated the first Mickey short, *Plane Crazy*, almost entirely – if not indeed entirely – by himself with phenomenal speed: it had taken him about three weeks from a standing start to get the cels ready for inking, which means he must have done something like 600 drawings per day. (If he worked a 15-hour day and didn't stop for food or the lavatory, that's about one drawing every minute and a half. But such feats were not entirely unheard of among the early animators.) Iwerks's contribution to *Steamboat Willie*, the one all the fuss was about, was not inconsiderable either: apart from animating it, he was the one who had dug out a gadget called the Cinephone (pirated and adapted by Pat Powers from RCA's sound-recording system) and used it to synchronize the soundtrack. As a result of all this he was assured of a steady job – and in 1929 he was provisionally promoted from just plain "animator" to "director." Moreover, for a time Walt was actually paying Iwerks a higher salary than he was paying himself. But, even so, it was Walt who was being feted and rapidly becoming wealthy.

The musician Carl Stalling, who was Disney Studios' primary source of scores for the shorts the company was now swiftly producing, had an idea for a new series to be run in tandem with the Mickey Mouse cartoons. Essentially, the notion was to produce musical scores based on the classics and then animate them. Quite how enthusiastic Walt was about this idea we don't know, but it seems that Iwerks was; and Walt gave the

two men permission to try the idea out. The result was *The Skeleton Dance*, released in 1929. Viewed today, this cartoon seems very much like a pilot, an exploration of an idea rather than the actual realization of that idea. Nevertheless, it was successful enough to engender what would be the studio's long-running Silly Symphonies series.

Iwerks directed a number of the other Silly Symphonies, but he was beginning to grow restive about working for someone else: from his viewpoint, *he* was the talent behind Disney Studios, and surely he should be striking out on his own. Pat Powers, Walt's distributor at the time, agreed, and offered to set Iwerks up in a studio of his own with a salary double what Walt was giving him. How could Iwerks refuse? Accordingly, he set up Celebrity Pictures and set to work producing a series of cartoons featuring a new character, Flip the Frog.

There was evidently a certain amount of animosity between Walt and Iwerks around the time of the split. Iwerks felt that his contribution to Walt's success was being not so much under-emphasized as written out of history, while for his part Walt felt betrayed by the man whom he'd regarded as his long-standing friend and whom he was paying the biggest salary he could. Both men were partially right, of course. In his years as an independent producer, Iwerks would frequently make little

The Brave Tin Soldier (1934)

♭color ╱animated ◎ 8 minutes
ComiColor

In a toymaker's workshop, a newly made tin soldier is dropped and his leg breaks off; he is therefore thrown in the waste bin. At night all the toys come out to play, him included; most taunt him, but the ballet-dancer doll takes pity on him and love blossoms. A fat king has also fallen for her and attempts to take her by force. After a fight, the soldier is tried (the judge is a Groucho Marx jack-in-the-box) and sentenced to the firing squad; the dancer throws her arms around him and dies with him. Both fall into the fire, where they melt to form a big red heart. Their souls go up the chimney to reach Toy Heaven, where they are reunited and the soldier's leg regenerates. Animated by Jimmie Culhane and Al Eugster.

Little Black Sambo (1935)

♭color ╱animated ◎ 8 minutes
ComiColor

Bathed by his Mammy, little Black Sambo is told to steer clear of the tiger: "That old tiger sure do like dark meat!" The family dog hears this, and as a prank — using the slats of a freshly painted fence to give himself stripes — disguises himself as a tiger. Predictably, the real tiger enters the scene; at one point during the fairly humdrum japes Sambo is so scared by the beast that he turns into a white boy. For obvious reasons, this short is rarely seen today.

Mary's Little Lamb (1935)

♭color ╱animated ◎ 8 minutes
ComiColor

It's Mary's last day of classes, and her lamb follows her to school. Her schoolmistress (an elderly, waspish woman who is a recurring character in other Iwerks toons) holds a "concert" of the kids' party pieces, and the lamb tries to join in — amid much looped animation. There are cameo appearances by Horace Horsecollar and Clarabelle Cow lookalikes. Mary's panties have as much of a screen presence as in a lower-grade anime movie.

barbed allusions to his resentment in the form of minor characters who resembled with astonishing closeness those stalwarts he had created for Disney Studios, such as Mickey Mouse, Clarabelle Cow, and Horace Horsecollar. Walt retaliated by making Iwerks a non-person at Disney Studios, downgrading perceptions of Iwerks's contributions to the extent that it was as if the man had never been there. (This may have been the origin of the long-term Disney policy, still evident today, whereby absolutely everything is claimed to have been Walt's doing — unless it was a disaster, of course.)

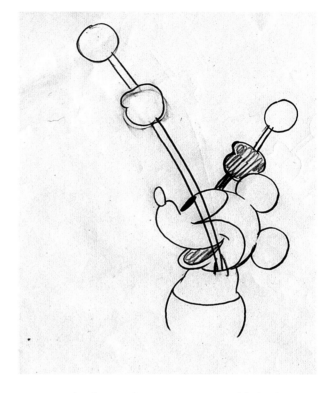

Animation drawing from *Steamboat Willie* (1928).
Private collection. © Disney Enterprises, Inc.

What neither Powers nor Iwerks had realized, however, was that Walt's contribution to the output of Disney Studios was much greater than it appeared on the surface. Just as it's a truism in the publishing world that a good editor can turn a poor manuscript into a great book, so Walt was uniquely able to draw the very best out of the animators working for him and subtly mold it so that it was even better. In particular, he was a master of *story*. In the early days of animation, story didn't seem very important: audiences were fascinated enough by the moving creatures on the screen that they were prepared to laugh at just about anything. All that seemed to be necessary to a successful short was the stringing together of a few visual gags. Walt himself followed this pattern in the early Mickey shorts and most of their predecessors. But, particularly in the Alice Comedies, he had realized that animated shorts could be much more successful, and animated humor much more effective, if the shorts told a properly formed story — with a beginning, a development, and an end — and deployed genuinely rounded characters rather than just recognizable shapes on the screen.

When Iwerks presented *Fiddlesticks*, the first Flip the Frog cartoon, to Powers, Powers knew there was something less than satisfactory about it but wasn't quite sure what. There was some

consternation: he had been planning to sell the Celebrity Pictures output to MGM, and here he was with a pilot that wasn't up to snuff. The animation was fine – as good as Disney Studios was producing, for obvious reasons – and there were one or two good gags, but the movie didn't spark any audience interest in its eponymous character. Powers concluded that it was the character itself that was at fault, and insisted that in future shorts Flip become less froglike and more human. Iwerks obeyed and, beginning with *The Village Barber* (1930), the third in the series, Flip was essentially no longer a frog in anything but name. The change was effective enough for the sale to MGM to go through (representing MGM's first foray into the animation field). In fact, the standard of the Flip shorts did steadily improve, but it was not enough to make the character in any way a rival to Mickey.

The two men tried just about everything to improve the popular appeal of the series – even sex: shorts like *The Office Boy* (1932) and *Room Runners* (1932) are sufficiently salacious that one might think twice, even today, about showing them on kids' television. Iwerks recruited an incredibly strong team to Celebrity Pictures: Carl Stalling provided most of the music, while his roster of animators included such legends of the industry as Shamus/Jimmie Culhane (who is credited by both names on different occasions), Norm Blackburn, Al Eugster, and Grim Natwick. A very youthful Chuck Jones had a job as a cel washer but didn't last long. In later years, Jones would identify another reason for Celebrity Pictures' long dark twilight of mediocrity: Iwerks "had no sense of humor." This was slightly unjust: the truth was that Iwerks's sense of humor remained stuck somewhere in pre-adolescence, so that a wobbling female bottom or bosom was regarded as thigh-slappingly funny – cows' udders being a particular favorite source of mirth. (Walt Disney had a similar weakness for "funny" udders, but in due course had the good sense to be talked out of it by those around him.)

The popularity of Flip, never high, slowly waned: the writing was clearly on the wall for the series. It was urgent that Iwerks and Powers come up with some replacement. This proved to be Willie Whopper, a little boy who, sparked by some incident in daily life, is inspired to tell his friends tall stories about his own supposed adventures. Thus, in the series pilot, *The Air Race* (made in 1933 but not released until 1936), a poster for an airshow has Willie telling of how he won the National Air Race and was kissed by Amelia Earhart. In *Viva Willie* (1934) our hero journeys in his imagination to the Wild West, defeating bandits and getting the gal (and wearing a cowboy hat that looks surely more than coincidentally like a condom). In *The Good Scout* (1934), spurred by scoutish talk of good deeds, he gets dragged into the rescuing of a kidnapped girl. The formula is pretty rigid, but, in fact, because these cartoons do genuinely have to tell a story – that's their very raison d'être – they're in general far more entertaining than their Flip precursors.

The public didn't think so, however, and most historians tend to agree with that judgment. Only 14 Willie Whopper shorts

The Air Race (1936)

🎞 b/w / animated ⏱ 8 minutes
Willie Whopper

This was the first Willie Whopper cartoon, made in 1933 as a pilot for the series but not released until much later, in 1936, after the series had been abandoned.

Willie and three pals are playing when they spot a poster advertising an airshow promising "Daredevils of the Sky." This is enough to drive Willie into one of his pseudo-reminiscences: "Did I ever tell you how I won the National Air Race?" Fade to the great day. Willie is the favorite of Amelia Earhart, who blows him a kiss, but a vast bully of a pilot decides he is Enemy Number One and uses every possible cheating strategy in his (of course unsuccessful) attempts to bring about Willie's downfall and win the race himself. The planes fly so high they pass the pearly gates, where St. Peter, disturbed by the racket, angrily gives them the finger. At one point, a fireworks factory is shredded by the racing planes and, once the debris has settled, some of the letters of its FIREWORKS sign have rearranged themselves to spell IWERKS. Willie wins and receives a trophy and a smacking kiss from Earhart. His friends are prepared to swallow the rest of the tale, but not that Earhart kissed him.

were made before the series was abandoned, the last – apart from the "posthumous" release of *The Air Race* – being 1934's *Viva Willie*. Since Flip had vanished after 1933's *Soda Squirt*, the studio's future depended on another series begun in 1933, the ComiColor Cartoons, which were, effectively, clones of Disney's Silly Symphonies, as developed after Iwerks's parting of the ways with Walt. These were much more successful than the Flip and Willie series, and they compare very well with the early Silly Symphonies – probably because, once again, they were of necessity story-driven. However, they showed no particular *progression*: they did not get steadily better, as one might have expected, but all remained of roughly the same standard and nature. Unlike the output from some other studios, it's impossible to establish any kind of chronological order simply by watching them: the early ones and the late ones are extremely similar.

Thanks to the ComiColor shorts, Celebrity Pictures struggled on another couple of years, until September 1936, when MGM canceled the series and, with it, all plans for a new series based on Gene Byrnes's long-running (1917–49) newspaper comic strip *Reg'lar Fellers*; the last of the ComiColor Cartoons to be released, *Happy Days* (1936), was in fact the pilot for this new series. It's a fairly pleasing little movie, and one's historical assessment of Iwerks's efforts might have been radically different had the series been allowed to proceed.

Meanwhile, Iwerks was out of a job. He was swiftly picked up by Leon Schlesinger of Warners, where, during a brief stay, he directed a couple of Porky Pig Looney Tunes – *Porky and Gabby*

(1937) and *Porky's Super Service* (1937) – before accepting an offer from Columbia to direct for their Color Rhapsodies series of shorts. During the next four years he directed 14 shorts for Columbia, most of them featuring Scrappy, a cheeky little boy created by Dick Huemer in 1931 and the studio's mainstay alongside Krazy Kat. A total of 14 shorts in four years suggests that Iwerks was not exactly over-employed – this was, after all, the man who could singlehandedly animate a short in three weeks. It seems that he stuck with Columbia as long as he did simply because there was no particular inducement for him to leave. Eventually, in 1940, he left; everyone *did* leave Columbia after a while, whether or not they had another prospect in view, because the animation studio was, by all accounts, a sweatshop and widely regarded within the business as the pits.

Iwerks then made a brief sojourn to the United Kingdom, about which not much is known save that he produced there a couple of short-lived and extremely obscure cartoon series: the Way-Out shorts, which were probably parody travelogues, and the Gran'pop Monkey shorts. There were at least three of the latter: *A Busy Day* (1940), *Baby Checkers* (1940), and *Beauty Shoppe* (1940). The central character was a wise and wily old chimp who had been created for a popular series of postcards by the prolific British illustrator (Clarence) Lawson Wood.

The friendship with Walt Disney had been patched up somewhere along the way, and on Iwerks's return to the U.S. he rejoined Disney Studios. This time, however, he was employed not as an animator but to head what was in effect Disney's special-effects department, although the term had yet to gain currency. He was the technical genius behind such animation/live-action movies as *Song of the South* (1946), *Mary Poppins* (1964), and *Bedknobs and Broomsticks* (1971), as well as the dramatic, Oscar-winning effects for Disney's *Twenty Thousand Leagues Under the Sea* (1964). Iwerks himself won two technical Oscars: the Technical Achievement Award in 1960 for "the design of an improved optical printer for special effects and matte shots" and the Academy Award of Merit (shared) in 1965 for "the conception and perfection of techniques for color traveling matte composite cinematography." His best-known Oscar, however, was the one he didn't get, although he was nominated for it – for Best Effects, Special Visual Effects for his work on Alfred Hitchcock's *The Birds* (1963). Much earlier he had devised the technique whereby drawings could be xeroxed onto cels rather than painstakingly traced in ink; its first major use was in *One Hundred and One Dalmatians* (1961). When he died – on July 7, 1971 – he was remembered mainly for his technical achievements rather than his animation. His son Don followed in his father's footsteps, spending 35 years at Disney designing film systems for Disneyland and Disney World before, in 1986, leaving to set up Iwerks Entertainment, now a successful provider of "location-based entertainment attractions" – i.e., roughly carrying on much as he had been doing for Disney.

Iwerks is certainly not a forgotten figure in the history of animation, but equally he is not the major figure one might have expected back in the late 1920s, when he and Walt Disney were together forming the cutting edge of this relatively young artform. What went wrong?

There have been earlier allusions to the rudimentary nature of his sense of humor and in particular to his lack of storytelling ability – even of the ability to recognize what a story actually *is* – but this doesn't account for his status as *the* major figure of early sound animation to be eclipsed by the passage of years: plenty of other animators whose names are still well known suffered the same failings. There must be something more, and I suggest it was this:

Iwerks's problem was that he never *matured* as an animator. This statement requires some qualification. The early animators were all, initially, like kids who have just been given a new computer and spend all their time playing video games on it – because video games are impressive and a novelty and easy fun. To those animators, it seemed that presenting audiences with comic cavortings of drawn characters on the screen was quite enough to constitute entertainment; the very novelty of seeing such a thing was supposed to enthrall. To egg the pudding, additional amusement was supposedly conveyed through the fact that the characters were (in general) not human beings but animals behaving as humans might: anthropomorphism was, it was assumed, of itself inherently funny. For these reasons most of the very earliest commercial animation – whether by Disney, the Fleischers, Terry, or whomever – is actually pretty dire to the modern audience and, one suspects, was little more palatable to the audiences of the day. Very soon, however, the best animators began to discover the true potential of animation and moved on from mere comic cuts to all the other things this new medium might be made to do. This is not to say that they abandoned comedy and knockabout farce, but more inventive animators swiftly discovered the form of surreal, reality-bending comedy that the genre has mined ever since. Iwerks was perfectly aware that this capability of the medium existed, and so naturally he incorporated such elements into his work; what he seems never to have realized, however, is that an important component of such humor – every bit as important as the visual surrealism – is the surrealism of the creator's mind. Genuine *wit*, in other words. Either Iwerks lacked it entirely or it never occurred to him that the ingredient was essential – one suspects a bit of both. Either way, the net result is that, watching his cartoons, one sees farm animal after farm animal being stretched into improbable forms or flattened by impact after impact, without the distortion of reality ever once really engaging the interest.

CHUCK JONES (1912–)

Still from *Duck Amuck* (1953). © Warner Bros.

Charles Martin Jones was born on September 21, 1912, in Spokane, Washington, the third of four children. His father had a habit of starting short-lived business ventures, each requiring its complement of printed, letterheaded stationery, much of which outlasted the businesses. The Jones children therefore always had plentiful supplies of drawing paper – probably as a direct consequence, all four ended up with careers in the field of art and design. It was also a very bookish household: reading was a way of life. These two factors combined to produce an artist whose mastery of the animated short has been second to none.

Oddly for such a highly literate and intelligent child, Jones dropped out of high school – seemingly just because he found it boring – continuing his formal studies at the age of 15 at the Chouinard Art Institute in Los Angeles. Here he learned about anatomy, and how to draw it; during his early career as an animator, in an era when most animators were entirely self-trained and thus lacked genuine drawing skills, this knowledge would set him apart from his peers. (Walt Disney, aware of the problem among his own animators, inaugurated art classes for his employees and also regularly imported animals and actors so that the animators could learn to draw movement. In the studio where Jones would spend much of his animating career there were no such luxuries, so it was significant that he brought these skills with him.) His characters may

129

The Night Watchman (1938)

color / animated / 7 minutes
Merrie Melodies

The first cartoon to be directed by Jones is charming but slight. Thos. Cat, night watchman to the kitchen, has the flu, so his enthusiastic but klutzy young son must do the job for him. The mice have a field day, eating everything in sight, then put on a musical floor show. As the kitten, intimidated one last time by the mouse ringleader, is about to give up, his good angel exhorts him not to take this lying down; he goes back and beats the stuffing out of the mice. The kitten physically resembles Jones's later series character Sniffles (even though Sniffles is a mouse).

Old Glory (1939)

color / animated / 9 minutes
Merrie Melodies/Porky Pig

A patriotic tub-thumper, released as Europe slid into war, that has Uncle Sam explaining to Porky why he should pledge allegiance to the Stars and Stripes. There are flashbacks to George Washington, Paul Revere, the Declaration of Independence, the Liberty Bell, Abraham Lincoln, and other appropriately stirring icons. This was a very Disneyish cartoon to make, and Jones was selected as the Warners director best able to emulate the realistic Disney style.

Sniffles Takes a Trip (1940)

color / animated / 8¼ minutes
Merrie Melodies/Sniffles

The fourth Sniffles cartoon has the little mouse setting off on a walking trip in the countryside and following a sign to the nature park Country Meadows. There he has various cute adventures with the wildlife. The best gag has him unknowingly slinging his hammock between the legs of a stork, which then, after he has fallen asleep, wades into the water. The lengthy closing sequence, in which Sniffles is terrified by the eyes of the night creatures, is beautifully executed.

not move like the animals they hypothetically are – no rabbit walks like Bugs Bunny – but nevertheless they move with a convincing pseudo-realism: if there were a creature like Bugs, then that is the way he would move, and the viewer never for one moment thinks otherwise. (Sometimes this observation of how creatures move could lead him up blind alleys. For example, his character Pepe Le Pew often goes into a curious, stiff-legged, bouncing mode of locomotion that seems artificial to the viewer and that many find profoundly irritating. In fact, this is a genuine – if occasional – gait of certain animals such as the springbok, called pronking; Jones uses it to indicate the anticipation of bliss. However, realism and "artistic realism" are not always consonant.)

A further element of note was that the family lived near the Charles Chaplin studios in Jones's formative years. The young Jones took full advantage of the opportunities presented to observe comedies being filmed, and in later years he would credit Chaplin's work as giving him his introduction to and instruction in the art of timing; as an animation director he would be markedly obsessive about the exact timing of visual gags, down to the exact frame. His first involvement in movies came when he served as a young extra in a Mack Sennett comedy.

On leaving the Chouinard, Jones found himself unemployed and unemployable: his classes at the Institute had not equipped him with any means of applying his art training. As he tells it, after a short period of near-starvation he was on the verge of accepting a job as a janitor when a friend – Fred Kopietz, later to animate at Disney – told him there was a way in which he could earn a living doing the one thing he was fully capable of doing: drawing. That way was animation.

In 1931 he got a job at Celebrity Pictures, owned by Pat Powers but, far more importantly, run by the pioneer animator Ub Iwerks, the man largely responsible for the creation of Mickey Mouse and who had done the bulk of Walt Disney's animation during the early years. Jones started at the studio as a cel washer. (Celluloid was expensive. It was thus common practice to clean off a used cel so it could be used again.) Also at the Iwerks studio was one of the legendary early animators, Grim Natwick, who had likewise had an art training. Natwick recognized the innate talent of the young cel washer, and before long Jones was working as an inbetweener (see page 83) under Natwick. Because of his art training and its concomitant anatomy lessons, Natwick similarly understood how creatures and people moved. He was able to teach Jones how to animate this movement.

Jones did not last long with Iwerks before being fired and striking out on his own, again briefly, as a freelance portraitist. The formative change in his career came in 1933, when he took a job at Leon Schlesinger Productions, the studio that supplied Warners with cartoon shorts. Leon Schlesinger himself was, Jones would later write, a man whose "sole method of determining the quality of an animated cartoon was how far it came in under budget." Schlesinger's creative ignorance was remarkably useful so far as Jones and the other – then much more significant – employees were concerned. Schlesinger very rarely interfered in anything they did, being content as long as they continued to churn out shorts at the requisite rate and as long as those shorts were acceptable to the distributors.

Schlesinger had just lost Hugh Harman and Rudolf Ising, and with them the series star Bosko. In some desperation, he promoted animator Friz Freleng to be animation director of both Looney Tunes and Merrie Melodies, a situation that didn't last long – the pressure on Freleng must have been intolerable. He then recruited other staff, notable among them being Tex Avery, Bob Clampett, Robert McKimson, and, as a humble in-betweener, the very young Chuck Jones.

Termite Terrace, where Tex Avery directed with Clampett and Jones on his staff, was so called because of its insect population; it was also the division of the studio where Schlesinger least often prowled, having little understanding of or interest in the cartoons that Avery and his team were producing, but glad they were getting excellent audience responses. There could not have been a better environment for Jones's future development as an animator. An integral part of Avery's genius was the realization that animation was an artform in its own right, and that such rules as had been imposed on it were in fact rules derived in other disciplines and applied to animation in blithe disregard for the fact that it was a *different* medium. So, while others worked in the belief that the most successful animation was that which most closely approached live-action, Avery was moving in exactly the opposite direction, away from the conventions of live-action cinema to explore the brand-new playground in which animation could, and, he felt, should, be playing; hence the tricks such as characters running out of the screen and into the audience, or the film seemingly slipping its sprockets, or characters from one cartoon inadvertently straying into another, to name just a few examples. In this exploration beyond the completely artificial boundaries that had been set for animation, Avery was more like an experimental animator than a commercial one, yet his cartoons were intensely commercial, as audience reactions showed. Jones took this lesson on board, and in his later career he was more than happy to push the boundaries back, as exemplified in the short *Duck Amuck* (1953). This depends in its entirety on two seemingly incompatible factors: that the audience and Daffy Duck alike are fully aware that Daffy is an artificial creation of artwork projected onto a screen; and that the audience identifies Daffy as a genuine, living personality, because if they did not do so then the cartoon would lose all of its humor and most of its imaginative affect.

There was a further lesson of Avery's that Jones fully absorbed. Avery once remarked that it wouldn't have mattered if Bugs Bunny was not a rabbit at all; the character would remain the same even if Bugs was to be a bird. This has often been taken as evidence that Avery was not interested in character animation, whereas almost certainly exactly the opposite was true (see page 12). Jones, building on this, realized that what defined an animated character was not appearance *per se* – although obviously it assists the audience to be given an instantly effective visual cue – but *movement*. Thus, in the short *What's Opera, Doc?* (1957), most of which Bugs spends disguised as Brunhilde, we never for one moment believe that the character we are watching *is* Brunhilde: even if the face itself were disguised, movement and other aspects of body language tell us that the person under the wig is Bugs. The result of this incongruity is, naturally, hilarious.

And, of course, there was still one further lesson Jones learned from Avery. Jones already understood timing well, as we've seen, but in Avery he witnessed a great instinctive master of the timing of gags. Jones had that same instinct, but while

The Dover Boys at Pimento University, or The Rivals of Roquefort Hall (1942)

🎨 color / animated ⏱ 8³/₄ minutes
Merrie Melodies
Parodying snobbish college novels of the *fin de siècle*, this tells of the three Dover brothers and their shared fiancée, Dainty Dora Standpipe. She is kidnapped to his hunting lodge by vile and dastardly Dan Backslide, who would have his wicked way with her if only she'd stop beating him up. The brothers, summoned by boy scouts, arrive to find him unconscious; the eldest, Tom, continues beating him up anyway, then clumsily knocks himself and his siblings out. Dora waltzes off into the romantic sunset with a goofy Pimento U. student who has made bit appearances earlier.

My Favorite Duck (1942)

🎨 color / animated ⏱ 7¹/₂ minutes
Merrie Melodies/Daffy Duck & Porky Pig
Porky, on a camping trip, is tormented by Daffy in customary fashion, the duck being super-confident because, as he keeps pointing out to Porky by use of signs and notices, the duck season is closed – as one of the signs says, "Do not even *molest* a duck." But the first of the final set of signs Daffy unrolls proves to say: "Duck Season Opens Today!" In the midst of the subsequent chase the film breaks. After a few moments of white screen, Daffy appears to tell the audience how the movie ended – with him thrashing Porky, of course. But then he is given the hook, and Porky trudges on-screen with a well-bashed duck in tow.

The Aristo-Cat (1943)

🎨 color / animated ⏱ 7¹/₄ minutes
Merrie Melodies/Hubie & Bertie
The butler Meadows is left to look after the cat while the mistress is away. The cat torments Meadows in various ways until the butler quits in disgust. The cat attempts to catch mice for food but doesn't know what a mouse is. Hubie and Bertie persuade him that the neighbor's vast, vicious dog is a mouse – with predictable results. The cat awakens in bed, saying: "What a terrible dream!" But from under the covers emerge the two mice and the dog, the latter saying: "Yeah, wasn't it!"

working with Avery he honed it until, in the years after Avery's departure from Schlesinger and Warners, he was turning it into an exact science, instructing his staff to the precise frame when an action should start or stop for best mirthful effect. To take a single example, when Wile E. Coyote falls off a cliff, as he so frequently does, the timing of what happens to him afterward is not arbitrary but precisely defined; Jones even specified the time between the falling coyote's disappearance into the distance

Odor-able Kitty (1945)

🎨 color / animated ⏱ 7¹/₄ minutes
Merrie Melodies/Pepe Le Pew

Marks the first appearance of Pepe Le Pew, although here he's called Henry and has a family. A disreputable alley cat — in desperation for food and to stop everyone, man and beast, from bullying him — disguises himself as a skunk. Unfortunately, he attracts the amorous interests of a lustful male skunk with an assumed "romantique" French accent, who thinks the tomcat is female. After various chase sequences, during which the cat even disguises himself as Bugs Bunny, the skunk's wife and children appear and tow him back to virtuous domesticity. Thereafter the cat, washed clean of any disguise, revels in the physical abuses he receives on the street as preferable to the amorous attentions of the skunk.

Inki at the Circus (1947)

🎨 color / animated ⏱ 7¹/₄ minutes
Merrie Melodies/Inki

A little African boy with a bone in his topknot, Inki was a racial stereotype who was featured in about five of Jones's shorts. In this example, Inki's bone attracts a pair of dogs, who seize it, along with Inki, and subject him to indignities. They meet their match, though, when a sinister mina bird (paired with Inki in other shorts) escapes from its pen and fights them back. Inki tries to make pals with the bird, but it isn't interested, flicking the bone in his hair so that it spins propeller-like. There is further clowning between the four before the bone ends up in the mina's topknot.

Duck Amuck (1953)

🎨 color / animated ⏱ 7 minutes
Daffy Duck/Bugs Bunny

This starts with Daffy in Three Musketeers guise, but almost immediately the background changes to a farm, and he immediately becomes a hoe-wielding farmer. From that point onward nothing is fixed: a skiing Daffy starts off in the Arctic and arrives in the South Seas, only to run out of scenery as he dances along; when he complains to the animator, the animator's eraser rubs him off the screen, repainting him in place as a Mexican flamenco guitarist, but now without sound, then with the wrong sound effects . . . After multiple changes, Daffy yells in frustration, "Let's get this picture started!" and "The End" appears. But this is far from the short's end, as the argument with the animator continues. After the film's ratchet has apparently slipped — so that the two Daffies from adjacent frames can climb into a single frame and fight each other — and various further humiliations, Daffy demands to see who's responsible for all this. We discover the animator is Bugs Bunny.

below and the emergence of the characteristic ring of orange dust to mark his impact.

All of this lay ahead for the young man who was inbetweening (see page 83) for Avery on Termite Terrace. It was soon realized that he had a bright talent, and this was encouraged by giving him increased responsibilities. Soon he was working as a fully fledged animator, and in about 1936 he was given his first short to direct, *The Night Watchman* (1938). There is something in this short of Tom & Jerry, although in fact Hanna and Barbera would not start that series for a couple of years yet. By no means a landmark short in any way other than marking Jones's debut, it is nevertheless surprisingly accomplished for a maiden venture; and its failings – such as a pretty grim song-and-dance showtime routine – seem imported ones, born from the nervousness of a young man to abandon entirely the conventions established by his elders.

And so to Bugs Bunny. Although his name is inseparably linked to the character, and although he was in there very close to the start, Jones did not create Bugs Bunny. Exactly who did is a slightly muddied issue, because a rabbit character of that name figured in a few Warners shorts before Avery picked it up by the scruff of its neck and created from it, in *A Wild Hare* (1940), the inimitable Bugs. The prototype rabbit character first appeared in a short done by Ben "Bugs" Hardaway called *Porky's Hare Hunt* (1938); before *A Wild Hare* appeared, Hardaway would direct one more short with the rabbit, *Hare-Um Scare-Um* (1939), and Jones two, *Prest-O Change-O* (1939) and *Elmer's Candid Camera* (1940). The latter is of additional interest because this was the short that introduced the fully-formed Elmer Fudd, developed in stages by the Termite Terrace crew from a series character Avery had created, called Egghead. Avery's version of Bugs was an immediate hit. In the hands of Jones and Bob Clampett the character was further molded, so that soon he had more or less the complete physical appearance of the Bugs we know today. (It is evidence of Avery's contention that characterization does not depend on appearance alone that the Bugs of *A Wild Hare* is physically quite different from the later Bugs, yet is unmistakably the same character.) Also involved in the rapid development at Warners of the new star was Friz Freleng. But, in a way, he went off on a path of his own, giving Bugs a semi-permanent antagonist in the form of Yosemite Sam, necessitating a different setting and ethos. This left Jones and Clampett to deal with what we can regard as the main line of Bugs's biography, the shorts in which he interacted with Elmer and Daffy.

Like all the important American commercial animators of the day, Jones made propaganda cartoons during World War II, notably 12 of the 26 Private Snafu training cartoons. Warners issued these as a segment of *The Army–Navy Screen Magazine* compilations put together for the benefit of American troops fighting overseas. Dr. Seuss wrote a number of them; it is roughly from here that his friendship with Jones dates, a friendship that was to bear animation fruit decades later. Like Goofy in the various Disney *How To* shorts, Private Snafu demonstrates exactly the wrong way of doing everything.

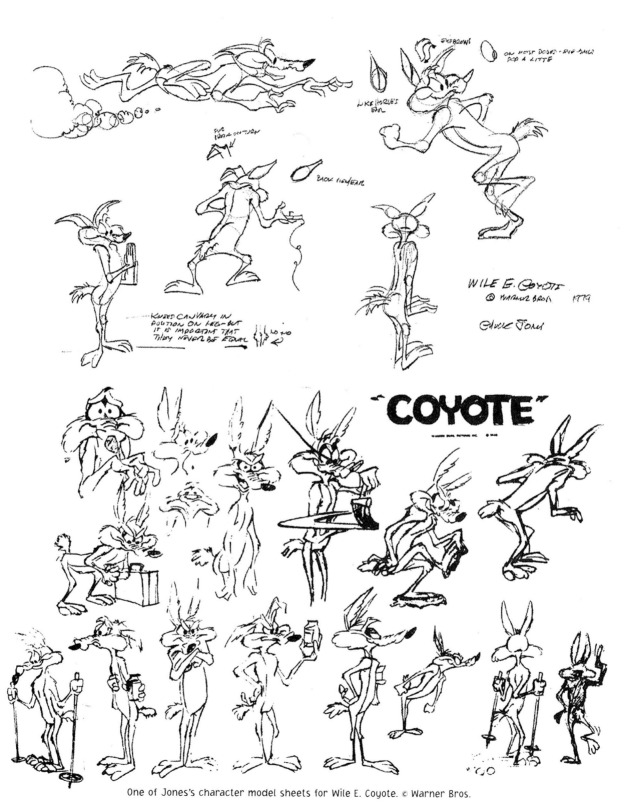

One of Jones's character model sheets for Wile E. Coyote. © Warner Bros.

CHUCK JONES

What's Opera, Doc? (1957)

🎨color /animated ⏱7 minutes

Widely regarded as both Jones's and Bugs's finest hour — or, at least, seven minutes — this translocates an almost standard Bugs/Elmer tale into Wagnerian opera, making a seven-minute Ring Cycle of it. Elmer is Siegfried; Bugs is most notably Brunhilde. Their sung and balletically scored courtship is almost moving before Bugs's wig falls off and Siegfried recognizes the Wabbit. Calling upon the elements — "typhoons, hurricanes, earthquakes, smog" — Siegfried smites Bugs, then tragically mourns him, the "dead" rabbit raising his head just long enough to say: "Well, what did you expect in an opera? A happy ending?"

How the Grinch Stole Christmas! (1966) tvm

(vt *Dr. Seuss' How the Grinch Stole Christmas!*)

🎨color /animated ⏱ 24 minutes

The Grinch, who lives with his intimidated dog Max 10,000 feet up a mountaintop north of Whoville, loathes Christmas — perhaps because "his shoes were too tight," perhaps because "if there's one thing I hate, it's the noise, noise, noise," or most likely because "his heart was two sizes too small" — and each year the sight of the jollifications in the valley below makes him madder. This year, after having endured it for 52 years in a row, he plots to "stop Christmas from coming." He makes himself a Santa outfit, dresses up Max as a reindeer, and sets off to sleigh into town, where he goes from house to house removing all the gifts, candies, food, and decorations. But the next morning, people are joyful for Christmas even without the gifts, and he suddenly realizes what the festival is all about. Still dressed as Santa, he goes back into Whoville, redistributes all the goodies, and celebrates Christmas with everyone else.

Cat and Dupli-Cat (1967)

🎨color /animated ⏱ 6¼ minutes
Tom & Jerry

One of the last in the rather unsuccessful series of Jones-directed Tom & Jerry cartoons, this is set on the dockside, where Tom and a disreputable waterfront cat do battle over possession of Jerry. In this contest, there can be only one winner, of course: Jerry. The title refers to a protracted sequence in which the two cats think the other is a reflection in a mirror.

By this time Jones had developed a series star of his own, the by now largely forgotten Sniffles, a sort of innocent abroad of the mouse species whose naïveté kept landing him in one scrape after another. Sniffles debuted in 1939 with *Naughty but Mice* and lasted somewhat unenthusiastically for twelve cartoons, until *Hush My Mouse* (1946) saw the last of him. The Sniffles shorts are pleasant

and funny enough, but they lack the bite associated with both Jones and the Warners stable in general. Somewhat later came Henery Hawk, who starred alongside such stalwarts as Foghorn Leghorn and Daffy in nine cartoons, from *The Squawkin' Hawk* (1942) to *All Fowled Up* (1955), and Marvin Martian, who vied with Bugs and Daffy in seven cartoons, from *Haredevil Hare* (1948) to *Spaced Out Bunny* (1980). But far more significant was Pepe Le Pew, who starred in sixteen shorts — in addition to at least one cameo appearance — from *Odor-able Kitty* (1945) to *Louvre Come Back to Me* (1962) and captured the hearts of millions, though never the heart of whichever new lovely he craved. Jones has admitted that Pepe is a partial reflection of himself in his younger days — ever eager to catch the girl but somehow always being "disqualified." But the reason Pepe has proved so enduringly popular, far beyond what the comparatively small number of his cartoons would suggest, is that most of us, male or female, can identify with the little skunk. We have almost all, at some point or another, resorted to desperate artificial stratagems, like Pepe's hilarious "Freunch accong," in order to appear as dashing, romantic hero(in)es, only to watch the object of our desires run for the hills. In laughing at Pepe and his antics we are laughing at ourselves and our pretensions.

The greatest of all Jones's creations, however, was not really a character but an oeuvre: the Road Runner & Coyote cartoons. There have been 43 of these, with more possibly in the pipeline, from *Fast and Furry-ous* (1949) to *Chariots of Fur* (1994). In addition, Wile E. Coyote has matched wits (unsuccessfully, of course) with Bugs Bunny in *Operation: Rabbit* (1952), *Compressed Hare* (1961), and *Hare-Breadth Hurry* (1963), but in these he seems almost a different character masquerading under the same name and appearance, even though the director of all three cartoons was Jones. The first interesting thing to note about the Road Runner & Coyote cartoons is that the series title is in a way a misnomer: they are really just Coyote cartoons, because Road Runner is merely what Alfred Hitchcock named a McGuffin, a device to drive the plot but having no actual relevance to it. It does not matter what the object of Wile E. Coyote's obsession is: the mainspring of these cartoons is the obsession itself and its consequences — which are, without exception, injurious to the coyote. Fittingly, the Road Runner goes uncharacterized: he (or it could even be she) lacks personality entirely, being merely a moving target that occasionally pauses to say "Beep! Beep!" — a line Jones and his favorite screenwriter, Mike Maltese, derived from hearing a heavily laden colleague making his way along a crowded corridor at Termite Terrace, just when they were seeking to vocalize the bird. For all that it matters, Wile E. Coyote might have been seeking to travel to the Moon or to swat an irritating fly: the joke is that he will go to absurd lengths — often, foolishly, involving the purchase of gadgetry from Acme, whose gadgetry always malfunctions in some slight but fundamentally important way — for the sake of achieving what is, in this instance, an exceedingly trivial goal. There must be other road runners in the simplified American West where the saga is played out; but Wile E. Coyote wants, *needs*, to catch *this* one.

Still from *One Froggy Evening* (1955). © Warner Bros.

Again, as with Pepe, a reason for the phenomenal success of the series is that we identify a part of ourselves with Wile E. Coyote and his obsession. We have all, at some point or another, done something exactly analogous: irate to discover, shall we say, that the one and only pen we want on this particular day has gone missing, we go in frenzied search of it, despite the fact that there other, equally serviceable pens readily available on all sides. Later, we see how crazily we were behaving and laugh about it; Wile E. Coyote, of course, never does. An ancillary point of identification is that Wile E. Coyote exemplifies the Gadget Man (or Woman) locked up inside most of us: just as he forever puts his faith in the products of Messrs. Acme, so do we clutter up our lives and our attics with miracle technological gadgets that promise much and, once bought and eagerly, childishly brought home and unwrapped, deliver little.

A further advantage of the Road Runner & Coyote shorts, so far as the Termite Terrace crew was concerned, was that they could be done relatively quickly. All that the bean counters of Warners required was that each animation director produce one marketable cartoon every four or five weeks. Anything that took substantially longer than that, as

determined by the worksheets the staff turned in, was a cartoon that had not earned its keep. Every now and then, however, a cartoon would come along which the team on Termite Terrace realized had to be done properly or it was not worth doing at all, a dilemma which creators probably as far back as Leonardo da Vinci have tried in vain to explain to those who hold the purse strings. Jones has described how the team got around this:

In order to create a piece like *What's Opera Doc?* the animation team had to cheat. We had so many Road Runners, we knew we could do them fast. All eight animators would work like crazy to finish a Road Runner picture in two and a half weeks, but would keep "Road Runner" on their worksheets after they'd started on something like *What's Opera Doc?* This meant we could produce an extra film over eight or nine weeks.

The Phantom Tollbooth (1969)

♭color /animated/live-action ⊙ 89 minutes

In live action, Milo finds the lessons at school boring and pointless. Suddenly, a gigantic gift-wrapped box appears in his bedroom; opened, it reconfigures itself to form a turnpike tollbooth, out of which pops a miniature car. From the map also supplied Milo chooses the Castle in the Air as his destination, and in the car he goes through the tollbooth and into animation. His first calls en route to the Castle in the Air (where the two princesses Rhyme and Reason are incarcerated) are at places called Expectations (where, to judge by the one person he meets, the Whether Man, nothing is ever determined); the Doldrums (where it is against the law to think, or to do *anything*); Dictionopolis (where words are more important than numbers, letters grow on trees, and no one uses one word where six will do); Digitopolis (where numbers are more important than words); and the Mountains of Ignorance (where dwell demons such as the Terrible Trivium, Demon of Petty Tasks and Worthless Jobs). He is befriended by characters like Tock the watchdog (one waits in vain for a "What's up, Tock?" joke), the mad scientist Kakofonous A. Dischord (*sic*), who adores noise, and the Humbug, a ne'er-do-well insect. Through allegory, dialogue, and rather dull songs Milo is taught many lessons about the value of thought and education, the dangers of too little knowledge, and the folly of being too lazy to enjoy oneself. (Based on the novel *The Phantom Tollbooth* (1962) by Norton Juster.)

The Cricket in Times Square
(1973) tvm

♭color /animated ⊙ 25 minutes

Chester C. Cricket is accidentally transported from Connecticut to the Times Square subway station. There he is befriended by newsstand boy Mario, the scruffy Tucker R. Mouse, and Harry the Cat. Newsstand customer Mr. Smedley gives Chester a Chinese cricket cage and tells the ancient Chinese legend of why crickets always tell the truth. It emerges that Chester can make beautiful music with his wings and can play anything after hearing it just once. Tucker dreams up the idea of Chester performing to bring new customers to the ailing newsstand, and sure enough the commuters flock to hear the cricket play, especially after Smedley informs the newspapers. (Based on the book *The Cricket in Times Square* (1960) by George Selden.)

In a way, it seems curious to ascribe the creation of any of these characters – Pepe Le Pew, Wile E. Coyote, and the rest – to Jones alone, because this was not really the way that Termite Terrace worked. Let me stress that these comments are not meant to imply that Jones did *not* create Pepe and the others. But anything that came out of Termite Terrace was to some greater or lesser extent, consciously or unconsciously, collaborative in nature. By way of analogy, when The Beatles were in their prime, there were some Lennon–McCartney songs that were by Lennon and some that were by McCartney; it was only after The Beatles split up and the two musicians began releasing solo albums that it became obvious how important the mere presence of the other was to each of these two songwriters. Similarly, Jones might have come up with Wile E. Coyote and Road Runner even if Clampett, McKimson, Freleng, and the rest had not been there, but would they have been the *same* Wile E. Coyote and Road Runner? Almost certainly not. This becomes most obvious when we start looking at some of the other Warners series stars, in particular Daffy Duck, Porky Pig, Elmer Fudd, and, of course, Bugs Bunny. All of these characters would not have become as we know them today had it not been for Jones. But the same can be said for Clampett, Avery, McKimson, and others, including Noble, Maltese, Blanc, and Freleng. In later years, Jones and Clampett, who had never much liked each other, would feud over this point. Clampett's perfectly natural resentment over the fact that blanket public credit was blindly being given to Jones for everything good that came out of Termite Terrace was in turn resented by Jones. It was a foolish feud, and neither man came out of it with much credit.

It shouldn't be thought that Jones devoted his entire time at Warners to series cartoons – far from it. There were some notable one-offs. There was *One Froggy Evening* (1955), in which a man discovers an all-singing-all-dancing frog and believes he can make his fortune from the creature; unfortunately, the fates conspire to ensure that, whatever fabulous performances the frog might put on, no one will ever witness them apart from its luckless owner, who dies not so much a broken man as one who continues to put his faith in something that all the empirical evidence suggests will never come about. Another memorable one-off is *High Note* (1960), whose "characters" are notes written on a staff and act during a performance of Strauss's *Blue Danube* waltz; the High Note is one that has over-imbibed before the concert and hence acts, to euphemize, unpredictably. Later, during his comparatively short tenure at MGM, Jones would revisit this territory in *The Dot and the Line* (1965) and win an Oscar for it. A great early one-off by Jones for Warners was *The Dover Boys at Pimento University, or The Rivals of Roquefort Hall* (1942), in which he expropriated ideas that were then at the cutting edge of graphic design and somehow made a very funny and in, some ways, moving limited-animation cartoon short from them.

Jack Warner, a man whose bean counter habits were so notorious that someone once suggested he had rubber pockets in his suits, so as to be able to steal soup, closed down the Warners animation studio in 1953, believing that animation was dead because the only thing audiences would want in the future was 3D movies. During the four months it took Jack Warner to realize that he'd been mistaken and should open the animation studio again, Jones worked for Disney; exactly what he drew there, apart from a paycheck, has gone unrecorded by history.

CHUCK JONES

In 1962, with cinema audiences plummeting as television took hold and the animated short increasingly seeming an expensive irrelevance, there was to be no reprieve for the Warners animation division. In conjunction with Les Goldman, Jones started a company called Tower 12 Productions, whose main aim was to produce shorts for MGM, which had closed down its animation department in 1954 but nevertheless saw a market for animated shorts. The ones produced for MGM by Tower 12 Productions were mostly Tom & Jerry cartoons, which with hindsight Jones realized he was not adequately fitted for. It might seem that Jerry and Tom could be treated much as Road Runner and Coyote, with in each case the latter engaged in an endless pursuit of the former, but the parallel is not exact: Tom and Jerry have a relationship and are thus genuinely co-stars, whereas, as noted, in the Road Runner & Coyote movies there is really only one participant. Jones's Tom & Jerry cartoons are by no means as embarrassing as he seems to think they are, but at the same time it is true to say they represent both him and the characters at less than their best. The finest of the Tom & Jerry cartoons by Hanna and Barbera gain their excellence from the fact that, while superbly imaginative in terms of their *mises en scènes*, they are in no sense arty. The Jones of *What's Opera, Doc?* and others had become a very arty director, and this was one of his great merits. The rather self-conscious application of this artiness to Tom & Jerry, as if he were over-aware of the need to surpass anything Hanna and Barbera had done, leads to cartoons that are in their own curious way rather good, yet are at the same time somewhat unengaging *Tom & Jerry* cartoons.

Also in 1962 was established Chuck Jones Enterprises (CJE), a company devoted to producing animation for television; a division of it, Chuck Jones Productions, concentrates on theatrical cartoons, including a few shorts and the animated sections of live-action features like the joyous technofantasy *Stay Tuned* (1992) and the mainstream Robin Williams vehicle *Mrs. Doubtfire* (1993). Under the CJE umbrella, Jones has done some remarkable work, including the tv specials *The Cricket in Times Square* (1973) and its sequels; the Kipling adaptation *Rikki-Tikki-Tavi* (1975) and its sequels; *A Connecticut Rabbit in King Arthur's Court* (1978), featuring Bugs Bunny; and a pair of tv specials featuring Raggedy Ann and Andy – *The Great Santa Claus Caper* (1978) and *The Pumpkin who Couldn't Smile* (1979). In addition, Jones has coproduced for television *Dr. Seuss' Cat in the Hat* (1971) and executive-produced the classic Richard Williams special *Charles Dickens' A Christmas Carol, Being a Ghost Story of Christmas* (1971). Amid a torrent of other work has been the feature *The Bugs Bunny/Road-Runner Movie* (1979), the co-writing, with his first wife, Dorothy, of the feature *Gay Purr-ee* (1962), the title animation for the feature *Gremlins 2 – The New Batch* (1990), and the direction of the live-action/animated feature *The Phantom Tollbooth* (1969).

All of these are eclipsed in the popular mind by the first tv special he did in conjunction with Dr. Seuss, *How the Grinch Stole Christmas!* (vt *Dr. Seuss' How the Grinch Stole Christmas!*), which since its first airing on CBS in December 1966 has been shown every Christmas by tv stations all over the world. Here one can witness the perfect combination of animation director (Jones) with original illustrator and writer (Seuss), but there's a little more to it than that: what resounds throughout the featurette is the love Jones has for Seuss's use of language; as Seuss's witty yet weightily oratorical lines, read by none less than Boris Karloff, resonate across the soundtrack, Jones's moving pictures resonate visually in seemingly divinely inspired accord.

Jones is still a player in the theatrical animation arena. During the 1990s, apart from those films noted, he has been responsible for *Another Froggy Evening* (1995), *From Hare to Eternity* (1996), *Superior Duck* (1996), *Pullet Surprise* (1997), and *Father of the Bird* (1997). He received an honorary Oscar in 1996. There have been exhibitions of his art in venues including the Museum of Modern Art in New York (1985) and the Capitol Children's Museum National Center for Animation in Washington, D.C. (1995). He has been the subject of the documentaries *Chuck Amuck: The Movie* (1989), *Chuck Jones – A Life of Animation* (1991), *Chuck Jones: Extremes and In-Betweens* (2000), and others, and has written books including *Chuck Amuck: The Life and Times of an Animated Cartoonist* (1989) and *Chuck Reducks: Drawings from the Fun Side of Life* (1996). For some years now, however, this creative dynamo has concentrated most of his energies, aside from those involved in the running of his businesses, on fine art, a book of which is planned for publication.

Someone once remarked that "Chuck Jones is up there near the top of everybody's personal pantheon," yet, for all that, the man himself seems somewhat diffident about recognizing the scale of his achievements. Entirely typical of him is this remark, from an interview he gave in 1988 to Steven Bailey:

> I'd say I did a lot of good cartoons that were enjoyed by a lot of people, and someone else pegged me as an "artist." We certainly didn't regard ourselves as artists when we were doing them – we were making films that we thought would last maybe two or three years.

The decades have passed on and, if anything, those short movies made to "last maybe two or three years" are, thanks to television and video, more popular now than they have ever been. Not always, but often, Jones dedicated to something thought to be ephemeral all the artistry that most others would reserve solely for the premeditatedly permanent. In doing this he was not alone among the animators of his generation, but Jones's offerings have survived better into the 21st century than almost anyone else's, so that today the best of them seem almost to have been made just yesterday for each new screening.

RENÉ LALOUX (1929–)

Born in Paris, René Laloux had already earned himself a reputation as a fine-art painter before he entered the world of animation. This was not where he started, however: his initial career was in psychiatric management, and by the age of 27 he had been appointed manager of the Cour Cheverny psychiatric clinic, where he opened a studio as occupational therapy for the patients. It was this which led to his first essay into animated moviemaking, the short *Les dents du singe* ("The Monkey's Teeth"; 1960), which was written and drawn by his patients; it was done in collaboration with Paul Grimault's studio.

He thereafter collaborated with Roland Topor on two extremely well received shorts, *Les temps morts* ("Dead Times"; 1964) and *Les escargots* ("The Snails"; 1965). In 1969, he and Topor were working on an animated feature, and on the strength of their shorts there was a fair amount of eager interest in what the result would be. In the end, *La planète sauvage* (*Fantastic Planet*; 1973), based on a Stefan Wul novel, took four years to complete, and on its first release many found it extremely disappointing: the limited animation offended eyes more accustomed to the Disney or Disneyesque "illusion of life," and, to many, this dreamy semi-science fictional fantasy seemed incomprehensible and willfully opaque. What all agreed upon, however, was that the designs and settings, mostly by Topor, were exceptional: the faces of the giant Draags, who regard the tiny human Oms as vermin, became iconographic images overnight and have remained so to this day, being instantly recognizable to many who have never seen the movie or even do not realize that the images are derived from a movie. Many of the other creatures who populate the planet Yagam (or Ygam) seemed conjured from the mind of a Hieronymus Bosch in a mood of particularly malevolent and gleeful hilarity – such as a plant–animal which, from within a cage of its own roots, seizes insects, or the evil-toothed quasi-shark-like mammals that the wild Oms use as weapons in their fights to the death. Whatever the reviewers thought, however, hippie audiences adored *La planète sauvage*; many recommended a sizable ingestion of marijuana beforehand. It received the Special Grand Prix at the 1973 Cannes Film Festival as well as First Prize at the Trieste Film Festival, the Gold Medal at the Atlanta Film Festival, and the Best Film Award at (perhaps surprisingly) the Teheran Film Festival.

Laloux's second feature movie, *Les maîtres du temps* (*Time Masters*; 1982) followed nearly a decade later. This time his collaborator responsible for the designs was the celebrated Moebius (Jean Giraud); it was based on a comic-book adaptation done in 1978 by Moebius of, again, a Stefan Wul novel. Certainly the movie is visually striking, and there was the same inventiveness in the settings that had characterized *La planète sauvage*; however, this time – at least in the appallingly dubbed English-language version – there genuinely was a murkiness of plot: there are stretches where either nothing happens or what does happen is inexplicable even within the imagined context of the movie. Both are

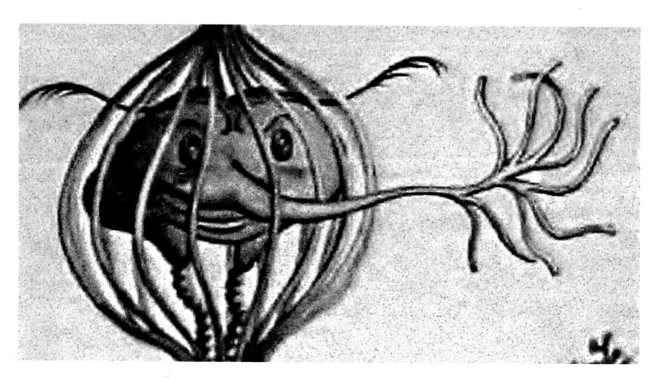

unforgivable sins in what is ostensibly a space opera. But, in places, there is great stylishness, and the visual feel of the movie seems to have contributed something to that of Don Bluth's *Titan A.E.* (2000).

His third feature movie was *Gandahar: les années lumières* (1988), this time adapted by Laloux from a novel (*Les hommes-machines contre Gandahar*; "Robots Against Gandahar"; 1969) by Jean-Pierre Andrevon (usually incorrectly listed as Androvan) and with Philippe Caza doing the drawings and designs; Laloux and Caza had started work on it as early as 1974. Unfortunately, this movie has never been properly released in an English-language version; instead, a thoroughly mangled cut was prepared by Harvey Weinstein, who listed himself as main director ahead of Laloux, and then Isaac Asimov was drafted in to concoct a script that had something to do with the original but, more importantly, attempted to graft some kind of consistent plot onto what Weinstein had done to Laloux's work. This mess was released as *Light Years*. The original plot depicts the adventures of a young servant, Sylvain, and his lovely girlfriend, Airelle. Sylvain has been despatched by Ambisextra, Queen of Gandahar, to find out what has been killing off the guardians of Gandahar's boundaries. They discover an entity called Métamorphe, product of a forgotten science, which has created an army of robots to invade the planet and turn its inhabitants into stone for transportation a thousand years into the future, from where Métamorphe is mounting this operation. The two young people find the Métamorphe of the present, which is still relatively young; it is ignorant of the activities of the being it will become in a millennium's time, and sympathetic to their cause. Thereafter, time paradoxes abound in a movie that cannot properly be taken in all at one viewing.

Since then, there has been no further feature from René Laloux, but he has produced a book on the animated movie: *Ces dessins qui bougent: Cent ans de cinéma d'animation* ("Drawings that Move: A Century of Animation"; 1996). In this, he tries to distinguish the two strands that make U.S. and European animation typically so different in affect, suggesting that U.S. animation is drawing-driven and European animation graphics-driven.

La planète sauvage (1973)

(vt *Fantastic Planet*; vt *Planet of Incredible Creatures*; vt *The Savage Planet*)

color / animated ⏱ 72 minutes

On the planet Yagam, ruled by large blue humanoid creatures called the Draags, live the tiny Oms, evolved descendants of the survivors when the inhabitants of distant planet Earth destroyed their civilization. Tiwa, a Draag girl, adopts the orphan Om boy Terr; like other Om pets he is put into a hi-tech collar so that he is ever under his owner's control. The Draags' main occupation is meditation, during which their souls float free of their bodies. They also periodically mount extermination programs (de-Omizations) against the undomesticated Oms, who are vermin to the Draags. Terr gains access to Tiwa's instructional headset and gets himself an education; later, he takes the headset with him as he escapes into the surreal landscape of Yagam to join the wild Oms. These have been feuding; Terr helps unite them in the wake of the latest de-Omization, and the survivors flee to an abandoned Draag rocket depot, where over the years they establish their own civilization. When Draag exterminators arrive, a few Oms, Terr included, use a rocket to flee to Yagam's satellite, the Fantastic Planet, which they discover is the place the Draags' souls go during meditation, there to engage in a form of spiritual reproduction with the souls of beings from other worlds, an essential process if the Draags are to be perpetuated. A truce must be established between the two species, who thereafter live in partnership and harmony, to their mutual benefit. (Based on the book *Oms en série* (1957) by Stefan Wul.)

Still from *La planète sauvage* (1973), showing the blop-blop, one of the many bizarre creatures inhabiting the eponymous world. Private collection.

Les maîtres du temps (1982)

(vt *Time Masters*)

color / animated ⏱ 78 minutes

A spacecraft is wrecked on the dangerous planet Perdide. Before he dies, the captain, Claude, sends his son, Piel, the sole survivor, into the Forest of the Dolons with a high-tech microphone that permits instantaneous voice communication across the light years; Claude also alerts his friend the spacefarer Jaffar — who possesses another of these microphones — to Piel's predicament. Jaffar makes the slow interstellar journey to Perdide, he and his companions sending a constant beam of survival instructions to the boy. But aboard Jaffar's spaceship is a renegade prince, Matton, on the run from his own people and irate that his flight should be diverted by the rescue mission; he tries to give the boy fatal instructions so that the journey may be resumed. Thwarted by the others — including his wife, Belle, and Jaffar's elderly buddy, Silbad — Matton escapes to the planet Gamma Ten, not knowing it is lethal. Jaffar follows to save him, but is likewise captured by the winged men there, who are mindless puppets of a nameless creature formed of pure thought, which insists on complete uniformity. Matton, changing his stripe, sacrifices himself to destroy the thought-being, free Jaffar, and restore to all the winged slaves their individuality. Other distractions to Jaffar's mission include an encounter with the militaristic Reform; a space storm that cripples both ship and crew; and an interception by servants of the Masters of Time, who are preparing to colonize Perdide by a method that involves throwing the world sixty years back in time. This opens the way to the final revelation — that Silbad is in fact Piel, who was hurled back into the past along with Perdide and rescued thence. (Based on the book *L'orphelin de Perdide* (1958) by Stefan Wul and, more directly, on the comic-book adaptation of it as *Les maîtres du temps* (1978) by Moebius.)

WALTER LANTZ (1900–1994)

Born on April 27, 1900, in New Rochelle, New York, the son of an Italian immigrant called Frank Lanza – arbitrarily renamed Lantz by the immigration officer – and Frank's second-generation Italian immigrant wife Mary, Walter Lantz became a prolific producer and director of animated shorts. Among his diverse character creations there is one, Woody Woodpecker, who will remain a part of commercial animation's pantheon as long as people remember animated shorts at all. Woody was a character who seemed very much to belong to the Warners stable – indeed, it is often pointed out that he could almost be a clone of the original, Tex Avery-created Daffy Duck – and in many ways Lantz can be regarded as the greatest Warners animation director that Warners never had.

When Lantz was 12, his father accepted a job in Beckley, Connecticut, which involved the boy having to finish his schooling in order to run a quarrymen's commissary. He had been drawing since an early age, being much encouraged in this by his father, who also kept him well stocked with books to read. Now Frank paid for a correspondence course in cartooning for his eldest son, followed by another in animation. Out of this latter course,

Lantz gained little except instructions on how to build an animator's drawing table. From that point on he was self-taught.

Frank Lantz's job in Beckley lasted only a year before the quarry closed down, and the family moved back to New Rochelle, where Walter got a job in a garage. He began caricaturing his workmates. The caricatures came to the attention of a client named Fred Kafka, who was impressed enough to fund the youngster in evening classes at the Art Students League in New York, where Lantz did very promising work as a fine artist. Kafka then found him a job as an office boy in the art department of the *New York American*, one of the Hearst newspapers, and Walter Lantz, then age 15, moved to a YMCA in Manhattan. At the newspaper, he was doing chores for strip artists who included George McManus, of *Bringing Up Father* fame, and George Herriman, of even greater *Krazy Kat* fame; one of his fellow office boys was Milt Gross. But the most important

of the artists working there was Winsor McCay. When Lantz went to see one of McCay's vaudeville performances, he was bitten all over again by the animation bug.

Morrill Goddard, editor of the *New York American*, encouraged him, recommending him as a talented young artist to Gregory La Cava, who was in the process of setting up William Randolph Hearst's new pet project, the Hearst International Film Service, which was intended to capitalize on the huge numbers of popular comic strips published in the Hearst newspapers by animating them. La Cava did indeed give Lantz a job, as a cameraman. Decades later Lantz recalled:

> We didn't have any animation cameras in those days, just Hearst-type newsreel cameras, and that's what we used. They were like a big wooden box. No motors, just a chain and a crank. We'd put the animation cel down and hold it down with a piece of glass and a lever. We'd press the lever to smooth the cel out so it didn't have any wrinkles, set the exposure, turn the crank, and make a picture.

If the technology was primitive the animation was just as much so — unsurprisingly, because commercial-quality animation was really still in the latter stages of being invented, and so animators everywhere were in the quandary of having to invent their art as they went along. The shorts that the Hearst studio was producing were rarely as much as three minutes long, so story was not their strength: the stories were another thing the animators were often expected to make up as they went along. It soon became clear that their cameraman, Lantz, knew just about as much as anyone else there about animation, and could draw better than most of them thanks to his lessons back at the Art Students League. He soon progressed to being an in-betweener for Vernon (always known as "George") Stallings, and then began to do more and more of Stallings's work for him. A particular stimulus came with the introduction to the studio of Grim Natwick, a complete novice to animation but a fully trained artist and illustrator. Animation came very naturally to Natwick, and because of his training he could do things that the other, more experienced animators could only dream of. Many animators have noted how generously Natwick helped them in their young days, and Lantz was no exception.

When he was still only 18, Lantz was given his first series of shorts to do, based on the comic strip *Jerry on the Job* by Walt Hoban. His colleagues, William Randolph Hearst, and, most importantly, the audiences were delighted with the results: Lantz was beginning to write some of what would become the basic rules of the commercial animated short. Notable among these was that actions rather than words should be foregrounded: an animated character is capable of *doing* just about anything the animator wants it to do, so this colossal level of freedom should be used rather than wasted in favor of words (in those days, written words). This was quite an important development.

Boy Meets Dog (c 1937)

🎞 b/w / animated ⏱ 8½ minutes

Adapted from Gene Byrnes's strip *Reg'lar Fellers*. Bobby's father won't let him do anything fun. One day Bobby bumps into a puppy who has had a tin can tied to his tail. He takes the puppy home, but the mean father is furious he has done so. Tired of how badly Bobby is being treated, the fairy folk leap from his bedroom wallpaper, seize the father, and carry him off to trial in Elfland (where there are some parodies of Disney's Seven Dwarfs). Chief witness against the father is the pup, and the judge is Bobby. The father is condemned to the Youth Machine, being turned into a baby — at which point he awakes and thereafter is a reformed character.

This short began as a cinema commercial for Ipana Toothpaste, which later backed out. With the plugs for Ipana removed, it premiered some years later as a home movie rather than theatrically.

Scrub Me Mama with a Boogie Beat (1941)

🎞 color / animated ⏱ 6¾ minutes

Somewhere way down upon the Swanee Ribber is Lazy Town, where the population of 123½ is entirely caricatured black, complete with thick rubber lips, and lazy. But then the paddle steamer pauses at Lazy Town for a lunch break, and from it comes a very pale-skinned, uncaricatured belle who immediately energizes the entire population. All perform a red-hot boogie, and as the paddle steamer leaves with the belle aboard, the Lazy Town "darkies" are still a-hoppin' and a-poppin', which all goes to show the get-up-and-go effects of having pale skin. American 1940s animated racial stereotyping at its ghastliest, this cartoon is, for obvious reasons, little seen today.

Animation was a new art form, but for some years — and, in many cases — animators often didn't seem to realize it, preferring to torment established artforms like live-action cinema and the comic strip into animated guise; at the Hearst studio, obviously, the earlier animations were just comic strips made to move. Lantz and others like him realized that the scope was there for animation to have an identity of its own, to be let out in the playground and told to play however it wanted to, rather than being confined to the classroom. It is notable that even in the much later shorts that Lantz produced — and he was still doing so into the 1970s — there is almost always very little by way of dialogue: they are visual stories told visually.

In July 1918, Hearst abruptly closed his studio; the Hearst comic-strip characters were farmed out to other studios. John Randolph Bray was one of the beneficiaries, and, like the others, he employed ex-Hearst men to carry on the work they had been doing. George Stallings and, alongside him, his bright young assistant animator, Walter Lantz, did a year-long stint at the studio,

run by Raoul Barré and Charles Bowers, working on Mutt & Jeff cartoons before, still together, they were hired by Bray, initially to work on the well established Colonel Heeza Liar cartoons; the first short in the series to be done by them was *Colonel Heeza Liar's Treasure Island* (1922).

Stallings, always a heavy drinker, was by now well into the darkness of alcohol dependency; it was often Lantz's job, aside from doing an unreasonable amount of his boss's work, to leave the office to track down Stallings at whichever speakeasy he'd gone to and haul him back. Bray was nobody's fool, and within a few months Stallings was out on his ear and Lantz was promoted to fill his shoes, as studio manager and as an animation director, beginning with (uncredited) *Colonel Heeza Liar in Uncle Tom's Cabin* (1923).

Lantz also introduced a new series character, Dinkey Doodle, who, with his dog friend, Weakheart (an only slightly modified version of Otto Messmer's cat Felix), appeared in a string of animated/live-action shorts, starting with *The Magic Lamp* (1924). The mixture of animation with live action was very popular in this era of animation history, but what Lantz succeeded in doing where others had failed was to have both the live-action and the animated components in motion *at the same time*. In Disney's Alice Comedies, the mixture comprises, almost all the time, a live-action girl moving around in an entirely animated world. In Lantz's Dinky Doodle shorts, however, there is a much stronger sense of genuine interaction in that both the live action and the animation are moving together. He achieved this through the device of a laborious technique whereby first the live-action footage was shot, then each frame was blown up

as a photographic positive print. The edges of these prints were then perforated to fit over the pegs of the animator's board like regular animation sheets. Thus, the photographic positives functioned as a moving background over which the animation cels could be placed. Special effects could be added by cutting out elements from extra photographic prints and animating them on top of the base prints.

Lantz had as his main assistant animator Clyde Geronimi, with Dave Hand helping later on. Both of these men went on to become important figures in the Disney animation setup. But the major person involved in the Dinky Doodle shorts, which ran until *Dinky Doodle in the Army* rounded off the series in 1926, was always Lantz himself, not just as animation director and animator but also as writer and live-action star. In later years, he claimed he was lousy as an actor in these shorts, but, in fact, his enthusiasm shines through and makes up for any thespian deficiency. Nevertheless, he was able to persuade Bray to let him hire actors for his next animated/live-action series, the Un-Natural History shorts – begun with *How the Elephant Got his Trunk* (1925) and ended with *The Hyena's Laugh* (1927) – presumably for no other reason than that these quasi-Aesopian, quasi-Kiplingesque shorts required children to play the human roles. For the twelve Hot Dog cartoons, which ran from *For the Love o' Pete* in 1926 to *The Farm Hand* in 1927, it was back to Lantz as star again.

Both series ended in 1927 for the very good reason that so did Bray's studio. Goldwyn had decided not to renew the contract for the Goldwyn-Bray Pictograph, and Bray seems suddenly to have grown tired of the game. None of the other studios had anything to offer Lantz except a major drop in pay and status. However, a friend he had made in his Hearst years, the live-action director Bob Vignola, suggested he should try Hollywood. He spent a few weeks working without pay for Hal Roach, doing some piecework animating for live-action shorts, and then a few months with Mack Sennett, doing much the same but also working as a gagman – and this time getting paid.

In early 1928, he met the woman who would later be his second wife and also the third (or so) voice of Woody Woodpecker: the stage actress Grace Stafford. Around then he also met Carl Laemmle, the boss at Universal. Laemmle had just finished rejecting Mickey Mouse as a possible cartoon star but had also inherited Walt Disney's earlier series star, Oswald the Lucky Rabbit, after Oswald had been abducted from Walt by Charles Mintz. Laemmle had decided that, in the future, Universal should produce its own animated shorts, and Lantz was the ideal man for the job. Oddly, even Walt Disney himself expressed pleasure that Lantz had inherited the character, perhaps because it represented the downfall of the "traitors" who had deserted to Mintz.

Laemmle was one of those in Hollywood who had accepted that the talkies were the way of the future, and so the first thing Lantz and his team had to do was add sound to those Oswald shorts that Mintz's men had already completed as silents but which hadn't yet been released. This he and his team did in the most primitive of ways: they made the sound effects and spoke the (very limited) dialogue while watching the movie, recording as they went. Thereafter they were expected to make twenty-six Oswald shorts, with sound, per year – a gruelling task, since Laemmle, as was his habit, also wanted the budgets kept tight. But Lantz, of course, was more than accustomed to such a constraint from his days with Hearst and then Bray. He brought in Bill Nolan as head of a second unit, so the two men could alternate cartoons, each thereby having four weeks rather than just two per short. Among the animators were George Moreno and a very young Tex Avery, who started as an inker but rapidly worked his way up; Avery would learn from Lantz that animation, as a visual medium, should deploy visual humor. Another animator of note who worked with Lantz during these years was La Verne Harding, for a long time the only female animator in the U.S. industry. Despite the talent on hand, the Oswald shorts – with the character remodeled by Lantz to be somewhat cuddlier than the old Iwerks-Disney version, and with the series title changed from Oswald the Lucky Rabbit to just Oswald the Rabbit – were of varied quality in terms of both animation and gags, not to mention storylines. A bigger team, or the same team with a schedule less hectic than a short every two weeks, could have done them better; as it was, the best the Oswald shorts could generally hope for was charm, and some of them attained that.

Woody Woodpecker (1941)

🎨 color / animated ⏱ 6³/₄ minutes
(vt *Cracked Nut*)
Woody Woodpecker
Although Woody had appeared as a supporting character for Andy Panda the previous year in the short *Knock Knock* (1940), this was the first Woody Woodpecker cartoon. Pugnacious and loudmouthed, the rebarbative bird soon squabbles with the other birds in the tree, and the small forest creatures conclude he's a nut case. To prove he's not, he performs the trick of transforming a tree trunk into a fully carved and painted totem pole in no time flat. Directed toward a stone monument of a tree, he tries again . . . with obviously painful results. By now half-convinced himself that he's crazy, he goes to see Dr. Horace N. Buggy, a supposedly Scottish fox who proves to be more of a nut case than Woody himself. But the real purpose of the short is to let Woody prove his credentials as a starring zany, so there is much irrelevant clowning to display wacky tricks before we find him finally seated in the audience, one of whose members crossly folds the bird up into his theater seat.

Even before beginning into the task of producing new Oswald shorts, Lantz had another animation job to do for Universal. The Jazz Singer (1927), popularly though wrongly regarded as the world's first talkie, had been a smash hit for Warners, and, naturally enough, the other studios were eager to imitate it. Laemmle's effort was King of Jazz (1930), featuring Paul Whiteman. It was Laemmle's idea that the movie have an animated prologue telling a fantasticated story that would culminate in Whiteman's being crowned king of jazz. In Lantz's effort, which in any event was the first color cartoon ever made, Whiteman is a hunter in the jungle, his singing voice supplied by a then little known Bing Crosby, who interacts with various jungle animals – including, incongruously, Oswald – before getting a bump on the head that swells and transmutes into a crown. The standard of this 4-minute sequence is as good as animation got in this early era; it was a creditable performance by Lantz and his cohorts.

Nevertheless, Oswald the Rabbit continued in black-and-white. And continue Oswald did, until 1939, over 160 cartoons later. He survived even the departure of Carl Laemmle from Universal in 1935 and the subsequent closure, late that year, of Universal's animation studio. This development was not unwelcome to Lantz: for some while he had had aspirations to set up his own independent studio, and now he was able to hammer out a deal with Universal whereby they would distribute his product. Two of the other series he had created did not survive: the Pooch the Pup shorts, of which there were thirteen in 1932–33, featuring a chummy little dog; and the Cartune Classics, six shorts in color that appeared in 1934–35 and were done along the same lines as the early Silly Symphonies (Disney) and Merrie Melodies (Warners). He did, however, recreate the latter series later, in 1938, and thereafter there were dozens before the series died in 1961.

Lantz became increasingly aware, however, in his newfound role as independent producer, that Oswald's days were numbered. In 1936, he did try to redesign the character and give him a new lease on life; thereby the stylized black rabbit (black because it was quicker and easier to animate) was transformed into a much more realistic white one, effectively becoming, at least visually, an entirely different character. This had little effect on Oswald's declining popularity, and so the hunt was on for new series stars. Meany, Miny and Moe, a trio of circus-dressed monkeys who had debuted in the Oswald short *Monkey Wretches* (1935), were promoted to have a series of their own, which lasted just thirteen shorts, in 1936–37. Baby Face Mouse, who was much the same as the Chuck Jones character Sniffles, introduced over at Warners that same year, starred in five 1938 shorts before vanishing again. Peterkin Pan, a jolly little satyr created by the wife of the artist Willy Pogany, who worked briefly for Lantz as a backgrounder, lasted exactly one short: *Scrambled Eggs* (1939). A little later came Homer Pigeon, who had two widely separated cartoons, *Pigeon Patrol* (1942) and *Pigeon Holed* (1956). It was in 1939 that Lantz struck gold with a character called Andy Panda.

Even before this, another idea that he toyed with was the making of an animated feature movie, to be called *Aladdin and His Wonderful Lamp*. Lantz issued a press release about this, saying that he proposed to raise $750,000 from independent financial backers, but in fact either the backers never materialized or, according to his own later recollections, he decided that the project was financially just too risky.

So it was back to the shorts, and in particular to Andy Panda. The first time a living panda, Su-Lin, had been brought to the West was as recently as 1936, and the event had sparked off a craze for the creatures. Lantz went to the Brookfield Zoo in Chicago to make sketches and take moving and still photographs of Su-Lin, who was later adapted for the screen by staff animator Alex Lovy. The character, who debuted in *Life Begins for Andy Panda* (1939), had all the requisites a cartoon star was then supposed to have – they can be summed up as cuddliness – and also caught the current tide of Panda-mania. But it's noticeable that, perhaps because of the legacy of Oswald and his slapstick, the Andy Panda cartoons also have an edge to them that's lacking from many of the other cute-style cartoons of the day. Looked at today, they give the impression that the Disney animators and the Warners animators had collaborated, with one team responsible for some aspects and the other for the others, the two not quite blending. In fact, this dissonance is a strength rather than a weakness: there is added hilarity in the fact that, at the centre of a maelstrom of visual gags and general wild mayhem is a cute, cuddly, juvenile animal.

Even so, all of Lantz's earlier career had predisposed him toward the Warners rather than the Disney style of cartooning,

and a supporting character he introduced into an Andy Panda short called *Knock Knock* (1940) could almost have been a cousin of Daffy Duck, created at Warners about three years earlier by Tex Avery. This character was, of course, Woody Woodpecker, who made his first starring appearance in 1941's *Woody Woodpecker*. Both Daffy and Woody were initially wild zanies whose supposed humor derived from the fact that they were irresponsible imbeciles proud of the fact that, had they been human, they would have been securely locked up somewhere. Daffy evolved into something rather different, but Woody never really did; as a result, while any particular Woody Woodpecker short is likely to evoke plenty of laughter through the quickfire gags and general inventiveness of the whole proceedings, the character himself has never engendered the same kind of fan loyalty that Daffy has. We identify with Daffy in his ups and downs and, particularly, his frustrations, regarding him perhaps as the spoiled child who lives inside each and every one of us, whereas Woody is somehow always *outside* us, not so much an acquaintance as someone whose jokes entertain us at a party but whom we promptly forget about afterward, until the next encounter. That this reflects no failing on Lantz's part is evidenced by the long-lasting popularity of the Woody Woodpecker shorts, as opposed to the character himself. Well over 150 of them appeared before, in 1972, Woody bowed out in the appropriately named *Bye Bye Blackboard*.

Back in 1940, Universal's bean counters had pulled the plug on Walter Lantz Productions, ceasing to pay the monthly advance that had been part of the distribution deal. For a while, there was no Walter Lantz Productions, and the animators, Lantz included, were unemployed. It is a measure of the atmosphere at the Lantz studio that, even though there was no job there, many of the animators got together regularly with Lantz at the studio for purely social reasons. On one of these occasions, La Verne Harding suggested it might be fun if everyone collaborated on an animated short. Lantz at once jumped at the idea, pointing out that, if this first short could be sold, it might make enough money to finance another, and so on, until the studio was back in paying production once more. This is what happened, the short in question being the Andy Panda outing *Crazy House* (1940), which, ironically, was bought by Universal. Lantz later paid those animators involved for the work they had done for free, not once but many times over as the profits of his reborn enterprise flourished – and flourish they did, in no small part because, in pulling the plug on him, Universal had foolishly handed over all the rights to his animated characters. The bean counters who had saved Universal $3750 per week in closing Lantz down thereby lost the company untold millions in merchandising rights alone.

Andy Panda said farewell in 1949 with *Scrappy's Birthday*, leaving Woody to keep Walter Lantz Productions going. Other series characters were produced. Chilly Willy, a mute little penguin with more than a touch of Charlie Chaplin to him, debuted in 1953 with *Chilly Willy* and appeared in about 35 shorts, though never really capturing the public's heart – despite being made over by Tex Avery between his first appearance and his second, *It's Cold* (1954). The abortive series Foolish Fables also began in 1953, lampooning children's tales according to a formula that had begun to grow tired at least a decade earlier; it lasted exactly two cartoons – fewer even than Musical Miniatures, a series of four shorts released in 1946–48 that put classical music backings to series stars like Woody and Andy; this was an attempt to repeat with the classics what had been achieved during 1941–45 by the Swing Symphonies, a relatively successful series, done in the manner of the early Silly Symphonies, but to jazz. Sugarfoot, a lame horse, proved equally lame as a series hero, managing only two cartoons, both released in 1954. In 1958, the bear Windy debuted with *Salmon Yeggs*, but lasted for only four shorts. The pretentiously debonair cat Doc starred in seven shorts, vying initially with two mice, Hickory and Dickory, in *Mouse Trapped* (1959) and later with a dog named Champ. Inspector Willoughby, a bumbling secret agent with more than a touch of Tex Avery's Droopy about him, was created for Lantz by Jack Hannah and arrived in *Hunger Strife* (1960), in which Windy, no longer in the running as a series star, was a supporting player. Willoughby did better than most of the Lantz introductions, starring in a dozen shorts, of which the last was *The Case of the Elephant's Trunk* (1965).

But really the most successful character introduction was not a star at all, and not even a single character: it was the notion of having a straight guy, against whose phlegmatism the antics of the star would hopefully seem even more hilarious. The idea was brought to the studio by Tex Avery, who in 1954–55 made a brief return to Lantz in what was to prove his swansong with theatrical animation, departing after just a few movies over a dispute concerning his pay. Daws Butler was hired to play the voice of this straight guy or stooge; audiences could readily identify the character by the voice even if the visual identity changed from one cartoon to the next.

In 1957, Lantz made the breakthrough into television with *The Woody Woodpecker Show*, which he hosted himself, in direct imitation of Walt Disney on the earlier Disney tv shows. There was some new animation in these shows, but the basic formula was of three cartoons linked by live-action and live-action/animated material. And the show was immensely popular. Nevertheless, it lasted in its first incarnation for only about a year, coming off the air after the September 25, 1958 broadcast. This was possibly related to the fact that the television censors demanded that about twenty-five sequences be cut from the original theatrical cartoons, cuts that Lantz was very unhappy to make: Woody's nervous breakdown in *Knock Knock* was one such excision, despite the fact that the short didn't have much point without it. After the demise of *The Woody Woodpecker Show*, Lantz immediately produced the syndicated *Woody Woodpecker and Friends*,

Apple Andy (1946)

🎨 color / animated ⏱ 6³/₄ minutes
Andy Panda

Our hero, out strolling, comes across an orchard and salivates at the sight of the juicy apples. Devil Andy urges him to hop over the fence and steal some; Angel Andy arrives to dissuade him, but is bopped with a mallet by Devil Andy. Andy eats a bushel or so of green apples (though painted red by Devil Andy), and in his subsequent illness has a nightmare hallucination of being danced around by the Apple Core-Us Girls, being treated to a rendition of the song "Up Jumped the Devil (With the White Nightgown)," and descending to a technological Hell where Devil Andy and his minions cram him with apples and apple products.

Banquet Busters (1948)

🎨 color / animated ⏱ 6¹/₂ minutes
Woody Woodpecker / Andy Panda

The first Woody Woodpecker cartoon in which Woody was voiced by Grace Stafford, Lantz's wife; she retained the role until the end of the series in 1972, although in this cartoon she had little voicing to do. In the big city, Andy Panda and his partner, Woody, are failing to earn a living supplying music for parties and special occasions. After the office mouse steals their last peanut, they see a society musicale and dinner mentioned in the newspaper, and all three gatecrash. There is much inventive clowning, culminating in a slapstick food fight, as they steal food, despite a watchful walrus butler.

which followed much the same format and ran successfully from 1958 to 1966. Using the original title of *The Woody Woodpecker Show*, the series was revived by NBC in 1970–72 and again in 1976–77, each time drawing most of the material from old shorts, but with some extra animation added.

In 1972, however, Walter Lantz Productions finally closed its doors. Lantz had hung on longer than virtually any other studio in producing animated shorts for the cinema, and the economics of such production were by now becoming impossible: it could take a decade or more for a new animated short to recoup its production costs, let alone start making a profit. It was time for him to get out, to retire on the money he had made over the years from such stars as Woody Woodpecker and would continue to make through television reruns, merchandising, and, in due course, video sales. He remained active for the next twenty years as an artist, producing both fine and character-oriented commercial art. He died in the hospital in Burbank, California, on March 22, 1994, of heart failure, and was greatly mourned: of all the animation producers there have been, Walter Lantz was quite possibly the most loved as a person by those who worked for him.

WINSOR McCay (1867?–1934)

Original drawing from *Gertie the Dinosaur* (1914).
Private collection.

Astonishing as it might be, the early years of the man regarded as the Father of Animation are so lost in obscurity that there is even doubt as to the place and date of his birth. It seems most probable that he was born in 1867 in East or West Zorra, Ontario, Canada; however, in later life, he gave his own birth date on different occasions as 1869 and 1871, and his birthplace as Spring Lake, Michigan. And there is even some confusion about his name, Zenas Winsor McCay (after his father's employer Zenas G. Winsor), the "Zenas" often being rendered as "Zenic" and the "McCay" being at the time of his christening "McKay," his father later changing the patronymic for reasons that are obscure. Further, while the son was in his teens, he changed "Zenas Winsor" to "Winsor Zenas."

Through childhood, he drew everything he could see using whatever he could lay his hands on. The drawings were done purely for the pleasure of drawing, with no notion that the finished products were of any value: if on paper, they were given, or most usually thrown, away; if on some other medium, like a fence or the side of a house, they were left for the elements to destroy. He got in trouble at school for drawing all over the margins and endpapers of his books. And these were not mere childish scrawls: according to all accounts they were extremely accurate, technically proficient, and highly detailed renditions

— and done at great speed, a characteristic that would remain with him throughout his life.

His father tried to groom him for a business career. In 1886, he was sent to Cleary's Business College in Ypsilanti, Michigan, where, instead of attending classes, he spent most of his time in a dime museum, Sackett & Wiggins's Wonderland, in nearby Detroit, earning money by doing portraits of the customers for 25 cents each, of which his share was half. The dime museums were an "art form" pioneered by the entrepreneur P.T. Barnum; they featured clowns and jugglers and other acts more usually associated with the circus, but really their prime attraction was the "freak" show — bearded women, Siamese twins, dwarfs, and the like. In Ypsilanti itself, the news of his precocity spread, and the Michigan State Normal School's Professor John Goodison offered to give him private tuition, an offer eagerly accepted. Although Goodison encouraged him to go for further training to the Art Institute of Chicago, and although in 1889 McCay did actually go to Chicago with that intention, he never fulfilled it, and so these private lessons represent the only formal art training he ever received.

In Chicago, he found employment for a short time as an artist with the National Printing & Engraving Company, whose prime output was posters and advertising features and brochures for circuses, carnivals, and the railroads; he was also getting work as a sign painter from at least one dime museum. In 1891, he was offered a more lucrative job in Cincinnati, at Kohl & Middleton's New Dime Museum, and here he stayed for a full nine years, churning out posters and advertisements. Also in 1891, he met and eloped with Maude Leonore Dufour, marrying her in Kentucky; she was only 14, ten years his junior.

His early career as a dime-museum artist was to make its mark on his later output as a strip cartoonist and animator. The opportunities for an artist were immense – not only could McCay depict the human form in far more extreme (and bizarre) varieties than could be dreamed of by any artist in a formal studio, he was also constantly having to capture the human form in *action*. This was, of course, fundamental to his success as an animator.

In 1896, Kohl & Middleton's New Dime Museum – by now called Heck & Avery's Family Theater – staged a demonstration of the Vitascope projection device that an assistant to the inventor Thomas Alva Edison had recently come up with. This was probably McCay's earliest exposure to motion pictures, although Edison's peepshow-style Kinetoscope (in fact devised by his assistant William K.L. Dickson) had been around since 1891, so it's possible McCay had encountered moving pictures earlier.

As was his practice throughout his life, while McCay held one job he was also moonlighting on others, and in this instance, spurred by the need to support Maude and, from 1896, their young family, his freelance assignments as a sign painter soon became more significant than his full-time employ at the dime museum. The execution of one technique he had developed – that of doing a figure's outline as a single line rather than piecemeal – soon proved a crowd pleaser.

The *Cincinnati Commercial Tribune* began to employ him for piecework, producing art depicting dime-museum "freaks", a chore at which the newspaper's regular artists looked down their noses. In 1898, he accepted a full-time job at the *Tribune* drawing pictures that were essentially the precursors of the photographs in later newspapers. Realism, accuracy, detail, and, above all, speed were required for this job; looking at these illustrations today, one is staggered to realize that it took McCay mere hours to produce artwork of such detail that would take a modern illustrator days and possibly weeks to perform. Two years after joining the *Tribune*, he was lured to the *Cincinnati Enquirer* by the offer of a higher salary.

He didn't restrict himself to reportage. The *Tribune* and the *Enquirer* featured his caricatures and – ever the moonlighter – he also became a stalwart of the magazine *Life*, which was later to achieve fame as a medium of photo-reporting, but, at this time, was a reactionary cartoon magazine. Amid the racist and sexist outpourings demanded of him by its editors, McCay also produced some sets of drawings that are highly reminiscent of sequential stills

Little Nemo (1911)

b/w (with some hand-coloring) /live-action/animated silent 10½ minutes

The bulk of this short is made up of a live-action comic quasi-documentary of how the cartoon itself came to be made. McCay makes a bet with friends that he can complete 4000 drawings in a month to make a motion picture, and, despite interruptions, does so. The finished animation, hand-colored frame-by-frame on the developed film, lasts two minutes and is basically just a demonstration: characters from McCay's *Little Nemo in Slumberland* comic strip bow, stretch and distort before one draws another and gives her a flower; thereafter, the two climb into the jaws of a dragon and make their way off-screen; finally, a car bearing two other characters explodes comically.

How a Mosquito Operates (1912)

(vt *The Story of a Mosquito*)

b/w /animated silent 5½ minutes

A mosquito, complete with top hat and briefcase, invades a man's home and, as he fitfully sleeps, sharpens its proboscis and repeatedly sucks blood from him. After performing some tricks for the audience, it has one suck too many and bursts.

Gertie the Dinosaur (1914)

b/w /live-action/animated silent 12½ minutes

In the live-action portion, on seeing a dinosaur skeleton in a museum, McCay bets a friend he can "make the Dinosaurus live again by a series of hand-drawn cartoons" and, six months later, the 10,000 drawings are done. The actual animation, which lasts a little over five minutes (including time for dialogue boards), shows Gertie performing simple tricks for the audience, being distracted by a sea serpent, munching down a tree, encountering a mammoth, dancing, being hosed by the mammoth and throwing a rock at it, scratching her head with her tail, drinking a lake dry, and, as the final and most dramatic stunt, taking onto her back a live-action McCay and walking off-screen with him.

The Sinking of the Lusitania (1918)

b/w /animated/live-action silent 9½ minutes

The live-action footage comprises merely a minute or so at the outset, showing McCay settling in to document the tragedy, plus propagandist narration boards and a few still photographs of the famous who died; the remainder is occupied by animation (25,000 drawings). We see the *Lusitania* setting sail past the Statue of Liberty, and then being struck by not one but a murderous two torpedoes from the German sub U-39, with flames and smoke filling the sky as passengers and crew escape as best they can.

The Centaurs (c 1918–21)

🎞 b/w / animated silent ⏱ 3 minutes
(surviving fragments only)
What remains of this movie very charmingly shows a family group of centaurs — an older couple, a younger couple and the latter's son — disporting themselves in a coastal glade.

Gertie on Tour (c 1918–21)

🎞 b/w / animated silent ⏱ 1³/₄ minutes
(surviving fragments only)
Much more lavishly drawn than *Gertie the Dinosaur*, this fragment shows her meeting a toad, swallowing the tip of her tail, toying with an anachronistic pullman coach, and dreaming of herself among a crowd of other dinosaurs as "the life and soul of the party."

Flip's Circus (c 1918–21)

🎞 b/w / animated silent ⏱ 8¼ minutes (surviving fragments only)
Flip, from the Little Nemo in Slumberland comic strip, clowns in front of a tent wall bearing the legend "Flip's Circus," first on his own and then with a hippopotamus-like creature, which swallows his hat, refuses to release Flip's head when he performs the stunt of putting his head in the beast's mouth, eats a car engine, swallows and regurgitates Flip, etc. Also featured are the characters Boo Koo and Toot-Sweet.

Bug Vaudeville (c 1921)

🎞 b/w / animated silent ⏱ 13¹/₂ minutes
Having eaten too many cheesecakes, a man lies down to doze in a glade. He dreams, as if they were performers in a stage show, of a grasshopper juggling an ant; of a dancing daddy longlegs (with beard and boots, which it juggles); of a cockroach which cycles around the rim of a plate; of a pair of tumblebug (dung-beetle) acrobats; of a pair of potato-bug boxers; of Mlle. Butterfly and "her Equestrian Marvel, Black Beetle," who canter around a circus ring; and, finally, of a spider that swings out to seize the orchestrator of all these proceedings, whose silhouetted head and shoulders have been visible in the foreground throughout.

from later animated movies — much as if he were already turning toward animation but did not know the medium in which to express his vision.

Through most of 1903, basing his work on Kiplingesque poems by George Randolph Chester that had titles like "How the Alligator Got His Big Mouth," McCay produced for the *Enquirer* a series of color illustrations for the proto-comic strip

Tales of the Jungle Imps, by Felix Fiddle. His artistic style is already unmistakable in these pieces; on first glance one assumes momentarily that they're episodes from the later *Little Nemo in Slumberland*, for example.

By the time the last of the *Felix Fiddle* pieces was appearing in the *Enquirer*, McCay had left the newspaper, having been headhunted by the *New York Herald* and its sister paper, the *Evening Telegram*. Soon he was producing caricatures and cartoons for his new employers with the same facility and speed he had displayed in his Cincinnati work. And in early 1904 he started to produce for the *Evening Telegram* his first comic strip, the short-lived *Mr Goodenough*; two further essays in the form, *Sister's Little Sister's Beau* and *Phurious Phinish of Phoolish Philipe's Phunny Phrolics*, were even shorter-lived, lasting only one episode apiece. In July 1904, however, he had greater success with the weekly *Little Sammy Sneeze*, which ran until December 1906.

Just a couple of months after *Little Sammy Sneeze's* inception, McCay began, in September 1904, to produce (under the pseudonym Silas) his longest-running and arguably his most famous strip of all: *Dreams of the Rarebit Fiend*. In each episode, a character undergoes a surrealistically nightmarish experience which builds to a climax before the individual, in the final frame, awakens in a disheveled bed ruing the previous night's consumption of something unwise – almost always a rarebit. Begun in the *Evening Telegram*, the strip moved to the *Herald* in 1911 and did not finally close until August 1913. Less successful were *The Story of Hungry Henrietta*, which ran in the *Herald* for a few months in 1905, and *A Pilgrim's Progress, by Mister Bunion*, which ran in the *Evening Telegram* until December 1910 but never succeeded in capturing the popular imagination in the same way as *Dreams of the Rarebit Fiend* had, and as McCay's next strip, *Little Nemo in Slumberland*, most emphatically would.

Inaugurated in the *Herald* in October 1905, *Little Nemo in Slumberland* continued in that paper until 1911; after McCay had been recruited to the Hearst stable in 1911, the strip was uninspiringly retitled *In the Land of Wonderful Dreams* and continued in the *New York American* until the end of 1914; it was revived briefly, a shadow of its former self, under the original title in the *New York Herald-Tribune* in 1924–27. It was adapted as a Broadway musical in 1908, and almost from the outset was translated and syndicated in numerous foreign countries. Book selections appeared in 1906 and 1909, and several adaptations appeared thereafter; much later, the book publication of the complete set of *Little Nemo* strips began in 1989, a project completed in six large volumes by 1993. Countless merchandising deals were done while the strip was still current in the newspapers. The first of the animated shorts McCay himself made – *Little Nemo* (1911) – was based on the series, and decades later a distinguished team of animators contributed to the international coproduction *Little Nemo: Adventures in Slumberland* (1989). What's astonishing is that, despite the late-20th-century book and movie incarnations, Little Nemo has not survived as an icon in the same way that, for example, the characters have from the roughly contemporaneous *The Wonderful Wizard of Oz* (1900) and its sequels by L. Frank Baum; perhaps it was the 1939 Judy Garland movie that made the difference.

The plot of an individual *Little Nemo* strip is always the same: for much of the page, Nemo dreams he is having an adventure in Slumberland, and in the last frame he wakes up. However, to summarize the strips thus is to miss the point. What the strips progressively did was slowly explore, in ever greater depth, the whole fantasticated otherworld that was Slumberland, populated by its diverse freakish denizens, obeying its own rules and regulations, and always with new marvels just around the corner to be encountered in the next week's episode. (In creating his own otherworld for *Cool World* [1992], Ralph Bakshi seems either consciously or unconsciously to have drawn some inspiration from the *Little Nemo* strips.)

Beginning in 1909 there was a further McCay strip in the *Herald*. This was *Poor Jake*, done as Silas and portraying the exploitation of the eponymous workman by his selfish master Colonel Stall, who takes all the credit for Jake's labors and of course makes sure Jake never has the spare time or energy to realize any higher aspirations he might have; unsurprisingly, it failed to linger in the popular consciousness after its demise in 1911. That demise roughly coincided with McCay's departure from the *Herald* to join the empire of William Randolph Hearst; a few years later, with the termination of *Little Nemo in Slumberland*, McCay effectively left the comic-strip arena forever. Hearst wanted him to do editorial cartoons and other less inspired work, and finances forced McCay to deliver what his boss desired.

In 1906, McCay also engaged himself in a successful part-time vaudeville career, based on his ability to produce drawings at incredible speed and to be entertaining while so doing. His animations became part of his act in 1911, leading up to the triumph in 1914 when, in Chicago rather than his hometown, New York, he presented for the first time *Gertie the Dinosaur*. This drew rave reviews from virtually all quarters except the Hearst newspapers, which, on the personal instruction of William Randolph Hearst, not only almost completely ignored the event but even refused to carry advertisements for it. Hearst called McCay to his office, told him that he was devoting more energy to his stage career than to what was theoretically his full-time job at the *New York American*, and gave him a stark choice. Always neurotic about money, McCay opted for the safety of the regular income and savagely curtailed his theatrical appearances. In 1917, while McCay was finishing work on *The Sinking of the Lusitania* (1918), Hearst laid down the law once again: his employee was to devote his energies full-time to the newspaper – although, to be fair, at the same time Hearst did immediately increase his salary by the amount of McCay's somewhat inflated estimate of his earnings from vaudeville. There were a few reprieves between 1922 and 1927, notably a three-year run in 1922–25 in New York, but once again Hearst had managed effectively to end a career in which McCay had demonstrated singular genius. McCay must have thought of his

Frame from *The Sinking of the Lusitania* (1918). Private collection.

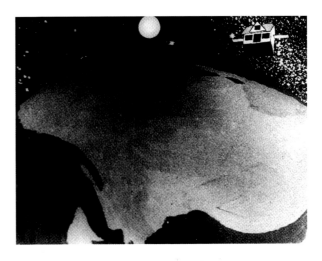

Frame from *The Flying House* (c 1921). Private collection.

old and minor comic strip *Poor Jake* and wondered if he'd been possessed of the gift of prophecy when producing it. Poor Winsor.

Today McCay is recognized as a giant of the early days of the comic strip; who knows what he might have achieved had Hearst given him the freedom to continue to develop that art form rather than straitjacketing him into hackwork. Even more so is McCay recognized as a giant of early animation; it is not at all uncommon to see him described as the inventor of the animated movie – which he was not: that title is generally given to J. Stuart Blackton (1896–1941) for *Humorous Phases of Funny Faces* (1906), although the animation historian Giannalberto Bendazzi notes the much earlier *Matches: An Appeal* (1899), made by Arthur Melbourne

The Pet (c 1921)

⏿ b/w / animated silent ⏱ 12½ minutes

After eating a rarebit at his club, a man falls asleep in bed with his wife . . . and dreams. To his great displeasure, a kitten has been adopted by the wife. It starts to grow at a prodigious rate. The next day, now the size of a Labrador, it eats the couple's existing cat and then their dinner. The man buys rat poison to get rid of the monstrous pet, which becomes horse-sized on eating all the coal in the cellar plus various items of furniture. It devours the entire barrel of rat poison but, although temporarily breaking out in buboes, survives and grows even more, then runs loose in the town, eating all it finds and growing to truly giant proportions. Finally, just before the dreamer wakes up, it must be blown to pieces by an armed airship and fighter planes.

The Flying House (c 1921)

⏿ b/w / animated silent ⏱ 16 minutes

A couple eats rarebits before going to bed. She dreams the house is threatened with repossession because of late mortgage payments; accordingly, her husband equips it with an engine, propeller, and wings, and they take to the skies, seeking somewhere the mortgage company will never find them. A ferocious thunderstorm blows them willy-nilly across the sky and into space. The fugitives think of settling on the Moon, but the Man in the Moon chases them away with a fly swatter. They are blown out of the sky by a rocket aimed for the Moon and tumble down to find themselves back in their own bed.

Cooper. Yet, after *The Sinking of the Lusitania*, McCay's glory days were over, his further animations being less groundbreaking by comparison and mainly less vivacious. Again, what might McCay have gone on to do had his ambitions not been so firmly trodden underfoot by his short-sighted employer? By the time of his death in 1934, animators all around him were going where he could have gone and making highly successful careers out of it, while a young man called Walt Disney was already building an empire.

When we look at McCay's animations today, it is important to see them in the context of McCay as showman — as vaudeville artist. He created ten animated shorts in all during the period of 1911–21, for each of them producing every single drawing himself; later animators would develop the idea of the composite animation cel setup, whereby sequences could be constructed in which only the foreground needed to be animated, with a static background behind, but McCay never thought of this. Or, if he did, he dismissed it as unnecessary for someone with his astonishing capability to "lightning sketch." Those ten shorts were: *Little Nemo* (1911), which required about 4000 drawings; *The Story of a Mosquito* (1912; vt *How a Mosquito Operates*), based on a *Dreams of the Rarebit Fiend* episode; *Gertie the Dinosaur* (1914), which

required about 10,000 drawings; *The Sinking of the Lusitania* (1918), the most ambitious of them all, which needed some 25,000 drawings, each done in much more detail than was the case for the earlier films; three movies made sometime between 1918 and 1921, of which only fragments remain, being *The Centaurs, Flip's Circus,* and *Gertie on Tour*; and three *Dreams of the Rarebit Fiend* movies, *The Pet* (c 1921), *Bug Vaudeville* (c 1921), and *The Flying House* (c 1921), the last done in collaboration with his son Robert McCay (1896–1962).

It is, of course, difficult to judge the merits of the three shorts of which only fragments survive, but it would seem that of these ten movies the outstanding achievements are *Gertie, The Sinking of the Lusitania,* and the late-period *Rarebit Fiend* movies. Of the others, *Little Nemo* is essentially an experiment with the new medium, being reminiscent of the sorts of tricks a child will play when drawing a flip book; *The Story of a Mosquito*, although it does have a rudimentary plot, has a similar ambience and is, frankly, a little dull, a sin committed to extreme by *Flip's Circus*, if the available fragments can be used as a basis for judgment; and *The Centaurs* seems a pleasant pastoral fantasy of classical Greece but also terminally bland. Hardly anything remains of *Gertie on Tour*, an attempt to resuscitate the animator's earlier great triumph, but contemporary accounts suggest that, while drawn with a far greater richness than its predecessor, it lacks the same spark of creative inspiration.

The great achievement of *Gertie the Dinosaur* was that McCay succeeded in creating an animated *character* — one with whom audiences could *identify*, bizarre though this might sound, bearing in mind that Gertie is a dinosaur. At the time, this might not have seemed like much, but it was actually a novel concept — one which later animators would pick up and run with to produce long series of shorts based on the adventures of a single character. If the creation of that character was a successful one, whether it be Oswald the Lucky Rabbit, or Mickey Mouse, or Betty Boop, or Felix the Cat, then the character alone would make up for any other deficiencies in the individual short or even series of shorts: audiences fell in love with the animated characters (even those designed to be hated) and followed their adventures with all the uncritical addiction that modern viewers display toward television soap operas. Walt Disney may have been the first to identify this trait and work to exploit it, driving his artists from early days to pay attention to the rounding out of the *personalities* of the creatures they portrayed. But it was McCay who first exemplified the principle.

The Sinking of the Lusitania is altogether a different animal. In place of *Gertie's* delightful whimsy we have angry propaganda — driven, unusually for such propaganda, by its creator's genuinely felt wrath. McCay was spurred to create a realistic recreation of the whole ghastly affair; and this he did with incredible industry — although, red-eyed with fury as he might have been, he did not neglect to indulge in his trademark self-promotion in the live-action sections of the short. Even by today's standards, when technological advances of all kinds have made us believe that animators (and perhaps their computers) can perform any magic they want to on the screen, the animation of *The Sinking of the Lusitania* is impressive. It might shiver and shake – inevitable, bearing in mind that McCay started afresh with each of his 25,000 drawings, and that his technique of registration was rudimentary – and on occasion the portrayal might be a touch primitive, but nevertheless it conveys the full grimness, despair, and violence of the event. The more straightforwardly propagandistic section of the film – a brief photo gallery of a few of the dead – is anticlimactic by comparison: the vividness and passion of McCay's animation speak far more loudly.

The three *Dreams of the Rarebit Fiend* shorts are much longer – at up to 16 minutes they approach in length what Disney would later dub "featurettes" – and they profit from several years' increased sophistication of style: a comparison between them and Disney's much-vaunted *Steamboat Willie* (1928), dating from seven years later (a long time during this early era of animation), would show the Mouse coming off a poor second. *Bug Vaudeville* is largely plotless, and could be regarded as a silent precursor of the early Disney Silly Symphonies. However, both *The Pet* and *The Flying House* are full-scale animated narratives; they would make excellent short stories if translated into the printed word. Visually, too, they are often superlative: there is true drama amid the comedy as the Flying House is swept looping and spiraling across the sky above Earth's atmosphere, and the drawing of this sequence is technically breathtaking. The movie's credits state that McCay's son Robert was the artist, but in sequences such as this it is evident that the father was still playing the major role, both as "animation director" and, more directly, in the drawing and animation.

Winsor Zenas McCay continued to work almost to the end – to within a day or two. On the morning of July 26, 1934, he collapsed at home, and by the late afternoon he was dead of a cerebral hemorrhage. Extensive obituaries appeared in newspapers far and wide, and official condolences came in from the likes of William Randolph Hearst, the Freemasons (McCay had been a Freemason since his youth), and the Society of Illustrators, but far more impressive was the sheer number of telegrams that poured in from friends and acquaintances – not to mention fans who felt personally touched by the death of a man they had known only through his work. In many ways, McCay was a prickly character, impatient of fools and driven by his neuroses concerning financial security and public status – what he valued most from his vaudeville career was the directly visible and audible acclaim, the thirst for which more than overcame the shyness that was also part of him. And yet, perhaps because of his puckish humor and his boundless energy, he seems to have had an infinite capacity to inspire friendship in others, who were only too willing to forgive his flaws.

As an animator, his greatness cannot be doubted. Had he continued to produce movies after 1921, there is no knowing

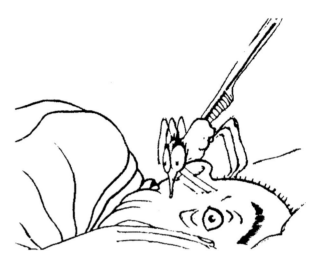

Drawing for *How a Mosquito Operates* (1912). Private collection.

where or how far he might have taken the medium he had done so much to create. That he abandoned animation in that year was certainly largely the responsibility of his employer, William Randolph Hearst. There is also the possibility that McCay was depressed by the course that animation as a whole was taking. Despite his vaudevillian soul, he had nurtured a dream of animation as a fine art; all around him, animators were churning out heartless, cynical movies that relied on cheap and often schoolboy-bawdy gags in search of no higher goal than a quick buck. Where he had had a vision, all these animators seemed to see was a profit margin.

There was much truth in this viewpoint, but also much falsehood. What is likely to have been a much more important factor in his attitude is the conscious or unconscious need to justify his decision to leave the field, a decision he may also have made in part because other animators were overtaking him in terms of technical proficiency and, indeed, on occasion, artistry.

His reputation as a comic-strip creator better survived his death than did his reputation as an animator – even though every animator since then has owed a debt to him. Not until the late 1960s did his prominence in the history of the art form become once more recognized by the public at large. In his book *Winsor McCay: His Life and Art* (1987), the standard work on the "Father of Animation," John Canemaker cites from a letter written to him in 1985 by Chuck Jones a remark that could well serve as McCay's epitaph:

The two most important people in [the history of] animation are Winsor McCay and Walt Disney, and I'm not sure which should go first.

ROBERT McKIMSON (1910–1977)

Still from Tortilla Flaps (1958), showing Speedy Gonzales being hotly pursued by Senor Vulturo. © Warner Bros.

Robert McKimson was born on October 13, 1910, in Colorado, one of five children and the middle of three brothers; the other two brothers, Thomas and Charles, would likewise become animators, often working with Robert at Warners and elsewhere. Their father was a newspaperman who eventually moved the family, via Texas, to Los Angeles, where the McKimsons arrived in 1926.

Two years later, in 1928, while Robert was still in his teens, he and elder brother, Thomas, got their first jobs in animation at the Disney studio, Robert being appointed as an assistant to Dick Lundy and Thomas in a similar position with Norm Ferguson. The prospect of more money lured them away to the short-lived studio opened by Romer Grey, son of the more famous Zane, where they worked on a few cartoons featuring a character called Binko the Cub; unfortunately, the studio died before any of these could get beyond the pencil-drawings stage. Their next port of call was the Harman–Ising studio, which was then working with Leon Schlesinger to release animated shorts through Warners,

the studio's main series star being Bosko the Talk-Ink Kid. Robert's first screen credit as an animator was on Bosko's Store (1932), and Thomas's was on the non-Bosko It's Got Me Again (1932). In 1932, Robert was involved in a car crash, after which, for some reason, he was able to animate much faster than before, a considerable asset in an era when most of the studios were more concerned about speed of production than quality. In 1933, Harman and Ising left Schlesinger for MGM and Thomas went with them. Robert, however, stayed behind with Schlesinger as part of what would, in due course, become the Warners cartoon studio.

Robert came to be regarded as among the very best of the Warners animators and an integral part of the team on Termite Terrace. So it was unsurprising when, on the departure of first Frank Tashlin in 1944 and then Bob Clampett in 1946, he moved up the ladder to have his own unit alongside those of Chuck Jones and Friz Freleng. Jones and Freleng were undoubtedly great directors of animated shorts, and McKimson was much in their shadow; moreover, there appears to have been a certain amount of ill will in the air. These two facts may help to explain, although they in no way excuse, the persistent habit among animation historians of denigrating McKimson and everything he did. Giannalberto Bendazzi, in his normally reliable *Cartoons* (1994), dismisses McKimson's contribution to the Warners output in a phrase, "the less creative Robert McKimson," while going on at length about the other directors. Leonard Maltin, in his likewise eminent *Of Mice and Magic* (revised edition, 1987), remarks: "A fine animator, McKimson turned out to be an uninspired director. Working alongside Jones and Freleng, with the same characters and access to the same talent pool, he missed the mark with alarming frequency" – this after describing how McKimson's creation Foghorn Leghorn totally eclipsed Jones's creation Henery Hawk. Jeff Lenberg, in his *Encyclopedia of Animated Cartoons* (2nd edition, 1999), takes the practice to hysterical pitch in his attempt to rob McKimson of credit for Speedy Gonzales and give the character to Freleng:

> The idea for Speedy's character originated in a Robert McKimson cartoon of 1953 called "Cat-Tails for Two." The story was about an idiotic cat-and-dog team who sneak into a Mexican strip in search of mice but discover that the rodents are too fast to be caught. The head mouse is unnamed in the film and bears little resemblance to the Speedy movie audiences grew up with.

It is hard to know where to start here. On the credit side, Lenberg gets the title and date of the short right. The movie features two cats, not a cat and a dog, who sneak on to a Mexican ship, not into a Mexican strip. There are no rodents, in the plural, just a single mouse, who, far from being unnamed, leaves a business card for us to read: "Senor 'Speedy' Gonzales. The Fastest Mouse in All Mexico." Physically, he differs only very slightly from the later Speedy, lacking the sombrero; in all other respects, including voice and dialogue, he is identical.

As noted, the "uncreative" McKimson created Foghorn Leghorn, in *Walky Talky Hawky* (1946), and Speedy Gonzales, in *Cat-Tails for Two* (1953). He also created the Tasmanian Devil. Add in lesser characters like the kangaroo Hippety Hopper, Pete Puma, Smoky the Genie, and Sylvester Jr., and one begins to wonder where this myth of McKimson's lack of creativity and/or inspiration came from. Certainly, there were many routine cartoons among the 175 or so that he directed for Warners, but exactly the same can be said for Jones, Clampett, or Freleng. His interpretation of Bugs Bunny makes the character less of a sophisticate and more of a slapstick zany than Jones's – but another way of saying this is that McKimson's Bugs is more like Tex Avery's. Indeed, the truth of the matter may be that, because

Daffy Doodles (1946)

🎨 color / animated ⏱ 7 minutes
Merrie Melodies/Daffy Duck/Porky Pig
The first cartoon directed by McKimson. "In a large eastern city a demon is on the loose. The people are terrified, the police baffled. With diabolical cleverness the monster strikes without warning . . . and draws moustaches on all the ads." The vile fiend is, of course, Daffy, here very much in a Tex Avery vein: he has no motivation beyond sheer anarchic nuttiness. Even Officer Porky Pig, intent on tracking the criminal, has a moustache painted on him before he can dodge, then another one during Daffy's mass moustache-painting episode in the subway. Many moustache-paintings later, the pig finally gets Daffy to court, where a jury of mustachioed Jerry Colonnas acquits him. Promising to switch to beards in the future, Daffy produces his brush and paintpot and paints the screen black for the short's finale.

Walky Talky Hawky (1946)

🎨 color / animated ⏱ 7 minutes
Merrie Melodies/Foghorn Leghorn/Henery Hawk
Foghorn Leghorn's debut (complete with his trademark repetitive speech pattern) and the second Henery Hawk vehicle; the new character, of course, soon eclipsed the old. Young Henery must fulfill his destiny as a chicken hawk by catching and eating his first chicken. In the farmyard, rooster Foghorn Leghorn has been feuding with a dog, and he persuades Henery that the dog is a chicken and he, Foghorn Leghorn, is a horse. Various farmyard japes ensue.

McKimson tended to put Avery-style characterizations into a distinctly non-Avery-style visual and conceptual environment, with little of Avery's surrealism, his cartoons tend to be judged by this negative yardstick rather than for themselves.

The first short he directed for Warners, *Daffy Doodles* (1946), owes much to Avery in terms of characterization and ending – with Daffy painting the screen dark as the cartoon's final blackout. It is also one of the funniest Daffy Duck shorts, with a pompous opening narration that accentuates the hilarious ridiculousness of its plot's premise: that the police of New York are hunting high and low for a serial criminal who is terrorizing the public by painting moustaches on the faces in display advertisements. That same year, 1946, saw McKimson make his debut Bugs Bunny short, *Acrobatty Bunny*, which has a traveling circus arrive and park the lion's cage directly over Bugs's rabbithole: as Bugs peers into the beast's gaping maw he calls, "Pinocchio!" The rest is a fine Bugs cartoon, if no classic. And again in 1946, in a short that was intended to star Jones's series character Henery Hawk, McKimson introduced a character who stole the show and went on to have a series of his own and

Cat-Tails for Two (1953)

♫color /animated ◷ 6¹/₂ minutes
Merrie Melodies/Speedy Gonzales
The first appearance of Speedy Gonzales. Two cats — little smart-aleck George and hulking dimwit Benny — are down in the docks to catch mice. "Do you like Mexican food?" asks George. "Yes," says Benny: "It gives me heartburn and I love it." So they go to a Mexican ship for Mexican "mouses." Aboard, the trap they set is robbed by a mouse who leaves his business card in place of the cheese: "Senor 'Speedy' Gonzales. The Fastest Mouse in All Mexico." As the chases continue, it is George who gets the worst of the battering, thanks to Benny's stupidity and Speedy's tricksterism. A final firework gag sees the two cats blown sky-high up the ship's funnel.

Tabasco Road (1957)

♫color /animated ◷ 6¹/₂ minutes
Merrie Melodies/Speedy Gonzales
After a celebration in Speedy's honor in a "cantinita" (a little cantina built by the mice within the walls of a cantina), two of the mice are rolling drunk and hence easy prey for the local cats. Pablo and Fernando mimic Tweety beside a bruiser alley cat: "I tink I saw una pussycato." "You deed, you deed saw una pussycato!" They then offer the cat a fight, from which they have to be saved by Speedy — more than once, with one of his tricks being done so quickly he has to rerun the film in slow motion for the benefit of the audience. Finally, the cat flees in terror of more, leaving Speedy congratulating himself that his pals are safe. But he promptly finds the pair now challenging an entire alleyful of cats to a fight, and has to pitch back into the fray.

become a member of Warners animation's small pantheon: Foghorn Leghorn.

A character with whom McKimson became much associated was Sylvester, sometimes with Tweety Pie but as often in combination with one of the other Warners stars. It was in the Sylvester cartoon *Hop, Look and Listen* (1948) that McKimson introduced Hippety (or Hippity) Hopper, a baby kangaroo who escapes from the zoo and is mistaken by the frenetic cat for a mouse – a very *large* mouse, and one who can box.

Speedy Gonzales was a much later creation, and here certainly the accusation is valid that too many of the Speedy cartoons are formulaic, comprising merely a chase in which the Fastest Mouse in All Mexico defeats and humiliates a much larger predator using a mixture of rank speed and tricksterism. In fact, although McKimson created the character, he directed only a small proportion of the further Speedy shorts, a high proportion of

which, like 1957's *Tabasco Road*, gloriously break free of the formula. (*Tabasco Road* brought McKimson his second Academy Award nomination; the first had been for *Walky Talky Hawky*.) The director who produced the bulk of the Speedy cartoons, at least in the early days, was Friz Freleng, who seems to have wanted to use the character as the basis for a rival series to Jones's Coyote/Road Runner shorts.

The Tasmanian Devil, usually known today as Taz (a name given to him in 1991, for television), was another McKimson creation. He arrived in a rather fine Bugs Bunny short called *Devil May Hare* (1954). The animals flee from Taz, who will devour anything and everything, past Bugs's hole, and the wily rabbit tries to bamboozle Taz with a succession of artificial animals he could try to eat. In the end, in desperation, Bugs places a Lonely Hearts ad for a female Tasmanian Devil who has matrimony in mind. One flies in immediately from, presumably, Tasmania, and Bugs, in the guise of a rabbi (geddit?), marries the pair, thereby calming Taz's savage soul. (The quasi-Freudian equation of Taz's violence with a lack of sex went remarkably unremarked-upon at the time.) As the pair flies off Bugs comments: "All the world loves a lover, but in this case we'll make an exception."

The character was obviously ripe for further development, but Eddie Selzer, who had taken over as producer after the departure of Leon Schlesinger, thought that Taz was far too violent and issued instructions that there be no further Taz shorts. This edict lasted about two years until Jack Warner, who generally took little or no interest in the activities of the animation studio that bore his name, heard that the public loved the creation and was eager for more. Orders came down, and McKimson made two further Taz cartoons in 1957, one each with Bugs and Daffy. Thereafter he did two more, *Bill of Hare* in 1962 and the exceptionally funny *Dr. Devil and Mr. Hare* in 1964, both with Bugs. A final Taz short was released in 1979, two years after McKimson's death and directed by Friz Freleng; this was *Fright Before Christmas* and was done as part of the television special *Bugs Bunny's Loony Christmas Tales* (1979). Much later, Taz became an emblem of Warners in the same way as, although obviously to a much lesser extent than, Bugs Bunny.

All of this was, of course, far in the future at the time Warners closed down its animation studio in 1962. McKimson and the other directors went their separate ways. Friz Freleng and David DePatie set up the new studio DePatie–Freleng, best known for its long string of Pink Panther cartoons but also producing continuations of the Warner Looney Tunes and Merrie Melodies series. McKimson joined the new company as an animation director. He continued to work on new cartoons in the Warners series until 1969, when the studio discontinued releasing such shorts, and on Pink Panther titles until more or less the day he died, which was suddenly, of a massive coronary, on September 27, 1977. He left behind a legacy of fine cartoons, a few truly great ones, and several fine character creations.

Norman McLaren (1914–1987)

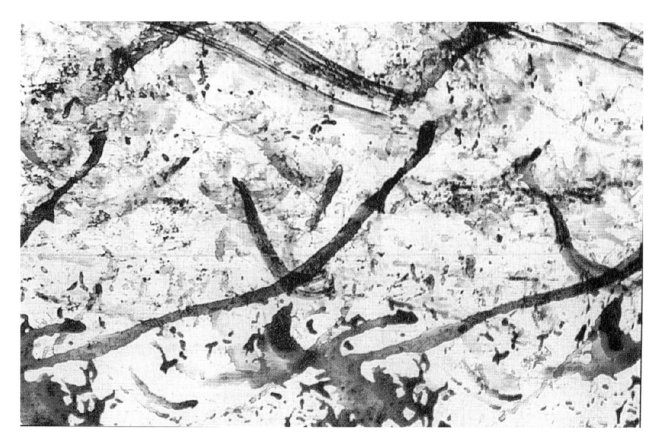

Still from *Begone Dull Care* (1949).
© National Film Board of Canada.

norman McLaren was one of the most influential of all animators, both through his nurturing of others and through his own brilliant, restless innovation. During his career he won 147 awards for his short movies, a record for any single moviemaker.

He was born on April 11, 1914, in Stirling, Scotland. In 1933, he enrolled at the Glasgow School of Art, and while there, in about 1934, he discovered an old 16mm movie projector in a basement. He naturally sought some way of putting this machine to use. Unfortunately, he didn't have a movie camera, but the idea occurred to him to attempt animation by drawing directly onto film stock. He therefore got hold of some old film, soaked off the emulsion, and painted directly onto it his first foray into animation. Although this didn't result in anything worth screening for others, it showed him that, in principle, the technique was sound.

He made various short movies from then on as an ancillary to his course work (when he finally chose a major it was actually in interior design). These were primarily live-action movies, although their *raison d'être* was experimentation with special effects and techniques. In 1935, a short film of his took first prize at the Second Glasgow Amateur Film Festival, but it was at the following year's festival that the future course of his moviemaking career was to be determined.

One of the judges at the 1936 event was the pioneer moviemaker and powerful advocate of the new medium of cinema John Grierson (1898–1972), a fellow Scot. Grierson's 40-minute documentary *Drifters* (1929), concerning the North Sea herring-fishing fleet, had been selected to open alongside the British premiere of Sergei Eisenstein's *Bronenosets Potemkin* (vt *Battleship Potemkin*; 1925), and was a landmark of British cinema, which up until that point had been dominated by studio-bound fictions rather than documentary location work. Because of his enthusiasm for informational moviemaking, Grierson was appointed first head of the GPO Film Unit – the GPO (General Post Office) being in those days responsible not just for the mail but for its savings bank and the telephones. Later, in 1939, he was appointed the first Commissioner of the National Film Board of Canada. Throughout World War II, he supervised the production by the NFB of scores of propaganda and training movies as well as documentaries about Canada. At the end of the war he left the NFB planning to pursue his moviemaking in more commercial spheres in the United States, but was unfortunately an innocent victim of the McCarthy-era witch-hunts and was blacklisted as a Communist (he seems to have been, rather, a good old-school Scottish socialist; McLaren, by contrast, had been a member of the Scottish Communist Party and retained a socialist morality throughout his life). Thereafter Grierson worked for UNESCO, for U.K. movie companies and, notably, for Scottish television, before returning to Canada late in life to take a chair at McGill University.

McLaren entered two of his works in the 1936 Glasgow Amateur Film Festival. He pinned high hopes on *Camera Makes Whoopee*, into which he had poured every special effect he could think of. His other entry, *Colour Cocktail*, he had included more or less to make up the numbers; it was apparently (no copy survives) a five-minute abstract piece done in live action and slow motion, interspersed with shots of the interplay of lights on colored paper; it accompanied a gramophone record with which it was synched sufficiently precisely to give the impression of a sound movie. To McLaren's considerable dismay, Grierson heartily disliked *Camera Makes Whoopee*, ripping it apart in his judgement as being technically proficient but artistically a worthless mess. McLaren was just saying goodbye to any thoughts of a future career in moviemaking when Grierson suddenly announced that *Colour Cocktail* had won the event. The experienced moviemaker later asked the student out for a drink and a chat, which served as enough of an interview for Grierson to offer him a job at the GPO Film Unit. McLaren started there in the Fall of 1936, but in early November was summoned by Grierson with the "request" that he go to Spain as cameraman alongside Ivor Montagu in order to make a pro-Republican propaganda movie about the Spanish Civil War. The resulting movie was the documentary *Defence of Madrid* (listed as 1936 but more likely 1937). The experience of making it enhanced the pacifism and abhorrence of violence which had always been a part of McLaren's makeup, as exemplified by an earlier live-action/animated movie, *Hell unLtd* (1936), a profoundly anti-war, anti-capitalist item that he had codirected with Helen Biggar.

In 1937, Grierson left the GPO Film Unit, being replaced by Alberto Cavalcanti. Under Cavalcanti's directorship McLaren began to make his first professional animated movie, *Love on the Wing* (1938), once again done by drawing directly onto film stock. This movie was intended to emphasize the theme important to the GPO that "It's heaven to receive a Greetings Telegram – be an angel, send one!" but caused a furor and at the time was not released. The cause of all the fuss was that, for a few brief moments, McLaren had made use of phallic imagery. Horrified, the postmaster general barred any release of the short, which is nowadays regarded as a classic. The movie is of further significance in that it deployed McLaren's first experiment with "animated sound." The soundtrack of a conventional movie is supplied (in simplest terms) by coding the edge of the film with patterns of light and dark generated by electrical fluctuations

derived from a microphone; when the film is projected, a light shines through this moving band of patterns onto a photoelectric cell, the electrical pulses from which drive the loudspeakers. McLaren's idea was that, if the visible part of the movie could be created by painting onto the film stock, then so could the soundtrack. McLaren was not the first to experiment with this technique – that was probably Rudolf Pfenniger, who announced something very like it in 1932 – but he was certainly the first to put it to any worthwhile artistic use.

The upset over the phallic images in *Love on the Wing* naturally made McLaren restless in his job at the GPO Film Unit, but even without this he would have departed Britain in 1939 as World War II loomed; he had seen too much slaughter in Spain while filming *Defence of Madrid* to be able to countenance any further direct confrontation with violence. He made one more animated short for the unit, *Mony a Pickle* (1938) – the title is Scots meaning "many a predicament" – before embarking for New York. There he was commissioned by Baroness Hilla Rebay von Ehrenwiesen of the Museum of Non-Objective Painting (later to be called the Guggenheim Museum) for a few experimental animated short-shorts, about two minutes long, such as *Allegro* (1939), *Rumba* (1939), *Dots* (1940), and *Loops* (1940), all of which deployed his technique of animated sound. However, his grants from Rebay could not make ends meet, and he was forced to take on in-betweening and other lowly jobs at commercial animation studios. He was able to continue making some movies for himself, however, of which the best known are *Stars and Stripes* (vt *Étoiles et bandes*; 1939), animated directly on the filmstock and featuring images of the U.S. flag to the accompaniment of the eponymous music, and *Spook Sport* (1939), the latter a more abstract piece, codirected with Mary Ellen Bute.

As early as 1939, soon after his arrival in New York, he had written to his old mentor Grierson at the National Film Board of Canada to see if there might be any jobs available, and Grierson had replied, regretfully, that there weren't. By the spring of 1941, however, things were different. The Canadian Government was in urgent need of funds for the war effort and accordingly asked the NFB to start producing propaganda movies aimed at encouraging people to invest in defense bonds and the like. Most of the NFB's output was being shown as packages of several movies in venues such as factory canteens, and Grierson felt that some light relief among the rest might improve attendance and generally make the audiences more receptive. Accordingly, he hired McLaren – after some resistance to the notion from the animator, who, as a pacifist, was nervous he might be asked to create pro-war propaganda – to join the NFB and in due course (1943) to kick-start a new animation unit for it. McLaren was to spend the rest of his professional life in the NFB's employ.

Through the end of the war, in 1945, McLaren created a string of short animations for the NFB, some of which were overtly connected to the war effort and some only vaguely related to it; titles include *V for Victory* (1941), *Mail Early for Christmas* (1941), *Hen Hop* (1942), *Five for Four* (1942), *Dollar Dance* (1943), *Keep Your Mouth Shut* (1944), *Chants populaires #5* ("Popular Songs no. 5"; 1944), *C'est l'aviron* ("This Is the Oar"; 1944) and *Alouette* ("The Lark"; 1944), these last two also done to French popular songs.

Grierson left the NFB at the end of the war, having accepted the post of commissioner only for as long as hostilities continued. McLaren, however, stayed on. In the succeeding three decades or so before his retirement he was to direct over 40 animated shorts for the NFB and produce further movies done by other animators. At the same time, he made the NFB an international Mecca for aspiring animators, who came to work with him and learn from him; two such were Frédéric Back and George Dunning. And, all the while, McLaren was making technical innovations – pixilation, for example, which he introduced in the Oscar-winning *Neighbours* (vt *Voisins*; 1952), allowing him to animate, in a process akin to stop-motion, human beings shot in live action so that they appear to glide and fly. (In *Neighbours*, two people come to blows over the ownership of a flower that grows on the boundary between their two properties. The anti-war message of this parable is obvious.) For the famous abstract short *Blinkity Blank* (1952), he produced images not by drawing and painting on clear film stock but by scraping the emulsion off completely exposed stock, so that the images appeared as white-on-black. Furthermore, because of the difficulties of registration involved in such a process, he devised the technique of using clusters that lasted for only a few frames, then leaving the film black for a score or more of frames before the next cluster of images. This preserves the illusion of motion but, at the same time, presents an excitingly stroboscopic effect that toys with the viewer's persistence of vision. He added a soundtrack of percussive effects in the same way. And in *Pas de Deux* (vt *Duo*; 1968), he exposed each frame as many as ten times to create striking multiple images of a pair of ballet dancers (Margaret Mercier and Vincent Warren) dancing, backlit on a stark black stage.

Of further interest were some of the musical soundtracks he used for these shorts. He was always concerned that the appeal of the movies should in no way be governed by national or ethnic boundaries, which is one reason why he made so little use of language in any form in them – except for the credits, which, after a while, he began to give in multiple languages. (Of course, most of the movies he made for the NFB were already bilingual in French and English insofar as they required language at all.) The music was similarly eclectic in style, varying from pan pipes in *Pas de Deux*, to Albinoni for the similarly danced *Ballet Adagio* (1971), to jazz by the Oscar Peterson Trio in *Begone Dull Care* (vt *Caprice en couleurs*; 1949), to sitar music by Ravi Shankar on another very famous short, *A Chairy Tale* (1957), in which a man performs a sort of *pas de deux* with a chair that declines to be sat upon: the movie shows the youth initially trying to exert mastery and then settling for understanding. The use of such tracks became of more interest to him than his earlier experiments in animated sound, and after using the technique in *Blinkity Blank* he did so in only three more shorts: *Rhythmetic* (1956) – where the soundtrack illustrates simple mathematical progressions performed, as if in a dance, by arabic numerals – *Mosaic* (vt *Mosaïque*; 1965) and *Synchromy* (vt *Synchromie*; 1971). That notion of dance is fundamental to much of McLaren's work, far beyond the obvious examples like *Pas de Deux*. His final movie, the long (nearly 22 minutes) short *Narcissus* (1983), in which he deployed many of the experimental and animation techniques derived through his long career, yet again makes use of dance in its telling of the classical tale of the youth who loses everything to his obsessive self-love.

In 1973, McLaren's work as a maker of animated movies and as head of the NFB's animation department was honored by his being made a Companion of the Order of Canada. The death of this genius of animation and very considerable humanitarian, on January 27, 1987, in Montreal, was mourned the world over.

OTTO MESSMER (1892–1983)

Still from *Feline Follies* (1919), the debut of the cat who would soon be called Felix.

Born in West Hoboken (now called Union City), New Jersey, on August 16, 1892, Otto Messmer was encouraged in art while a student at the Holy Family School there. Later he took a correspondence course in art and attended New York's Thomas School of Art. He did a form of apprenticeship illustrating fashion catalogs for the Acme Agency, but his real yen was to be a cartoonist. His ambition changed on seeing one of Winsor McCay's performances: he was keener than ever to become a newspaper cartoonist, but only as a stepping stone toward animation. While selling cartoons to the newspapers, including the *New York World*, he also tried, therefore, to get a job as a set painter in the movies.

His break came in late 1915, when Universal's Jack Cohn commissioned him to try his hand at making an animated movie. This Messmer did using a character he devised called Motor Mat, a child driver who could perform amazing feats. He employed the same "straight-ahead" method of animation that his hero McCay did; that is, he drew each frame separately, background and all, knowing nothing of the new techniques that fellow animators John Randolph Bray, Earl Hurd and Raoul Barré had introduced. His pilot movie was, accordingly, not good enough to be released, but, nevertheless, Cohn was sufficiently impressed by both the quality and the speed of execution to show Messmer's work around. Two of the people to whom he showed it – Hy Mayer, one of the many cartoonists of the era who was dabbling in animation, and the Australian-born animator Pat Sullivan – offered Messmer employment. Messmer initially chose Mayer, and with him made a short commercial cartoon for Auerbach's chocolates called *The Travels of Teddy* (1914) – Mayer was a political associate and friend

of Teddy Roosevelt. Later he did some work, although it's not clear exactly what or how much, on Mayer's live-action/animated Travelaughs series of shorts, begun with 1915's *To 'Frisco by the Cartoon Route* and running fairly successfully until 1918's *New York by Heck*.

Beginning in 1915 or 1916, Messmer was primarily working with Sullivan, and for a period of a few years it is difficult to work out which of the two men did precisely what. Sullivan, whose earlier life reads like something out of a Jack London novel, had managed to get a job in about 1910 as assistant to the comic-strip artist William F. Marriner and, after Mariner's death in a fire in 1914, he continued to produce the strips. One of these was *Sambo and His Funny Noises*, featuring a Little Black Sambo character; the strip did not thrive long under Sullivan's hand, but, two years later, now an independent animator, Messmer revived the character – under the new name Sammie (or Sammy) Johnsin, to avoid copyright problems – producing ten shorts during 1916, beginning with *Sammie Johnsin Hunter*. Others of Sullivan's character-led cartoon series that Messmer worked on were Boomer Bill (two or three shorts – records are hazy – in 1917) and Charlie (ten shorts in 1916), a cooperative venture with Charlie Chaplin; later in life Messmer was to say that working on the latter revolutionized his ideas of timing and body language in animation. The short that received the most prominence, however, was one done as a humorous prologue to Universal's feature movie *20,000 Leagues*

Under the Sea (1916) and released on its own the following year as *20,000 Laughs Under the Sea* (1917).

The year 1917 saw a break in the animating activities of both men. Messmer was inducted into the U.S. Army and went off to fight in Europe. Sullivan, by contrast, was discovered to have had sex with an underage girl (Marjorie Gallagher) and, even though he promptly married her, was convicted of statutory rape; he was sentenced to two years in Sing Sing, although in the end he served only nine months. Despite this inauspicious beginning and his lifelong difficulties with alcohol, the marriage of Pat and Marjorie lasted until 1932, when she died after falling out of a hotel window.

After Messmer returned from the war in 1919, he rejoined Sullivan, and the two of them seem to have done freelance animation hackwork for a while. By now, Sullivan's main focus was on drumming up business, and soon he would give up animating for good; throughout, however, he kept his name on every cartoon his studio produced and publicly claimed the credit for the work that was, in fact, being done by Messmer. One contribution to the studio's income was the occasional commission from John King, producer of the new Paramount Screen Magazine, created to replace the very similar Paramount–Bray Pictograph now that John Randolph Bray had deserted Paramount for Goldwyn. Each release of this weekly anthology contained several pieces of animation, some of which were one-offs but many of which were series; the Bobby Bumps series, by Bray's erstwhile collaborator Earl Hurd, was a popular item, but the vast bulk of the output came from Paul Terry's studio. Sometimes even Paul Terry could not keep up with the frantic schedule, and on those occasions King would fish around for others who could produce something in a hurry to fill the gap. One such commission came Sullivan's way at a time when his studio, too, was busy, and he came close to turning it down; instead he asked Messmer to knock out a cartoon in his spare time. This Messmer did.

The cartoon was called *Feline Follies*, and it appeared in the issue of the Paramount Screen Magazine released on November 9, 1919. Its star was a black cat called Master Tom, and even viewed today it is a charming and highly amusing piece. King liked it enough that he promptly commissioned a series: one cat cartoon a month for two years. Soon Hal Walker was hired to help Messmer cope with the workload. It was King who changed the cat's name to Felix.

In late 1921, Adolph Zukor, boss at Paramount, decided that the Paramount Screen Magazine was too expensive, and closed it down. According to Sullivan in later years, it was only at that moment that he realized the copyright to the character had been assigned to Paramount (in technical point of fact, to Famous Players–Lasky). Sullivan's tale was that, roaring drunk, he went to Zukor's office and threatened the man with all hell unless the copyright in Felix was handed back to him. When, in a final act of desperation, he urinated on Zukor's desk, the studio boss agreed.

Sullivan went to Warners to try to interest them in Felix but was turned down. However, a staffer there, Margaret J. Winkler, saw

Feline Follies (1919)

b/w / animated silent ⏲ 5½ minutes
Felix the Cat

The black cat Master Tom, scourge of mice and shatterer of female hearts, falls in love with Miss Kitty White, and she with him. "They select as a rendezvous that hallowed spot of feline lovers: the Back Fence — in a thickly populated neighborhood, of course." Fleeing incensed humans, they part with Tom's injunction: "Tomorrow night at the ashcan!" While they disport themselves there, the mice in the house where he lives trash the joint and steal all the food, so later that night his owner throws him out. He hurries to tell Kitty White, but is so horrified when he discovers she has already given birth to a big litter of black kittens that he finds a gas tap and starts sucking on it.

Felix in Fairyland (1923)

b/w / animated silent ⏲ 9½ minutes
Felix the Cat

Felix, reading a book of fairy stories, comes to the conclusion that Fairyland must be a great place to live. Just then, a fly stuck to flypaper begs him for help; he releases it, and it proves to be a beautiful fairy, who grants him one wish. A little later, without thinking, he wishes he were in Fairyland, and that is sure enough where he finds himself. Befriending Little Miss Muffet, he chases away the spider that frightens her; but it turns into a wicked witch, who then chases Felix on her broomstick. He outwits her and steals the broomstick, then flies to the rescue of The Old Woman Who Lived in a Shoe. Discovering that the local landlord, the Ogre, refuses to rent rooms in his castle to children (or cats, for that matter), Felix goes to sort him out — which he does, by tricking the Ogre into turning himself into a mouse. The short ends as the Old Woman moves her army of children into the castle.

the possibilities, and in February 1922, having signed a contract with Sullivan in December 1921, she left Warners to become animation's first female producer and distributor. She demanded from Sullivan an improvement in quality and got it, thanks to increased industry from Messmer and his team – to which in 1923 was added Bill Nolan, later the animator for Krazy Kat. (Another who animated Felix was the great Raoul Barré, who joined Messmer for a couple of years in 1925–27.) Winkler rapidly became a powerful mover in the distribution of animation, with such goodies as the Fleischers' Out of the Inkwell series and Walt Disney's Alice Comedies soon added to her stable. Under her guidance, and with help also from Sullivan, Felix the Cat became a coast-to-coast sensation, with additional huge popularity building up abroad as well. In 1922, the New York Yankees made Felix their mascot; in 1925 the popular song "Felix Kept Walking" was released in his honor; when Charles Lindbergh made his solo flight

Poster for *Felix Tries to Rest* (1924). Private collection.

By the end of the 1920s it seemed there was no mountain so high that the animated Felix the Cat could not climb it. But there was, in fact, one obstacle: Sullivan's conservatism. In late 1929 the first sound cartoons appeared, such as Paul Terry's *Dinner Time* and Walt Disney's *Steamboat Willie*, and to most it was obvious, from the rapturous reception given the latter and its sequels, that from then on sound was a prerequisite to any animated series's success. Strangely, Sullivan did not see this: he was reluctant to expend money or effort on what he seems to have thought was a passing fad. By this time, his alcohol difficulties were mounting, which may have muddled his judgment. In 1932 his wife died, and thereafter his descent was rapid.

When Sullivan died of alcoholism on February 15, 1933, he left his business affairs in a shambles. Messmer attempted to carry on the animated Felix, but it was impossible to unravel who actually held the copyright to the character – although the comic-strip incarnation seems to have been unaffected. In 1936 the Van Beuren studio tried its luck with three Felix the Cat sound shorts in color – *Felix the Cat and the Goose that Laid the Golden Egg*, *Neptune Nonsense*, and *Bold King Cole* – but there was a feeling that somehow this was a character whose time had passed, that he should have been left undisturbed as a figurehead of animation's silent past. Two decades later, in 1958, Joe Oriolo, who by now owned the rights in the Felix comic strip and who, *inter alia*, co-created Casper, the Friendly Ghost, launched a syndicated series of 5-minute Felix cartoons for television. In 1991, *Felix the Cat: The Movie* was released, directed by Hungarian animator Tibor Hernádi – among whose earlier credits was animation direction of René Laloux's *Les maîtres du temps* (*Time Masters*; 1982) – and produced by Don Oriolo, Joe's son; unwisely, this transports Felix into a *Star Wars*-ish territory and plot, although the animation is fine. In 1994 CBS produced 55 5-second-long Felix "bumpers" for use as links between its cartoons on Saturday morning television, and in 1995 this was developed, with Don Oriolo as an executive producer, into the tv series *The Twisted Tales of Felix the Cat*, which ran until 1997 and mixed traditional-style Felix cartoons with some live-action sequences and computer animation.

Having given up the weekly Felix the Cat comics page in 1943, Messmer did a little story work for Famous Pictures in the mid-1940s, but otherwise he steered clear of animation for the rest of his life. In 1955, having abandoned even the daily comic strip, he entered what proved to be a long retirement. He might have been an almost forgotten figure of animation – remembered merely as a comics artist – had it not been that Oriolo made a point of giving Messmer full credit during Felix's revival on television in the late 1950s. From the 1960s onward, Messmer's true position in animation's pantheon was established, and during the final two decades of his life he thoroughly enjoyed the fame and respect his achievement so richly deserved and which for so long had been kept from him. He died in Teaneck, New Jersey, on October 28, 1983.

across the Atlantic in 1927, he took with him a stuffed-toy version of Felix (although it's unclear whether this was because of personal inclination or paid sponsorship); and in 1928 a Felix doll was the subject of the U.S.'s first experimental television transmission. Felix also became the first animated character to be seriously merchandised, which happened on a scale that would not be equaled until Disney got into its stride with Mickey Mouse.

In 1923, Messmer began to draw a syndicated weekly cartoon page of the character, distributed by King Features, and to this was added a daily comic strip in 1927. The weekly page ended in 1943, some years after it had become obvious that Messmer's interest was flagging. He struggled on with the daily strip until 1955 and then retired, having sold the rights in the character to Joe Oriolo. Various artists continued the strip until 1967, when finally it died. There was a brief revival in 1984–87.

Hayao Miyazaki (1941–)

A journalist once dubbed Hayao Miyazaki "The Japanese Disney," and the epithet has stuck. While it was intended as a compliment, and while it must certainly have drawn additional Western viewers to the movies of this exceptional animator, it nevertheless does him a very great disservice: although his animation generally lacks the incredible polish that Walt Disney insisted upon from at least the days of *Snow White and the Seven Dwarfs* (1937), Miyazaki's movies are considerably richer in terms of storytelling, subtext, palette, and emotional depth. He is also much more of a hands-on animation director: to cite a single example, of the almost 150,000 cels in *Princess Mononoke* (1997), Miyazaki personally altered or touched up no fewer than 80,000. His love for his chosen artform shines through almost every frame that hits the screen; although he has become a commercially successful director, there is never the remotest sense while watching a Miyazaki movie that he is driven by anything other than the joy of creation.

Hayao Miyazaki was born on January 5, 1941, in the Bunkyo-ku district of Tokyo. His uncle was head of the family firm, Miyazaki Airplane, and his father a director of it; his inherited fascination for flight and for flying machines of all types is evident throughout his oeuvre. His mother was a strong-minded woman; even though she fell ill of tuberculosis when he was barely out of infancy, she obviously – to judge by some of the female characters portrayed in his movies – had a major influence on him, as did the situation of being a small child made vulnerable by the threatened loss of one

of the world's pillars, specifically a parent: this theme is a recurring one. His childhood was overshadowed by World War II and its aftermath, and here again there is a detectable thematic influence, although it is not overtly expressed in movies that are very often sunny: the motif recurs of individuals doing their best to survive under the threat of faceless or omnipotent forces, and of the ability of love, not necessarily romantic, to transcend these adversities. Also from childhood came a reverence for lore and mythology.

A further important influence appeared later. Miyazaki is a creator not just of animated movies but of manga. These graphic narratives are not regarded or conceived as mere throwaways, like most English-language comics: usually published in installments, rather like a Dickens novel and often just as ambitious in aim, they are probably better considered as the Eastern equivalent of the graphic novel, but generally done on a vast scale. Because of the time frame over which they tend to be published, their plots are often infernally complicated, with digressions and sub-stories galore, and frequently lurching from complex to ramshackle – again not unlike some Dickens novels. Miyazaki's own manga, some of which have been translated into English, include *People in the Desert* (1969–70), *Nausicaä of the Valley of the Wind* (1982–87, 1990–91,

1993–94), *The Journey of Shuna* (1983), *Miscellaneous Memorandum – The Age of Floatplanes* (1990), and *Tiger in the Mire* (1998).

Of more general importance in consideration of his movie work is the nature of the relationship between manga and anime. In the West, it is not uncommon for popular comics to have an animated incarnation, and on rare occasion there may be interplay between the two versions. But this is trivial by comparison with the situation in Japan between manga and anime, where it is probably more accurate to regard the two as being simply different manifestations of the same medium: anime are manga that happen to show motion. We can see this exemplified in one of the major complaints Western critics often make about Japanese animation: that the animators seem to have no conception of acting, so characters' emotions are conveyed through a limited series of stylized facial expressions. This is true, but misses the point: it is an attribute of comics art the world over that facial expressions are quite deliberately stylized rather than accurately depicted, in order to convey emotions in symbolic – and therefore instantly assimilable – form to the reader.

The young Miyazaki was, from a very early age, extremely interested in drawing. This interest was fed by his reading of manga, and played out by drawing manga illustrations. As he entered high-school, his desire to become a manga author was growing but when, in the final year of high school, he saw *Legend of the White Serpent*, he was so inspired that he decided to become an animator and gave up on the idea of being a manga artist. In his early twenties, after gaining a degree in political science and economics, he obtained a job that was related to his favourite artform: Toei-Cine took him on as a trainee in-betweener(see page 83).

Miyazaki soon found himself inbetweening for such projects as the feature movie *Watchdog Woof Woof* (*Wan Wan Chushingura*; 1963), the tv series *Wolf Boy Ken* (*Okami Shonen Ken*; 1963–65) and the theatrical Short *Gulliver's Space Travels* (*Gulliver no Uchu Ryoko*; 1965). The tv series *Wind Ninja Boy Fujimaru* (*Shonen Ninja Kaze no Fujimaru*; 1964–65) saw a new development for him – he was allowed to do not just inbetweening but also some key animation – and with the tv series *Husle Punch* (*Hassuri Panchi*; 1965–66) he had graduated to doing solely key animation.

Little Norse Prince Valiant (*Taiyo no Oji: Horusu no Daiboken*; vt *The Little Norse Prince*; vt *The Great Adventures of Little Prince Valiant*; vt *Prince of the Sun: The Great Adventure of Horus*; 1968) represented another major step forward, although it may not have seemed so to him at the time. This Toei theatrical feature, for which Miyazaki did some key animation but, far more importantly, was scene designer, has nothing to do with the Prince Valiant of the comic strips but is instead the tale of a young boy's adventures in a curiously Japanese version of mythological Scandinavia where magic still walks the land and gods vie with each other and with mortals. It is a fairly rudimentary piece of work, both visually and conceptually, but it has a certain clumsy charm and, although hindsight is an easy deceiver, seems to contain something of Miyazaki's vision: it has a little of the *feel* of a Miyazaki movie, as if

a child had somehow imitated the work of the later adult.

Further work for Toei in various capacities followed: he did key animation for four episodes each of the tv series *Little Witch Sally* (*Mahotsukai Sally*; 1966–68) and *Akko-Chan's Secret* (*Himitsu no Akku-chan*; 1969–70), and for the theatrical features *Puss in Boots* (*Nagagutsu o Haita Neko*; 1969) and *The Flying Ghost Ship* (*Soratobu Yureisen*; 1969). He took on additional responsibilities for the theatrical features *Animal Treasure Island* (*Dobutsu Takarajima*; 1971) and *Ali Baba and the Forty Thieves* (*Ali Baba to Yonjuppiki no Tozoku*; 1971).

While at Toei he developed what has been a lifetime friendship with Isao Takahata, a great director. In 1971 the two men decided to cut their ties with Toei and moved together to A–Pro, which often undertook work for Tokyo Movie (later to become Tokyo Movie Shinsha). The grass was not much greener here, but at least the pair was given greater responsibilities. In short order Miyazaki contributed to the development of a proposed tv series based on Astrid Lindgren's *Pippi Longstocking* children's books, *Nagakutsushita no Pippi* (ditched when A-Pro failed to secure screen rights); directed much of the tv series *Lupin III* (*Lupin Sansei*; 1971), a good deal of the time in collaboration with Takahata; saw Takahata direct a couple of shorts (really featurettes) based on Miyazaki screenplays and designs, *Panda & Child* (*Panda Kopanda*; vt *Panda, Little Panda*; 1972) and *Panda & Child: Rainy Day Circus* (*Panda Kopanda Amefuri Saakasu no Maki*; 1973); and did key animation and a little storyboarding for the tv series *Akado Suzunosuke* (1972–73). Another development during his time at A-Pro was that he and Takahata met the younger Yoshifumi Kondo, whom, a decade and a half later, the pair would groom to inherit Miyazaki's mantle at Studio Ghibli.

Miyazaki and Takahata jumped ship from A–Pro in 1973, this time joining Zuiyo (later to be renamed Nippon Animation). Miyazaki's first task was to develop scene designs and layouts for the tv series *Heidi: Girl of the Alps* (*Arupusu no Shoujo Haiji*; vt *Alpine Girl Heidi*; 1974), the first of what became the World Masterpiece Series; this was based on Joanna Spyri's children's novels and directed by Takahata, and it took Miyazaki to the Alps for an extended sketching tour. More piecework followed, even as friend Takahata's star had most definitely risen: a little assistant key animation for the tv series *A Dog of Flanders* (*Flanders no Inu*; 1975); scene design and layout for the tv series *3000 Leagues in Search of Mother* (*Haha wo tazunete sanzenri*; 1976), which Takahata directed; and key animation for some episodes of the tv series *Rascal the Raccoon* (*Araiguma Rascal*; 1977).

And then came the challenge, at last: to direct the 26 episodes of the tv series *Future Boy Conan* (*Mirai Shônen Conan*; 1978), based on *The Incredible Tide* (1970) by prolific U.S. children's novelist Alexander Key. In addition to directing, Miyazaki was responsible for character and other design, for layouts and for storyboards; in short, this was very much Miyazaki's own series. The story – a young orphan boy quests to save a kidnapped girl

Still from *Laputa* (1986), showing the flying fortress itself.
© 1986 Nibariki, Tokuma Shoten.

quasi-orphan in an underpopulated, feudalized post-nuclear-holocaust world – contained much that was close to Miyazaki's heart, and both plotting and thematic elements of it would recur in his own later independent moviemaking, notably in *Nausicaä* – the manga and the 1984 movie – in *Laputa* and in *Porco Rosso*.

Although *Future Boy Conan* was a major and rewarding project, it was still television – with television's tight budgets and deadlines – rather than the cinema, which was what Miyazaki hankered for. When Tokyo Movie Shinsha offered Miyazaki the chance to direct a theatrical feature, he leapt at it. To be sure, this feature was to be the second in a series, so the opportunity was hardly there for groundbreaking work; but the series was a prestigious one – based on Monkey Punch's highly popular manga *Lupin Sansei* – and there was plentiful scope for someone as full of ideas as Miyazaki. The movie's immediate series precursor, *The Secret of Mamo* (*Lupin Sansei: Mamo Karano Chousen*; 1978), directed and cowritten by Soji Yoshikawa, had not been an especially good piece of work, but it had been a lot of fun to watch and, importantly, had shown the potential the series characters and format possessed to generate something entirely more interesting. Miyazaki pitched into the new assignment, eventually to be called *The Castle of Cagliostro* (1979), with fervor, cowriting the screenplay himself (with Haruya Yamazaki), deepening and mellowing the characters – some of whom had been brashly rebarbative in the previous movie – toning down the violence, tightening both plotting and pacing, and in general bringing to it all the qualities which one would come to expect of Miyazaki in his later prime.

The Castle of Cagliostro (1979)

(*Rupan Sansei: Kariosutoro no Shiro*; vt *Arsene Lupin and the Castle of Cagliostro*; vt *Lupin III: Castle of Cagliostro*)
♭color /animated ⏱ 100 minutes
Bright-witted, wisecracking, toughly romantic master-criminal Lupin III, fresh from robbing a casino and discovering the plundered bank notes to be forged, spots a young girl (Clarisse) in a bridal gown being chased by bad guys. He fights them off, but they eventually succeed in kidnapping her. With various loyal sidekicks he traces her to the tiny Monaco-style country of Cagliostro, whose eponymous count, the forger of the dud bank notes that are flooding Europe and endangering national economies, plans to force his young relative Clarisse into marriage and thus unite the evil and good sides of the family. Also on the scene are the bumbling Inspector Zenigata and the sexily dynamic Fujiko, who is, like Lupin III, a master criminal wanted by the authorities in more countries than most of us have heard of. In due course, the forced marriage is thwarted. Lupin, Zenigata, and Fujiko combine forces to destroy the count's criminal plans. Lupin and Clarisse fall in love but realize that, coming from such different worlds, their love is futile: they must part, and choose to do so sooner rather than later. The lead character is variously named in different territories because of copyright problems with the estate of author Maurice Leblanc, upon whose *Arsène Lupin* series Monkey Punch had based his manga, Lupin III supposedly being the grandson of Arsène.

163

nausicaä of the Valley of the Wind (1984)

(*Kaze no Tani no Nausicaä*; vt *Nausicaä*; vt *Nausicaä of the Valley of Wind*; vt *Warriors of the Wind* – the last a savagely cut version disowned by Miyazaki)

(color / animated 116 minutes)

The Earth has been devastated in the dim past by a presumably nuclear holocaust (the "Seven Days of Fire") and by technology-derived pollution. Though social structures have reverted to the clan stage, the people are perfectly aware of a past that was unaffected by these twin evils, and of what happened to destroy that past; they are conscious that one day some form of return to the pre-catastrophe conditions may be possible. But no one really knows how to bring this about, a problem exacerbated by the fact that survival is a matter of battling against a supremely hostile natural world where plant spores can kill within seconds if inhaled, where gigantic carnivorous insects can attack without warning and gobble you up, and where the sea is acid.

Only a few understand that survival and the re-creation of a habitable world must depend not on warfare with nature but on cooperation with it. One such person is Nausicaä, the young princess of the clan that occupies the Valley of the Wind, a place whose pure breezes are innocent of the virulent plant spores. She can communicate in some way with the denizens of plant and animal worlds — in particular, as far as the movie is concerned, with ohmu, huge semi-sentient creatures that look and move rather like gigantic wood lice — and her own secret research is showing her that it is possible to grow non-toxic plants.

One day, a giant aerial battleship crashes into the valley, and the sole human survivor blurts out before dying that the aircraft's cargo must at all costs be destroyed. Despite this warning, the villagers are in confusion about what to do with an enigmatic ball of life they have recovered from the wreckage. Before they can make up their minds, the valley is conquered by the technological might of the Tolmekians, led by the beautiful but ruthless Princess Kushana. Conquest is, for Kushana, not an end in itself but a means toward her ultimate aim: to rid the world (or at least the region) of the poisonous spores that emanate from the forest, something she believes can be achieved only by destroying the forest in its entirety. To help her do this, she managed to obtain one of the great God Warrior death cyborgs used by the ancients during the Seven Days of Fire; this cyborg is the ball of life that emerged from the wreckage of the plane crash. In these efforts she is opposed by Nausicaä and by Asbel, a princeling whom Nausicaä picks up during the course of her many convoluted adventures. The movie concludes as Nausicaä, fulfilling an ancient prophecy, saves the Valley of the Wind from destruction under the feet of stampeding ohmu, also saving the human world from eventual extinction through her discovery that the trees of the forests are filtering the poison out of the planet's water, thus slowly restoring the balance of nature.

The merging of Miyazaki's talents and sensibilities with what was essentially crime-caper material was destined to be one of two things: disastrous or genre-transcendingly exquisite, with no middle ground . . . rather as if, say, Australian director Peter Weir had been assigned to direct a James Bond movie. In the end it was closer to the latter. What had been commissioned in expectation of an artistically minor outing proved a triumph, a movie satisfying and rich in incident, verve, humor, wisdom, and subtext, not to mention frequent beauty. The pace rarely flags, and the pyrotechnics are spectacular. There are respectful tips of the hat to countless screen and prose precursors, most notably to Alfred Hitchcock's Grace Kelly/Cary Grant vehicle *To Catch a Thief* (1955), with its sumptuous Riviera settings and air of being set in a "France that should have been." The backgrounds, in part based on Miyazaki's European researches for *Heidi: Girl of the Alps* and the aborted *Pippi Longstocking*, are a delight. Throughout the movie, there is the sense that every sequence – every *cel*, even – has been designed with loving care. As a further shock to the systems of Western viewers, the characters don't burst into inappropriate song every ten minutes – any more than they would in any other crime caper. Indeed, it's interesting to note in this context that the Lupin III movies, despite being animated, are rightfully included along side their live-action counterparts in the *Gangsters* volume (1998) of Phil Hardy's *Aurum/Overlook Film Encyclopedia*. And Steven Spielberg has listed it among his favorite actioners of all time.

After this significant accomplishment, what next was the successful young director set to do? The sad answer is more television, in the form of directing two 1980 episodes of the revived *Lupin III* series (1977–80). In addition, that same year he did the key animation for a single episode of the television series *New Adventures of Gigantor* (*Tetsujin 28 Go*; 1980–81). Although it's perfectly possible that he relished these tasks, it seems more likely that it was at about this time that he – along with Takahata – conceived the notion of founding Studio Ghibli (or something like it) to avoid in the future the need to take on minor, ephemeral animation projects unless they actually wanted to.

However, the next project on offer to the two men from Tokyo Movie Shinsha, in conjunction with the U.S. company Hemdale, was a seemingly delicious one. This was the animated feature *Little Nemo: Adventures in Slumberland*, reviving Winsor McCay's youthful hero to create the sort of movie McCay himself might have made had he enjoyed the benefits of a more sophisticated technology. As if this were not enough, there was the prospect of encountering the multi-talented artist and writer Jean Giraud (better known under his pseudonym Moebius) and an astonishingly impressive gallery of other creators: Ray Bradbury, Oliver Johnston, Frank Thomas, John Canemaker, Brian Froud . . . All must have seemed rosy for the two friends, but everything rapidly turned sour, and soon afterward, blaming artistic differences, they walked out of the enterprise.

Miyazaki went back to doing minor work. He directed the first six episodes of *Great Detective Holmes* (*Meitantei Holmes*), a 26-

part series for Italian television that, due to breaks in production was not completed until 1985, being aired in Italy in that year and not on Japanese television until 1984–85. He did some key animation on Osamu Dezaki's feature *Space Adventure Cobra* (1982) and on the tv series *Zorro* (*Kaiketsu Zorro*), which was never released in Japan.

Paradoxically, a more significant event in the development of his animation career was a return to manga: he began to publish *Nausicaä of the Valley of the Wind* (*Kaze no Tani no Nausicaä*; 1982–87, 1990–91, 1993–94) and issued the single-volume *The Journey of Shuna* (*Shuna no Ryoko*; 1983).

The manga *Nausicaä* was exceptionally well received, and it was soon perceived by those around him that it should be translated into an anime. Apparently with some reluctance, Miyazaki agreed. After funding had been raised, work began later in 1982, with Takahata as the movie's producer. The problems involved in transferring *Nausicaä* to the screen were considerable, for all the reasons earlier alluded to: the story had become exceptionally complicated – far too complicated for any movie to handle – and in fact was still unfinished, yet for the maintenance of audience belief in the situation and the characters it was deemed essential that the screen version in no way conflict with the printed one. In the West, the temptation to grossly simplify would not have been resisted; Miyazaki and Takahata, by contrast, were determined to remain faithful to the original's richness.

The result, *Nausicaä of the Valley of the Wind* (1984), produced by Tokuma Shoten in conjunction with Hakuhodo, is an astonishing piece of work. This is not to say that it is necessarily, in absolute terms, a good movie: the often congested plot staggers around (especially in the appallingly cut U.S. version, released in 1986 as *Warriors of the Wind*; this version however, was created without Miyazaki's approval), and there is a profusion of what seem to be *di ex machinae*; the animation is often clumsy or oversimplified – or both – and the characterization of all but Nausicaä herself and the icily beautiful warrior princess, Kushana, is stylized or scant.

These are mere nitpicks in light of the movie's many virtues. The world it creates very soon becomes utterly convincing as a self-consistent fantasy otherworld, and Nausicaä is such an appealing protagonist that one identifies with her entirely and becomes deeply involved with her struggle. Moreover – and this is the work's most important strength – there are frequent moments of quite stunning beauty of vision, of sheer marvel at the miracle of life and of the natural world.

Kushana in particular is a complexly drawn character. Although she is in the wrong of the argument and possesses many of the traits of a villain, she is not evil and indeed has much of the heroic. Her motivation is admirable; only her somewhat ruthless methods are misguided and undesirable. The omission of a true villain – of true individual human evil – recurs throughout Miyazaki's canon. Where there are genuine villains, as in *The Castle of Cagliostro* and *Laputa*, they are male and are, rather than dastardly brutes, of the highly plausible, smooth-talking, outwardly civilized variety. This lack

Laputa: Castle in the Sky (1986)

(*Tenku no Shiro Rapyuta*; vt *Tenku no Shiro Laputa*; vt *Castle in the Sky*)

🎨 color / animated ⏱ 124 minutes

Pazu is a gutsy young orphan from a mining village. (Miyazaki conducted a research trip to Wales in order to make the social and physical background authentic, and the situation there at the time — with Margaret Thatcher wilfully destroying the mining industry — ended up affecting his plot in numerous ways.) Sheeta is likewise an orphan, but reared in a distant pastoral valley. Unknown to her, she is heir to the throne of Laputa, now regarded by the general populace as mythical but in fact still aloft among the clouds, the last of many flying islands that once tyrannically dominated the earthbound nations. She possesses an amulet whose meaning she does not understand but which she was told by her mother always to wear. This amulet proves its worth when she — having been kidnapped by government forces led by the sinister Mushka (who proves also to have a claim to the Laputan throne, and hence to be double-crossing his masters) — falls from the aircraft in which she is being "escorted" and, after a long and sickening plummet, is gently lowered by the glowing amulet the rest of the way to the ground and literally into Pazu's arms. As the two young people compare notes, he tells her that his father, a brave aeronaut, once saw Laputa during a storm, but that everyone save Pazu assumed he was a liar or deluded.

However, the two adolescents are very soon being hunted not only by Mushka's thugs but also by the gang of aerial pirates led by Ma Dola: Mushka, as rival heir, is eager to attain and abuse the global power that possession of an aerial fortress and its superweapons would give him; the Dolas are merely keen to get their hands on the treasures still assumed to exist on Laputa. Mushka wins the race to capture Sheeta and the amulet; Pazu allies himself with the pirates to rescue the girl. The parties make their way to the flying island, where they discover a beautiful but empty kingdom populated only by small animals and, at most, a handful of the ancient Laputans' terrifying war robots, now turned to peace and the tending of the royal gardens (shades here of Ridley Scott's *Silent Running* [1972]). There is a titanic battle of wills between Sheeta and Pazu on the one hand and Mushka on the other, all set among the vast and enigmatically silent machine that lies at the core of the flying island (shades here of Fred McLeod Wilcox's *Forbidden Planet* [1956]), followed by an equally titanic showdown between the government's vast military might, under Mushka's command, and the two young folk plus Ma Dola's plucky if rather dimwitted gang of pirates. Finally, the bad guys are destroyed while our heroes, the pirates, and, very significantly, Laputa itself escape. Disencumbered of the machineries of war, the island floats to higher altitudes where, more distant from Earth, it and its animals and peacefully aging robots can continue their existences untainted by the greed and power lust of humankind.

My Neighbor Totoro (1988)

(Tonari no Totoro)

color / animated ⏱ 83 minutes

Two young sisters, ten-year-old Satsuki and four-year-old Mei, are brought by their father to live in a country cottage so they can be near the hospital where their mother is being treated for some unspecified disease. Although their father is loving, parental supervision of the two girls is minimal. From the outset it is obvious to the children that there is something magical about their new home. Mei one day spots a little furry creature trundling through the unkempt garden. Following it and a medium-sized version that joins it, Mei eventually falls into a hole in a huge camphor tree and discovers a gigantic version of the creatures she has been pursuing. The two become friends — soon three, as Satsuki likewise becomes acquainted with the creature, called Totoro (strictly speaking, Big Totoro, the other two also being totoros) after Mei's mispronunciation of a Japanese word meaning "troll." Thereafter the two girls have adventures with their giant friend — flying on a spinning top, playing ocarinas with him on the topmost branch of the camphor tree, chanting seeds into prodigious and near instantaneous growth, journeying in a Cat-Bus (a cross between a cat and a bus), and so on. Finally, after the Cat-Bus takes them to visit their mother in the hospital so that they can reassure themselves her condition is not as grave as feared, Totoro seems to feel that his job with them is done: just like all the adults, they can no longer see him, although of course they will always know he is somewhere in the forest, watching out for them.

Kiki's Delivery Service (1989)

(Majo no Takkyubin)

color / animated ⏱ 102 minutes

Kiki is a witch, and it is the custom that trainee witches must leave home at the age of 13 to spend a year living alone in some distant area, supporting themselves purely through their magical abilities. Kiki is rather short on magical abilities, but at least she has more or less mastered the art of flying a broomstick. With her companion, the black cat Jiji, she arrives in a strange town, almost causing a serious traffic accident through her erratic flying and escaping a police booking only through the intervention of the boy Tombo, who is attracted to her on sight. He gets no thanks: she disguises her fear and insecurity (her lack of self-esteem) by being almost spitefully dismissive of him. She finds lodgings with a pregnant baker, Osono, and sets up a flying messenger service to deliver items around the town. Tombo is persistent, but Kiki always rejects him, although eventually softening; however, it is only through using her powers of flight to save his life in a dirigible disaster that she can gain the confidence to accept him as the honest suitor he is.

of full-scale hate figures may be regarded as a weakness, but only by those whose world view is so simplistic that they must see the human condition depicted only in black and white: unalloyed good versus absolute evil. The complex adversaries he produces allow stories that are infinitely more satisfying and credible than those of his commercial Western counterparts.

Nausicaä was immediately a colossal success in Japan and — in relative terms — the rest of the world. The future of both Nibariki and, when it almost immediately came into existence, Studio Ghibli was assured. It is a measure of *Nausicaä*'s success as a movie (ignoring for a moment its commercial success) that Miyazaki became an internationally recognized director during the years when his sole movie available in any Westernized form was *Warriors of the Wind*, the garbled U.S. dub of *Nausicaä*.

One movie does not make a studio, as Miyazaki and Takahata were only too well aware. They jumped almost immediately into their next feature, again directed by Miyazaki and produced by Takahata: *Laputa: Castle in the Sky* (1986) — generally known in its Western releases only as *Castle in the Sky*, since in Spanish "la puta" means "whore." This change of title may seem a trivial matter, but, in fact, it is depressingly trivializing: the central image of the movie is Jonathan Swift's flying island, Laputa, from his *Gulliver's Travels* (1726), and to call it anything else is cultural craziness. However, the story of *Laputa* is about much more than a flying island; indeed, Laputa itself, although marvelously depicted, is almost no more than a symbol in what is in point of fact a coming-of-age tale.

In most discussions of *Laputa*, terms like "science fiction" and "alternate world" abound, and there are certainly several allusions in the movie to science-fictional precursors. However, just as with *Nausicaä*, it is unprofitable to consider *Laputa* as a work of sf. The story is set in an unnamed otherworld whose technology might match that of various periods of our own history but which, for that very reason, has never had and never will have any direct counterpart on this world. Just as Swift's satire is, at its root, a work of fantasy rather than of sf, so is Miyazaki's partially recursive tale — even though his purposes are, for the most part, not directly satirical. In this fantasy world it is perfectly reasonable that love can conquer all: not only do the two loving adolescents beat off the threats of principal bad guy Mushka and military stupidity, they also conquer the previously flinty, ruthless heart of the pirate Ma Dola, who, at the start of the movie, is unabashed by the prospect of mass murder but, by its end, has become a sentimental old dear. In most hands this theme of love's omnipotence would almost certainly become trite and bathetic, but in Miyazaki's it is a perfectly rational statement of an ideal.

Aircraft and flight play a major role in *Laputa*. This fascination for flight is evident in all but one of Miyazaki's movies — to skim, we also have the Heath Robinsonish escape plane that appears in *The Castle of Cagliostro*; the various flying machines that are central to *Nausicaä*, but, most notably, the little glider which Nausicaä herself uses to travel about; the spinning top that carries the eponymous elemental and the children aloft in *My Neighbor Totoro*; the broomsticks and

Still from *Nausicaä of the Valley of the Wind* (1984).
© 1984 Nibariki, Tokuma Shoten, Hakuhodo.

airship of *Kiki's Delivery Service*; and the winged angel in the music film *On Your Mark* (1995). Only in *Princess Mononoke* is it not overtly expressed, although it is often hard to believe that San cannot fly, so surely does her strange, non-human scuttling gait take her over all obstacles and up to the rooftops. As we saw, the obvious genesis of this preoccupation of the director is his youth as a member of an aircraft-manufacturing family, but more important seems to be that, perhaps subconsciously, flight – with its escape from the mundane concerns of the ground – has come to symbolize in his own personal mythology the ability human beings have to aspire to and attain something better and more fulfilling than the straightforward business of physical existence. In *Laputa*, Sheeta and Pazu realize their dreams in the sky, and the fitting farewell of the flying island is that it distances itself yet further from the mundane. Nausicaä transcends the hell of existence in a devastated world through her companionship with and travel on the winds; Kiki must master flight in order to become truly herself; Totoro takes the children for what is to Mei merely a thrilling adventure but to her elder sister Satsuki is symbolic of far more than that. In all cases flying is as much a spiritual matter as a physical one.

The three central characters of *Laputa* are Sheeta, Pazu, and, perhaps oddly, the aerial pirate Ma Dola. Although Mushka is important as the movie's villain, he is, in a strange way more a catalyst than an individual, more a cipher than a personality: he is necessary to drive the conflict that underpins the plot, but plays little part in the emotional, interpersonal dynamic of the movie. Dola – supposedly modeled on Miyazaki's mother, who had died in

1984 – becomes central primarily through strength of personality rather than plot function, important though that is. Essentially, she is one of animation's great zanies; most often in the West such characters are relegated to the position of sidekick, their purpose being to conquer hearts with their exuberance and wisecracking. Miyazaki doesn't normally create zanies – Teto, the little animal sidekick of Nausicaä, is left deliberately unzanified, and Jiji, Kiki's cat familiar, is much more obtrusive in the crassly voiced English-language dub than in the original – but with Dola he shows he is just as capable of this particular art as any other animator. It would have been too easy for him, indeed, to have allowed Dola's personality to swamp those of the two leads, Sheeta and Pazu; with great skill he keeps her just on the right side of a very fine line.

Miyazaki has yet to show himself as adept at creating involving male central characters – with the glorious exception of Marco Pagott in *Porco Rosso* – and Pazu exemplifies this. In the mind's eye it is difficult to determine the difference between Pazu and *Nausicaä*'s Asbel or *Mononoke*'s Ashitaka: all three are just variations on the standard Miyazaki boy lead. Pazu is certainly more three-dimensional than Asbel, as befits the fact that this movie is as much about him as it is about Sheeta, and he is perhaps more fully realized than Ashitaka. However, although we can admire Pazu's good humor and his incredible resources of pluck, somehow it is

Porco Rosso (1992)

(*Kurenai no Buta*; vt *The Crimson Pig*)
🎨 color / animated 🕐 93 minutes)

The setting is the Adriatic at a time when Italian Fascism is on the rise. Some years before the story's start, the pilot Marco Pagott became so world-weary that he decided to distance himself from the rest of humanity by turning himself into a pig; this is the only fantasy element of the plot, whose adventure component is made up of a series of skirmishes, both on the ground and in the air: between Marco and the largely faceless forces of Fascism, which seek to clench him and everyone else in their conformist iron fist; between him and the Mamma Aiuto Gang, a rather amiable bunch of airborne pirates (reminiscent in many ways of Ma Dola's crew in *Laputa*) who have tired of Pagott's rescuing of their intended victims; and between him and the Aero Viking Association, a bunch of bad guys who have hired a smooth-talking, small-brained American-immigrant pilot, Donald Curtis, to blast him out of the skies. There are thrills and spills aplenty along the road toward the resolution, whereby Marco retains his independence with the minimum of bloodshed.

hard to become entirely involved with him as he proceeds from one hair-raising escapade to the next: it is difficult to identify with him because there is not really much there to identify *with*. To an extent much the same can be said of Sheeta, although Miyazaki has something more to work with in her case, as girl, woman, tomboy and princess all wrestle with each other in her psychological makeup. Yet Sheeta does not stand out as a personality in the same way as do Nausicaä, Satsuki, Kiki, Fio, and Mononoke.

Ignoring its subtexts concerning coming-of-age, the abuse of technology, the human potential to attain higher things, the importance of the common people (remember those Welsh miners; see synopsis) in the grand scheme of things – however much the tyrannies that seek to govern them may decree otherwise – and the ability of love to transcend all and to defeat the seemingly undefeatable, *Laputa* is to most audiences little more than an imaginative rollicking adventure. Even at this level it is brilliantly successful. It follows a peculiarly British tradition of boys' adventure stories whose prime exponent is usually regarded as Robert Louis Stevenson: elements of *Treasure Island* (1883), *Kidnapped* (1886), and even *Catriona* (1893) are detectable here. There is also some influence from Jules Verne.

Miyazaki turned next to pastoral fantasy, with *My Neighbor Totoro* (1988). *Totoro*'s was not an easy birth. The proposal had been around for a while, but none of the possible investors in the project could see the commercial possibilities of a simple tale of two little girls and a friendly woodland spirit; in particular, they couldn't see the merchandising potential of the central creature, the woodland spirit himself. In the end, *Totoro* came into existence solely because of a complicated two-movie deal. The

publishing house Shinchosa had for some time been contemplating the possibility of branching out into cinema. They had published a novel by Akiyuki Nosaka that Ghibli house producer Toshio Suzuki persuaded them was ideal as the basis for an animated movie. This tragic tale of a Japanese boy's wartime and postwar childhood and death was duly assigned to Isao Takahata and, made as *Grave of the Fireflies* (*Hotaru no haka*; 1988), proved to be one of anime's finest moments. There was, however, a brilliant further idea. As the movie *Grave of the Fireflies* would be of a historical/ educational note, schools would send busloads of children to see it; so why not, on the pretext that such a gloomy movie required accompanying light relief, present it as one half of a double bill, with *Totoro* as the other half, thereby guaranteeing the latter a huge audience and an equally huge demand for associated merchandising? The ploy worked, and Studio Ghibli set about making the two movies side-by-side. In the end, *Totoro* proved perhaps the most popular movie ever to have come out of Japan, and certainly among the most commercially successful.

What immediately strikes one about this movie – aside from some memorable sequences – is the animator's observation of the two children. This is so comically true to life that it is little wonder the movie has a huge following among adults as well as children. The best example occurs early on, when Miyazaki is establishing the relationship between the sisters: whenever Satsuki says something of importance, Mei has the habit of joining in a split second later and speaking slightly faster, so that the two girls finish the statement almost simultaneously – Mei clearly assuming that she has thereby deceived the rest of the world into believing she has had the same thought as Satsuki and is therefore as grown-up as her big sister. There are also some nice moments when a boy from the neighboring farm tries, with desperate prepubertal ill grace, not to show that he is attracted to Satsuki.

It is Satsuki who is the movie's central character, even though that position might seem to belong to either Mei or Totoro. Satsuki is the axle around which the rest of the story rotates. With her mother in the hospital for who knows how long and with who knows how severe an illness, Satsuki is caught neatly between the freedom of childhood and the responsibilities of adulthood. Not only must she do her best to care for her little sister; she must also care for a temporarily wifeless father. Mei learns some simple lessons from her friendship with Totoro, but Satsuki is transformed by that relationship. This transformation is not a simple coming-of-age affair: only just young enough to be able to see the totoros at the start, she learns not only how to begin becoming an adult but also how to *hold onto her childhood* – something all adults must do if they are to be complete human beings.

Subliminally, to underscore this point, Miyazaki equates the three totoros with the three members of the human family. Little Totoro is clearly an equivalent to Mei; they both have the same adorable propensity to get into trouble. Big Totoro is equally clearly a daddy figure: he is a big, cuddly furry creature, which is what all

the best daddies of ten-year-old girls should be, and of course they should also be that girl's best friend in all the world, and the one who watches over her to make sure she comes to no harm. Big Totoro has much screen time and Little Totoro has a fair amount, but Middle Totoro – the equivalent of Satsuki herself – has only a tiny role. At first, this might seem to be a pragmatic decision by the animator: Middle Totoro offers less potential for fun than the other two. But, on further thought, it becomes clear that the difference in emphasis between the three is a reflection of Satsuki's perception of the three forest spirits (or three aspects of the same spirit, a point Miyazaki allows to remain moot) and hence, by extension, of her perception of herself within her human family. By the end of the movie, of course, she has, without realizing it, learned through her adventures with Big Totoro that she, too, is important. This gain of proper self-esteem is one reason she can no longer see (*need* no longer see) the totoros.

Such considerations lead one to acknowledge that *My Neighbor Totoro* is, as a fantasy, far more than the superficial children's outing Western critics have too often assumed it to be. With the focus so much on Satsuki's *perceptions* and on the inability of all but children to *see* the woodland spirits, it is legitimate to speculate that the entire story, wonderful supernatural entities and all, may be simply a product of those perceptions of hers – that she has conjured the magical events and personages into a subjective form of reality through the subconscious exercise of her own imagination. This sort of play with the nature of reality, and with the importance of perception in molding reality, is an intermittent concern of the most sophisticated written fantasies; and, in *My Neighbor Totoro* it is masterfully and very delicately handled.

Miyazaki's next feature, *Kiki's Delivery Service* (1989), again focuses on a girl, the rather older (age 13) Kiki, a trainee witch, and her gaining of adequate self-esteem in preparation for adulthood. The message is obvious here: Kiki's gaining of womanhood (that is, full witchhood) and independence is something she earns, not simply something that comes about because she says it is so; only once she has earned her status, not so much in the eyes of the world but in her own mind, can she start forming fulfilling relationships at an adult level. Because Kiki is the central female character of a film quite deliberately aimed at girls, this becomes a profoundly feminist message, although not one that can be expected to go down too well among cocktail-party feminists: Kiki attains the joys of completeness but must also accept its responsibilities.

Miyazaki produced *Kiki's Delivery Service* himself. Increasingly, he was to serve as producer of those Ghibli movies which he did not himself direct, beginning with Takahata's *Only Yesterday* (1991), a rather long-winded non-fantasy that explores a woman's childhood in parallel with developments in her adult life, in the end conveying much the same message as *Kiki's Delivery Service*. Later, Miyazaki proposed the idea of using racoons as main characters in Takahata's *Pom Poko* (1994), which Takahata went on to write and to direct; the tale of raccoons mounting a war against the people destroying Tokyo's surrounding countryside to establish suburbs suffers from extreme long-windedness.

Much more significant than either of these two is Yoshifumi Kondo's *Whisper of the Heart* (1995), which Miyazaki not only produced but wrote and storyboarded. This movie bears all the hallmarks of a Miyazaki movie, as if Kondo were merely his mentor's hands; and it comes as no surprise to learn that Kondo was being groomed to fill Miyazaki's shoes at Studio Ghibli (a plan thwarted by Kondo's death at the tragically early age of 47 in January 1998). *Whisper of the Heart* is again a tale of young people earning their adulthood in order to be able to properly establish interpersonal relationships. Schoolgirl Shizuki must run the rite-of-passage gauntlet of writing her first novel, the eponymous *Whisper of the Heart* – even though that novel is by implication an embarrassing work of purple prose – in order to feel herself worthy of entering an equal relationship with schoolboy Seiji, who, if he is to merit *his* half of the relationship, has his own gauntlet to run: a promising young violin-maker, he must study at a specialized school halfway around the world if he is to become a great one. With digressions into the fantastic and a constant sense of magic realism, the movie exerts an unflagging fascination, so that it seems much shorter than its two-hour running time. *Whisper of the Heart* is possibly the most emotionally successful of all the Ghibli movies.

Miyazaki's next movie as director after *Kiki's Delivery Service* was *Porco Rosso* (1992), known throughout the English-speaking world under this title (with Jean Reno voicing the title role) for the simple reason that – astonishingly and shamefully – the only English-language version yet to be made has been a crude dub done by Japan Airlines for in-flight use. Where *Kiki* had been overtly directed at young people, *Porco Rosso* – a tale of aerial derring-do in the Adriatic between the wars – was designed for grown-ups. The real name of the central character – the "Crimson Pig" of the title – is Marco Pagott, a tribute by the director to the Italian producer of that name who has been his good friend since 1981, when they met while working together on *Great Detective Holmes*. (Miyazaki approves of pigs, so the bestial casting of his friend was a compliment, not an insult.)

Porco Rosso is an excellent action caper, but much more interesting than all the flamboyant adventures is the interplay between Marco and the two women in his life. The first of these is the beautiful Gina, whom he has known since his youth, when the two of them were part of a quintet of inseparable friends; it is never overtly stated that Gina and Marco were lovers during his pre-pig days, but it is understood. Gina has married the quintet's three other men, one by one, and each has died young. While she genuinely mourns them and did genuinely love them, it is clear that of the four it was Marco who always was and still is her true soulmate and the object of her affections. Stately and gracious, she now runs a hotel on the Adriatic coast which seems isolated out of time: the ambience there is such that it feels as if the political torment in the rest of Europe was a million miles away. Her face betrays always wistfulness, for, despite the fact that she loves Marco

Princess Mononoke (1997)

(*Mononoke Hime*; vt *The Princess Mononoke*)

🕮 color / animated ⏱ 135 minutes

Ashitaka kills a crazed boar-god and is cast out by his clan, doomed to wander the land. In due course, he encounters the Lady Eboshi, who is trying to create an island of stability and prosperity in the midst of a tormented country: she has taken in society's rejects — whores and lepers — and is giving them not just food and shelter but also a purpose, that of advancing technological well-being through the extraction and purification of iron ore from mines carved out of the forest lands. Unfortunately, to succeed in this she must destroy the forests, in so doing driving out the many nature gods who live there. She and the citizens of the mid-forest town she has erected, Tataraba ("place of the bellows"), are opposed philosophically by Ashitaka, and physically by the nature gods themselves and by San, a wild girl who has been reared by the goddess-wolf Moro.

The greatest of the forest gods is Shishi (or Didaribotchi), who by day takes the form of a mighty-antlered, sad-faced deer and by night that of a vast, not quite corporeal creature. Eboshi wishes to destroy Shishi because he is an obstacle to the progress of her fledgling civilization, and is assisted by crooked lords who seek the severed head of Shishi, said to grant immortality. She starts a determined campaign to strip away the forest, destroy the gods, and seize the desired head. But while she is away with her army in the forest, one of the lords mounts an assault on Tataraba, intent on razing it and slaughtering all of its population still left there — essentially, the women and children.

Somehow, Ashitaka must bring out of all this potential disaster the least-bad resolution. He allies himself with San (with whom he has by now fallen in love) and the gods, but not to the extent that he will aid them in their stated aim of extirpating all of the humans. He will not slay Eboshi because she is not evil. He must protect the friends he has made in Tataraba from wholesale slaughter at the swords of the corrupt lord's samurai and mercenaries. He knows he cannot succeed in returning everything to the status quo, but he can ameliorate the effects that humankind's inexorable advance has on the forest and its gods — if nothing else, he can delay their demise. It is an almost impossible complex of seemingly irreconcilable tasks that he has set himself, but, in the end, he succeeds in at least the greater part.

and is sure that in his porcine way he loves her, she believes he will never be hers.

In strict contrast to the mature Gina is the tomboyish young ingenue Fio Piccolo, whom Marco first encounters when he needs to bring his plane to the Piccolo family's airplane repair shop. Barely out of adolescence and full of sprightly youthful ebullience, Fio falls head-over-heels for the mature, experienced male who erupts into her life. He is mightily tempted by her charms, but in the end realizes that the only honorable thing he can do — despite her violent protests — is to send her away from him, so that in due course she can meet and fall in love with someone of her own age

rather than become just another notch on an aging womanizer's belt. In so doing he discovers that his assumption that Gina would no longer be interested in him now that he's a pig has been false from the start.

Production and other work on *Pom Poko* and *Whisper of the Heart* was part of the reason why no Miyazaki-directed movie (save the 7-minute music film *On Your Mark* [1995]) appeared between 1992's *Porco Rosso* and 1997's *Princess Mononoke*. The other part of the reason was that this latter movie was by far the most ambitious project either director or studio had yet attempted. It was ambitious in every sense, not only because it has a complicated yet tightly controlled plot involving matters of great seriousness — of Miyazaki's own creation — , or because, at about two and a quarter hours, it is one of the longest animated movies ever made, but because Miyazaki — believing at the start of the project that it would be his last movie as director — determined that it should be his masterpiece. There is barely a skimped cel throughout its prodigious length, and very few that are not embellished with an attention to detail that staggers the imagination. This is a movie made with love, and it shows.

Despite the movie's title, the story is really that of the princeling Ashitaka, expelled from his village for having incurred a supernatural wound while saving his people from a rampaging, crazed god-boar, and set to roam the world; in plot terms, San (the *mononoke*, or monster) plays only a subsidiary role. This idiosyncrasy of titling arose because the movie was initially intended to tell San's story; during the project's development, however, the focus shifted to Ashitaka. Miyazaki was dickering with such title notions as *The Legend of Ashitaka* when a Ghibli executive, reluctant to see the studio throw away what he regarded as a commercially potent title, pre-sold the movie as *Princess Mononoke*. After that there was no turning back.

In fact, while it is true that the movie is Ashitaka's story and he is certainly the central character in terms of screen time and the role he plays, it is San, the Princess Mononoke — the orphan who has chosen to reject humanity, having been raised by the goddess-wolf Moro alongside her own brood — who offers the most powerful icon of the movie. Like Pazu in *Laputa*, Ashitaka is as an individual worthy of all the respect we can offer him for his courage, fortitude, wisdom beyond years, strength of character, and so forth, yet from this movie he does not emerge as a particularly distinct personality. San is an entirely different animal and, although her part is the smaller one, steals the movie — more than that, she becomes its thematic and emotional fulcrum. Miyazaki has always been, at his best, excellent at characterization, and for the princess-monster he pulled out all the stops. She has the almost alien hostility of the wild animal in her gaze, and when she moves in her crouching scuttle, nearly on all fours, it is with a speed and gait unknown to the human species. There seems to be about her unkempt form a nimbus of silver-gray negative light that sets her apart from the ordinary mold of humanity, yet she is in very human

terms extraordinarily beautiful, a child-woman and a fully mature female creature all at once.

Princess Mononoke (1997) is high fantasy of a conceptual sophistication and complexity rarely found in the written form of this subgenre and hardly at all in the cinematic form. Although the movie's resolution is in fact perfectly satisfying from a philosophical viewpoint, it does not concur with the demand by Western commercial moviemakers that there must always be a happy-ever-after ending. In this way of thinking, conclusions without all the ends tied off neatly are fine for art-house movies, but commercial animated movies are axiomatically regarded as products for children; children are incapable of dealing with good and evil in terms other than straightforward black and white – so the bad guys should be destroyed and the good guys should emerge as complete, not partial, victors. *Mononoke* exemplifies the reasons why such a line of thinking is fallacious. First, it is an animated movie primarily designed for adults rather than children – and Miyazaki has the sense to realize that such sweeping divisions of audiences into adult and child are artificial, grafted onto movies by the preconceptions of the movie industry and of the public alike: they are not inherent to the movies themselves. Second, even if the movie were aimed particularly at children, children are perfectly capable of appreciating indefinite conclusions to conflicts and of perceiving the many shades of gray that exist in the debate between right and wrong. Third, the human condition itself hardly ever leads to trite, simple resolutions; there is no reason why animated movies should not attempt to reflect real life rather than fairy tale in this respect.

The movie received rather mixed reviews from Western critics on the release of its Miramax version, dubbed into English in a good adaptation by Neil Gaiman that was unfortunately flatly voice-directed and -acted. In part the critics were, whether they realized it or not, reacting to the deficiencies of that voice track: watching this version is to realize that one is in the presence of a masterpiece, but a masterpiece that oddly fails to stir the soul.

In much larger part, however, what the critics were objecting to was that *Princess Mononoke* is not a *Disney* animated feature. It has become the subconscious habit of critics in the West to judge all feature-length animations by this yardstick. It is therefore very difficult for independent voices to make themselves heard, and Miyazaki's is above all an independent voice: he has sculpted his own aesthetic form which, while it has absorbed many influences (even including Disney), is nevertheless uniquely his. And *Princess Mononoke*, while not necessarily the most straightforwardly enjoyable of his movies – that title probably goes to *My Neighbor Totoro* or the Kondo-directed *Whisper of the Heart* – can be seen as the ultimate statement, the ultimate summation, made in *his* voice.

To date.

NICK PARK (1958–)

Born in Preston, England, on December 6, 1958, Nicholas Wulstan Park is a stop-motion animator who, in his comparatively short career, has made a habit of picking up Oscars. He dates his interest in animation to his childhood, when he found that his parents' 8mm home-movie camera had a stop-motion button; by the age of 13 he was making animated movies in the family attic. He was still a teenager when, in 1975, one of his amateur 8mm efforts, *Archie's Concrete Nightmare*, was screened by BBC Television. At school one of the subjects he was good at was art, and for some time before discovering animation he had dreams of becoming a comic-strip artist. In 1980 he graduated from Sheffield Art School with a B.A. in communication arts and went to the National Film & Television School in Beaconsfield, Buckinghamshire. It was while there that he started his graduation film, *A Grand Day Out* (1989), starring the characters Wallace and Gromit, whom he based on earlier notebook ideas and sketches. The movie was still unfinished when, in February 1985, he joined the company Aardman Animations.

Aardman Animations had been founded in 1972 by David Sproxton and Peter Lord. Like Park, these two had both begun animating while still at school, making movies on the kitchen table using a 16mm camera that belonged to Sproxton's father. Among their first inspirations as animators they list Ray Harryhausen and Terry Gilliam. Their first (apparently untitled) animated movie, done with cut-outs and chalk drawing, was completed in 1970, and they optimistically sent it to the BBC. A children's producer there liked it enough to commission the two teenagers to produce short pieces of animation for *Vision On*, a series in which popular television presenter and artist Tony Hart encouraged children to develop their creativity and showed them drawing and painting

tricks and techniques. The first piece of Lord's and Sproxton's that appeared on *Vision On* (it was, atypically, a piece of cel animation) featured a clumsy superhero called Aardman, and it was in acknowledgment of this breakthrough that they so named the company they later founded. In 1976 they moved to Bristol, where *Vision On* was made at the BBC's Bristol studios. In that same year they created a character called Morph (originally for *Vision On* but appearing in the successor progam, *Take Hart)*, a simply stylized clay man with a cheery grin who could alter his shape at will into a bowl of fruit or a dinosaur or anything else, and who interacted with tv artist and presenter Tony Hart. Largely but not entirely because of Morph – Hart's presentation also appealed across a wide spectrum of ages – *Take Hart* began to pick up a significant adult audience. The BBC accordingly commissioned from Aardman a series of 26 five-minute shorts, *The Amazing Adventures of Morph* (1981), which was shown in the for-children-but-much-watched-by-adults early-evening slot made famous by such programs as *The Magic Roundabout*. Morph remains a popular character, and his adventures are widely available on video, though he has tended to be eclipsed by Aardman's later triumphs.

Although obviously delighted with the success of Morph, Lord and Sproxton were impatient with being categorized as animators solely for children, and as early as 1978 offered the BBC a couple of clay-animated shorts directed at an adult audience. Rather than being formally scripted or storied, these two shorts, *Down and Out* and *Confessions of a Foyer Girl*, seem to be voice-track recordings

•

made of people talking about their lives and thoughts; complete with false starts and hesitations, these have the semblance of *vox pop* collages. The BBC broadcast the two shorts as late-night curios but wasn't interested in taking the idea further. However, a couple of years later Jeremy Isaacs, the first controller of the newly launched Channel Four, saw the shorts and liked them. He commissioned from Aardman five further pieces done in the same style and broadcast them as the series *Conversation Pieces* (1982–83). This was followed some years later by the roughly similar series *Lip Synch* (1989–90). The fifth short in this latter series, *Creature Comforts* (1989), was directed by Nick Park (who had by now completed *A Grand Day Out*); and it brought Aardman Animations its first Oscar. In that year there were just three animated movies on the Oscar shortlist, and two of them were *Creature Comforts* and *A Grand Day Out* – an astonishing achievement for a young director at the start of his career. (The third was Bruno Bozzetto's excellent *Grasshoppers* [*Cavallette*; 1990], so it's not as if Park were up against weak opposition.)

Although it missed out on the Oscar, it was *A Grand Day Out* that radically altered the fortunes of both Park and Aardman. It might seem strange that a tale, however lunatic, featuring a man and his dog in a dour northern-English town might sufficiently appeal to U.S. audiences to be an Oscar contender, but the attractions of Wallace and Gromit go far beyond any considerations of geography or culture. The great strength of this movie and its successors is the strong characterization: Wallace, the outwardly normal-seeming, middle-aged, terrace-living North of England perpetual bachelor, with his obsessive love of cheese and cream crackers, is in fact, behind the mundane facade, an inventor of not inconsiderable genius who has packed his cramped terrace house with elaborate "labor-saving" gadgetry; while the never-speaking Gromit, his dog (in Park's original plans a cat) and the sole being with whom he has managed to establish any emotional relationship, is the sensible one of the duo, although he generally has no way of communicating his advice to Wallace save through usually ignored facial expressions.

In any story involving a duo of protagonists, whether for the movies or otherwise, it is the strength and profundity of the relationship between the two characters that carry much of the audience's interest – more, really, than the characters themselves – so that the story can be almost tertiary (although it is not in the case of these three featurettes, which are almost too strongly plotted). The relationship between Wallace and Gromit is stamped with masterful firmness very early on in *A Grand Day Out*. The two are a family as much as if they were a married couple.

It is this that gives the dynamic to the second of their movies, *The Wrong Trousers* (1993), rather than the plot, which centers on the titular roboticized garments (devised by Wallace to take Gromit for walks). For much of the movie it seems as if an incursive criminal penguin is dislodging Gromit from his natural place in Wallace's heart, a shocking disruption of the duo. More profoundly, this is a duo that cannot even be added to, as we realize in *A Close Shave* (1995), when Wallace and Wendolene, owner of the local wool-

The Wrong Trousers (1993) tvm

color / stop-motion animated ⊙ 28³/₄ minutes

An Oscar-winning short. For Gromit's birthday, Wallace has made a pair of "technotrousers," robotic legs programmable to take Gromit for walks. Gromit loathes the device. Broke, Wallace rents out Gromit's room to a mysterious penguin with a penchant for playing Mighty Wurlitzer music late at night. When the penguin seems to be taking over Gromit's place in Wallace's heart, Gromit packs up his bag and runs away from home. Wallace wakes the next morning to find the penguin has adapted the technotrousers. Trapped in them, he is sent by the penguin on a nightmarish trip through town. Meanwhile, Gromit has discovered that the penguin is a wanted criminal. Donning the mantle of a P.I., he exposes the penguin's evil plot to rob the local museum of diamonds, using the technotrousers and the sleeping Wallace to evade the laser security. The theft is accomplished, but after one of the most thrilling toy train chases in cinematic history Wallace and Gromit serve up the penguin to the police. And the reward money pays all those bills.

shop, seem set on forming an amorous partnership, despite all the vicissitudes created by her enforced life of crime. But there is no room within the relationship between Wallace and Gromit for the intrusion of a third party – no way for the duo to be extended to become a trio without the destruction of the original duo. This is wryly recognized by Park when, at the movie's end, he invokes an outrageous, deliberately self-conscious *deus ex machina* to ensure that Wallace and Wendolene pursue their relationship no further: she is allergic to cheese, a great obsession of Wallace's life, and so cannot be a fit mate for him. The cheese allergy, in other words, symbolizes all the myriad other reasons why she cannot be his partner, as well as the core, unspoken one: that, for the rules of Story to be obeyed, the duo of Wallace and Gromit must remain intact.

Another highly important characteristic of the three movies is Park's evident love of bizarre, over-complex gadgetry: aside from the sequence of machines that rouse Wallace daily and painfully dump him fully clothed at the breakfast table, where further machines prepare (or disastrously misprepare) his breakfast, there are the cockamamy spaceship of the first movie and the roboticized trousers of the second, and in the third the elaborate device used by the villainous Preston in his attempts to turn sheep into dog food in a single pass, the Mutton-o-Matic. All three gadgets are effective devices of the plot. The over-reliance on gadgetry as a plot underpinning is a dangerous business in animation, and it has been suggested that this is the reason why Park did not immediately create more Wallace and Gromit movies after the success of the first three. It must have been a difficult temptation to resist, however: not only did both the second and third movies carry off Oscars, but the two characters has sparked a vast and presumably extremely profitable merchandising exercise in the U.K. and, to a lesser extent, in the U.S.

A Grand Day Out (1989) tvm

color / stop-motion animated ⏱ 22¾ minutes
Nominated for an Oscar, which *Creature Comforts* won. While Wallace and Gromit are trying to decide where to go on vacation, Wallace discovers that they have run out of cheese. They decide to go on a trip to the Moon — after all, "Everybody knows the Moon's made of cheese." So Wallace and Gromit build a spaceship in their cellar and off they go for a picnic to the Moon, which indeed proves to be made of cheese. But on the Moon they encounter a coin-operated lunar being in the shape of an old cooker (stove). The cooker reads one of Wallace's holiday brochures and conceives the idea of taking a ski trip on Earth. Despite its attempts to break into their spaceship, Wallace and Gromit manage to escape and head back home with a basket full of cheese.

Creature Comforts (1989) tvm

color / stop-motion animated ⏱ 5¼ minutes
An Oscar-winning short. In parody of a television *vox pop* documentary, a series of animals speak into a microphone about the advantages and disadvantages of living in the zoo, grumbling about the food and the confinement, or even favorably comparing the situation to working in the circus.

A Close Shave (1995) tvm

color / stop-motion animated ⏱ 30 minutes
An Oscar-winning short. An escaped sheep invades the home of Wallace and Gromit, who are now operating a window-cleaning service, and causes havoc. While Gromit is busy cleaning windows at Wendolene's Wool Shop Wallace falls in love with Wendolene. Upon returning home, they discover the sheep and decide to adopt him. After being washed and accidentally shorn by a device called the Knit-o-Matic, the sheep is named Shaun by Wallace. But Preston, Wendolene's evil cyberdog, is a ruthless sheep rustler and, in these times of wool shortage, is also murdering stolen sheep to manufacture dog food. Gromit manages to free the stolen flock but is set up by Preston. He is jailed for sheep rustling. Wallace and Shaun spring Gromit from jail, and they later catch Preston and the enforced Wendolene in the act of re-stealing the original flock of sheep. Preston turns against Wendolene, and after a thrilling chase both she and Wallace are loaded into Preston's own machine based on the Knit-o-Matic, the Mutton-o-Matic. But Shaun and Gromit save the day and it is Preston who ends up being crushed in his own sheep-mincing machine.

But soon, anyway, there were bigger things on the horizon. Ever since the company's founding in 1972, it had been the idea that one day Aardman would move into the business of feature animation – feature stop-motion animation, at that. The history of animation is not marked by many successful stop-motion features

– Tim Burton's *The Nightmare Before Christmas* (1993) is a glaring exception to the general rule – but this did not deter the Aardman crew's ambitions. It was just a matter of waiting for the right time and, importantly, the right movie. It has been suggested that the idea of a Wallace and Gromit feature was briefly considered, but wisely discarded: a small cast of characters wouldn't carry a feature movie while a large cast would dilute the power of the duo. Park, however, had made notes of ideas for an escape movie with chickens as stars. Although chickens have thin legs, heavy bodies, and feathers, so presenting great difficulties for animators working in plasticine, gradually, he, Lord, and Sproxton came to believe this might be the germ of the feature movie they craved to make. The Oscar wins and nominations (Aardman had by now chalked up more than just those by Park) meant that the big Hollywood studios were interested in whatever Aardman might come up with. To assist them, Aardman was partnered with Canadian producer Jake Eberts, best known as a founder of the movie company Goldcrest. Through his new company, Allied Films (backed by Pathé), he agreed to fund the development of an Aardman idea, with everyone committed to bringing in a Hollywood studio as co-financier and distribution partner later in the process. With independent backing, Aardman could now achieve far better terms with a studio than had previously been possible. Throughout 1995, Aardman looked at well over a hundred outside ideas, many of them direct pitches from the studios, in a series of meetings set up by Eberts. But it soon became apparent that Aardman would be happiest working on an idea of its own.

Among the studios actively interested was the newly formed DreamWorks, founded by Steven Spielberg, David Geffen and Jeffrey Katzenberg. Thanks to the good offices of Eberts, Lord, Park and Michael Rose (who, along with Eberts, would be the new movie's executive producer) Aardman found itself pitching to Spielberg and Katzenberg what was at the time little more than the notion of making an escape movie about chickens.

Spielberg and Katzenberg were immediately enthusiastic and offered to commit there and then. As third-party funding was not immediately required, it was agreed that everyone would continue informal discussions while the project developed. This would allow Aardman and Dreamworks (primarily Katzenberg) to see how they got along before tying a knot. The relationship did prosper, and by 1997 DreamWorks was fully involved financially in the movie. (That the relationship was indeed happy was further emphasised with the announcement in October 1999, almost a year before the release of *Chicken Run*, that Aardman and DreamWorks had agreed to a further four feature movies.)

Of course, everyone's faith in the movie was fully justified. Released in the U.S. in June 2000, *Chicken Run* was an immediate sensation, being not just a box-office but a thunderous critical success. Here, it was felt, was the breath of fresh air that feature animation so desperately needed: a strong story with strong characterization and a greater emotional depth than had

traditionally been associated with the medium. Consider the situation at about this time. Disney was seeking to amaze audiences with its technological achievements in *Dinosaur* (2000), which was paradoxically a retrogressive movie, despite the high-tech wonders, being in effect a return to territory which Don Bluth had explored years earlier in *The Land Before Time* (1988); the studio had recently released another backward-looking movie, *Fantasia 2000* (1999), while through its Pixar affiliate it was offering *Toy Story 2* (2000) – an excellent sequel, but a sequel nevertheless. Late in the previous year the two major animated features had both been modern classics that had made only minimal impact through over-tentativeness on the part of the distributors: Bard Bird's *The Iron Giant* (1999) and Hayao Miyazaki's *Princess Mononoke* (US release 1999); more to the point, they were both triumphs of traditional cel animation, their actual innovativeness being well hidden. Only Don Bluth seemed to be trying anything new in the field, with his *Titan A.E.* (2000), but that fine movie, too, was being stabbed in the back by half-heartedness on the part of its distributor (and, indeed, Fox closed down Bluth's studio there almost the instant the movie was released).

This was a mistake DreamWorks had no intention of making: *Chicken Run*, directed by Park and Lord, was launched with the kind of fanfare Hollywood reserves for only its predicted blockbusters. The technique of stop-motion clay animation was novel for a commercial animated feature, and this was what the movie critics first saw when they commented on *Chicken Run*'s originality. But what they soon began to realize was that, beyond the medium, beyond even the story, the movie was truly original because its characters were *grown-ups*. Buzz Lightyear and Woody – to choose from *Toy Story 2* by way of example – may *look* as if they are adults, but in fact they are children in every respect except appearance. *Chicken Run*'s Ginger, Mac Fowler, and the others might *just* be chickens – talking animals – but they have the mature emotions and reactions of *adults*. Not only did this make the movie infinitely more satisfying for a grown-up audience, it actually did the same for the children whom the cinemas assumed would be their core market. Decades earlier, Aardman had learned that character transcended external form in its creation of Morph, who was, visually, the simplest of clay figures: he had such a strong personality that in the end he dominated Tony Hart's show and had to be given a series of his own. Park had brought to the studio his instinctive understanding of the importance not just of characters but of the relationships between them. All of these lessons were brought to bear on *Chicken Run*.

Even as this inaugural smash-hit feature was being released, Aardman was not being idle. The studio has produced a second tv series of Rex the Runt, and also one for the Internet, Angry Kid. Nothing can be predicted with certainty, of course, but it looks as if commercial feature animation will, for perhaps the next decade or so, be dominated by two studios, Disney and the currently relatively tiny, Bristol-based Aardman, and it would be a fool who bet too much money on which of them, if either, may prevail over the other.

Still from *Chicken Run* (2000), showing Rocky (left) and Ginger having a romantic moonlit tryst.
© DreamWorks/Pathe and Aardman.

Chicken Run (2000)

color / animated 🕐 84 minutes
Co-directed with Peter Lord. Every P.O.W. movie you've ever seen rolled into one and relocated to a chicken run, where the hens, headed by the enterprising Ginger, are trying to escape — not just the run, but entirely from Tweedy's Farm to find freedom. Into the enclosed world of the run crashlands Rocky the Flying Rooster, escaped from the circus. Blackmailed by Ginger, he promises to teach the hens to fly — with spectacularly unsuccessful results. All becomes more urgent as the Tweedies receive delivery of a monstrous chicken-pie-making machine. Ginger is chosen as test chicken, and Rocky — now half in love with her — must rescue her. After a rapidly paced Indiana Jones-style stampede through the heart of the device, narrowly escaping death myriad times, the two are spat out unscathed, having also by happenstance disabled the machine. The hens' hopes are dashed, though, when it emerges that Rocky cannot fly, except in the sense of being a "human" cannonball; he deserts them. Ginger realizes the sole answer must be to build an airplane, and there is a race as the hens construct it while Tweedy repairs the pie machine. The plane somehow works and, with the aid of a returned Rocky, the entire populace flies off to an island that becomes their sanctuary.

It is a very long time indeed since Disney has faced a serious challenge, and this one has come from an unexpected quarter. While Aardman is a team enterprise and it would be stupid to undervalue the contributions of any of its members — for Lord, Sproxton, and others at the studio are themselves set to become major figures in animation's history — much of that situation can be ascribed to the character-creating genius of Nick Park.

BILL PLYMPTON (1946–)

Born on April 30, 1946, in Portland, Oregon, as one of six children, Bill Plympton drew throughout his childhood; he blames Oregon's rainy climate for keeping him and his siblings indoors much of the time. At the age of 12 he sent some of his drawings to Disney, offering himself as an animator on their forthcoming feature *Sleeping Beauty* (1959); their response was politely encouraging.

After graduating in 1964 from Oregon City High School, he attended Portland State University, where he earned a B.A. in graphic design. He was also a member of the film society at college, for whom the making of a promo movie represented his first attempt at animation; this was *The Great Turn On* (1968), a silent movie done as a joint venture with B. Summers, another student animator, in simple line. In 1968, he moved to New York, attending the School of Visual Arts for a year and thereafter trying to make a career for himself as an illustrator, cartoonist, and designer; his work appeared in newspapers and magazines such as the *Village Voice*, *Rolling Stone*, *Screw*, *Vanity Fair*, *National Lampoon*, *Penthouse*, *Playboy*, *Viva*, and the *New York Times*, and he designed the magazine *Cinéaste*, among others. In 1975 the *Soho Weekly News* began to run his political strip *Plympton*, later syndicated by Universal Press.

In 1977, he made his second foray into animation, the uncompleted *Lucas, the Ear of Corn*. For children, this darkly comic "coming-of-age story" (by Gene Gorelik), done in cut-out animation, shows the young corncob Lucas making the transition from life in the field to being eaten by a boy. Jerky and poorly lip-synched, it nevertheless has charm.

In 1983, Valeria Vasilevski, one half of the singing duo The Android Sisters, asked him to make an animated short. Jules Feiffer had written a song for National Public Radio called "Boomtown," satirizing military spending, and the scheme was to turn this into a short, with the song sung by the Android Sisters, as the soundtrack. The result, *Boomtown* (1985), won a Director's Award at the London Film Festival, and has been widely shown ever since.

Plympton then began work on a live-action/animated/stop-motion short, *Drawing Lesson #2* (1987). At the same time, since shooting of the exteriors was being held up by the weather, he began work on the all-animated *Your Face* (1987). In the former, the protagonist is a "magic line" who starts by giving and simultaneously drawing an art lesson and then falls into an account of his unhappy love affair and marriage to ex-model Vera, who finally abandoned him for vile patron Bruno. Plympton drew the animation under the camera, rather than use traditional one-sheet-per-frame animation, so that the drawing grows from left to right with a sort of frenetic flow that irresistibly drives the cartoon forward; the result is that a fairly simple comedy actually becomes quite exciting, almost as if it were a thriller. In the closing credits there is a wry line: "Funded by a grant from the pocket of Bill Plympton." The latter short, *Your Face*, was scored and sung (with the voice distorted so that it sounds male) by Maureen McElheron, leader of a country & western band in which Plympton once played pedal steel guitar; Plympton has frequently worked with her since. Nominated for an Oscar, *Your Face* shows a crooner: as he sings the eponymous song, his own face goes through bizarre and surreal distortions until in the end the grassy slope on which he has been sitting becomes a face that swallows him.

Further shorts came fast and furiously, especially since Plympton was by now planning his first feature movie and, in order to fund it, released sections from it as shorts as and when they were complete – *Your Face* is one, as are *The Wiseman* (1992) and *Push Comes to Shove* (1992). This accounts for the very episodic structure of that feature, *The Tune* (1992), which he financed entirely himself – and indeed animated entirely himself, all 30,000 drawings or so, an astonishing rarity in an era when the credits at the end of an animated feature generally seem to run longer than the movie itself. Keeping everything under his own control in this way is important to Plympton, in that it gives him total artistic freedom; more recently, he has also taken charge of the promotion and distribution of his own movies. His short movies are not only self-financing but also sufficiently profitable to contribute to the costs of producing his features, which are themselves of course profitable and help finance further shorts and features. In addition, like most animators, he has taken on commercial work to fund his own ventures – such as the animation for the excellent music video *245 Days* (1989), done for a Peter Himmelman song.

Aside from *245 Days*, 1989 saw the release of a number of Plympton station IDs for MTV and a couple of his best-known shorts: *25 Ways to Quit Smoking* and *How to Kiss*. The former is more like a series of moving comic-strip gags than an animation, with the methods recommended varying from tying a knot in your neck to mounting heat-seeking missiles on top of your head. *How to Kiss* is a hilarious parody of a popular-information short whose various segments – such as a demonstration of the French kiss in which the lovers' tongues appear to explore every corner of each others' skulls – combine in an attempt to put one off kissing for life. Also of note from this era is *Plymptoons* (1990), in which Plympton animates a longish series of the gag cartoons he did in his earlier career as mini-shorts of no more than about 10 to 15 seconds each. The result is rather like seeing examples of some of Gahan Wilson's more surrealistic artwork come to life.

Boomtown (1985)

♪color / animated ⏱ 6 minutes

The Android Sisters introduce themselves, then present in semi-song (lyrics by Jules Feiffer) the arguments in favor of overspending on defense. A hugely muscular American Eagle sees off marching Russian Hammer & Sickles by waving a bomb at them. As for the economic benefits, coins rain from the skies and, planted like seeds, give rise to factories, schools, houses, and happy smiling faces. But that industrial economic boom fails to happen because of high technology, which brings a further rain of coins from the sky, the "crop" this time benefiting only the few. But without an economic boom, why should the Russians come? The over-muscled American Eagle is left holding a useless bomb.

In that same year, 1990, Plympton had the satisfaction of turning down Disney, who had failed to give him his big break when he was a tender 12-year-old. This time Disney offered him a great deal of money to work on the character of the Genie in *Aladdin* (1992), a character whose screen presence is a matter of frequent surreal transmutations. Plympton could well have been ideal for the animation, as Disney clearly realized, but, having carved out his own path as an independent animator, there was no way he was going to devote two or three years to bringing other people's ideas to the screen, with his efforts judged by a committee. Furthermore, like so many others, he was not going to sign the standard Disney contract whereby, during his time of employment by the company, every creative effort he might make would be deemed to be the property of Disney.

While Plympton had shown his mastery of the short form, it might have been anticipated that *The Tune*, being episodic in nature, would prove to be little more than a strung-together series of shorts. It does have something of that feel, inevitably, but at the same time it all adds up to very much more: as protagonist Del wanders through Flooby Nooby in search of enlightenment, there is a sense of this being a quest parallel to that of Alice through the Looking-Glass World, with the entirety building toward a finale that seems at one and the same time contrived and satisfyingly inevitable. The animation was done using a three-stage process – Plympton worked on paper, assistants cut out the relevant images and pasted them on cels, and then, finally, Plympton repenciled these elements and added shading, color and detail. The end-product betrays nothing of these travails, however, instead having the freshness of loose pencil work. Not all of the sections are as successful as others – the segment in which Del consults a nonsensically enigmatic guru seems labored and spun out, whereas that concerning the mating habits of fast foods is hilarious and of perfect length. Overall, the movie might be judged as a series of experiments toward a feature movie, the experiments being successfully bound together to form a feature movie themselves.

The Tune (1992)

♭color / animated ⏲ 69 minutes

Abrasive music boss Mr. Mega tells fledgling songwriter Del he has 47 minutes to come to Mr. Mega's office with a new song or he will lose his job — and the love of Didi, Mr. Mega's secretary. Driving to the meeting, a panicking Del takes a wrong turn and finds himself in Flooby Nooby, whose kindly mayor explains that "In Flooby Nooby, songs like that, they write *themselves*"; what Del must do is not so much write songs as *find* them — learn the music of the heart. Bemusedly, he tries to understand the advice of incomprehensible guru The Wiseone, observes the amatory practices of diner foodstuffs, is sung the blues by a noseless taxi driver ("You got more beaux than Little Bo Peep"), and so forth; even once he reaches the headquarters of Mega Music his troubles are not over, for he and Didi lose their way en route to Mr. Mega's office. Mr. Mega rejects all Del's songs . . . except the one he and Didi sing when they assume all is lost.

I Married a Strange Person! (1997)

♭color / animated ⏲ 76 minutes

Two mating birds collide with Grant Boyer's satellite dish, and a high-energy beam shoots through him. Hereafter he is a changed man, as his new bride, Keri (sometimes written as Kerry), discovers: thanks to a sentient boil on the back of his neck vastly enlarging the Imagination sector of his brain, there occur all around him, wherever he goes, gross and surrealist alterations of reality. This premise permits Plympton to produce a series of often scatological and violent sketches, including: the trailer for a tv show called *Belch Opera*; a giantized blade of grass seeking homicidal vengeance on a gardener using his own lawn mower; Keri herself being invaded by the legendary 40 pounds of unsightly fat; and one of cinema's more bizarre sex scenes, during which Grant molds Keri's breasts as if they were modeling balloons. Grant's appearance on a tv chat show inspires the boss of the Orwellesquely named Smile Corp tv company to send a military force to seize Grant and steal the Imagination lobe. Keri rescues him from the Smile Corp clutches and, after much chasing, the two resume marital bliss.

Before embarking on his next animated feature, Plympton made two live-action features: *J. Lyle* (1994), which has some animation, is a cheery little comedy in which a New York lawyer learns about life from such characters as a magic dog with animated eyes, while in one scene his innards emerge from his body and communicate with him; and in *Guns on the Clackamas: A Documentary* (1995), another comedy, this time in mockumentary form, the financiers pull out midway through the shooting of a new Western movie and the producers have to forge on as best they can, resorting to such stratagems as marketing the stars' dirty underwear and filming scenes using the corpses of actors. Both have great moments; neither can be regarded as a complete success.

By contrast with *The Tune*, only one section of Plympton's second animated feature, *I Married a Strange Person!* (1997), had been previously released as a short; that section was *How to Make Love to a Woman* (1995), a sort of R-rated version of *How to Kiss*. Animated much more orthodoxly than *The Tune* — Plympton's animations, done in pencils, were xeroxed onto cels and then painted by his assistants — *I Married a Strange Person!* has a similar episodic structure, although now the binding of the overall plot is somewhat tighter. What is particularly interesting about the movie is protagonist Grant Boyer's unwitting ability to mold reality, usually with disastrous results because of his lack of control over the power. The realities that Grant calls into existence are reifications of the subjective realities our imaginations conjure during our everyday lives; for example, as we watch an obnoxious neighbor on his power lawn mower we do not *expect* that the grass will rise up in revolt against him, but our fantasies may call that image up; in *I Married a Strange Person!* Grant's imaginative gizmo reifies that alternative.

Since completing *I Married a Strange Person!* Plympton has been less productive, although shorts have continued to appear. *Sex and Violence* (1997), a collection of animated gags in the same vein as *Plymptoons* but in general (though not exclusively) raunchier, has been followed by *More Sex and Violence* (1998); others have included *Surprise Cinema* (1999) and *The Exciting Life of a Tree* (1999). Generally, Plympton's later work has resorted more to sex humor — always part of his repertoire — than before, a trend that is not necessarily for the best: the self-appointed wag of the school playground tends to resort to sexual obscenity in a desperate attempt to wring laughs when he has run out of wit. It is to be hoped that this is a temporary phase in Plympton's case, because the sharpness of his humor and satire and the almost unspeakable charm of his drawing have given much to animation as it has moved into the 21st century. Unfortunately, too many of his would-be imitators have seen only the taboo-flouting elements of Plympton's work and not the intelligent sardonic wit that lies behind it.

LOTTE REINIGER (1899–1981)

Frame from *Die Abenteuer des Prinzen Achmed* (*The Adventures of Prince Achmed*; 1926).

Lotte Reiniger pioneered the art of silhouette animation; this art might not seem very important to the history of animation, but even today the earliest of Reiniger's animations possesses a beauty and fascination that far transcends anything on offer from most animators of that era, who were largely concerned with churning out productions of mind-numbing mediocrity that were just good enough to stop the audience from walking out. Reiniger's animations, by contrast, are touched by a love for the form and by a joy in the very act of creation, ensuring they are today as magical as they ever were.

Born Charlotte Reiniger in Berlin on June 2, 1899, she became involved in the movies after seeing a lecture on trick photography and special effects given by Paul Wegener, the actor and director probably best known today for *Der Golem* (1915). Her imagination fired, she was determined to become a part of Wegener's team. Since he was a member of Max Reinhardt's theater, she persuaded her parents to let her go to the acting school attached to that theater. The actors and students did not, in general, mix, so as a way of attracting the attention of the stars

she began to cut silhouette figures of them in their starring poses; these were good enough to be published in a 1917 book. Wegener himself was impressed enough that he commissioned from her the captions for *Der Rottenfänger von Hameln* (*The Pied Piper of Hameln*; 1918); he also let her be an extra in various of his movies. In 1919 Wegener introduced her to a group that was in the process of setting up an experimental animation studio – Hans Cürlis, Berthold Bartosch, and Carl Koch – with the suggestion that they should animate her silhouettes. She made her first silhouette movie with them, a short called *Das Ornament des verliebten Herzens* ("The Ornament of the Lovestruck Heart") in late 1919. Audience reaction was good, and Reiniger never looked back: all told she made over 50 shorts.

In 1923 she was approached by a banker, Louis Hagen, who offered to finance a feature-length movie of her silhouette

animation; he also offered her a studio, specially built above his garage. Thus began the production of the world's first animated feature – an accolade usually, but erroneously, given to Walt Disney's *Snow White and the Seven Dwarfs* (1937). With Bartosch, Koch (whom she had married in 1921), and Walther Ruttmann she started work on *Die Abenteuer des Prinzen Achmed* (*The Adventures of Prince Achmed*; 1926), she animating the action with silhouettes and Ruttmann doing the backgrounds. The plot of the 90-minute movie is derived from several of the tales of *The 1001 Nights* and involves magic, romance, and adventure, as one might expect. It was filmed in black-and-white and then hand-tinted; in addition to the silhouettes there was animation using wax and sand, and there was some use of multiplane camera.

Unfortunately, during the Allied bombing of Berlin in 1945, the negative and all the known prints of *Prinzen Achmed* were destroyed. However, in 1954 a surviving black-and-white print was discovered in the archives of the British Film Institute. Later, the coloring instructions that Reiniger had written back in 1925 were discovered, so the process of restoration could begin, being completed by 1970. However, because at the time the movie was made projectors ran at 18 frames a minute rather than the modern 24 frames a minute, the restoration runs faster than the original (90 minutes reduced to about 65). A new score by Freddie Phillips was added to replace the original by Wolfgang Zeller; this, apparently, is not a change for the better. Moreover, much of the fine detail of the backgrounds has been lost.

The movie was rapturously received in 1926 and earned the admiration of other significant moviemakers including Jean Renoir and René Clair; Renoir, in particular, became a close friend and colleague.

A second animated feature followed, in 1928: *Doktor Dolittle und seine Tiere* (*Dr. Dolittle and His Animals*), based on Hugh Lofting's novel *The Story of Dr. Dolittle* (1920), with a score by Paul Dessau, Paul Hindemith, and Kurt Weill. Unfortunately, the only version available today has a new score and a new voice-over, and again the movie is shown at an artificially accelerated speed. At the time of its release, of course, the movie suffered the very considerable disadvantage that it wasn't a talkie – between the time Reiniger started work on it and its completion, sound movies had largely taken over from the silents. A third animated feature would have followed, based on Ravel's opera-ballet *L'Enfant et les sortilèges* (*The Child and the Witcheries*; 1925), with libretto by Colette, but in the end – after some scenes had been animated and some sequences designed – getting the necessary copyright clearances from all concerned proved impossible. A live-action movie she codirected with Rochus Gliese, *Die Jagd nach dem Glück* ("The Pursuit of Happiness"; 1929), starring Renoir and Bartosch, suffered the same problem as *Dr. Dolittle* – being made as a silent when everyone wanted sound – and an attempted dubbing of the dialogue was apparently a disaster.

Reiniger and Koch were politically left-leaning, and with the ascendancy of the Nazis to power in 1933 they realized they should get out of Germany. This was more difficult than it might seem, because Britain, France, and other countries refused them emigration visas. Reiniger continued to make animated shorts much as before, but with subliminal anti-Nazi messages. In 1936 she and Koch did in fact leave Germany, but were able to do so only using a succession of temporary visas for countries determined by where they could get work, and they were often apart. Renoir was helpful to them here, employing them on his own movies when he could; and on the outbreak of war he took them with him to Italy, where he was directing *Tosca* (*The Story of Tosca*; 1941), a task he in due course turned over to Koch. The couple remained in Italy until 1944, when the Allied advance compelled them to return to Germany. In Germany, Reiniger was forced to work on a new animated movie, *Die goldene Gans* ("The Goose that Laid the Golden Eggs"), but she never finished it.

Finally, in 1948, the couple was permitted to leave Germany for Britain, which is where Reiniger pursued the rest of her career. The two founded the company Primrose Productions, and she did silhouette animation for advertising as well as for BBC Children's Television. Koch, who had never fully recovered from the psychological traumas of the blitz in Berlin, died young, but Reiniger continued to work until very late in life. Her last film, *The Rose and the Ring* (1979), based on the William Makepeace Thackeray story, was released when she was 80. Her most significant movie in later years was *Aucassin and Nicolette* (1975), done in conjunction with the National Film Board of Canada and based on a medieval fable. She died on June 19, 1981, in Dettenhausen, Germany.

It is criminally hard to see any of Reiniger's work today aside from the contents of a compilation video that is itself extremely difficult to obtain. However, the restored version of *Die Abenteuer des Prinzen Achmed* pops up not infrequently at animation festivals and the like (and was released on video in 1999), and sometimes one can be lucky enough to catch one of her later shorts on British television. It is worth all efforts, as her work exerts a strange, compelling fascination that is utterly unique in animation. And, to recall, it was she who made the world's first animated feature.

Jan ŠVANKMAJER (1934–)

Still from *Něco z Alenky* (*Alice*; 1988).
© Jan Švankmajer/ICA.

The *New Yorker* once remarked of the work of the Czech moviemaker Jan Švankmajer: "The movie-going world is split into two camps: those who have never heard of Jan Švankmajer; and those who happen upon his work and know that they have come face to face with genius." One might go further: many of those familiar with his work regard him as either the most significant moviemaker active today or a purveyor of nonsense – an attitudinal dichotomy that has greeted, and continues to be associated with, all the great artists of Surrealism.

Švankmajer's works typically mix clay and other stop-motion animation, puppetry, and live action into a surrealistic mix that is simultaneously bewildering and extremely entertaining. They strain the unwritten rules of moviemaking nearly to the breaking point – the rules as to what you can and cannot do on a cinema screen and still expect people to watch – and consequently go almost entirely ignored by the major movie distributors in the English-speaking world. Yet whenever they are shown they tend to draw dedicated and large audiences. Their video sales are healthy, even though the videos

are released largely through specialized companies. He is a cult moviemaker whose worldwide "cult" is larger than the following of many mainstream directors. The release of a new Švankmajer movie is a cause for excitement in many quarters and many countries. He has won scores of awards. Yet there could be no movie director who accords less with the commercial "Hollywood" ideal.

Švankmajer was born in Prague on September 4, 1934, the son of a window-dresser and a dressmaker. He enrolled in 1950 at the College of Applied Arts in Prague, where he worked in sculpture, painting, and engraving, and where he first became interested in the art and writings of the Surrealists. In 1954, he continued his studies at the department of puppetry, Prague Academy of Performing Arts (DAMU), becoming increasingly interested in moviemaking. The Soviet cultural thaw in 1956 allowed him to also pursue his

Jan Švankmajer

Alice (1988)

(vt Neco z alenky)

🎨 color / stop-motion animated/live-action/puppetry

⏱ 85 minutes

Alice, bored, sits alongside her elder sister by a stream and lets her mind wander. She is in her bedroom, and her eyes roam around the accumulated stuff there: toys, sewing equipment, dolls, cup of tea, partially-eaten food, a stuffed rabbit, etc. Suddenly, the stuffed rabbit (*Lepus cuniculus*, according to the label) begins to move creakily in its case, and the tale is begun. The White Rabbit flees across a wind-blasted wasteland to vanish into the drawer of a desk, and Alice follows; the drawer's knob comes loose in her grip, but she pries the drawer open and is swallowed by the desk, thereby entering a bizarre Wonderland that contains elements of, but is radically different from, Lewis Carroll's original vision. (Based on the book *Alice's Adventures in Wonderland* (1865) by Lewis Carroll.)

Tma, Svetlo, Tma (1989)

(vt *Darkness, Light, Darkness*)

🎨 color / stop-motion animated ⏱ 7½ minutes

Beginning with a pair of forearms, the parts of a human body, acting almost like conspirators, accumulate themselves in a tiny room, the form going through grotesque metamorphoses as they add themselves to the assembly. When the man is complete, he is left jammed like a fetus in the cramped room.

studies of the Surrealists, including Luis Buñuel. His final production at DAMU combined puppetry with live actors, some of whom were dressed as puppets; it was a combination – presenting as it does a confusion of realities and perceptions – that he would return to often in his later work.

After graduating from DAMU in 1958, he worked as a director and designer in Liberec with the Czech State Puppet Theater. His first professional movie experience came when he was employed as a puppeteer by Emil Radok on *Johannes doktor Faust* ("Johannes, Doctor Faust"; 1958), doing conceptuals and sculpture as well. The movie was inspired by folk puppetry, which was also a major inspiration for Švankmajer's own movie version of the Faust legend, decades later. In an interview with Peter Hames done in 1992–93, Švankmajer remarked:

> I must say that nothing I have seen from modern puppet theater compares with the old folk puppet art. Perhaps for the reason that they tried so stubbornly to meet the standards of great theater while the technical means at their disposal hampered their attempts, something authentically stylized emerged which could be compared only to traditional oriental theater: Japanese kabuki or Chinese opera.

Švankmajer's career was interrupted by conscription. On returning to Prague and civilian life in 1960 he joined the Semafor Theatre, founding there the Theatre of Masks; his interest in masked theater had developed alongside his interest in puppetry – a not unnatural link, since what is a puppet but the ultimate mask? He produced a number of plays here, including another version of the Faust legend, and also met and married a young Surrealist painter: Eva Svankmajerová has been an important collaborator on his movies ever since.

After a falling out with the Semafor Theatre – whose focus was narrowing toward traditional stage musicals – the Theatre of Masks moved in 1962 to join Prague's Laterna Magika ("Magic Lantern") theater. After a couple of years, however, Švankmajer left Laterna Magika to make his first film, the short *The Last Trick* (*Poslední trik pana Schwarcewalldea a pana Edgara*, literally "The Last Trick of Mr. Schwarzwald and Mr. Edgar"; 1964), whose subject is a battle between two wizards, conducted by actors dressed as puppets. Various members of Prague's Black Theatre were involved in the project; the filming was done at Krátký Film in Prague. His second short, *J.S. Bach: Fantasy in G-minor* (*J.S. Bach: fantasia g-moll*; 1965), done in black-and-white, uses natural objects, mundane architectural details (such as doors and locks), etc., in strange juxtapositions as a Surrealistic/Manneristic accompaniment to the music. The abstraction of this is counterpointed by the very down-to-earth introduction, wherein a man unlocks a room, sits down at an organ, and takes a bite of an apple before beginning to play. Even here, the apparent naturalism is subverted; why should the organ be locked away in a seemingly deserted house, and why should the organist be initially wearing street clothes over his performance costume?

In the same year that he made *J.S. Bach* Švankmajer went to Austria to make the short *A Game with Stones* (*Spiel mit steinen*; vt *Hra s kameny*; 1965); old musical toys provide the sound accompaniment to a set of animated sequences in which stones dropping from a bizarre gadget arrange and rearrange themselves. The patterns the stones make are not arbitrary, however: taken together the sequences can be seen as representing the evolution of human life from the dawn of life on Earth through the final human self-annihilation; afterward, the gadget is incapable of emitting further stones.

Already Švankmajer was making a name for himself, his movies picking up various awards at film festivals. Mass appeal still eluded him, of course, and the continued hard-line policies of the Czech regime were preventing the full flowering of his Surrealistic genius. The first of these two deficiencies was in part solved by his fourth film, *Punch & Judy* (*Rakvičkárna*, literally "The Lych House"; vt *The Coffin Factory*; 1966); the common English title of the movie is actually misleading, because the two characters involved are Punch and Joey, Joey being another figure from traditional puppetry. The pair vie, increasingly destructively, for the possession of a guinea pig; in the end, only the guinea pig survives. In the visually less ambitious *Et Cetera* (1966) Švankmajer used simple animation of simple

Jan ŠVANKMAJER

figures to convey messages concerning the endlessly repeating cycles of progress and their ultimate futility. The movie ends with a device that could have come from Termite Terrace: just before yet another repetition of a cycle, the film itself seemingly catches fire in the projector. *Historia Naturae (suita)* (1967) ostensibly explores Švankmajer's interest in the Holy Roman Emperor Rudolf II. This is perhaps more a tribute to Švankmajer's lifelong fascination for the art of Rudolf's court painter, Giuseppe Arcimboldo, direct or indirect visual references to whose work are found littered throughout the animator's oeuvre.

The short-lived Prague Spring of 1968, in which the iron grip of Soviet control was momentarily relaxed, encouraged Švankmajer to enjoy both a frenzy of moviemaking and an artistic/philosophical flowering. The Surrealism that had never been far from the surface now came triumphantly to the fore. In the live-action short *The Garden* (*Zahrada*; 1968), a visitor asks why the fence around his host's property is made of human rather than wooden fenceposts; he is told that this is because the host knows such secrets about all the people there that they are willing to serve him in any way, even as his fenceposts. The visitor eagerly joins them. The satire of the reign of the Stalinist secret police and the whispering informers

who served them seems obvious. *The Flat* (*Byt*; 1968), done like *The Garden* in black-and-white live action but this time with the benefit of much trick photography, is more ostentatiously Surrealist: a room locks inside itself a man who discovers that nothing is as it should be (e.g., when he looks in a mirror, he sees the back of his head). More central to consideration of Švankmajer's animation is *Picnic with Weissmann* (*Piknik s Weissmannem*; vt *Picknick mit Weissmann*; 1969). The "white man" (*weiss Mann*) of the title is, in fact, a white suit, the most nearly human occupant of a roomful of animated objects. One of these, a shovel, digs a trench in front of the room's closet; at the end of the movie the closet opens and a trussed-up, nearly naked man falls out of it and into the grave the shovel has prepared. In *A Quiet Week in the House* (*Tichý týden vy domě*; 1969) a fugitive takes refuge in an empty house and, through holes he bores in the various doors off its hall, watches animated objects disport themselves. *The Ossuary* (*Kostnice*; 1970), a live-action short, gains satirical effect through juxtaposition of visuals and soundtrack. The movie was filmed at the Sedlec Ossuary near Kutná Hora,

The Death of Stalinism in Bohemia (1990)

◊color /live-action/stop-motion
animated/photomontage/archival footage ◷ 9³/₄ minutes
A brief political history of Czechoslovakia since the Soviet occupation at the end of World War II. Gottwald, the country's first Communist premier, is seen as born from Stalin's brain, delivered in a Caesarean section of the dictator's sculpted head by an anonymous pair of hands. That same pair of hands then runs an assembly line, casting people in clay and running them along a conveyor belt to where they are hanged and their bodies returned to the original bucket of clay. Later politicians are seen as photographs on sheets of paper that are eventually crumpled up; the invasion of the Soviet tanks to crush the Prague Spring of 1968 is represented by a series of rolling pins rolling down a stepped slope and flattening anything in their path. At last comes Perestroika and a new freedom, but once again that anonymous pair of hands cuts open Stalin's sculpted head to deliver a new brain child . . .

Czechoslovakia, where the bones of countless victims of the Black Death were used to construct bizarre tableaux in the 19th century; Švankmajer counterpointed shots of these with a soundtrack comprising the bland, officially sanctioned tour narrative delivered drearily by one of the guides. Unfortunately, the censors were not so stupid as not to realize the effect, and in the released version the voice soundtrack was replaced by a jazz tune.

A big step forward was taken with *Don Juan* (*Don Šajn*; 1970), at 33 minutes by far his longest movie to date and indeed his longest until he began to create full-length features. Based on versions of the tale drawn from the European puppet tradition, and featuring one of Švankmajer's favorite motifs – the characters being played sometimes by puppets and sometimes by actors dressed as puppets – this tells of Don Juan's evil stratagems to seduce Maria, who loves and is loved by Don Juan's brother Filip. After Don Juan has killed both Maria's father and Filip, he is tormented by the ghost of the father and consigned to Hell. In an envoi drawn straight from puppet theater, as the villain awaits his doom he warns the children in the audience to take heed of his fate and avoid such deeds. It was followed by *Jabberwocky* (*Žvahlav aneb šaticky Slaměného Huberta*, literally "Jabberwocky, or Straw Hubert's Clothes"; 1971), which mixes live action with much stop-motion in a sort of sarabande inspired by Lewis Carroll's poem; it can be regarded as a forerunner of Švankmajer's later, much more ambitious feature based on Carroll's *Alice in Wonderland*.

There was to be only one more movie in this first phase of Švankmajer's career. *Leonardo's Diary* (*Leonardův deník*; 1972) animates drawings from Leonardo's sketchbooks and interpolates live-action images drawn from archival footage. This might seem innocuous enough, but unfortunately the Communist authorities declared (probably correctly) that the precise selection of the scenes from past and present Czech life and their juxtapositions with the sketches constituted a political statement antagonistic to their regime. Švankmajer was, as a consequence, banned from making further movies. For the next seven years, although he did some special-effects work and title sequences, he devoted his artistic endeavors to projects outside the field of cinema.

He was permitted to return to moviemaking in 1979, with the proviso that he stick to adaptations of acknowledged and approved literary works. Accordingly, he made *The Castle of Otranto* (*Otrantský zámek*; 1979), which he had started before his artistic exile, and the black-and-white *The Fall of the House of Usher* (*Zánik domu Usherů*; 1980), both mixing animation with live action and based respectively on the tales by Walpole and Poe. Needless to say, neither is a straightforward adaptation; however, the authorities were content to accept the fiction that he was obeying their ordinance.

The truce could not long be maintained. *Dimensions of Dialogue* (*Moznosti dialogu*; 1982), his next short, is an ambitious effort, done in three parts. In the first, humanoid figures composed of crockery, vegetables, and so on repeatedly devour each other and vomit, until the end result is a perfect human head that persistently vomits replicas of itself. In the second section, a man and a woman fuse; when they separate again, a little piece of matter is left over which neither wants. In their increasingly violent efforts to force it on each other, they tear themselves to shreds. In the third section, two clay heads initially vomit complementary objects (e.g., one vomits a shoe and the other shoelaces); however, the pairs of objects become increasingly disparate, until finally the heads are destroyed. The clay and stop-motion animation is superb, as in Švankmajer's previous two films, and the direction exemplary. These are pretty depressing messages that Švankmajer is conveying: that dialogue between us is, at least in this stage of our development, impossible, and that we find any differences between ourselves to be so intolerable we would rather destroy everything than attempt to understand and adapt to those differences; only a featureless uniformity is acceptable to us – as in the ultimate sterility of the head's being able to reproduce only perfect replicas of its perfect self. One way of looking at tyrannies is as attempts to impose uniformity on human beings, even though human beings are by their very nature individual; and the Communist regime in Czechoslovakia was exactly such a tyranny: despite winning several international awards, *Dimensions of Dialogue* was banned in its homeland.

Nevertheless, Švankmajer was able to make in that same year *Down to the Cellar* (*Do pivnice*; vt *Do sklepa*; 1982), a less ambitious movie that yet again features fine stop-motion animation. Švankmajer has described it as his most autobiographical movie, in that during childhood he was terrified whenever sent to fetch something from the family cellar. As he once remarked in a different context: "I am not interested in the imaginary world of

J a n Š v a n k m a j e r

the child as a general category; that's a problem for psychologists. I'm interested, in the first instance, in a dialogue with my own childhood. Childhood is my alter ego." This short was followed by another Edgar Allan Poe adaptation, as if Švankmajer were intent on mollifying the authorities by showing he was really a good, obedient little puppet: *The Pendulum, the Pit, and Hope* (*Kyvadlo, jáma a nadĕje*; 1983).

He devoted the next few years to the making of what is widely acknowledged as a masterpiece, his first feature movie, *Alice* (*Neco z Alenky*, literally "Something from Alice"; 1988). To call this an adaptation to the screen of Lewis Carroll's classic surrealistic fantasy (it was written too early to be Surrealistic) would be a stretching of terms further than they should be stretched; and yet in a curious sense — and even although radical differences are immediately visible should one lay the synopses of the two works side by side — it *is* an adaptation, for it uses elements from Carroll's tale and adapts them to accord with Švankmajer's own Surrealistic vision, which is so close to Carroll's own: "But you must close your eyes," says Alice at the start of the movie, "otherwise you won't see anything."

It would be impossible to detail here the constant intertwinings between Švankmajer's vision and Carroll's, but a few should be mentioned. Of the various sequences in Wonderland, the most nightmarish is the Mad Hatter's Tea Party: insanity (although not violent insanity) is played for real in what is in effect almost a miniature psychological thriller. Elsewhere, Alice enters a new room and discovers that its wooden floor is perforated by the holes made by living socks as they pour through it like giant woodworms. Opening the drawer of the desk in this room she finds in it a glass containing false teeth and two glass eyes. A sock pounces past her to seize these, and uses them to accoutre itself; snatching a darning-mushroom from a sewing-basket nearby, it perches itself atop this and thereby becomes the Caterpillar. When its scene with Alice is finished, it falls to sleep by darning shut the holes over its glass eyes.

One further disturbing element is of note. When Alice, who is perhaps seven years old and beautifully played by Kristina Kohoutová, drinks the ink, she grows but remains a young child; on shrinking, however, she becomes a doll of herself — a chilling effect. On one occasion, the doll-Alice swells to become not the child but a gigantic version of the doll, which is tied and towed away (like Gulliver by the Lilliputians) by the various animals that have been attacking her. Left alone, the doll starts to ripple and is then ripped open by the child, who climbs from the shell like an insect emerging from its pupa case. It is not surprising that some people find *Alice* so disturbing — far more than any horror movie — that they cannot bear to watch it. To many it clashes intolerably with their perception of Carroll's original as a cozy nursery tale; this is odd, because at the heart of the appeal of the original is the very fact that it is unsettling, and disturbing — a realized nightmare.

Six more years were to pass before Švankmajer made another feature, but with *Alice* he established himself as a major moviemaker

Faust (1994)

(vt *Lekce Faust*)
color /live-action/stop-motion animated/puppetry
92 minutes

A citizen of a modern city proves to be just the next in an endless cycle of Fausts. He is lured by two emissaries of Lucifer to a derelict building, which he discovers is both a dual theater — of puppetry and opera — and the alchemical laboratory of Dr. Faustus; here he witnesses and aids the creation of a homunculus. Both within the theater and in the real world, he is driven by a force from outside rationality or logic to be Faust in two separate senses: as opera singer and as puppet he must *play* Faust for an audience; and in the wider world he must *become* Faust, ever following the script that he sometimes finds lying around. Mephistopheles is summoned and also proves to be Faust — a mirror of the man. Faust's damnation is predetermined, as he comes to understand too late to deviate from the script: in his instance the moment of that damnation occurs when, fleeing the theater, he is run over by an empty car.

not just in the eyes of animation fans or art-movie buffs but in the appreciation of a much broader international public. In the year of *Alice*'s release, 1988, one of the shorts Švankmajer made — the other was *Virile Games* (*Mužné bry*), a Surrealist, Pythonesque treatment of soccer violence — was the commissioned music video *Another Kind of Love*, done to promote the song by British punk rocker Hugh Cornwell. In 1989, as well as the highly acclaimed *Darkness, Light, Darkness* (*Tma, Svetlo, Tma*), he made two commissioned very short shorts for MTV: *Meat Love* and *Flora*.

That year, 1989, also saw the downfall of Communism in Czechoslovakia. Other artists, on release from the Soviet yoke, promptly began to produce works that in some way or another reflected the release; it has been noted, for example, that in the five years following the fall of Communism the Czech publishing industry released as many works of fantasy as it had in the preceding four decades. Elsewhere, there were literary and other artworks that served either as Communism's obituaries or danced on Communism's grave. Yet, aside from such commissioned works as those noted, Švankmajer continued, to a considerable extent, in his moviemaking as he had done before. There was one exception, his sole overtly political movie: *The Death of Stalinism in Bohemia* (1990). Of it, Švankmajer remarked in his interview with Hames:

When someone from the BBC came to see me to ask whether I would make a film about what was happening in Bohemia, I refused. It did not seem possible. However, it started to take off of its own accord (as had many other projects). Despite the fact that this film emerged along the same path of imagination as all my other films, I never pretended that it was anything more than propaganda. Therefore I think it is a film which will age more quickly than any of the others.

Jan Švankmajer

Loath though one is to contradict the movie's creator, Švankmajer is probably wrong in that last assessment. Certainly precise identification of the personalities and events depicted in *The Death of Stalinism in Bohemia* requires the average non-Czech viewer to scrabble for the reference books, but that hardly affects one's appreciation of it *as a movie*; it works superbly well as a satirical, semi-Surrealistic portrayal of the phases of totalitarianism, culminating in its inevitable downfall – *any* totalitarianism, not just a Communist one – and therefore particularization is not essential.

In 1991 Švankmajer established, together with his long-time colleague Jaromir Kallista, the company Athanor, whose purpose is to produce original Czech movies. This has more or less marked the end of his career as a maker of shorts – only *Food* (*Jídlo*; 1992) has since appeared – leaving him to concentrate on features. It has also seen animation decline as a component of his moviemaking – although it is still important.

His second feature, *Faust* (*Lekce Faust*; 1994), is a case in point. Whereas *Alice* had been a movie in which live action and puppetry definitely played second fiddle to diverse forms of stop-motion animation, *Faust* – based on various versions, including those drawn from traditional puppet theater, of a legend that has obviously haunted Švankmajer throughout his creative life – is really a live-action movie with extensive sequences done using puppetry (and actors dressed as puppets) and only comparatively short animated sequences. In fact, the tale is told using a stimulatingly bewildering variety of media, with even "Faust" himself being at one moment a puppet and the next a human being (though even then, of course, it is made clear that he is in a different sense still a *puppet*). Other main characters are likewise always ambiguous: aside from the diabolical emissaries Cornelius and Valdez, who remain human, they seem to be puppets; yet their scale is ever uncertain and they are sometimes capable of independent action far from the strings of the never-seen puppeteer. The setting shares this uncertainty: as if the theatrical stage on and around which much of the action is set were a portal to another world, sometimes it briefly blossoms to become a real-world exterior, which in turn can sometimes be seen to be merely a puppets' stage. There is much of nightmare in this movie as it locks one in its paranoid grip, just as "Faust" is locked in Lucifer's. Apart from one or two longueurs, it is so dense with fantasy notions, icons and imageries that repeated viewing is necessary before one has the feeling one has watched it completely – as if Švankmajer had made *Faust* with video in mind. On occasion, it has to be said, there is also a sense that some element or other is too arbitrary. But this cannot diminish the importance of *Faust* in the context of modern fantasy cinema: it has the completely unsettling effect that is unique to the best of fantasy, in whatever medium. (It

should be noted that the excellent dubbing of the English-language version, with all voices played by Andrew Sachs, is in itself no mean feat.)

This tendency away from animation is continued in Švankmajer's most recently released feature, *Conspirators of Pleasure* (*Spiklenci slasti*; 1996). This can be viewed simply as a Surrealistic sex comedy – and it works very well on that basis, being chilling, imaginatively exhilarating, and hilarious by turns. But a subtext can be read concerning the need for people of disparate philosophies to form silent, tacit alliances, or conspiracies, as a defense against the repression of even the most seemingly open of societies. To extend this, and to extend Švankmajer's analogy, the obsessions that link the conspirators are themselves harmless freedoms. But they are, nevertheless, likely to be regarded as crimes by a supposedly liberal society, just in the same way as freedom of thought, which most of us would regard as not only harmless but indeed so highly desirable as to be worth fighting for, was regarded as a crime by the totalitarian regime under which Švankmajer suffered for so much of his life.

By all reports, Švankmajer's fourth feature, *Otesánek* (provisional English title *Greedyguts*) – originally expected to be released in 1999, then 2000, and then 2001 – shows a return to animation, being done as a live-action movie intertwined with a (perhaps surprisingly) 2D-animated movie, the latter recounting a Czech folk tale from a little girl's fairy-tale book, which tale is being mirrored in real life. As long ago as 1996 the screenplay won first prize in a screenwriting competition set up to mark the centenary of cinema by the State Fund of the Czech Republic for the Sponsorship and Development of Czech Cinematography.

Summarizing the art of this great moviemaker and master of 3D animation is not easy – as difficult as summarizing the plot of one of his groundbreaking feature movies. However, in a 1985 interview with Peter Král, Švankmajer responded to a question about the materials he prefers to work with when doing stop-motion animation with an answer that seems to point to the core of his art:

> I prefer objects which to my way of thinking have their own interior life. Along with the esoteric sciences I believe in the "conservation" of certain contents in objects that have been touched by beings in a state of heightened sensibility. Objects "charged" in this way are then susceptible under certain conditions of delivering up their contents and, on contact, of revealing associations of ideas and resemblances from our own unconscious impulses. Several of my films thus have their origin in a found object – or in a group of objects – to which I had previously "listened." Of course, one cannot make such films except as improvisation recorded directly by the camera. It's a game of internal truth, in other words – The Great Game.

PAUL TERRY (1887–1971)

Setup for an unidentified Mighty Mouse short.
Photograph: S/R Laboratories.

A native of San Mateo, California, where he was born on February 19, 1887, Paul Houlton Terry studied in San Francisco before dropping out of high school to take various newspaper jobs, thereby following in the footsteps of his elder brother John. In 1911 he moved to New York with the ambition to become a newspaper cartoonist. After a brief stint in advertising he took a job as an illustrator with the *New York Press*. However, a night out with his colleagues to see one of Winsor McCay's performances of Gertie the Dinosaur changed the direction of his life: what he wanted to be was an animator – again following the example of John Terry, who had done some animation by that time.

The first animated movie he made, *Little Herman* (1915), earned him barely more than the cost of the film it was made on, but that didn't deter him. He approached Bud Fisher with the suggestion that an animated series could be based on the cartoonist's Mutt & Jeff strips. But, even though Fisher was eager, the idea came to nothing – at least for Terry. Soon afterward, Charles Bowers had the same idea, and persuaded Fisher to go with him and Raoul Barré for the production of what proved to be an extensive series, done by various hands, of Mutt & Jeff cartoons. Unsuccessful with Fisher, Terry took a job at the studio of John Randolph Bray, and it was here that he devised his first series character, Farmer Al Falfa.

Terry had not been with Bray long when he was called away, in 1917, to do war service, specifically to make medical films that mixed animation and live action. In the process he learned a great deal about anatomy, although there is no evidence that he ever thought to put this knowledge to use in his animation, the drawing of which remained as rudimentary as ever. Afterward, he was one of a New York-based consortium of animators – the others included Earl Hurd, John Terry, and Frank Moser – who set up their own studio, but this venture didn't last long before John Terry got the opportunity to establish himself as the John Coleman Terry Studio, employing most of the staff and inheriting many of the cartoon properties – such as the Bringing Up Father series, based on the strips by George McManus – of the Hearst Studio, which had just been closed down. So, for Paul Terry, it was back to churning out Farmer Al Falfas.

Farmer Al Falfa also starred in many of the next major series Terry produced, the Aesop's Fables. The idea was that of a writer named Howard Estabrook, but Terry deserves full credit for immediately recognizing the potential. The basic formula for these cartoons was that an Aesopian-style funny-animal fable would be told – in the early days the fables were indeed Aesop's, or mangled versions thereof, but as time went on the Aesopian well began to run dry – and then, after the telling, there would be a moral supposedly drawn from the story, or at least from Aesop (although often there was just a made up gag-line by Terry or his animators). It became obvious that the final gag-line was actually more important than the preceding cartoon, and this was a very good thing, for Terry had contracted with the Keith–Albee Theater chain of movie theaters – which held a majority holding in the studio he set up especially to cope with the series, Fables Pictures Inc. – to

Farmer Al Falfa's Wayward Pup (1917)

b/w / animated silent ◷ 10 minutes
Farmer Al Falfa
Fido keeps stealing and smoking Farmer Al's pipe, eventually burying it as if it were a bone, then torments the ducks. After further canine pranks, Farmer Al buys a fighting gamecock to teach the mutt a lesson. But the dog has the last laugh when Farmer Al accidentally flattens his own gamecock.

Wolf! Wolf! (1944)

color / animated ◷ 6¼ minutes
Mighty Mouse
Little Bo Peep's lost sheep are spotted by a wolf family, one of whom is dressed up as a decoy Bo Peep. He lures one by playing the flute, but at the last moment his disguise is seen through; a trumpet proves more successful. The lamb is just saying its last prayers when, from his treetop home, Mighty Mouse spies the predicament; by the time he flies to the rescue the lamb is actually in the stockpot. In customary fashion, Mighty Mouse beats the stuffing out of the wolves, prevailing even when their entire cottage becomes an anti-aircraft artillery battery. The lamb returned to its mama, the cartoon concludes: "And Mighty Mouse proves again that he's the champion of sheep and men."

The Talking Magpies (1946)

color / animated ◷ 6¼ minutes
Heckle & Jeckle
The two magpies, seeking new lodgings, are for the price of a worm sold an empty nest directly outside the bedroom window of Farmer Al Falfa, and soon cause a noise nuisance through their incessant bickering. A series of sequences follows in which, each time Farmer Al attempts to cope with them, he receives violent retribution, the two birds echoing his earlier yell at them of "Qui-i-i-i-et!"; the only interesting routine is when Heckle gets inside a radio and speaks a pretend radio announcement to the effect that magpies are a farmer's best friend. In the finale, Heckle and Jeckle have taken possession of the bedroom while Farmer Al and his dimwit dog are bruisely confined to the nest.

produce a new Aesop's Fable cartoon each week, a horrific schedule. Obviously, much re-use of animation from one short to the next was employed to ease the pressure, but, even so, it is likely that only Terry could have managed to meet the demand. He had recognized, as soon as he'd discovered how little profit his production of *Little Herman* was going to make, that perhaps the only way of deriving much immediate money from animated shorts

was to reduce the whole process to an assembly-line operation. Whereas some of the other studios, most notably Disney, reckoned (correctly, in the long term) that the way to profitability in animation was through the quality of production, Terry opted to take the route of speed. Fables Pictures Inc. (later renamed Fables Studio) thus became a sweatshop that mainly attracted inexperienced or talentless animators.

In 1928 Keith-Albee — which would go onto become RKO — sold its interest in the studio to Amadee J. Van Beuren and his company Van Beuren Productions. It was at the behest of Van Beuren that Terry experimented with the newfangled craze, synchronized sound, to produce the short *Dinner Time* (1928); although the precise release date of this short is hazy, it is known to have preceded Disney's *Steamboat Willie* (1928), generally heralded as the first synchronized-sound cartoon, by a few weeks. (The Fleischers probably predated them both.) Van Beuren believed that sound was the way of the future; Terry thought it was just a flash in the pan, in that it prohibitively increased the costs of producing animation shorts — in his view no cinema-owner or distributor would bear the increased expense. The two men quarrelled, and in 1929 Terry left Van Beuren Productions to set up, with his old colleague Frank Moser and a movie consultant, Joseph Coffman, a new company: Moser-Terry-Coffman. They drew up a contract with a company named Audio Cinema to produce cartoons that would be distributed by Educational Pictures; although under the contract Audio Cinema would finance the actual production of the cartoons, Terry and Moser would go unpaid until the cartoons showed a profit. Ironically, bearing in mind the nature of his disagreement with Van Beuren, these were to be sound cartoons, the production of sound movies being the specialty of Coffman's consultancy business. Production of the first Terrytoons, as they were called, began in 1929, with the first short, *Caviar*, being released on February 23, 1930.

Although these were sound cartoons, there was very little dialogue in them — lip sync was difficult and time-consuming and therefore expensive — the synchronization instead largely involving the actions of the characters in time to a piece of music. Unlike the other studios, which either paid rights fees for the use of existing material or, like Leon Schlesinger's Looney Tunes done for Warners, were in a sense promotional exercises to stimulate sales of the songs on which they were based, the Terrytoons almost from the start had original soundtracks, done by the composer and orchestrator Philip A. Scheib, using either freshly composed or traditional, non-copyright tunes. This was all the more remarkable because Terry had contracted to produce a new short every fortnight — only half the frequency of his earlier cartoons, but in fact a schedule even more hectic because of the complexities of using synchronized sound.

Farmer Al Falfa was finally put out to pasture. This was not quite the relief to movie lovers worldwide that it might seem, because the required rate of production of the Terrytoons necessitated all the same old time-saving techniques, notably the reuse of animation

and, indeed, story lines. Thus, even though new series characters were introduced, it is difficult to think of the Terrytoons individually rather than as one vast mass of mediocrity and monotony that, begun in 1930, went on well through the 1950s. Of these series characters, only a few are remembered today. Gandy Goose, based on the persona of comedian Ed Wynn, was launched in *Gandy the Goose* (1938) and, after initially flopping, was teamed with a cat called Sourpuss; in one of the classic examples of the sidekick becoming more important than the main character, Sourpuss saved the day. The suddenly popular Gandy shorts continued until 1955's *Barnyard Actor*. Heckle & Jeckle debuted in 1946 with *The Talking Magpies*; the two birds – one Brooklyn-accented, the other English-accented – underwent various, and variously similar, madcap-chase escapades several times a year until 1954's *Blue Plate Symphony*, after which a resurgence in their popularity brought about through the rerunning of the shorts on television prompted the production of a few extra Heckle & Jeckle movies, their last outing being as late as 1966, with *Messed-Up Movie Makers*. In 1956 they began a television career in *The Heckle and Jeckle Cartoon Show*, which ran from 1956 to 1971 and saw them hosting collections of old theatrical Terrytoons featuring themselves and other characters such as Dinky Duck, Gandy & Sourpuss, the mouse Little Roquefort and his perennial foe Percy the Cat. In 1979–82 the pair were the support act in *The New Adventures of Mighty Mouse and Heckle and Jeckle*; these were newly made animations, but by now the pair's popularity hinged exclusively on that of their costar, Mighty Mouse.

Mighty Mouse was developed by Terry from an idea by I. Klein to produce a spoof Superman character (in Klein's version, a fly). Initially, this character was called Super Mouse, and was thus billed for the first four of his shorts, begun with *The Mouse of Tomorrow* (1942). The regular adversary in the earliest cartoons was Powerful Puss, from whose clutches Mighty Mouse would dutifully save Pearl Pureheart (reminiscent, at least in name, of Dick Tracy's girlfriend Tess Trueheart), a little mouse heroine; but thereafter resurrected as bad guy for the series, redesigned as a cat, was Oil Can Harry, who had been the villain and suave seducer in the four Fanny Zilch "mellerdrammers" Terrytoons had made in 1933, and had later appeared in an even shorter series of two Terrytoons shorts in 1937. Initially, the dialogue in the Mighty Mouse cartoons was conventional, but from *Mighty Mouse and the Pirates* (1945) on they were given an opera-style treatment that became a hallmark of the series. Mighty Mouse, after a cinema career that was basically over by the mid-1950s, saw his last theatrical release with *Cat Alarm* (1961), but by that time his career in the shorts had been entirely eclipsed by his astonishing success on television through the latter half of the 1950s and the first half of the 1960s. In 1956 *The Mighty Mouse Playhouse* (whose run lasted 1955–66 before various revivals) captured an astonishing 70.8 percent of the audience, trouncing even *The Mickey Mouse Club*. The most significant of the non-Terrytoons revivals was *Mighty Mouse: The New Adventures*, done by Ralph Bakshi in 1987–89 (see page 27).

Frame from *Farmer Al Falfa's Wayward Pup* (1917).
Private collection.

But long before much of this Paul Terry was no longer a part of Terrytoons. He was one of the first animation producers to realize that television was going to kill the animated theatrical short, and that one must either come to some arrangement with the new medium or in due course perish. Accordingly Terrytoons was the first major animation studio to sign up for television. Old Terrytoons shorts – including even some of the Farmer Al Falfa series – were bought by CBS for the network's *Barker Bill's Cartoon Show* (1953–56), the first networked weekday cartoon series. There were typically two shorts per show with surprisingly few, if any, reruns, so that during its mere three seasons the show chomped its way through something like a quarter of the entire Terrytoons output.

In 1955, CBS realized that a profitable arrangement could be even more profitable if they owned the operation, and offered Terry $3.5 million for Terrytoons and all its assets. This was a formidable sum, and Terry accepted it. Without further ado he retired entirely from animation, living for the rest of his life – he died in October 1971 in Rye, New York – in luxury on the proceeds of the sale. To the astonishment and bitterness of many of his staff, who had been with him for two or even three decades, he kept the entirety of his massive windfall to himself, leaving them to forge on with Terrytoons under the new CBS management. Although it is fair to say that most of Terrytoons' enduring work – almost all for television – was done between Terry's departure in 1955 and the final closure of the studio by the CBS subsidiary Viacom in 1971, it is also true that the sweatshop conditions in the studio became, at least for a while, even worse. But that is another story.

Vladimir "Bill" Tytla
(1904–1968)

Concept art for the *Ave Maria* section of *Fantasia* (1940).
Private collection. © Disney Enterprises, Inc.

Vladimir William Tytla – usually known as either "Vlad" or "Bill" – is animation's lost genius. Although he worked for other studios and for a while had a studio of his own, it was only really during the nine years that he worked with Disney that he was able to flourish; he had an obsession with perfectionism that other commercial studios regarded as economically undesirable, their priority being to produce cartoons at speed and regularly. Chuck Jones has described Tytla as "the Michelangelo of animators"; Art Babbitt called him "the greatest animator of all time."

His parents were immigrants to the U.S. from the Ukraine, he himself being born on October 25, 1904, in Yonkers, New York; he was often to recall his Ukrainian heritage in his later animation, especially when working on Chernabog in the *Night on Bald Mountain* section of Disney's *Fantasia* (1940). At age nine he saw a presentation by Winsor McCay of the recently

completed *Gertie the Dinosaur* (1914), and this turned him early toward animation. While at high school, he attended evening classes in art at the New York Evening School of Industrial Design, eventually quitting high school in favor of a career in art. By 1920, when he was only 16, he was working for Paramount, lettering title cards; while there, he was nicknamed "Tytla the Titler." Thereafter, he did some animation work for Raoul Barré on the Mutt & Jeff shorts and for John Terry, who had a studio in Greenwich Village; for years afterward he regarded John Terry as a sort of mentor, and frequently asked his advice on artistic and career decisions. However, it was John's brother Paul who really plunged the young Tytla into the mainstream of commercial animation, poaching him from John's studio to work at Terrytoons on the long Aesop's Fables series of shorts that the studio was then producing.

Terrytoons was not precisely an atelier. Nevertheless, Tytla stuck it out for several years, catering to his fine-art aspirations by attending evening classes at the Art Students League. In 1929, he and a couple of commercial artists with whom he had been rooming quit their jobs and headed for Paris to study painting and, in Tytla's case at least, some sculpture under Charles Despiau. Also in Paris, he saw some of the early Disney cartoons, and was much taken by them. On a visit to London, he met with the Russian Embassy in the hopes that they might help a wild scheme of his to start up an animation studio in Moscow in imitation of Disney's in Burbank; but, perhaps unsurprisingly, there was no interest.

Back in the U.S. again, he accepted a new job with Terrytoons, having decided he simply wasn't good enough to emulate the fine-art masters whose work he had seen in Europe: if he couldn't be better than Brueghel, he reasoned, it was silly to pursue the matter further. Being a commercial artist rather than a fine artist is one thing, but the anti-culture atmosphere he found still prevailing at Terrytoons was quite another. Nevertheless, he stayed on, probably purely because the money was respectable. About the only good thing for Tytla that came out of this second period at Terrytoons was that it was here he met another of the great, undeservedly obscure (to the public) figures of animation's history, Art Babbitt; it was a meeting that would do much to mold Tytla's later career.

In 1932 Babbitt went to California to join Disney, and immediately began recommending that the studio recruit Tytla, too. Since Walt had heard about Tytla from other respected animators as well, he was definitely interested, and asked Babbitt to informally explore the situation further. However, Paul Terry was well aware of this major talent he had on his staff – even though he wasn't really using it – and responded by giving Tytla a pay hike. A few weeks later, at Walt's prodding, Babbitt wrote again; another pay hike followed. Deciding to do his old pal Bill a favor, Babbitt wrote a third time, this time just generally saying there were lots of good animation jobs in California; sure enough, Tytla got yet another pay hike.

Despite the money, however, Tytla eventually gave in to Babbitt's urgings and flew across to at least have a look at the Disney studio. He liked what he saw and, even though Walt offered him a starting salary less than what he was getting at Terrytoons, accepted a job. It wasn't to be long before his salary was vastly in excess of anything he could have hoped for from Paul Terry; Walt recognized he'd hired an animation genius.

At Disney, Tytla served his apprenticeship on the shorts, animating under Ben Sharpsteen on *Cock o' the Walk, The Cookie Carnival, Mickey's Fire Brigade,* and *Broken Toys* (all 1935). By this time, though, Walt was already heavily involved in *Snow White and the Seven Dwarfs* (1937), and Tytla was one of the earliest

animators he drafted onto the project; he and Fred Moore were made supervising animators, with specific responsibility for the Seven Dwarfs.

After animating the giant who is Mickey Mouse's adversary in the short *Brave Little Tailor* (1938) and the sorcerer Yensid in the short *The Sorcerer's Apprentice* – which in due course became the central section of *Fantasia* – Tytla plunged straight into work on Disney's next feature, *Pinocchio* (1940), on which he was primarily responsible for the creation and animation of Stromboli. Of the three villains in *Pinocchio* – the others are the sinister Coachman and the wily J. Worthington Foulfellow – Stromboli is probably the one with the least screen time, and yet, as animated by Tytla, he packs more than enough punch to make up for this. Ollie Johnston and Frank Thomas, in *The Disney Villain* (1993), propose that the reason Tytla was so good at portraying larger-than-life, emotionally volatile characters was that he was one himself, a man who habitually followed his heart rather than his head.

Stromboli might have seemed a hard act to follow, and doubtless Tytla felt this was so. According to Art Babbitt, who roomed with him for some time, and to Adrianne, who married Tytla in 1936, it was his custom to come home after each new assignment and worry about whether or not he was capable of doing it – and then, of course, he would produce something way beyond anyone's expectations. (Johnston and Thomas also declare that Tytla had a vast ego. But it seems far more likely that the converse was true, and that, as so often is the case, in public he hid his insecurity behind a brash mask.) There was one thing, though, that Tytla was adamant he could *not* do: "Ducks I don't like, I do not. Ducks I got no patience with." As it proved, his follow-up to Stromboli would be a character quite literally larger than life: Chernabog, the Slavonic dark god of evil and destruction, who features in the *Night on Bald Mountain* section toward the close of *Fantasia*.

The model for the animation of Chernabog was supposed to be the famous horror actor Bela Lugosi, whom Walt hired to come into the studio. However, Tytla was not entirely happy with Lugosi's rendition of the role, and so, in the end, he got fellow animator Wilfred Jackson to act the part instead. From such humble origins sprang what is generally regarded as one of animation's greatest triumphs.

Fearful of being typecast, Tytla asked for a quite different character as his next assignment, and was accordingly given the eponymous star of *Dumbo* (1941), whom he modeled on his own son Peter. Here he showed that he was equally a master of the tender as of the powerful. But *Dumbo* was a movie whose making was complicated by the 1941 strike at the Disney studio, a strike precipitated by Walt's foolish firing of Tytla's oldest friend at the establishment, Art Babbitt. Most of the studio's star animators broke the strike, but, to general astonishment, Tytla – although he did not actively picket or otherwise agitate – was not one of them. He had considerable loyalty toward Walt, but he had other loyalties too, to his fellow workers and to Babbitt. In later years he told the tale of how, during the strike, he and Walt bumped into each other in a diner and agreed that two sensible men like themselves should be able to work out a solution. They agreed to meet at the studio, but, unfortunately, by the time Tytla had changed into more appropriate clothes, either one of the union organizers or one member of the Disney management team had persuaded Walt that the meeting would be pointless, and so Walt canceled.

After the strike was over, Disney was not an easy place to work; although Tytla was welcomed back into the fold and there was no question that his participation in the strike would ever be held against him (uniquely, Walt's affection for him remained unscathed), a man as sensitive to atmosphere as he undoubtedly was had great difficulty coping with the inevitable tension in the air. He did some work on Pedro the plane for *Saludos Amigos* (1943), the shorts *The Grain that Built a Hemisphere*, *Education for Death* and *Reason and Emotion* (all 1943), and the propaganda feature *Victory Through Air Power* (1943), but he had the sense that his time at Disney was over. The clincher came when Paul Terry, having heard through the grapevine about Tytla's unhappiness with the situation, flew across from New York in order to blandish him with offers of a job at Terrytoons. In February 1943 Tytla left Disney.

The rest is swiftly told. For a few years he worked as a director of animation at Terrytoons, but he had considerable difficulty adapting back from the pursuit of perfection to the need for fast product. No one was really surprised when he moved on, this time to the Paramount/Famous Studios, where, by all accounts, he was equally unhappy: the animator once responsible for Stromboli and Chernabog was now working on shorts featuring Popeye, Casper the Friendly Ghost and Little Lulu. For Little Lulu (and, when Paramount lost the rights

to her, Little Audrey), Tytla used his daughter Tammy as the model, which must have added at least some interest to what may have otherwise seemed a mere chore. He did some work for Tempo – the studio run by his one-time Disney colleague David Hilberman – including some stop-motion animation, but then Tempo was closed down by the McCarthyite witch-hunts. After a stint with Academy Pictures he founded William Tytla Productions. By this time he was a sick man, and anyway he had never been much of a businessman; the company apparently produced some good work but eventually foundered.

He did some piecework for Hanna–Barbera, but his only real credit of much significance during his final years was as a director of animation on *The Incredible Mr. Limpet* (1964) for Warners. In this live-action/animated movie, Don Knotts plays a Walter Mitty type with a penchant for aquaria; with the outbreak of World War II, he is eager to do the right thing, and therefore wishes himself into a fish (and into animation), in the guise of which he aids the U.S. Navy against U-boats. In fact, because Tytla was so unwell by then, most of the actual animation had to be done by his fellow animation directors – Gerry Chiniquy and Hawley Pratt – and sequence director Robert McKimson.

He suffered a series of minor strokes that left him blind in his left eye – a fact he successfully concealed from his professional colleagues. In 1968 he approached his old employers, Disney, both asking for animation work in general and trying to sell them the idea he had developed for an animated movie featuring Mousthusula, The 2000-Year-Old Mouse, but Disney was going through its own hard times and didn't want to take on an extra animator. So much for sentiment. He had a final and much bigger stroke while in the hospital for a routine operation, and later, on December 29, 1968, died on his farm in East Lyme, Connecticut.

The animation industry had squandered Bill Tytla.

WILL VINTON (1947–)

Will Vinton was born on November 17, 1947, and grew up in McMinnville, Oregon. His initial interests were some distance away from animation: when he enrolled in the University of California at Berkeley, it was to study an unusual combination of physics, architecture, and moviemaking. Oddly enough, it was the architecture that guided him toward clay animation, in that he became fascinated by the fluid-seeming designs of the great Spanish architect Antonio Gaudí, the leading exponent of the Catalan Modernist school of Art Nouveau; perhaps Gaudí's most famous work was on Barcelona's Church of Sagrada Familia. It was Gaudí's practice to initially model his designs in clay. Through emulating this and matching such work with his moviemaking studies, Vinton was led to an interest in clay animation.

It is often thought that Vinton invented clay animation – an understandable misconception given that he has made this artform most emphatically his own, developing it to a sophistication and versatility undreamed of by the earlier pioneers: he has justifiably been called the Walt Disney of clay animation. (There are those who believe, analogously, that Disney invented animation.) Clay animation dates from just a few years after the invention of the motion picture itself, and was spurred in particular by the invention of Plasticine in 1897 by British chemist-entrepreneur William Harbutt. In one of his last movies, *Chew Chew Land, or The Adventures of Dollie and Jim* (1910), the animation pioneer James Stuart Blackton had a sequence in which clay – not Plasticine – was used for the animation. Willie Hopkins was another pioneer of clay animation, with such shorts as *Swat the Fly* (1919). The Fleischers' Out of the Inkwell short *Modeling* (1921) was a further early example of clay animation being used in a commercial cartoon; while in the Buster Keaton movie *Three Ages* (1923) the star interacts with a clay-animated dinosaur. The clay-animated tv series *The Gumby Show*, done by Art Clokey, was aired by NBC in 1957; it had been preceded by the one-shot *Gumbasia* (1953) and by Gumby episodes from 1956 in *The Howdy Doody Show*. Clay animation was also an important technique in early stop-motion special effects. The most notable modern practitioners, aside from Vinton, are Jan Švankmajer and the crew at Aardman Animations.

While at Berkeley, Vinton met a fellow student named Bob Gardiner, and the two worked on some early projects together. Clay animation featured as one element of their first collaboration, *Culture Shock* (1969), a short that used diverse media to convey its topical message. After graduating (in architecture) from Berkeley, Vinton worked briefly for the production company Northwestern in San Francisco before joining Odyssey Productions in Portland, Oregon, where he made live-action movies. At the same time, he was moonlighting with Gardiner in his basement to produce the clay-animated short *Closed Mondays* (1974), which shows an elderly wino staggering around an art exhibition and being taken over by the fantasy worlds his perception of the artworks conjures; in the

Still (detail) from *The Adventures of Mark Twain* (1985).
© Will Vinton Studios.

Mountain Music (1975)

🖌color /stop-motion animated ⏲ 8 minutes
An extended pastoral prelude shows us the forests of a mountain region, and we hear the music of the creatures there: hooting owls, croaking frogs, a howling wolf. Cut to a glade where a trio of musicians is performing. Slowly, their music becomes more and more technologically derived as speakers, amps, and other not necessarily musical totems of a technological society spring up around them, the music all the while becoming wilder and louder, utterly drowning the natural music of the forest creatures. At last, a volcano erupts in the background, destroying all, its thunder drowning even the electronic blare of the musicians. Then, slowly, the forest's own music comes back again until we hear the first few tentative notes played by a human being as the whole cycle starts again.

a Christmas Gift (1980)

🖌color /stop-motion animated ⏲ 7 minutes
From the freezing cold sidewalks a street waif watches in wonder all the signs of Christmas going on indoors — toystore window displays, a boozy party, etc. — with a look of innocent wonderment on his face. After all the stores are shut he spies, through a candlelit window, an old woman who has nothing. From her door, he offers to share his own Christmas repast, a piece of bread and a piece of cheese. As they become friends, the two share the happiest Christmas of all the town.

James Weldon Johnson's
The Creation (1981)

🎨 color / animated ⏱ 7³/₄ minutes

Featuring the art of Joan C. Gratz and narrated by James Earl Jones, this is a highly dramatic piece of semi-abstract animation recounting the Judeo-Christian Creation myth. Shapes flow and swirl naturalistically from one to the next until finally Man is born, with part of the soul of God within.

The Adventures of Mark Twain
(1985)

🎨 color / stop-motion animated ⏱ 86 minutes

Tom Sawyer, Huck Finn, and Becky Thatcher inadvertently stow away on Mark Twain's balloon bound for Halley's Comet. (In reality Twain, born in a year of the Comet, was convinced he would die in the year of its next return, which indeed he did. So this balloon trip symbolizes his journey to meet his destiny with the Comet.) En route, Twain regales the kids with stories, which are animated as vignettes; these are drawn from "The Celebrated Jumping Frog of Calaveras County" (1867), "Adam's Diary" (1893), "Eve's Diary" (1905), "The Mysterious Stranger" (1916), "Captain Stormfield's Visit to Heaven" (1907), and other items from his notebooks and journals. Much of Twain's dialogue is also made up of *bons mots* drawn from his writings and diaries. A sort of trans-dimensional elevator, the index-o-vator, transports the kids from one level to another within the balloon's superstructure, and thus from one area to another of Twain's fiction and indeed psyche. There are some showcase pieces of clay animation, notably the sequence in which the balloon encounters a thunderstorm. Tom does his best to sabotage the ship, and near the end of the voyage almost succeeds, but at last the comet is attained; at this moment a dark alter ego of Twain, which has haunted proceedings intermittently, appears and fuses with him, so that the two sides of his nature are reconciled.

final segment the wino himself becomes a gilded sculpture. To everyone's surprise, this movie walked off with a 1975 Oscar as Best Animated Short. Vinton never looked back.

Closed Mondays has a striking sophistication of story and of camera techniques, but it was really with the following year's *Mountain Music* (1975) that Vinton – by now established as the senior member of the team – and Gardiner began to display the full sophistication of the *medium*. This short has a visual impact that could probably not be achieved by any other means, as the landscape flows and mutates in seeming response to a group of musicians whose performance likewise shifts from a simple folk rendition to hard rock. Cel animation could have drawn the same pictures and, much more recently, CGI could render those in seeming 3D; but only the use of clay allows the ever-changing landscape the sense of ponderous solidity manifest in this short – a realism that transcends mere visual appearance. Although not

a recipient of an Oscar – surprisingly, it wasn't even shortlisted – *Mountain Music* can be regarded as one of the key shorts in the history of animation.

Other notable shorts from this pre-1985 period include *James Weldon Johnson's The Creation* (1981), nominated for an Oscar and based to a large extent on the clay art of Joan C. Gratz, a long-time Vinton stalwart, and *Dinosaur* (1980). The latter is essentially a documentary about the dinosaurs, given in the form of a class presentation. The voice track, aside from the narration, is filled with the sound of the kids in the class chattering, bitching, and arguing about the topic. *A Christmas Gift* (1980) is one of the great classic Christmas animated shorts, beautifully rendered and beautifully told, although its moral is somewhat confused.

As a result of the reception accorded to *Closed Mondays*, Vinton founded his own production company, Will Vinton Studios, and also registered the trademark Claymation. So influential has his work in the Plasticine medium been since then that it is not at all uncommon to find the term Claymation used (erroneously) to describe any piece of clay animation.

In the same year *Mountain Music* was released, Vinton made his first foray into tv commercials, a strand of his work that has dominated the studio's output ever since. This was not just in immediate economic terms but also in that his most popular series characters, The California Raisins, were to be born from a 1986 tv commercial for the California Raisin Advisory Board. This goofy band of musicians, whose foibles and idiosyncrasies offer hilariously observed and genuinely affectionate snapshots of California rock-music culture from the 1960s and 1970s, first strutted their stuff to an obvious choice of song – "I Heard It Through the Grapevine" – which has been their theme tune ever since. They've starred in the tv specials *Meet the Raisins* (1988) and *The Raisins Sold Out!* (1990), and have made guest appearances in other Vinton enterprises, such as *A Claymation Christmas Celebration* (1987).

The first Vinton tv commercials, done in 1975, were for Pacific Mountain pears and Rainier Ale. Advertising agencies were a bit slow to pick up the message that Claymation could be an enormously popular selling tool: there was an ad for Levi's Youthwear in 1978, but it wasn't until 1981 and an ad for Benjamin Franklin Savings & Loan that the dam really burst. Since then, the studio has done hundreds of other ads in an almost continuous stream, including extended series not just for the California Raisin Advisory Board but also for such companies as Kentucky Fried Chicken, Purina, Domino's Pizza, and, in 2000, the National Football League, which commissioned six 15-second ads featuring sportscasters James Brown and Terry Bradshaw in clay incarnations. M&M/Mars has, so far, used about sixty Vinton-animated commercials. Other clients for Vinton commercials have included Nintendo, Nike, Coca-Cola, and Nissan.

It was obvious from fairly early on that Vinton had his sights set on a Claymation feature. Three featurettes released between 1976 and 1979, each 27 minutes long, can be regarded as trial

Still from the award-winning *Michael Raisin* tv commercial.

runs for the major enterprise. Later combined as the theatrical compilation feature *Little Prince and Friends* (1980), the three were *Martin the Cobbler* (1976), based on a Tolstoy story, *Rip Van Winkle* (1978), based on the famous Washington Irving story, and *The Little Prince* (1979), based on the equally famous Antoine de Saint-Exupéry story. All three are exceptional pieces of animation, but the third is the most interesting. As noted in discussing *Mountain Music*, one of the great advantages of the clay-animation medium is that it can convey a sort of magic-realist version of reality through the evident solidity and mass of the material being used – the depiction is realer than real, as it were – and it was this characteristic that Vinton exploited in all his earlier movies; but in *The Little Prince* he tried to do something quite different, to get precisely *away* from any literal depiction of Saint-Exupéry's almost metaphysical tale. (Vinton has ascribed this urge in part to his detestation of the clodhopping literalness of the 1974 Lerner–Loewe movie musical based on the story; as *Halliwell's* accurately remarks of this movie, it is "an arch musical which falls over itself early on and never recovers.") This stripping away of the realism from Claymation's habitual effect of magic realism, to

leave only the magic, was achieved by the use of special camera techniques, stylized character movements, and other methods, perhaps most notably, the occasional use of a clay version of the smeared motion developed in 2D animation by practitioners as widely different as Chuck Jones and Norman McLaren.

Despite these early practice runs at a Claymation feature, Vinton has, perhaps surprisingly, created only one such film, *The Adventures of Mark Twain* (1985). In an eerie echo of the general critical predictions decades earlier, before Walt Disney released his *Snow White and the Seven Dwarfs* (1937), the reviewers of the Vinton movie patiently explained to the public that Claymation was incapable of sustaining the interest of viewers through the duration of a full-length feature movie, and gave the impression that there was something clumping and stodgy about clay animation as a medium. This concert of disagreeable voices drowned the truth: there is nothing dull or slow about the movie

A Claymation Christmas Celebration (1987 tvm)

🎨color / stop-motion animated with some conventional animation ⏱ 24 minutes

Herb and Rex, two dinosaurs, introduce a selection of carols, variously mangled: the Three Kings try to sing "We Three Kings" soberly but their camels keep rocking it up; "The Carol of the Bells" is performed in Notre Dame by the Paris Bellharmonic under the baton of Quasimodo, with one idiot bell almost ruining the recital; "Angels We Have Heard on High" is interpreted by ice-balletic walruses and penguins; "Joy to the World" is (quite impressively) given an African beat and accompanies a piece of experimental animation; and the California Raisins give a rather flat (for them) rendition of "Rudolf the Red-Nosed Reindeer." A running gag is offered by various choirs misinterpreting "Here We Go A-Wassailing" as "Here We Go A-Waffling/Waddling/Wallowing." The highlight in terms of animation, is "The Christmas Tree Carol," where each nest of settings reveals a setting tinier than itself within a Christmas-tree ornament.

Meet the Raisins (1988 tvm)

🎨color / stop-motion animated with some conventional animation ⏱ 27 minutes

Mock-rockumentary about the rise to stardom of the supergroup The California Raisins (A.C., Beebop, Stretch and Red), complete with all the clichés — the prissily pretentious musicologist as presenter, the early success in a tv talent show, the embittered original group member (Zoot the grapefruit) who was fired and now works on a fish-canning assembly line, the appalling British rock rival Lick Broccoli, the movie career, the comeback tour of the Arctic Circle (where they sing to an audience of snowmen), and even the obligatory plane crash. (All that's missing are the groupies and the drugs.) Clips of their movies offer lively parodies: *Ben Herb*, *The Good, The Bad and The Wrinkled*, *Two Thousand Some*, and *Star Truck*. Highlights are their attempts to make money in the early years, first as live elevator music and then as a singing telegram; their attempt to deliver a love greeting to a mountaineer is especially amusing.

at all, in part because of the sheer technical brilliance of the animation and *mises-en-scènes*, but in even larger part because of its episodic construction, with a frame story containing a series of stories that could stand on their own as independent shorts (and two of which had, in fact, been released together in 1981 as just that, *The Diary of Adam and Eve*). The result of this fix-up construction decreases the movie's overall storytelling power, but in no real way diminishes it as a movie or as a piece of entertainment.

Vinton's other forays into features have come in the form of contributions to other people's live-action movies, including the "Speed Demon" section of the Michael Jackson music movie *Moonwalker* (1988). By far the most meaningful of his feature-movie participations, however, has been his first, the Claymation special effects for the Disney/Silver Screen *Return to Oz* (1985). Again the critical reception given to this movie was not favorable — although later reassessments are increasingly rating it highly. There has never been any doubt, however, about the quality of the Vinton studio's contribution to it, which won a well deserved Oscar.

There has also been extensive work for television, again mainly in the form of contributions to larger items. Significant among these have been the "Cecille" segments done in 1990–91 for *Sesame Street* and the series of clay-animated shorts that appeared from 1992 on Disney's *Adventures in Wonderland*. There have also been some excellent tv specials mixing new with earlier animation, and these are widely re-aired to this day: *A Claymation Christmas Celebration* (1987), *Meet the Raisins* (1988), *The Raisins Sold Out!* (1990), *Claymation Comedy of Horrors* (1991), and *A Claymation Easter* (1992). A new step was *The Online Adventures of Ozzie the Elf*, a 1997 tv special based on a Web site character and done in conjunction with Web provider America Online (AOL). Even more significant was *The PJs*, a prime-time tv series done with Eddie Murphy and airing on Fox in 1999, moving to Warners in 2000. Based on the adventures of a group of black people in a housing project, the series had some considerable success despite the accusations of some African-American groups that it was racially offensive; even Spike Lee joined the chorus. Such criticism must have been especially painful for Vinton, a liberal who has never been afraid to make his anti-racist sentiments plain.

In reviewing Vinton's career to date it is hard not to get the impression that all his incredible zeal, talent, skill, and technical expertise have so far been devoted to producing . . . well, not very much. The bulk of his landmark achievements in animation fall in the first part of his career, before the mid-1980s or so, with not a huge amount to show thereafter, except the occasional tv special and, of course, the more recent tv series – plus those hundreds of tv ads. Will Vinton Studios – now operating in CGI as well as Claymation – is a thriving business employing a large staff. So, in commercial terms, one can hardly argue with the course he has chosen; yet one aches for some new enterprise that would be as *permanent* as those early shorts and featurettes – and, especially, *The Adventures of Mark Twain*. Perhaps in this new century, now that Nick Park and Aardman Animation has proved so emphatically that clay animation can be a commercially successful medium, Vinton will return to the business and the art of making movies – an art at which he so conspicuously excels.

RICHARD WILLIAMS (1933–)

Setup for *Charles Dickens' A Christmas Carol, Being a Ghost Story of Christmas* (1971). Photograph: S/R Laboratories.
© Richard Williams Productions.

Although in fact Canadian by birth – he was born in Toronto on March 19, 1933 – Richard Williams is more usually referred to as a British animator because of the long period he worked in the U.K. Despite having earlier won awards and been widely recognized among the cognoscenti, it was only really in 1988, with the release of *Who Framed Roger Rabbit*, that Williams's name was thrust into the forefront of public consciousness. He is now regarded as the man who could have single-handedly turned commercial theatrical animation on its head had it not been for the bean counters of Hollywood.

As a young man, Williams worked briefly with George Dunning in Montreal before moving to Spain to paint and study. Soon, however, he had an idea for an animated movie; as there was no chance of producing or financing it in Spain, he moved to London and got work in television advertising. In 1958 he released the featurette in question, *The Little Island*, and it immediately gained high praise: in this philosophical piece, Beauty, Truth, and Goodness, represented by horrid little monsters,

pursue their obsessions to an inevitably disastrous conclusion. In terms of its style, it was both an acknowledgement of and a rebuff to Disney; as such, it could be said to epitomize Williams's career.

On the strength of the reception given to *The Little Island*, Williams founded his own studio in London, and over the years this became a mecca for animators. Other shorts followed, such as *Love Me Love ME* (1962) and *A Lecture on Man* (1962). But, for the most part, Williams had to concentrate on commercial work, mainly tv advertisements. Some of these, such as a short series of ads for Truman's Bitter (beer), have become collectors' pieces in their own right. A major step forward, in terms of public recognition, came when he was commissioned to do the animated titles and interpolated sequences for Tony Richardson's *The Charge of the Light Brigade* (1968); the animation was the

Charles Dickens' a Christmas Carol, Being a Ghost Story of Christmas (1971) tvm

(vt *a Christmas Carol*; vt *Charles Dickens's a Christmas Carol*; vt *Richard Williams's a Christmas Carol*)

🎨 color / animated ⊙ 25 minutes

A stripped-down version of the classic tale. Marley's Ghost warns Scrooge of the error of his ways. The Ghost of Christmas Past shows him how he lost the love of Fezziwig's daughter through his worldliness; the Ghost of Christmas Present shows him Christmas at the Cratchits (with the doomed Tiny Tim), in poor mining and fishing communities, and at the home of Scrooge's nephew Fred, also introducing him to the waiflike spirits of Ignorance and Want; the Ghost of Christmas Yet to Come shows him how he will go unmourned, and how Tiny Tim will die as a consequence of his family's poverty. Awoken from his visions, a reformed Scrooge spreads Christmas goodwill and saves Tiny Tim.

most lauded part of this otherwise not terribly well received movie. Other movies for which he did the title sequences included *The Return of the Pink Panther* (1974), *What's New, Pussycat?* (1965), *The Liquidator* (1965), *Casino Royale* (1967), and *Sebastian* (1968) – all comedies, mainly comedy quasi-thrillers.

In about 1964, Williams read some of the tales of Mulla Nasrudin, the wise fool of Sufi folktales. He contacted the London-based writer Idries Shah and encouraged him to prepare a new edition of the tales illustrated by Williams; the result was the book *The Exploits of the Incomparable Mulla Nasrudin* (1966), published by the prestigious publishing house of Jonathan Cape. More to the point, this was the genesis of the animated feature, the dream of which would impel his career for the next three decades.

Another turning point came in 1968, when he saw the Disney version of *The Jungle Book* (1967). He and his staff had, up until then, thought they knew everything there was to know about character animation, but Williams realized while watching the movie that he still had a lot to learn. In particular, he was impressed by the character animation of the tiger Shere Khan, so he got in touch with the Disney animator responsible, Milt Kahl. It was the beginning of a friendship that would last until Kahl's death in 1987. Kahl and other "old timers" of animation took the time to teach the younger animators at Williams's studio what they knew; the most important of these training exploits was the regular series of classes run by Art Babbitt.

All this time, Williams was taking on commercial animation in order to fund his continuing work on the Nasrudin project, which went by various names throughout its production (and even after its release). Sometime in 1967–68, an early version of the soundtrack was recorded with Vincent Price (as the sorcerer

ZigZag) and other actors, including Sean Connery, Donald Pleasence, and Anthony Quayle. In 1969, the BBC produced a documentary about the project, which at the time had the provisional title of *The Golden City*. A few clips of the work-in-progress were shown, and it was evident from them that Williams was doing something new in commercial animation while at the same time continuing, with a sort of profound respect, in the great tradition. What emerged during this documentary was that Williams was reverting to full cel animation. Moreover, the backgrounds Williams's studio was producing were dramatic in their lavishness and stylization, drawing upon both the Western and more importantly the Persian/Islamic tradition, with its strong emphasis on geometrical pattern and richness of color.

The project, thanks to the BBC documentary, acquired considerable fame and prestige; but fame and prestige don't pay the bills, and none of the major studios was prepared to put money into it. The income from television commercials could go only so far. It was against this background that in 1970 Williams accepted the commission to create a half-hour tv special version of Charles Dickens's novella *A Christmas Carol*. In accordance with a recurring motif of his career, Williams had difficulty finishing on time and within budget *Charles Dickens' A Christmas Carol, Being a Ghost Story of Christmas* (1971 tvm), and in later stages Chuck Jones had to be called in to help (Jones is credited as executive producer). The result was one of the great landmarks of tv animation, even though the shortness of the film meant that the story had to be compressed more than was desirable. That said, this is an exquisitely beautiful short movie. An extra delightful touch is that actors Alistair Sim and Michael Hordern supply the voices of Scrooge and Marley's Ghost, reprising their roles from the definitive live-action version of the tale, *Scrooge* (1951). While Marley's Ghost is visually and verbally rendered much as in the earlier movie, Sim's reinterpretation of his role is delightful. The visual depiction of Scrooge owes, if anything, more to Reginald Owen's appearance in the role in the 1938 U.S. live-action version *A Christmas Carol*.

Charles Dickens' A Christmas Carol was deservedly rewarded with an Oscar, and, possibly because of this recognition, Paramount began negotiating a deal with Williams for the Nasrudin project. At first, all seemed to be going well, but then Idries Shah's sister, who had done some if not all of the translations for the book Williams had illustrated, claimed that her copyright was being infringed. With the threat of litigation hanging in the air, Paramount nervously withdrew, leaving Williams to contemplate several years' worth of wasted animation. He was forced to trash all the work that had been done with the characters (including Mulla Nasrudin, despite the fact that he was a traditional figure and hence free of copyright) and situations that appeared in the tales as rendered in the book and start all over again, salvaging what he could. He devised a

Setup for lobby card for *Who Framed Roger Rabbit* (1988).
Photograph: S/R Laboratories.
© Touchstone Pictures and
Amblin Entertainment, Inc.

new plot for what now came to be called *The Thief and the Cobbler*. (One of its later provisional titles was, ironically, *The Thief who Never Gave Up*.)

In about 1974, Williams was commissioned by 20th Century-Fox to act as animation supervisor on a feature movie to be based on Johnny Gruelle's nursery characters Raggedy Ann and Raggedy Andy; the director was to be the venerable Abe Levitow. Unfortunately, Levitow soon fell ill, and Williams was pressured to direct the movie in his place. By all accounts, the production was torturous, and, yet again, Williams went over time and over budget so that the movie had to be hastily finished by other hands. The end result, *Raggedy Ann and Andy: A Musical Adventure* (1977), can hardly be described as a satisfactory movie, although it is filed to the brim with all kinds of excellences, most notably in some of the animation. Not surprising, given some of the animators who worked on the project: among them, Art Babbitt animated the Camel with the Wrinkled Knees, Tissa David did Annie, Emery Hawkins did Greedy, Hal Ambro did Babette, Charlie Downs did the Captain, John Kimball did the Loonie Knight, and Gerry Chiniquy did King KooKoo, while Grim Natwick also contributed. The movie's biggest problem is that it is heavily overladen with largely mediocre songs, most of which had to be given the song-and-dance treatment, thereby excruciatingly

Who Framed Roger Rabbit (1988)

🌀 color / animated/live-action ⏱ 103 minutes
It's 1947 and private eye Eddie Valiant has turned to alcohol since the murder of his brother by a Toon — one of the animated characters who coexist in Toontown with humans in the contiguous Tinseltown. So he loathes all Toons and has to be truly desperate for money to take the job when commissioned to follow Jessica, sexy wife of cartoon superstar Roger Rabbit, to see if her rumored adultery with Marvin Acme, human owner of Toontown, is true. Acme is murdered, and the sadistic Judge Doom, arbiter of the law in Toontown, declares Roger guilty of the crime. Acme's will, reputedly leaving Toontown to the Toons, has gone missing. Valiant is reluctantly pulled ever deeper into the mystery, discovering that Toons aren't so bad and that the murderer, not just of Acme but of Valiant's own brother, was Judge Doom, who is in cahoots with others to dispossess the Toons, demolish Toontown, and develop the land for freeways and superstores. Doom is destroyed; Roger and Jessica are reconciled; and Valiant gets his own girl. (Based on *Who Censored Roger Rabbit?* (1981) by Gary K. Wolf.)

Raggedy Ann and Andy: A Musical Adventure (1977)

♭color / animated with a few live-action moments
⊚ 84 minutes

For her seventh birthday Marcella gets a new doll, Babette. In Marcella's playroom, the piratical Captain of a ship in a bottle falls in love with the Frenchly sophisticated Babette and abducts her to the outside world. Concerned for Marcella's happiness, rag-doll siblings Ann and Andy pursue. They fall in with the Camel with the Wrinkled Knees; narrowly escape being devoured by the rapacious candy-swamp monster, Greedy; and are ensnared by the Loonie Knight in the practical-joking hell run by the lunatic King KooKoo. But, in the end, the heroes prevail, the Captain repents the abduction, and order is restored to the playroom — in which, too, the lonesome Camel at last finds a home. (Based on the stories and characters created by Johnny Gruelle.)

The Thief and the Cobbler (1995)

(vt Arabian Knight; vt The Princess and the Cobbler)
♭color / animated ⊚ various running times (see text)

Baghdad, sometime during the era of the Arabian Nights. Evil King One-Eye marches on the city. Within, cobbler's apprentice Tack is seized on a trumped-up charge by evil vizier ZigZag and falls in love with the Princess Yum Yum, and she with him; her father, the Caliph/King, has effectively abdicated his throne through insouciance. Meanwhile, a fly-infested thief has become enraptured with the three golden balls which, atop a tower in Baghdad, symbolize the city's security: if these are lost the city shall fall. The thief steals the balls; ZigZag, who thereafter seizes them, promises the Caliph their return in exchange for Yum Yum's hand in marriage. This offer rejected, ZigZag sells out to One-Eye. The Caliph's only hope is to call upon the witch who is sister to One-Eye; Yum Yum and Tack act as his ambassadors to her. The witch advises "attack," and indeed the cobbler's apprentice uses "a tack" to demolish One-Eye's siege of Baghdad. The lovers are wed and the Thief becomes an inadvertent hero.

holding up the action; apparently, 20th Century-Fox steadfastly refused all requests by Williams that he be permitted to drop a few of them.

However, the revenue Williams received enabled him to resuscitate the Arabian project — this time only briefly, alas, because the poor box-office take of Raggedy Ann meant that his money rapidly ran out. It was back to a matter of taking on any commercial hackwork he could get in order to keep the studio's doors open.

Then, in 1978, Saudi Arabian prince Mohammed Feisal stepped in with funding for Williams to make test footage for the revised project — a sequence called The Battle Scene. This was supposed to take only a few months, but in the end it was not

until the end of 1979, and at over twice the cost that Feisal had originally been quoted, that the sequence was completed. Although the screening of the test sequence was reportedly so well received that its audience spontaneously leaped to its collective feet for a standing ovation, Feisal looked at Williams's track record of budgetary and time over-runs, considered his own recent experience of this characteristic with the test sequence, and understandably declined to fund the movie any further.

A second BBC documentary about the Arabian project, done in 1981, failed to enthuse any new backers. However, in that same year, Williams was approached by auhor Lena Tabori to coproduce and direct a half-hour tv special called Ziggy's Gift, based on the character created by Tom Wilson in the book When You're Not Around (1968) and thereafter syndicated by UPS as a daily comic panel done by Wilson. Shown on ABC on December 1, 1982, Ziggy's Gift won an Emmy for Best Animated Program. The tale sees the balding, mute Ziggy and his dog, Fuzz, take work as a street-corner Santa Claus in order to raise money for the poor.

Once again, acclaim did not bring anything material by way of sponsorship for the Arabian project, and it was back to the unglamorous business of making tv ads. In 1984, Gary Kurtz – producer of Star Wars (1977), Return to Oz (1985), Little Nemo in Slumberland (1989), and many others – injected some money into the project and gave it some promotion to the studios; again there were no takers. However, Williams did put together a 12-minute sample reel for the movie, and while in San Francisco arranged for a screening of this for his old friend Milt Kahl, who was by then extremely ill. Stephen Spielberg, Robert Zemeckis, and others involved in a planned feature movie based on Gary K. Wolf's wry cult classic Who Censored Roger Rabbit? (1981) heard about the sample reel, begged for a screening of their own, and, although they didn't fund Williams's project, they promptly commissioned Williams to be animation director of their own movie, eventually released as Who Framed Roger Rabbit (1988). Of the sample reel, Spielberg is reported to have said: "He warped perspective and had absolutely no respect for convention. He [Williams] was just what we were looking for." (Among those who watched the sample reel around this time and later were many Disney staffers involved in Roger Rabbit; a recurring rumor is that they either intentionally or unwittingly borrowed various plot points for the studio's forthcoming animated feature Aladdin (1992). Comparison shows, however, no more similarities than one might expect between two movies operating in approximately the same territory.)

Bearing in mind that Williams was desperate for funding for his lifelong dream, one might have thought that his immediate answer on being offered the lucrative work on Roger would be a resounding yes!, but in fact his first response was negative. In my

Two frames of storyboard art for Raggedy Ann and Andy (1977).

Encyclopedia of Walt Disney's Animated Characters (3rd edition, 1998) I summarize the situation thus:

> Williams thought that animation/live-action mixtures were dreary and doomed to failure. He pinpointed the way in which, in previous efforts, animators decided beforehand what could and could not be done, and then did it, leaving the directors of the overall movies to fit the rest in as best they could around their animators' efforts. Before Williams could be persuaded to take the job on (and we shouldn't lose sight of the fact that he regarded it as a money-making enterprise which would help underwrite *The Thief*), he wanted to establish that the boot would be on the other foot: Zemeckis was to dictate exactly what he wanted from the movie, and it was to be up to Williams to supply it. As has been widely quoted, he said to Zemeckis: "I'm your pencil." One can see the attraction for Williams in adopting this approach: it is much more exciting to take on a seemingly almost insuperable challenge than just to churn out the adequate.

Williams was given a budget of $100,000 to produce a single minute of specimen animation for the movie – seemingly a ridiculous sum, but in that single minute he had to solve a host of technical problems that affected the movie as a whole. The main challenge was, of course, the blending of animation and live actors to make a seamless whole; in earlier attempts, as in Disney's own *Mary Poppins* (1964), the audience had been perfectly conscious of the fact that the animation was merely that, animation, and that what was on display was a clever technical trick; but for *Roger* to work it was necessary to create the illusion that the animation and live action were both firmly locked into the same reality. Williams's test minute of animation was reportedly sensational; after Spielberg and Zemeckis had satisfied themselves that Disney was genuinely aware of the astronomical sums involved in maintaining this standard throughout the full length of the planned feature movie, the show was on the road. Again from *Encyclopedia of Walt Disney's Animated Characters*:

> It was a very slow vehicle. From the outset it had been plain to Williams that there could be no short-cuts in the production of 82,080 frames, each done by hand on a photostatic blow-up of a single frame of live action. The animation crew numbered 326 – 254 directly under Williams in London, 72 others in California. . . . A further handicap to speed was the use throughout the film, for the sake of verisimilitude of the animation/live-actors interaction, of moving cameras – as is customary in live-action movies but heretical in animation, where conventionally the camera is locked in position and everything else is moved. It is small wonder that, as deadlines and revised deadlines passed and as fixed budgets

began to look anything but, the people at Disney were tearing their hair out. All the signs seemed to be that they had been pouring money into a movie that might prove to be a *flop d'estime* . . . During the delays in *Roger*, Hoskins was able to find the time to star in not just one but two other movies. There were even shy suggestions, late in the production, that enough was enough: the material that was already prepared should be cobbled together as best as possible and released so that there would be at least *some* financial returns, however dismal, on the colossal investment that had by now been made.

Who Framed Roger Rabbit was, of course, a phenomenal box-office hit, despite the reservations of many critics concerning, in particular, its screenplay; essentially, to generalize, the animation was adored but there were many severe reservations about the live action. Later, Robert Zemeckis was to acknowledge in almost so many words that without the participation of Williams the movie would have been impossible, and no one was surprised when Williams carried off an Oscar for his efforts.

Williams was very much the animator of the moment, and, naturally, considerable attention was focused on the great project about which there had been so much talk over the years – indeed, over the *decades*. Some funding came in from Japan, but the most important development was that Warners stepped in with a deal to complete the Arabian feature. Work went into high gear at Williams's London studio, with a planned release date that was gradually pushed further back as time went on. In spring 1992, Warners got wind of the upcoming Disney feature *Aladdin* and of its vaunted similarities to the Williams movie; not optimistic about its commercial chances in a head-on contest with Disney, Warners backed out of the deal.

It seemed for a while that all was not lost. Budgetary over-runs had been insured against by the Completion Bond Company, who could be expected to pick up the tab that Warners had so abruptly dropped. However, the Completion Bond Company itself was beginning to wonder if the movie would ever in fact be completed. After a highly successful June 1992 screening of the work so far revealed that there was still some 15 minutes' worth of animation to be done, the Completion Bond Company decided it was time to cut its losses. It stepped in and fired Williams and everyone else involved in the project. The television animator/producer Fred Calvert was hired to finish the movie as best he could and as quickly and cheaply as possible; Williams was compelled to hand over everything to Calvert.

Exactly what happened next is uncertain, and Calvert has repeatedly and unjustly been cast as the villain of the piece. As far as can be established, he completed the project with as much integrity as was possible, given the stringent constraints placed upon him. For commercial reasons, some song sequences were added; these were largely done by Don Bluth's studio. Some sequences were eliminated from the original, for reasons unknown. In 1994, Calvert's version of the movie, for which no U.S. distributor could be found, was released in Australia and South Africa under the title *The Princess and the Cobbler*. It was received as no masterpiece – indeed, as a bit of a disappointment – and its performance at the box office was only moderate. In early 1995 Miramax stepped in and bought the movie for a song from the ailing Completion Bond Company. The fans in the U.S., Britain, and the rest of the world eagerly awaited the release of at least the Calvert version; but then Miramax decided the existing version was still not commercial enough and the entire project should be reworked. A new voice track was added (the original had very little dialogue, and both Thief and Cobbler were dumb) – complete with the occasional anachronistic Disney-plugging pseudo-witticism. Much of the animation was cut, including everything pertaining to a witch who had been of some importance in the original. The order of events was shuffled.

The Miramax version – the only version most U.S. and U.K. viewers will ever see – was released in August 1995 as *Arabian Knight* and is a complete mess. The screenplay and voice track, in particular, represent an attempt to blandify out of existence everything that was original and strong that the movie possessed. Just to add to the bizarreness, because of the paucity of dialogue in Williams's version, which relied heavily on mime, much of the time the characters in the Miramax version are speaking without moving their lips! Sequences of aesthetically fabulous, quite electrifyingly beautiful animation are rudely shouldered aside by dull, Hollywood-cliché sequences that inspire nothing so much as the urge to throw something at the screen.

It is hard to find anything cheerful in the story of what happened to Richard Williams's Arabian project, but Edward Summer – whose exemplary 1996 chronology of events relating to the movie in the magazine *Films in Review* has been of considerable help in piecing together this account – finds a couple of causes for hope. First, somewhere in a vault there still exists the working version of the movie that Williams handed over to Fred Calvert, and it can be only a matter of time before some enterprising company manages to find a way to release this on video and DVD; sales of such an item would obviously be extraordinary. Second, Williams's unfinished masterpiece, though never released in a proper form, set new standards for future animators; and in the making of the movie a whole new generation of animators, many now holding the highest positions in the creative staffs of the major studios, were trained in the art of animation at its very finest. Referring to the Greek myth, these animators have collectively nicknamed themselves the Children of the Dragon's Teeth: the "teeth" that Williams sowed in making – or attempting to make – this movie have given rise to a vast army of animators fully schooled in his ideals.

Williams retired from commercial animation after his movie had been taken from him by the Completion Bond Company. He is believed to be working on an animated movie of his own based on one of the plays of Aristophanes.

Select Bibliography

Note: Editions cited are those used, and may not be the first.

Adams, T.R.: *Tom and Jerry: Fifty Years of Cat and Mouse*, Crescent, New York, 1991

Adamson, Joe: *Bugs Bunny: Fifty Years and Only One Grey Hare*, Hutter/Holt, New York, 1990

Adamson, Joe: *Tex Avery: King of Cartoons* (revised edn.), Da Capo, New York, 1985

—*The Walter Lantz Story, with Woody Woodpecker and Friends*, Putnam, New York, 1985

Arseni, Ercole, Bosi, Leoni, and Marconi, Massimo: *Walt Disney Magic Moments*, Mondadori, Milan, 1973

Beck, Jerry (ed.): *The 50 Greatest Cartoons, as Selected by 1,000 Animation Professionals*, Turner, Atlanta, 1994

—*"I Tawt I Taw a Puddy Tat": Fifty Years of Sylvester and Tweety*, Holt, New York, 1991

Beck, Jerry, and Friedwald, Will: *Looney Tunes and Merrie Melodies: A Complete Illustrated Guide to the Warner Bros. Cartoons*, Holt, New York, 1989

Bendazzi, Giannalberto (trans. Anna Taraboletti-Segre): *Cartoons: One Hundred Years of Cinema Animation*, John Libbey, London, 1994

Blair, Preston: *Cartoon Animation*, Walter Foster, Tustin CA, 1994

Blitz, Marcia: *Donald Duck*, Harmony, New York, 1979

Brion, Patrick: *Tex Avery*, Chêne/Collection Cinéma de Toujours, 1984

Brion, Patrick: *Tom and Jerry: The Definitive Guide to Their Animated Adventures*, Harmony, New York, 1990

Burke, Timothy, and Burke, Kevin: *Saturday Morning Fever: Growing up with Cartoon Culture*, St Martin's Griffin, New York, 1999

Cabarga, Leslie: *The Fleischer Story* (revised edn.), Da Capo, New York, 1988

Canemaker, John: *The Animated Raggedy Ann & Andy*, Bobbs-Merrill, New York, 1977

—*Before the Animation Begins: The Art and Lives of Disney Inspirational Sketch Artists*, Hyperion, New York, 1996

—*Felix: The Twisted Tale of the World's Most Famous Cat*, Pantheon, New York, 1991

—*Paper Dreams: The Art & Artists of Disney Storyboards*, Hyperion, New York, 1930

—*Tex Avery: The MGM Years, 1942–1955*, Turner, Atlanta, 1996

Canemaker, John (introduction): *Treasures of Disney Animation Art*, Abbeville, New York, 1982

—*Winsor McCay: His Life and Art*, Abbeville, New York, 1987

Cawley, John: *The Animated Films of Don Bluth*, Image, New York, 1991

Clute, John, and Grant, John (eds.): *The Encyclopedia of Fantasy* (revised edn), Orbit, London, 1999

de Bono, Edward (ed.): *Eureka! An Illustrated History of Inventions from the Wheel to the Computer*, Thames & Hudson, London, 1974

Finch, Christopher: *Jim Henson: The Works – The Art, the Magic, the Imagination*, Random, New York, 1993

Frierson, Michael: *Clay Animation: American Highlights 1908 to the Present*, Twayne, New York, 1994

Gilliam, Terry (with Lucinda Cowell): *Animations of Mortality*, Eyre Methuen, London, 1978

Grant, John: *Encyclopedia of Walt Disney's Animated Characters* (3rd ed.), Hyperion, New York, 1998

Grossman, Gary H.: *Saturday Morning TV*, Arlington, New York, 1987

Hahn, Don: *Animation Magic: A Behind-the-Scenes Look at How an Animated Film is Made* (revised ed.), Disney Press, New York, 2000

Halas, John: *Masters of Animation*, Salem House, Topsfield, 1987

Hames, Peter (ed.): *Dark Alchemy: The Films of Jan Švankmajer*, Praeger, Westport CT, 1995

Hanna, Bill (with Tom Ito): *A Cast of Friends*, Taylor, Dallas, 1996

Holliss, Richard, and Sibley, Brian: *The Disney Studio Story*, Octopus, London, 1988

—*Walt Disney's Snow White and the Seven Dwarfs & the Making of a Classic Film*, Simon & Schuster, New York, 1987

Horn, Maurice: *100 Years of American Newspaper Comics: An Encyclopedia*, Gramercy, Avenel NJ, 1996

Hyatt, Wesley: *The Encyclopedia of Daytime Television*, Billboard, New York, 1997

Johnston, Ollie, and Thomas, Frank: *The Disney Villain*, Hyperion, New York, 1993

Jones, Chuck: *Chuck Amuck: The Life and Times of an Animated Cartoonist*, Farrar, Straus & Giraux, New York, 1989

Jones, Chuck: *Chuck Reducks: Drawing from the Fun Side of Life*, Warner, New York, 1996

Kanfer, Stefan: *Serious Business: The Art and Commerce of Animation in America from Betty Boop to Toy Story*, Scribner, New York, 1997

Kenner, Hugh: *Chuck Jones: A Flurry of Drawings*, University of California Press, Berkeley, 1994

Lenburg, Jeff: *The Encyclopedia of Animated Cartoons* (2nd ed.), Checkmark, New York, 1999

—*The Great Cartoon Directors*, McFarland, Jefferson NC, 1983

Lewis, Jon E., and Stempel, Penny: *Cult TV: The Essential Critical Guide*, Pavilion, London, 1993

Lord, Peter, and Sibley, Brian: *Cracking Animation: The Aardman Book of 3-D Animation*, Thames & Hudson, London, 1998

McCabe, Bob: *Dark Knights and Holy Fools*, Universe, New York, 1999

McCarthy, Helen: *Hayao Miyazaki: Master of Japanese Animation*, Stone Bridge, Berkeley, 1999

McCarthy, Helen, and Clements, Jonathan: *The Erotic Anime Movie Guide*, Titan, London, 1998

Mallory, Michael: *Hanna–Barbera Cartoons*, Hugh Lauter Levin, Southport CT, 1998

Maltin, Leonard: *Of Mice and Magic: A History of American Animated Cartoons* (revised ed.), Plume, New York, 1987

Merritt, Russell, and Kaufman, J.B.: *Walt in Wonderland: The Silent Films of Walt Disney* (revised ed.), Le Giornate del Cinema Muto,

Pordenone, Italy/Johns Hopkins University Press, Baltimore MD, 1993

Morgan, Judith and Neil: *Dr. Seuss & Mr. Geisel: A Biography*, Random, New York, 1995

Peary, Danny, and Peary, Gerald (eds.): *The American Animated Cartoon: A Critical Anthology*, Dutton, New York, 1980

Schneider, Steve: *That's All Folks!: The Art of Warner Bros. Animation*, Holt, New York, 1988

Sibley, Brian: *Chicken Run: Hatching the Movie*, Abrams, New York, 2000

Smith, Dave: *Disney A–Z: The Updated Official Encyclopedia*, Hyperion, New York, 1998

Solomon, Charles: *The Disney that Never Was: The Stories and Art from Five Decades of Unproduced Animation*, Hyperion, New York, 1995

—*Enchanted Drawings: The History of Animation* (revised edn.), Wings, Avenel NJ, 1994

Woolery, George: *Animated TV Specials: The Complete Directory to the First Twenty-Five Years*, Scarecrow, Metuchen and London, 1989

Woolery, George: *Children's Television: The First Thirty-Five Years* (2 vols.), Scarecrow, Metuchen and London, 1983

Owing to both pressure of space, it is not possible to list the many hundreds of articles and Web sites that have been consulted during the writing of this book. An exception must be made, however, for Michael Brooke's quite astonishing Web site on the art of Jan Švankmajer, which is longer than many books and provides an enormous wealth of information about this great artist and moviemaker. Although most of the information is available elsewhere in printed form, Brooke's task in bringing it all together must have been Herculean and his skill in so doing is inestimable. The site is at http://www.illumin.com/svank.

Index

Alternate titles are indicated thus: = .
The sites of boxed synopses are indicated in **bold**
The sites of illustration captions are indicated in *italics*

206

I N D E X